D0518495

Pevsner on Art and Architecture

Nikolaus Pevsner

Pevsner on Art and Architecture

THE RADIO TALKS

Edited and with an introduction by
Stephen Games

Methuen

10 9 8 7 6 5 4 3 2 1

Published 2002 by Methuen Publishing Limited
215 Vauxhall Bridge Road, London SW1V 1EJ

Methuen Publishing Limited Reg. No. 3543167

Broadcasts © The Estate of Nikolaus Pevsner 2002

Preface, Introduction and Notes © Stephen Games 2002

The rights of Stephen Games and of the Estate of Nikolaus Pevsner
to be identified as the Authors of this work have been asserted by
them in accordance with the Copyright Designs and Patents Act
1988.

A CIP catalogue record for this book is available from
the British Library

ISBN 0 413 71220 6

Designed by Bryony Newhouse

Typeset by Deltatype Ltd, Birkenhead, Merseyside

Printed and bound in Great Britain by
Creative Print and Design (Wales), Ltd, Ebbw Vale

To Bracha

CONTENTS

Pevsner on Art and Architecture

PREFACE

I first read Pevsner's *Pioneers of Modern Design* as an art student in 1971 and it decided me in my wish to go on to study architecture, not necessarily in the hope of becoming an architect but in the belief that all questions relating to design had their basis in architecture. The ideas of the Bauhaus still dominated much of what we were taught in those days and Pevsner's writings were their principal intermediary. As prospective practitioners in the applied arts, we also saw ourselves as the main beneficiaries of Pevsner's vision of a new enlightenment.

Coming from this background, I had no anticipation of the storm about to break over Pevsner's reputation in 1977, the year of my graduation. I also had no idea that its centre in Cambridge was located just a few yards away from my student drawing-board, such was the barrier between the architects and art historians who occupied opposite ends of Scroope Terrace. When the storm did break, unleashed by David Watkin in *Morality and Architecture*, I felt, as did most of Britain's architectural community, that Pevsner's authority as an advocate of modern architecture had been improperly defamed in order to advance a separate agenda of Classical Revivalism and I said as much when I reviewed the book in the *Sunday Times*. Five years later, on Pevsner's eightieth birthday, I felt sufficiently protective of his reputation to make a largely hagiographic radio programme about him for the BBC and when I signed a contract to write his biography, I still imagined going into battle on his behalf.

In the years that followed, the initial shock of Watkin's iconoclasm passed and it became possible to see his monograph, for all its revanchism, as a brilliant piece of analysis, far better informed about Pevsner and his quality of thought than most of Pevsner's followers had been. Since then, *Morality and Architecture* has itself become a watershed in perceptions of the modern agenda, its ideas influencing a range of thinking far wider than its author's own conservative aesthetic preferences. As for my own biographical research, this has inevitably forced me to look afresh at

Pevsner's career and to allow his vast eminence to take care of itself in the light of new evidence. I have not gone native, however, as one London publisher suggested on meeting me after a fifteen-year gap, and my instincts on modern architecture are perhaps more Pevsnerian now than they ever were before.

The idea of bringing together Pevsner's radio talks in time for the centenary of his birth gives me the opportunity to collate a body of work that has never been publicly available before and at the same time to present a brief interim report on Pevsner's life. This report is based on research that has taken me all round Germany investigating the circumstances of Pevsner's early life and talking to people who had known him, including family members, neighbours and former students. That work would not have been possible without the assistance of the German Academic Exchange Service (the DAAD) and the Interior Ministry of the former East German government. I have also, since 1985, made numerous visits to the Getty Research Institute in Los Angeles to work through the 140 shelf feet of papers that constitutes the Pevsner archive and I acknowledge with considerable thanks the Getty organisation's generosity, the interest shown by Wim DeWit and the patient help I have always received from GRI staff, especially Beth Guynn. As for my efforts in getting to grips with Pevsner's radio talks, I thank the staff of the BBC Written Archives Centre in Caversham and John Davies in particular.

In addition, I owe a debt of gratitude to hundreds of Pevsner's friends, family, colleagues, associates and others in England and around the world who have helped me over the years. Their names make up a long list but that list must wait until the full biography appears. For now, I must restrict myself to thanking Leonie Cohn who produced more of Pevsner's radio talks than anyone else, Anthony Moncrieff, formerly of the Third Programme but now living in Thailand, the late Sir Ernst Gombrich who helped me twice, and at length, on issues for which no written sources existed, Sir Denis Mahon, Tom Read, Christine Penney at Birmingham University, Roger Carey, Asher Rozenberg and Nadia Kempster. I must also mention Jutta Krug for her support in the early days of my Pevsner expeditions, Fred Wyatt for his help more recently with translations and interpretations, my typists Angela Judd and Nathan Lyons, Ilsa Yardley, who read the proofs with an expert eye, and Louise Greenberg, my agent on this book but twenty years ago the producer who first brought me into the BBC and indirectly got me started on my long Pevsner journey.

A number of editorial difficulties presented themselves in the course of transcribing Pevsner's radio talks. In most cases, I worked from typescripts that Pevsner had amended in studio and I had to decide whether to leave in or reinstate anything from single words to whole paragraphs that he may have changed or deleted for reasons of accuracy, style or lack of time. My final decision, assisted by my own acute and thoughtful editor Max Eilenberg at Methuen, depended on the circumstances in each case and the result is therefore a composite. In that sense, this book is not a scholarly edition and I have not annotated each decision because there were so many. I have instead tried to treat the original texts as any editor might have done had this been a new book rather than an archive. In the same way, I have standardised Pevsner's punctuation, made minor changes to spellings and in a few places anglicised his more Germanic word order where his version made the meaning difficult. His tendency to refer to England and Britain interchangeably, however, remains unchanged.

I was able to trace almost eighty English-language radio talks given by Pevsner between 1945 and 1977. Of these, about two thirds were on architecture, one third on art; two thirds on history, one third on contemporary issues; two thirds about England, one third on other countries. I did not feel that all of them demanded inclusion. Some of the earlier ones were minor or unsatisfactory in other ways; the later talks were often little more than travel pieces with not very much to say. But this left getting on for another fifty very remarkable pieces of writing – expansive, engaging, persuasive and wry – and it is these, including the 1955 Reith Lectures, that make up this first ever compendium of Pevsner on the air. I selected the talks purely on the strength of their writing. Having done so, I found to my surprise that I had discarded most of his contemporary subjects, which had not been my aim. At first sight, these exclusions seem to misrepresent the focus of Pevsner's gaze but any reading of his talks quickly reveals exactly where his heart lay. If only we all had his penetration and power of expression.

Stephen Games
London, September 2002

INTRODUCTION

Sir Nikolaus Pevsner is one of the most complex scholars of the twentieth century. Born in Germany in 1902 but naturalised as a British citizen in 1946, he was both an art historian and a critic though he sometimes wrote as if the two activities were interchangeable. His historical works were also attempts at persuasion; his critical works were also attempts to secure a particular version of history. Throughout his career, his writings broke new ground – notably in the field of Mannerist Italian painting and English nineteenth-century architecture – but he was locked into a set of methodological conventions not his own and had as his primary audience the public rather than his peers. Behind his work lay an agenda that made sense only in Germany but which he tried to fulfil in Britain. He spent his professional life uncovering truths about art and buildings but making sure that events in his own life remained disguised. Perhaps oddest of all, the building he chose to exemplify his lifelong principles of purpose and anonymity – a factory built for the Werkbund Exhibition in Cologne in 1914 – was not a real building but a model designed by an architect, Walter Gropius, whose identity and reputation Pevsner actively promoted. As for its purpose, what he actually praised it for was its 'effortless mastery of material and weight' and for being the greatest example of art 'triumphant over matter' since Sainte-Chapelle and the choir of Beauvais Cathedral in the thirteenth century.

Inconsistencies do not alter the fact that both as a historian and a critic, Pevsner became the single most prominent figure in his field. After anti-Jewish legislation in Nazi Germany made it impossible for him to carry on teaching at Göttingen University where he been since 1929, he moved to England. Within eight years he had written four trailblazing books in his newly adopted language and Birkbeck College, London University, had created a lectureship for him which became a full professorship in 1959. He was the first Slade Professor of Fine Art at Cambridge ever to be reappointed for a second three-year term and the first to be made Slade Professor at Oxford as well. He went on to receive honorary doctorates from Oxford, Cambridge, East Anglia, Heriott-Watt, Leicester, Leeds, Keele, the Open University, Pennsylvania, York and Zagreb. Meanwhile as a critic, he enjoyed a parallel association with architecture and the applied arts, carrying out original research into English industrial design in the mid 1930s, acting as wartime editor of the *Architectural Review* from 1942–45, serving on two national councils that supervised art school teaching from 1959, becoming a member of the commission that advises Government on new buildings in 1966 and winning the Royal Gold Medal of the Royal Institute of British Architects in 1967.

As Pevsner became a national institution, his twin careers inevitably attracted negative as well as positive attention. Questions began to be asked about his ability to reconcile the objectivity required of a historian with the advocacy that accompanies criticism and from the 1970s to the 1990s his professional reputation started to suffer. Art historians found they disliked the way he treated history; architects found themselves constrained by his Gropius fixation; and both tended to see him as an obstacle to the development of their respective fields. Throughout this time, however, he continued to be regarded with affection and respect by appreciative former students and colleagues, by users of his forty-six-volume Penguin Guides *The Buildings of England*, and by those who remembered hearing and enjoying the radio broadcasts in which his scholarship most became flesh and blood. In recent years, as the memory of him has become more distant and the threat he once posed has receded, it has become possible to look at him more dispassionately as the figurehead of new thinking on art history and contemporary design in the English-speaking world for a large part of the twentieth century.

Pevsner was born to and brought up by Russian-Jewish parents in the fashionable new Music Quarter of Leipzig, near the Gewandhaus, the city's world-famous concert hall. As a boy, he wanted to be a writer like the celebrities who attended his mother's literary and musical salons but he showed his greatest originality in the obsessive cataloguing of the minutiae of his everyday life. After several attempts at writing short stories in the style of Thomas Mann, he took stock of his talents and decided to become an art historian. So seriously did he take his new calling that he listened in on art history lectures at Leipzig University while he was still a pupil at the Thomasschule – the school at which Bach had been organist and choirmaster.

Art history in Britain at the time was not yet a university subject and architectural writing tended to be about the romance of old houses, of *Highways and Byways* as one popular topography series was called. In Germany, by contrast, where art history had been an academic discipline since the 1830s, not only had a huge body of information about art been compiled but also standardised methods of approaching it. Indeed, one of the greatest achievements of German art history in the nineteenth century was the development of systems – systems of categorisation such as 'style' and 'period' that made it possible to create linkages between works; and systems of interpretation that made it possible to say what the significance of those works and linkages might be. It was this process of systematisation that allowed German art historians to think of their subject not just as art history – *Kunstgeschichte* – but as art science – *Kunstwissenschaft* – and of themselves as intellectual leaders in the world. The application of art-historical systems also contributed to Germany's sense of national revival in the nineteenth century and to the redeeming of its reputation as a second-rate artistic power. In this way, art history in Germany had an importance out of all proportion to its status in Britain.

For centuries, every German state had had its own university and in the normal German way, Pevsner made an academic tour of those he regarded as the best, comparing Munich, Berlin, Leipzig and Frankfurt-am-Main for one semester each before coming back to Leipzig and taking his doctorate in 1924. Leipzig was the university of the state of Saxony and had a modern outlook and a reputation for science. Its art history combined a classical training in the idealisation of form with an interest in art as a reflection of *Volksgeist* or national character. This mixture had been laid down by Leipzig's first chair of art history, the Czech dissident and political historian Anton Springer, whom it appointed in 1872. Art history, said Springer,

should represent the appearance of beauty in its progress through time; describe the inner essentials of artistic ideals; provide historical accounts of particular types of art; but at the same time sketch a graphic picture of the creative imagination of various nations and show the connection between that and the rest of what history deals with.

In 1893, two years after Springer's death, August Schmarsow was chosen as Leipzig's new chair of art history. Schmarsow introduced ideas similar to those of the Swiss theorist Heinrich Wölfflin but also incorporating work being done in Leipzig by Wilhelm Wundt, Germany's first experimental psychologist whose ideas on anthropology Freud critiqued in *Totem and Taboo*. Among Schmarsow's innovations was the study of the spaces contained within buildings rather than simply the buildings themselves. He also described buildings biologically or anthropomorphically, as if they had energy and psychological yearnings. Pevsner's *Outline of European Architecture* of 1942, which summarised German teachings on architecture for an English audience, encapsulates both approaches. Writing of Gothic cathedrals, he feels the smooth spatial rhythm at Notre Dame cathedral in Paris, the speed of the eastward drive at Chartres, the sense of being pressed forward in the nave of Reims, Amiens and Beauvais. The Baroque church, over four hundred years later, becomes a 'full-blooded organism' and he gives the example of Borromini's S. Carlo alle Quattro Fontane, begun in 1663. Its oval plan, he says, introduces a suggestion of movement in space. Its 'intertwined' elements produce 'a rolling, rocking effect', its compound spaces 'touch' and 'merge' and this feeling communicates itself to us, he says, in a luscious wave of empathy in which 'we can stand nowhere without taking part in the swaying rhythm'. Of German Baroque, Pevsner told his doubting English readers, anyone who feels repelled by its exultation but can admire a Gothic Devon screen is either not really looking or wearing 'the blinkers of puritanism'.

Outline also reflected the teachings of Wilhelm Pinder, Schmarsow's maverick successor whose presence in Leipzig attracted large numbers of students. Pinder was a radical conservative who challenged the philosophical excesses of German art history by appealing to his students' and readers' instincts. It was Pinder's lectures that excited Pevsner while still at school and confirmed his interest in art history. 'He spoke like in the movies, at unbelievable speed,' his mother told him after attending a Pinder lecture that her son couldn't get to, on the subject of Oswald

Spengler as poet of the scientific. Pinder brought theatricality to teaching. He also threw very good parties.

As a former student of Schmarsow's, Pinder had dutifully explored the ideas of spatial rhythmic analysis, but in the 1910s he became more interested in how art and architecture related to two other systems of interpretation: national character and the *Zeitgeist*. This 'spirit of the age' was held to permeate every facet of life in a given period, producing similar ideas, forms and behaviours – all of which taken together constituted 'style'. Historians today often tiptoe round the *Zeitgeist* as if it were one of German Romanticism's more difficult concepts. It was in fact easy to understand and use, and just as appealing to the Manchester Free Trade Utilitarians as it was to Herder, Hamann, Kant and Hegel. It allowed Pevsner in *Outline* to connect national differentiation in mid-thirteenth-century architecture with the experience of Crusader knights, and to write of the late eighteenth century as a period when artists 'were no longer satisfied with being servants of a ruling class' and when a new type of patron emerged, 'self-made, self-assured and cultured'. The equally colloquial idea of national character enabled him to make comparative generalisations – Spain was a more 'restless' country than Italy whereas French and English architecture in the thirteenth century had an ultimate identity of spirit. It also allowed him to predict what sort of art a country would produce and to rescue artistic reputations. He praised German architecture, for example, for the 'authenticity' of its national spirit as opposed to the inauthentic 'virtuosity' of the Italians, an interpretation that grew out of Germany's defensive response to what had for centuries been regarded as the superiority of Italian and French art.

This kind of writing, with its presuppositions and its habit of putting carts before horses, may seem too loose to qualify as history today. For Pinder and his students, that looseness – the fact that anyone could understand it and anyone might say it – was what gave it its power. Pinder certainly regarded himself as an art scientist in his handling of analytical and interpretational systems; but at the same time he regarded his science as defiantly anti-theoretical. He quoted with approval Georg Dehio, the German historian on whose early 1900s architectural guidebooks Pevsner based his *Buildings of England*, as saying: 'School? I have no school! Method? I have no method!' What characterised Pinder was a rift between his view of himself as objective and his uncritical tolerance for personal insight and gut response, none of it amenable to empirical testing. Pinder's susceptibility to instinct also swept him up in the political currents of the day and he became increasingly focused on the superiority of German art and the German *Volk*, arguing that those who disagreed with him did so because they did not have it in their blood and could not feel it.

Under Pinder's influence, Pevsner wrote and published his doctoral thesis on the Baroque town houses of Leipzig, and three years later brought out his first major book, *Die italienische Malerei vom Ende der Renaissance bis zum ausgehenden Rokoko* (referred to in English as 'Italian Painting of Mannerism and the Baroque' although never translated). This, the first of a two-volume set on Baroque painting in the Romance lands for the leading *Handbuch der Kunstwissenschaft* series, also applied Pinder's methods. Among other things, it sought to salvage late sixteenth-century Italian art from its limbo between the Renaissance and Baroque periods by defining its redeeming features and naming it 'Mannerism'. While working on this project and writing papers for various scholarly journals, Pevsner was also developing two side careers as a curator and as an art journalist. In 1924, after leaving Leipzig, he became an unpaid assistant curator for five years at the Dresden Painting Gallery and did additional volunteer work two years later as assistant to the director of Dresden's big International Art Exhibition. At the same time, he became the art critic on the *Dresdner Anzeiger*, one of Dresden's daily papers.

His exposure to the world outside academia opened him up to contemporary developments and two crucial encounters changed the focus of his work, both in 1925. The first was his visit to Gropius's new Bauhaus building going up in Dessau; the second was his visit to the Paris Exhibition where he saw Le Corbusier's famous Pavillon de l'Esprit Nouveau, with the tree growing up through its roof. The idea of modern architecture was not new to him. There had always been art magazines in the family home showing what progressive architects and designers in Europe were doing, and Pinder had given German modernism his own spin by presenting it as the ultimate encounter between the *Zeitgeist* and German rigour. Pevsner was nonetheless so overcome at seeing these two contemporary architectural landmarks for himself that he was never again able to devote himself exclusively to the art of the past.

As a historian, Pevsner was captivated by Gropius's Bauhaus school and its teachings because it seemed to open up a new intellectual system – one that took Pinder's pragmatism to its obvious conclusion. The Bauhaus was, he felt, engaged in solving contemporary 'stylistic' problems – problems of ideas, forms and behaviours – while at the same time driven by an historical precedent: the communitarian anonymity then thought to characterise the Middle Ages. As Pevsner wrote of the builders of St Denis in *Outline*, 'in the earlier mediaeval centuries the names of these men, immortal as their work seemed, did not count. They were content to be workmen working for a cause greater than their own fame.' Pevsner was overwhelmed by the idea that the anonymity that had supposedly produced the great cathedrals of the thirteenth century was now being recreated by urbanisation and the modern state. It became obvious that painting had had its day; that because the Age of Reason and the Industrial Revolution had made artists free, it had also made them irrelevant; and that because they could now work for themselves, they were at the mercy of their own self-indulgence. The only arts that mattered, Pevsner now felt, were architecture and design. They alone had to exist in a social context and were therefore more truthful.

With the publication of his book on Italian painting, Pevsner got a job as a *Privatdozent* or self-funded lecturer at Göttingen University, ostensibly to teach general courses on art from mediaeval times to the present day. Shortly after arriving in Göttingen in 1929, however, he obtained funding from the government of Lower Saxony for a research trip to England to take place the following year, supported by the university's Department of English. His aim was a first-hand study of English art in general – at the time as overlooked a field as German art had been until the late nineteenth century – and in particular of William Morris, who Gropius had apparently told him personally was one of his main sources of inspiration. Over the next two years, alongside more conventional courses on German and Italian art, Pevsner lectured and wrote about the origins of German modernism and fleshed out the interpretational system that traced the antecedents of Gropius to English nineteenth-century engineering and to the Arts and Crafts movement.

xxii   PEVSNER ON ART AND ARCHITECTURE

It was these lectures and writings that formed the basis for his first English-language book in 1936, *Pioneers of the Modern Movement*, reissued by the Museum of Modern Art in New York in 1949 as *Pioneers of Modern Design*. Pevsner normally gets the credit for assembling the chain of events that led from English utilitarianism to German functionalism. The idea for this may have come from any number of sources – possibly even from his mother Annie, an activist in Germany's emerging feminist movement as well as a *saloniste*, who had joined a women's philosophy group in Leipzig and translated into German a volume by the French philosopher Jean-Marie Guyau on English utilitarian ethics. But Pevsner did not have a monopoly on the idea. The linkage between modern architecture and utilitarianism was already sufficiently familiar in the 1920s for Evelyn Waugh to satirise it in his 1928 novel *Decline and Fall*. Waugh's book introduces the terrifying German architect Professor Otto Silenus who at the age of twenty-five is invited to tear down Margot Beste-Chetwynde's Tudor manor in the Hampshire country-side and put up a house designed like a factory – 'the only perfect building' – made out of polished aluminium and vita-glass. In a memorable piece of dialogue, two characters discuss the merits of Silenus's house. 'It's said to be the only really *imaginative* building since the French Revolution,' one says. 'He's got right away from Corbusier, anyway.' 'If people realised,' says the second, 'Corbusier is a pure nineteenth-century, Manchester school utilitarian, and that's why they like him.'

Although Pevsner's work on the modern movement was not original, he presented it in an unusually forceful way, identifying the birth of a new *Zeitgeist* as a comfort to anyone distressed, as he had been, by the outcome of the First World War and by Spengler's pessimism about the future of Western civilisation. 'The only fact that matters to the historian', he wrote twelve years later in *Outline*, 'is that the Modern Movement is a genuine and independent style. This fact is full of promise. For over a hundred years no style in that sense had existed. As Western civilisation had become more and more subdivided, it had lost its faculty to create a language of its own. An atomised society cannot have an architectural style. Can we not take it then that the recovery of a true style in the visual arts, one in which once again building rules, and painting and sculpture serve . . . indicates the return of unity in society too?'

Pevsner's work at Göttingen and his contributions to scholarly publications marked him out as one of the most promising young academics of his generation and someone prepared to challenge what he regarded as the complacency of more senior figures including his former employer at the Dresden Painting Gallery. With the backing of Wilhelm Pinder, with whom he had had a warm relationship, and of Pinder's former war comrade Georg Graf Vitzthum von Eckstädt, the chair of art history at Göttingen, Pevsner could have risen to the very top of the German academic hierarchy. Instead, Adolf Hitler was installed as Chancellor on 30 January 1933, Pevsner's thirty-first birthday, and in March was given dictatorial powers. Less than two months later, on May Day, new racial laws were introduced banning Jews from state employment and Pevsner among many others was put out of a job.

Pevsner, it must now be said, was a keen supporter of the Nazis. This has been hinted at occasionally in the past but only on the evidence of his literary style which in the 1930s began to take on some of the features of Nazi propaganda. Mention of Gropius made him particularly ardent and some remarks in *Pioneers of the Modern Movement* are reminiscent of Führer-speak:

> . . . the artist who is representative of this century of ours must needs be cold, as he stands for a century cold as steel and glass, a century the precision of which leaves less space for self-expression than did any period before.
>
> However, the great creative brain will find its own way even in times of overpowering collective energy, even with the medium of this new style of the twentieth century which, because it is a genuine style as opposed to a passing fashion, is totalitarian . . .

When *Pioneers* was republished after the war as *Pioneers of Modern Design*, some of these more extreme phrases were toned down, 'the great creative brain' becoming 'genius' and 'totalitarian' 'universal', though whether this was at Pevsner's instigation or his publisher's is not known. But because he came to be adopted by the British as one of their own and because he never allowed himself to talk about politics in public, the inference of Nazi sympathy has always been greeted by his friends and followers as if it were meant to demean him, which it often was. It is nonetheless true. During the 1920s and 1930s, Pevsner was as excited by the Nazis as his fellow countrymen, and for the same reasons.

This was observed by the sister-in-law of an English lecturer at Göttingen who met Pevsner in May 1933 and was intrigued by the ambiguities of his position. He was a 'fair type, very refined and cultural', wrote Francesca Wilson, a Birmingham schoolteacher and refugee worker, in her diary, 'a Jew but feels himself entirely German. Very nationalist in sympathy. Absurd situation for him . . . He had a *dringende Bitte nicht zu lesen* [urgent request not to teach]. They warned him that the students would make a row if he did.' Later in the month, she wrote an article in the *Birmingham Post* in which she quoted him at length:

> One of the most interesting conversations I had (and people still speak their minds out very frankly) was with a Privatdozent, who the day before had been asked not to lecture. He was tall and blond – only a German with a sixth sense would have known that he wasn't Aryan – dignified and refined, not only in appearance, but in cast of mind. 'I love Germany,' he said. 'It is my country. I am a Nationalist, and in spite of the way I am treated, I want this movement to succeed. There is no alternative but chaos, and I cannot want my country to be plunged into civil war. There are things worse than Hitlerism; I think your Press in England does not realise that. And there is much idealism in the movement. There are many things in it which I greet with enthusiasm and which I myself have preached in my writings. I consider the compulsory labour which is to start next January an excellent thing. All young men will have six months' service for the State, and no matter what their rank in life they will all work together. Hitler is planning public works on a vast scale to cure the unemployment problem, and I believe that he has the courage and will to do what he says. Then there is much that is Puritan and moral in the movement – a great drive is to be made against luxury, vice and corruption . . . For fifteen years we have been humiliated by the outside Powers. No wonder that Hitler appeals to our youth when he tells them to believe in themselves again, that the future is theirs to mould, that if they are united Germany will no longer be the pariah of the world . . .'

For Pevsner and his generation, the early years of Nazism were

Germany's glory years. The entire population was caught up in its fever, including not a few assimilated Jews, Jews being no less immune than anyone else to – can one say this? – the spirit of the age.

There were understandable reasons for Jews in Germany to gravitate to German nationalism. For centuries, they had been barred from entry into the upper echelons of German public life. A degree of liberalisation in the nineteenth century allowed them to escape these restrictions and live normally but only if they gave up their religion. They did so in droves. Pevsner's father Hugo (originally Hillel), who was a business-man and synagogue-goer, fully expected his son to train for religious initiation at the age of thirteen, but Pevsner took advantage of his father's absence in Sweden during the First World War to avoid doing so. Instead, at the age of nineteen, he converted to Evangelical Luther-anism, Northern Germany's dominant religion. So adverse did he feel conditions were for Jews in Germany, even after the Weimar government had removed all racial barriers in 1919, that in the personal documents he lodged with Leipzig University, he recorded that he had been born a Christian. Having done so, he continued to suppress his true identity all his life, claiming on BBC radio in 1954 that 'my origins are in a part of Germany which is Protestant and in this country I would certainly be called very low church indeed'. He also married into a German family with a blue-chip pedigree as legislators to the state of Saxony and was devoted to his wife's father, Justizrat Alfred Kurlbaum, one of the country's most distinguished appeal lawyers in the *Reichsgericht*.

Pevsner's Leipzig years were overshadowed by the war and its consequences. In 1916, there had been food shortages and riots; in the 1920s, the great inflation. He shared the common view that Germany's pre-war militarism was a justified assault on Britain's global economic monopoly, that Germany's subsequent defeat was not a defeat but a betrayal, that the post-war social-democratic Weimar regime in which his mother was an activist was incompetent, and that Hitler offered those things that conservative Germans had always seen as the answer to their political woes: unity, leadership, power, purpose. Nazism also rein-forced the basic concepts that he had acquired from art history: the link between the soul of the *Volk*, its art and its destiny – ideas with their roots in Greek idealism but central to the Romantic movement, Richard

Wagner and the rise of German nationalism. It was therefore Pevsner's common ground with Nazi sentiment that led him from the study of history to the practice of modernism.

Pevsner's only point of conflict with Hitler, apart from *Mein Kampf* which he dismissed as mere propaganda, was on this point of modernism. Hitler regarded modernism – and the practice of art history – as Jewish, degenerate and unGerman. While Pevsner shared Hitler's contempt for abstract art, the irrationality of which he regarded as beyond the comprehension of the ordinary man, he thought Hitler's view of abstract architecture immature and unsophisticated because, unlike art, it was more logical, not less. Nonetheless, he continued to find Hitler dazzling even after his dismissal from Göttingen, and in 1933 and 1934 wrote articles for the German press broadly supporting Reichsminister Josef Goebbels on the question of the state's right to interfere in artistic output. (His conclusion, in one piece called '*Kunst und Staat*', was that the demands of the state took priority over those of art, though he added that if the Government were more broadminded it could avoid checking the creative spirit and even recruit artists who had kept a distance from the Nazi regime.)

Pevsner spelled out his view of his new function in *Academies of Art, Past and Present*, a book on the social history of the artist which appeared in 1940 but which was written and ready for publication in Germany by 1933:

> In this century of ours . . . the historian can no longer shut himself off from contemporary needs. Everywhere he finds himself entangled in topical questions, or pushed aside into academic seclusion. Is it not one of the most urgent tasks for twentieth-century historiography to reconcile scholarship and direct utility? Too often has the journalist . . . provided meretricious biographies or monographs written without any of that conscientious respect for facts that characterizes genuine historical writing. But it is not by . . . picking up a few scattered facts and forging them into a chain . . . that an understanding of topical problems and difficulties can be attained. On the contrary. Only by throwing into relief the individual oneness of any given period or style or nation, and the logical coherence of all its utterances in the most varied fields of human activity, will the historiographer in the end be

able to make his reader discover what form a certain problem must take at
the present moment.

This shows Pevsner laying out what he sees as the crucial political
function, achievable only by the art historian, of defining a nation's
cultural essence so that it can play to its strengths.

The British were mercifully unaware of what they were taking on
when Pevsner arrived on their doorstep at the end of 1933. Had his
background been better known, it is unlikely that he would ever have
made the headway he did. Instead, as a refugee aided by Birmingham
Quakers and the Academic Assistance Council, he was automatically
taken to be an opponent of the regime that had rejected him. Even
today, twenty years after his death, he is still routinely described as a
socialist or having socialist leanings – mainly because English-speaking
countries always tended to stress the Modern Movement's socialist
origins and its reforming ideals. In Germany, by contrast, nationalists
could see it as the final step in the long march of German destiny.

In 1977, prompted by the dismal quality of most modern architecture
in England and by Pevsner's part in either propagating it or failing
adequately to criticise it, one of his former students launched a
fundamental attack on Pevsner's ideology and motives. David Watkin's
book *Morality and Architecture* was the first substantial challenge to the
idea, by then widely accepted, that only modern-looking architecture
was appropriate in a modern age. It followed the lead of Karl Popper
whose 1957 book *The Poverty of Historicism* had exposed the social
determinism of Marxism. *Morality and Architecture* questioned the
legitimacy of the *Zeitgeist* as an intellectual construct and contested its
currency in contemporary English architecture. Watkin's treatment of
Pevsner was immediately savaged not only by the architectural
profession but by some who had come to find Pevsner's teachings too
narrow, including the architectural historian Reyner Banham, also a
former student. It led, however, to a complete unravelling of Pevsner's
intellectual and moral authority. By that time, Pevsner had come to be
regarded in Britain simply as a fussy and out-of-date but still lovable
uncle. Now, art historians and architectural theorists alike began to
retreat from his writings or to use them only as a springboard for their
own writings. It also became increasingly common in some circles to talk

about Pevsner as an unwelcome figure in his adopted country and an alien implant.

This scapegoating of Pevsner by historians was itself ahistorical, however, because it took him to task for methodological failings that were still invisible to most people or which had certainly not yet been properly articulated. Far from offending against English empiricism, Pevsner's principal message – moral outrage against aesthetic shoddiness, a call to arms for an architectural style to suit the age – was welcomed by most of the people he ever came in contact with and no doubt by many more who only ever read his books or heard him on radio. In 1936, he slipped easily into the arms of the *Architectural Review* as it moved from 'cultivated and rather dilettante eclecticism' at the start of the 1930s towards 'unremitting advocacy of the modern movement'; and he rose steadily into a position thirty years later where he was equally in demand by the Establishment and the anti-Establishment as someone who could best defend their aspirations. The rejection of him after 1977 has far more to do with cultural changes that affected the whole of society at the time – exasperation with the failed rhetoric of the modern project and the rebirth of nostalgia – than with any long-standing objection to missionising per se. Indeed, what was intriguing about Watkin's critique of Pevsner was its perpetuation of what it claimed to be fighting against: a moral mission of its own, confusion of objectivity and subjectivity, belief in the appropriateness of a particular architecture to a particular culture and the attempt to harness England to a particular expression of European idealism. (Watkin even subtitled his next book but one, on the eighteenth-century architect Athenian Stuart, 'Pioneer of the Greek Revival' in faux-homage to Pevsner's *Pioneers*.)

So any challenge to Pevsner's reputation over the last two-and-a-half decades must not be allowed to colour the way in which he was seen while he was active. But how was he seen? Initially he was an unknown quantity. He arrived at a time when attitudes towards the new Germany were polarised along cultural and class lines; and because of his aversion to Judaism, he was not always as open as other exiles were about why he was in England, which made his identity ambiguous. There was also an issue of personality: he took himself and his project of cultural renewal very seriously. In Göttingen, his students had called him '*des Herrn Gottes Bleistift*' – 'the Lord God's pencil' – because he was tall, thin and all-knowing; the head of the English Department had also made up a little rhyme about him:

> Den lange Pevsner sieht man lungern
> Privatdozenten müssen hungern!
>
> Lanky Pevsner's on the street
> Tutors can't get much to eat!

In England, no one knew what to make of him. He was obviously energetic but it was impossible to say why. 'Immer fleissig, immer fleissig [always busy, always busy],' gibed Kenneth Clark one day when he found Pevsner scribbling away while waiting outside his office at the National Gallery. Companies approached by Pevsner in connection with a two-year research fellowship that he was offered by Birmingham University between 1934 and 1936 found him inscrutable and mainly unsympathetic. His work, which required him to mislead and eventually misrepresent his prospective interviewees, aimed to show how public taste was being betrayed by manufacturers of domestic goods and furnishings. A few acute minds may have sensed this. One firm responded to his overtures by telling him that it had no interest in public taste; another suspected that he was a spy – not unreasonably, in view of the number of art historians who spied as a sideline: Anton Springer, Kenneth Clark and Anthony Blunt to name but three.

Francesca Wilson, who had met Pevsner in Göttingen in 1933 and became his landlady in Edgbaston the following year, took a long time to begin to feel she knew and liked him. She had a messy household and found him too orderly and 'stiff upperlipped' at first. It was almost a year before she could record in her diary that he was 'water rather than wine but good water, pleasant to have every day. He is much more interesting because of his disasters. They have brought out the latent energy of his character – whereas success would have made a rather complacent and commonplace professor out of him, hardship has showed him up well. I admire every day the admirable dignity with which he beats his ridiculous situation and accomplishes his rather tiresome tasks.' Five months later she wrote that another member of her household had commented on Pevsner's 'smooth and easy urbanity, very soothing, nothing insolent about him . . . no corners'.

If Pevsner's personality was at odds with the relaxed, upper-class manners that the socially aspirant still gravitated to in Britain in the 1930s, he nonetheless had a message that attracted him to social progressives: the need for reform.

Following the end of the First World War, there was immense enthusiasm in the country at large for sweeping away the past and creating a new society and Pevsner was embraced because this was evidently a task that he could contribute to. He was mocked by a small element that included the poet John Betjeman and whose schoolboy ridicule of 'Granny' and 'Herr-Doktor-Professor' became part of the glue that held their group together, but their significance was tiny compared with the number of his admirers. Even Betjeman, in ganging up against him, was only ingratiating himself with the clique he most wanted to be liked by. In his earliest dealings with Pevsner he was respectful and appreciative. A letter of his from the late 1930s applauded Pevsner's writings on England's nineteenth-century rustic architects ('I loved your article on M[ack]murdo which was a wonderful eye opener for me') and confessed to having 'spent a lot of time trying to discover "pioneer" architects of my own but never had the time or the ability to be as thorough as you are'. He also invited Pevsner to join the Art Workers' Guild, the successor to William Morris, and to meet for a conversation.

The truth is that Pevsner impressed most of the people he ever met, as he must have done in the early 1930s to have cut a swathe through a new country as a complete unknown. He benefited from the sympathy felt in English academic circles for the victims of Nazi Germany but that alone cannot explain all the doors that opened for him. His detractors have called him dry and dogmatic, a 'blinkered fanatic', 'Der great Kategorist', but he could be charming and entertaining, had a fine sense of humour and many of his innumerable contacts became loyal friends, their friendships memorialised in the dedications to his *Buildings of England* books.

It is possible, in fact, to track Pevsner's career through the personalities he dazzled. In 1934, Professor Philip Sargant Florence, an American who had done pioneering research into workplace fatigue before moving to England in 1921, gave Pevsner a two-year fellowship in the Department of Commerce at Birmingham University in a field unrelated to history of art, out of sheer conviction that he would perform. In 1935, Gordon Russell, the Cotswolds furniture manufacturer, created a job for him again in a new field – fabric buying – because he seemed to know more about it than anyone else. In the same year, Frank Pick, the genius behind London Transport, pushed the Ministry of Labour and the Home Office into giving Pevsner a work permit, and a couple of years later helped find him a house in Hampstead. When Pevsner was locked up as an enemy alien in an internment camp outside Liverpool in 1940, it was Pick again – with Josiah Wedgwood of the Wedgwood ceramics firm, the writer P. Morton Shand, supposedly one of Pevsner's enemies, and Kenneth Clark at the National Gallery – who helped get him released. In 1936, James Richards, the editor of the *Architectural Review*, spent time grooming him as a writer on design and felt so well rewarded for his investment that just five years later he gave Pevsner the editor's seat when he left the magazine to do war work for the Ministry of Information. In 1941, Allen Lane, the founder of Penguin books, was bowled over by Pevsner as by no one else, commissioned *Outline* from him and made him editor of the *King Penguin* series. In 1945, Lane also gave instant assent to Pevsner's proposals to write the *Buildings of England* series and to edit a *Pelican History of Art*, both based on the *Handbuch der Kunstwissenschaft* to which he had contributed in 1928. And Gordon Jackson, the master of Birkbeck College, said of the remarkable German who spent the nights watching for incendiary bombs on the roof, then writing the text of *Outline* on an upturned bucket in the basement, 'I hear we've got a rather bright chap on the roof; I think we might invite him down.' There were also armies of ordinary people – local schoolteachers, vicars and county librarians – whom Pevsner met on his month-long research tours for *The Buildings of England* during the 1950s and 1960s who knew that he was something special.

Later in Pevsner's career, some of his fellow committee members on the Victorian Society, which he co-chaired from its inception in 1958 to 1976, felt that he was not as committed to the cause of preservation as they were and that if he had to choose between saving an undistinguished old building and erecting an undistinguished new one, he might easily argue that the *Zeitgeist* demanded demolition. For them, the importance of all old buildings was that they continue to shape contemporary life; for him, it seemed, only the best old buildings mattered; the rest were archaeological conundrums to be solved, documented and passed by. But by far and away the majority of the Victorian Society's members looked on Pevsner as a force for good and so valued his presence among them, in the full knowledge of his commitment to contemporary architecture, that in 1976 he was created president for life. Their affection for him was vividly recalled at a conference in 2001 where Jane Fawcett, the Society's former long-standing secretary, gave a moving talk about Pevsner which brought her to tears and which was met with a hugely sympathetic response from her audience.

One measure of Pevsner's enduring popularity is the hallowing of anecdotes about him – the time he was flung by a goat on Lord Farringdon's lawn, his habit of eating spaghetti at lunchtime because it went down quickly and left more time for work, his pictorial shorthand ('∩ x 4 N' meaning four bays of Romanesque arches on the north wall), his encounters with bewildered Wodehousean aristocrats like the Duke of Beaufort at Badminton whose conversation stopped at 'what is it y' said y' do?' and whose brain only seemed to engage when the talk came round to home-made butter, his difficulties with machinery or cars or simple cooking equipment. Apparently casual remarks made while lecturing were also instantly memorable – 'First there was Noyon Cathedral, that was 80 feet; then there was Paris, that was 115 feet; then there was Reims, 125 feet; then Amiens, 140 feet; then Beauvais which was 157 feet and fell down!' – or his habit of drawing exactly the right quotation scribbled on a piece of paper from his pocket the moment he needed it, or suddenly illuminating his face by the light of his slide-projectors to dramatise a point, or putting up a slide of a clock tower at exactly the time shown by the hands on its face. These stories are all evidence of a much loved presence.

But while Pevsner's adjustment to life in Britain seemed easy, his transition into an Englishman was much more tentative than is normally thought. Far from being an enthusiast for England, he had not wanted to leave Germany even after his dismissal by the Nazis, nor did he see England as an enticing alternative. As a young boy, he had gone with his mother on a visit to her parents who had settled in the London suburb of West Hampstead and been left with the impression of a mean, miserable city. His next visit in 1930 reinforced his sense of the country's shabbiness and inefficiency, its ignorance of anything outside itself and its lamentable sense of design – dull and dusty or jazzy and jerky. Britain had been an inspiration in the nineteenth century but had not systematised its own achievement and therefore had not learnt by its own example. The most advanced countries in the world – led by Germany, he believed – were now forging ahead with a brilliant new aesthetic but Britain was hiding in its past. Its idea of modern architecture ran, in his own words, from 'utterly uneventful' Neo-Georgian for the wealthy to 'rubbishy spec-built' Neo-Tudor for the masses with a 'vast and hollow' Neo-Palladian set aside for government and industry. No one was addressing the challenge of the modern. He sympathised with what he believed was the common view of foreigners that Britain was a dying culture in which 'conservatism comes dangerously near inertia'; the country was evidently in retreat. As for art history, it barely existed – and there were no jobs in it. 'Baroque? Baroque? There's no such thing!' said Sir Albert Richardson, professor of architecture at University College, London, some years later. 'It's nothing but the Spanish word for pearl!'

The idea of embracing England was therefore not his first reaction to his teaching ban in Göttingen. Instead, he tried to find alternative work within the world he knew best, and to dig himself in with the Nazi regime. He wrote energetically to publishers – sometimes under a pseudonym – with ideas for articles, which were accepted, and for books, which were not. He also applied for new posts with German connections, especially in Italy where he offered himself as a lecturer in German art at the University of Rome and at the German Institute of Art History in Florence. So hopeful was he that there was still a place for him in German society that he applied opportunistically to join Germany's Imperial Chamber of Culture, the *Reichskulturkammer*, very probably asking it to confirm that his activities in London were in the interests of the German state, just as Gropius – with whom he was in touch – did after moving to London. It was only after Pevsner's rejection by the *Reichskulturkammer* in March 1935 and the offer of work by Gordon Russell that he began to feel that England might have something to offer. Later in that same year, he went back to Göttingen, packed up his belongings and family – his wife Lola and their three children Uta, Tom and Dieter – and brought them back with him to England. Even then, he and Lola kept sending their children each summer to see his parents in Leipzig and to Lola's father in his summerhouse near Naumburg. So blind were they to the impending storm and to warnings from English friends that after the children's visit to Naumburg in the summer of 1939, Uta got stranded and had to live out the war in Germany under a false identity.

In addition to his loyalty to Germany, Pevsner remained loyal to the conservative German academic establishment and continued to correspond with art historians who thrived under Hitler's regime. In 1940, he dedicated his book *Academies of Art, Past and Present* to his former teacher, Wilhelm Pinder, who had gone from Leipzig to Munich and from there to the chair of art history at Berlin and, it later turned out, become an adviser to the Nazis on looted art. Then, after the war, he invited numerous German historians to contribute to his fifty-two-volume *Pelican History of Art* including at least two who might easily have qualified for denazification.

None of this seems to have registered with the English but it rankled with his fellow refugees. The most prominent – Fritz Saxl, Rudolf Wittkower, Edgar Wind and Ernst Gombrich – had been associated not with the German university system, as Pevsner had been, but with the Warburg Institute. The Warburg was based in Hamburg and was started and funded by members of the Warburg banking family in 1921. As a private foundation, it could stay out of German nationalistic polemics and concentrate on the liberal-humanist tradition which, among other things, had made Jewish emancipation a point of principle in the early nineteenth century. Immediately after the Nazis came to power in 1933, the entire institution moved to London where its academic staff would seize the high ground of English-speaking scholarship. By contrast, those historians who stayed within the university system in Germany tended to disappear from view, along with their work. Pevsner is a rare example of a German nationalist art historian who got out and became known. Although cordial to him professionally, most of the Warburgers found that he stuck in their throat. One measure of the gap between him and them is that Gombrich had been converted by Karl Popper from his already declining faith in *Geistesgeschichte* at a seminar in 1936 while for Pevsner, *Geistesgeschichte* was a late discovery and next in importance to him after Pinder. 'Of the early development of the Warburg school at Hamburg I noticed little or nothing,' he said in 1969.

Pevsner's fidelity to Germany and German officialdom must surprise anyone who has come to think of him as a wholly British phenomenon. This unawareness of Pevsner's background is partly explained by his success in erasing a period in his life that would always require too much explanation for outside observers. It is also explained by the fact that once Pevsner had escaped the cauldron of German politics, qualities in him that seem perhaps disturbingly stereotypical in their historical context – extreme self-discipline, an overriding sense of mission, excessive and uncomplaining industry – took on a more benign expression and could even be smiled at as amusing eccentricities. His relocation to England, whether he sought it or not, therefore proved a moderating influence, the full extent of which can be seen in his BBC talks.

With Pevsner's relocation to England, he set himself on a mission with the intriguing idea of putting the purely theoretical idea of *Geistesgeschichte* to practical use. *Geistesgeschichte* taught that a culture revealed itself in its artefacts. Impoverished artefacts must therefore represent an impoverished culture, which is how Pevsner saw England. But if the situation was reversible and artistic standards could be improved, the rest of the culture could be brought up with them. Pevsner had found a precedent for this in Prince Albert's mission in the mid-nineteenth century, a precedent he referred to twice on radio. Albert had set out to educated uneducated tastes 'by applying most efficiently the fine arts to our manufactures, in order to wed high art to mechanical skill'. His aim was essentially commercial, as was all ambition, according to Pevsner, in the Victorian age: to make Britain 'the headquarters of the skilled industry of the world'. Pevsner's was more poetic: to make Britain once again the headquarters of an idealistic utilitarianism.

His first attempt to achieve this, at Birmingham University, took the fight directly to the enemy. What he seems to have wanted to do was to write a manifesto accusing manufacturers of betraying their culture by foisting bad design on a gullible public – an accusation in which he set himself against a virtual caricature of commercial interests, just as William Morris had done. But because his work was being undertaken under the auspices of a university, he found himself forced to conduct it in a more responsible manner. An academic goal was set: that of establishing how design in household furnishings was created – whether it was imposed on the public by manufacturers in what they made available, or demanded of manufacturers by the public in its buying decisions, or whether it occurred somewhere in between, in the way that travelling salesmen or shops and stores interpreted it. He was also required to carry out an extensive research exercise using questionnaires, and ended up talking to 150 manufacturers in the Midlands area during 1934 and 1935, discovering a huge amount of information about the production and marketing of furniture, fabrics, ceramics and wall decorations. A more neutral writer might have turned this into a revealing report on the interrelationship of taste and trade; instead, once his research fellowship at Birmingham was over, he produced what is probably the most slanted piece of writing ever produced by an art historian: a piece of blatant propaganda that failed to test any of its starting assumptions and blithely manipulated most of its results. It appeared in 1937 as *An Enquiry into Industrial Art in England*, published by the Cambridge University Press.

Eight years later at the start of 1945, Pevsner was introduced to the BBC and attempted to use his soapbox in the same way. The introduction was effected by his next-door neighbour in Hampstead, the poet and publisher Geoffrey Grigson. Grigson was a combative figure in London art circles and may have seen in Pevsner an outsider to ginger up the Corporation's coverage of the visual arts. Pevsner's first broadcasts were as confrontational as Grigson could have wished, attacking the Royal Academy as a modern irrelevance and bludgeoning listeners to improve their taste in contemporary furnishings. The talks were not a success. Even allowing for the fact that intellectuals in the 1940s still behaved as if pomposity was an acceptable way of engaging the masses, Pevsner came across sounding strident, stilted and unintentionally condescending, even in his lighter moments.

'I have the greatest respect for people who can do things with their hands – probably because I never can,' he told listeners in a talk on the function of craft in January 1946. 'They hold the world together, the people who of a Sunday settle down to repairing fuses and carburettors and grandfather clocks and the people who for sheer fun bind books and weave scarves and graft trees and make kitchen dressers.' A talk he gave on soft furnishings ten months later managed to sound both patronising and insulting. 'It's rather hard on you to be talked to about [carpets, curtains and upholstery] – indeed it's hard on anybody. But on you especially because somehow I don't think the curtains, covers and carpets which you see day in, day out, are up to very much ... Rich women if they choose [a material for a frock] rashly can give it away and try again – even today I'm told – but you can't. You'll have to wear the damn thing even if you are sick of it.' In his most Orwellian and wooden talk, on art's duties to the state, he invented the scenario of having met in a pub ('at the local') an architect who wanted to be more artistic, only to go on and accuse him of the crime of bourgeois self-centredness.

With the war over, Pevsner's talks did at least coincide with the new cultural agenda of national reconstruction. They coincided also with the interventionism that many within the BBC saw as their proper role ('This problem of art and the State is one which should be *made* to interest "the man in the street",' one of his producers, Noni Wright, had told him). The tone he adopted, possibly on the advice of James Richards, his former editor at the *Architectural Review*, would have been familiar from the way that government tended to address the public through its Ministry of Information films. But in trying to act as an ambassador for the national interest, Pevsner was also compromising his private mission as a polemicist and his creativity as a writer. After receiving an almost Stalinist list of demands for rewrites from one particular BBC department, he refrained from pursuing other programme ideas that had been received enthusiastically some months earlier and directed his efforts elsewhere within the Corporation.

Fortunately for posterity, two things happened that rescued him from these early, crude offerings. The first was that at the end of September 1946, the BBC had launched a new service – the Third Programme – offering very much what Francesca Wilson had argued for before the war in a column in the *Birmingham Post*: 'a station for highbrows' with 'the best people in the country giving the best of themselves in proper lectures – lectures which are not a little potted knowledge but which have the gift of making the far seem near, the dark luminous'. The Talks Department was invited to find speakers to balance the preponderance of music programming on the station and quickly identified Pevsner as a potential contributor. His other saving grace was that Anna ('Niouta') Kallin, the producer who looked after him in the Talks Department, teamed him up with a young producer called Basil Taylor, another of Grigson's finds, who was much more interested in observational essays than aesthetic mentoring. This combination of events proved decisive to Pevsner's future career. Moving him off the Home Service and onto the Third Programme diverted him from mass audiences to audiences he was likely to engage with more respectfully; teaming him up with Taylor forced him to find a lighter touch, free from his clumsy moralising. Taylor was Pevsner's first real immersion into what English intellectuality meant. Although the campaigning Pevsner could occasionally break through – in his talk on Washington and monumentality, for example – his Teutonic self was largely suppressed, alongside his Jewish self, even in a potboiler on the origins of the Bauhaus.

In the nine talks that Taylor produced him in between 1946 and 1950, Pevsner became expansive, authoritative and detached. He could now tackle subjects that were difficult or unfamiliar to English listeners such as Bruegel or the art of the German Reformation. He could also indulge the antiquarian side he had developed at the *Architectural Review*, retrieving obscure literary quotations – in a couple of cases about sex, in two others about mediaeval torture – or dropping in odd phrases in Latin or old French. He could be funny too. One talk dealt with the writings of an eighteenth-century writer who had dismissed the Elgin Marbles as second rate and conceived of casting a plum pudding in a mould taken from a female breast. Another talk quoted the alleged co-author of William Chambers's *Dissertation on Oriental Gardening* of 1772, one 'Tan Chet-Qua of Quang-Chew-Fu, Gent., FRSS, MRAAP, also MIAAF, TRA, CGHMW, and ATTQ'.

Some of these talks took him back to material from his student days and to favourite textbooks: Emile Mâle's *L'art religieux*, Bruno Gebhardt's *Handbuch der deutschen Geschichte* and Siegmund Hellmann's *Das Mittelalter bis zum Ausgange der Kreuzzüge*, which Pevsner had read three times in quick succession in April and May 1924 in preparation for the oral examination its author would give him. Other talks gave him an opportunity to exploit his own incessant research. For almost any subject that Taylor might suggest, Pevsner had a ready-made set of references and an almost instantaneous recall of the entire history of European civilisation. That encyclopaedic range is evident in almost all his talks.

Between 1945 and 1977, Pevsner gave some seventy-eight talks to the BBC's domestic audience and another fifteen in its German-language service. These broadcasts, more than any of his other activities, established Pevsner as a national phenomenon in Britain – 'a man very much of our own', as one writer said of him in 1960 – and served to divorce him as far as that was possible from his pre-war self. He was highly valued both inside and outside the BBC as a speaker who always had something intriguing to say. He was also a novelty. Not all German-speaking art historians were considered fluent enough in English to be allowed on the air: in 1954, Erwin Panofsky who had moved from the Warburg Institute to Princeton and New York University was still regarded as having too thick an accent to be acceptable for the Third; and Gombrich was not allowed to broadcast until 1963. ('We should love to put Gombrich on – but we can't, he agrees himself,' said one of Pevsner's producers.) Pevsner's mild German accent by contrast became so well known that when the BBC Governors started casting around for someone to give its flagship Reith Lectures for 1955, his was name they lighted on. The seven talks that he went on to give, on the Englishness of English art, were the first Reith Lectures on a subject other than politics and power and were greeted by the *Journal of Education* as 'far and away the best . . . so far'. He visualised them as an opportunity to fulfil the goal he had set for himself in *Academies of Art* – applying Pinder's various techniques for 'throwing into relief the individual oneness of any given . . . nation', helping England to discover and exploit its strength, and at the same time validating *Kunstgeschichte* as a practical science. Although he was never fully satisfied that he had achieved this aim, they were probably the highpoint of his career as a visible public presence in England. In the years that followed, he gradually became more of a background figure, serving on a growing number of strategic, advisory, national and campaigning bodies as a member of the Great and the Good, and lecturing widely but no longer shaping the emerging agenda of architectural or historical thought.

In 1969, Pevsner took retirement from Birkbeck College and was given a knighthood for his services to art and architecture, which the Federal Republic of Germany matched by awarding him its Order of Merit. These and other public honours were only partly a consolation, however, for a wave of depression that swept over him in the latter half of the 1960s. His wife Lola, who organised and drove him on his exhausting twice-yearly expeditions for *The Buildings of England*, had died suddenly in 1963 of an embolism on the lung while he was in

America, and his recovery from the shock was slow. Lola's absence also
made the already huge burden of *Buildings of England* even greater and
Pevsner increasingly regretted the amount of time it was taking up,
though without ever feeling that he could hand over the project to
anyone else. His vision for a new Dessau in England's green and pleasant
land was not materialising either. He became nostalgic for the recklessness
of his younger writings, which he called 'lusty generalisations', and sad
that he had allowed minor work, including work for the BBC, to distract
him from serious scholarship and from his mission as a cultural interpreter.
To the very end, he could not understand why his intellectual models had
been found wanting in either of his two main fields – history or
architecture – and came to the conclusion that he had failed.

Perhaps his failure was inevitable for a German ideologue who took
on English empiricism on its home ground. Having accepted as
uncontentious a body of ideas forged in the exceptional circumstances of
Germany between the wars, he arrived in Britain with expectations that
proved, with hindsight, to be vastly misconceived – especially about
Britain's receptivity to the unfamiliar. ('The English seem to move
together when they are ready to do so, and no amount of exhortation
will move them,' his Reith Lectures producer, Donald Boyd, told him
kindly; 'they resist and resent it.') He also failed to see that his practical
insights needed to be detached from the mysticism in which *Kunstgeschichte* had framed them; and that even the most persuasive ideas lose
their appeal with the passage of time. Nonetheless, his impact on Britain
was immense and we can now look back with fondness at a man who
made a unique contribution to intellectual inquiry in the middle third of
the twentieth century, who was able to convince large sections of society
that aesthetics mattered and deserved attention, and who inspired others
to follow him into areas of inquiry that no one had yet taken seriously.
He brought to Britain – and to other countries in which his work was
translated – a new voice, a new body of thought, new ways of talking
about buildings and suggestive new texts. No other individual was as
passionate as he was about architecture and art or as energetic in
promoting the need to know and do more about it. His years of greatest
activity can without exaggeration be labelled as Britain's 'Pevsner years';
and of those years, his BBC talks are the most valuable and vivid
summary.

CHRONOLOGY

1902	Born 30 January in Leipzig
1919	Older brother Heinrich commits suicide
1921	Converts from Judaism to Evangelical Lutheranism
1923	Marries Karola 'Lola' Kurlbaum
1924	Ph.D., Leipzig University
1924–29	Assistant Keeper (Voluntär), Dresden Art Gallery
1929–33	Lecturer (Privatdozent) in Mediaeval and Later Art History, Göttingen University
1933	Moves to England
1934–35	Two-year fellowship, Department of Commerce, Birmingham University
1935	Joined in England by Lola and their three children, Uta, Thomas and Dieter
1936	Starts writing for the *Architectural Review*; *Pioneers of the Modern Movement* published
1937	*An Enquiry into Industrial Art in England* published
1940	Interned in Huyton internment camp outside Liverpool; *Academies of Art, Past and Present* published
1941	Works as road sweeper clearing bomb damage in Camden by day; fire watching on roof of Birkbeck College in the City of London by night
1942	Mother commits suicide in Leipzig to avoid being sent to a concentration camp; *An Outline of European Art* published
1942–45	Acting editor, *Architectural Review*
1942–59	Lecturer in the History of Art, Birkbeck College, London University
1945–77	Talks presenter, BBC Radio
1947	Member of editorial board, *Architectural Review*
1949	Hon. Associate, Royal College of Art; *Pioneers of Modern Design* published
1949–55	Slade Professor of Fine Art, Cambridge University
1950	Fellow of Society of Antiquaries
1950–55	Fellow, St John's College, Cambridge University

1953	Commander of the Order of the British Empire; publishes first volume of the *Pelican History of Art*
1955	BBC Reith Lecturer; Council member, William Morris Society
1958–76	Becomes Founding Co-chairman, Victorian Society
1959	Becomes member, National Advisory Council for Art Education
1959–69	Professor, History of Art, Birkbeck College, London University
1961	Becomes member, National Council for Diplomas in Art and Design
1962	Becomes member, Arts Panel, British Council
1963	Howland Memorial Prize, Yale University
1963–68	Commissioner, Royal Commission on Historical Monuments
1964	*Sources of Modern Art* published; reissued 1968 as *Sources of Modern Art and Architecture*
1965	Fellow, British Academy
1966	Becomes member, Historic Buildings Council, and of the Royal Fine Art Commission; awarded Alice Davis Hitchcock Medallion, Society of Architectural Historians of Great Britain; Hon. D.Litt., Leicester University
1967	Hon. Fellow, Royal Institute of British Architects; Hon. Fellow, St John's College, Cambridge University; Hon. D. Litt., Leeds University; Hon. Fellow, York University; Royal Gold Medallist, Royal Institute of British Architects
1968	Hon. LL.D., Oxford University
1968–69	Slade Professor of Fine Art, Oxford University
1969	Knighthood, for services to art and architecture; Hon. D.Litt., East Anglia University; Grand Cross of Merit, Federal Republic of Germany; Vice-President, William Morris Society
1972	*Some Architectural Writers of the Twentieth Century* published
1976	Life President, Victorian Society; *A History of Building Types* published
1983	Dies 18 August in London.

Pevsner on Art and Architecture

The rise of academies

Home Service
FRIDAY 25 MAY 1945
Producer: Not known

'That angry genius, Turner.' He was.[1] But what an explorer. What violent contrast between his mist and sea and storm and the accepted landscape painting of the early nineteenth century. Yet Turner went through the Royal Academy schools, was made a Royal Academician at the age of twenty-seven and the Academy's Professor of Perspective at the age of thirty-two. That was in 1807. Would it be likely in the case of a Turner today? No.

So, what has happened to the Royal Academy in the last hundred and fifty years or so? How has it lost touch with contemporary art? And why does its Annual Exhibition now belong, as *The Times* said some years ago, to the same order of things as the Boat Race, the Derby and Eton and Harrow?

To answer these two questions at all adequately, I think we must have a look at how and when the Royal Academy – and other art academies – came into being and how they developed. In the Middle Ages there were no artists in our sense. Painters and sculptors were craftsmen like goldsmiths and saddle-makers. Their crafts were taught under the apprenticeship system – the system common to all trades.

Opposition to this state of affairs came with the Renaissance. If a painter knew the mysteries of mythology Greek and Roman, of anatomy and perspective, he could consider himself on the same social level as humanists and scientists. And Renaissance patrons were indeed prepared to honour a Michelangelo, a Raphael, as much as any great men of letters. However, these were the privilege of the few. To extend it to the artists as a class, they – the artists – would have to combine, to start some association grand enough to impress patrons and efficient enough to ensure a high standard of competence among members and potential members. Impressiveness they could achieve by limiting numbers, efficiency by establishing organised training in those humanistic and scientific subjects which distinguished art as a profession from art as a trade. So the first academy of art was founded in 1563 in Florence, under the patronage of the Grand Duke of Tuscany and by Giorgio Vasari. Vasari belonged to the generation following that of the High Renaissance. He was what we call a 'Mannerist' and a boundless admirer of Michelangelo. Michelangelo's style, adapted but never contradicted, was the one and only style of the academy. Incidentally, the name 'Academy' was wisely chosen: at that time it was the most popular name for associations of amateurs, literati and scientists.

So we find already, at the very start, these two characteristics of art academies: court and society patronage and a bias towards standards of the past.

Vasari's academy never succeeded in becoming a real power. To achieve this was left to the Paris Academy of the great Colbert. In Paris, under Richelieu and then Louis XIV, academies assumed a new, wider function. The first of the French academies was the Académie Française. Its job was to establish law and order in the French language. Law and order were also what Colbert was after in supplementing his administrative re-organisation of France by a whole string of academies: an academy of science, an academy of belles-lettres, an academy of music, an academy of architecture and an academy of the fine arts. For 'Fine' the arts became, now that their practitioners could show academic titles and decorations. At the same time, the academic make-up tied the artist closely to the taste and requirements of court and aristocracy, partly by holding out all the advantages of income and status which royal patronage could ensure and partly by setting up academic classes in which young painters and sculptors could be shaped to purvey academic art.

The example of Paris was imitated all over Europe. I have counted over a hundred art academies in the eighteenth century. One of them is the Royal Academy in London, which received its charter in 1768. Its main function – I needn't repeat it – was to secure for the English-born artist a place in polite society. Hence its Annual Dinners, hence its exhibitions with the traditional emphasis on portraits of celebrities, hence its small and selected school with its professors of history, perspective and so on. Sir Joshua Reynolds was the ideal first president, cultured, competent, a friend of literati and virtuosi, and an untiring advocate of that grand manner in painting, which he didn't practise very often himself.

At first nearly all artists who mattered were members. However, on the example of the Immortals of the Académie Française, membership was confined to forty, plus the lower order of Associates. As the English school grew in numbers and importance, some artists were bound to be left out. And as the English school grew in originality, some of the best artists remained outside.

Gainsborough's was the first battle royal with the Academy. Blake never belonged to it. Constable wrote in a letter: 'Academicians are singular beings. Sometimes I almost wish I could write on my tombstone: *Here lies John Constable who was nothing, not even an Academician.*' Constable could not do so, since he was elected, though late and without enthusiasm. And Turner, as I told you, was a convinced R.A. It is only the great innovators of the generations born after 1825 who never got in at all, and – a thing which is new and typical of the last hundred years – never wanted to.

You see, the Romantic Movement had established the artist's freedom from serving a patron, a class, society or indeed anything but his own genius or caprice. This conception of the artist's function has its pros and cons. Anyway, it was highly understandable in Victorian England where the Industrial Revolution had eclipsed so much visual sensibility. The new patrons appreciated nothing but an art of easy appeal, entertaining or sentimental. Bold young painters found no response, or certainly less than they had found in pre-academic days. The Royal Academicians – rightly, one is inclined to say – did not regard it as their job to encourage the untried. The Academy provided what the wealthy wanted and thrived on it more than ever. The presidents were Sir Francis Grant, Sir Frederick Leighton, Sir John Millais in his last, the 'Soap Bubbles', years and Sir Edward Poynter, while, say, Rossetti and Madox Brown, William Morris, Alfred Stevens, Whistler, never even put their names forward for election.

A pretty anthology of invective could be made up of anti-academic sayings between 1840 and 1940. Young Ruskin said: 'The system of Academy teachings destroys the greatest number of its pupils and hinders and paralyses the greatest.' Whistler wrote: 'Whom the Gods want to make ridiculous, they make Academicians.' Roger Fry spoke of 'laboratories for inoculation against art'.

But such sweeping statements are the artist's privilege. The historian has to keep away from them. All he can try and do is to explain these two things: the dependence of the Academy on the partialities of a wealthy and settled class and the natural relationship between the Royal Academy of today and the taste of the day before yesterday.

1   This broadcast was the third in a series of programmes called 'The Arts' and coincided with the Royal Academy's annual exhibition. It featured two fourteen-minute contributions, the first by John Betjeman and the second by Pevsner. Pevsner's opening words refer to what Betjeman had just said about Turner in his talk called 'Looking at Things'. Five years earlier, Pevsner had published a history of academies called *Academies of Art, Past and Present* which he always regarded as his best book.

Richard Payne Knight

Third Programme
THURSDAY 16 JANUARY 1947
Producer: Basil Taylor

If any of you remember the name of Richard Payne Knight, it'll probably only be because, when the Elgin Marbles were offered to the nation, he (among others) was asked to give evidence for or against the purchase.[1] In opposition to the others, he pronounced them to be 'in the second rank of art'.

A blind art critic, is that all he was? There is nothing so remarkable in that. The impact of the Elgin marbles to eyes used to the gentle charm of the *Apollo Belvedere* and the cool reticence of Roman copies must have been violent. Just as violent as the impact of Benin bronzes was to us some thirty years ago after all the Monets and Whistlers we had seen. However, Payne Knight has by no means only this negative interest for us. He was in fact, in spite of his evidence, a distinguished archaeologist and in addition to that a pioneer – in fields as widely apart as the comparative history of religion and the philosophy of art. His approach to these fields is original, provocative and of considerable historical significance.

He was born in 1750 – that is, he was twenty-one years younger than Burke, one year younger than his friend Charles James Fox, seven years older than Blake and twenty years older than Wordsworth. His grandfather had made a lot of money as an ironmaster. His father was a clergyman. In 1777, he went on the Grand Tour to Italy and Sicily. His Sicilian diary curiously enough survives only in translation into German by Goethe. It's dry and well stocked with quotations from Roman authors. Immediate reactions to things and to people you will not find in it – rather a dull document for a young man of twenty-seven. It reveals no aesthetic sensibility whatsoever.

Knight made a reputation, in the world of dilettanti, for antiquarian learning in the years after his return. He published two folios of specimens of Antique Sculpture, of which the second was to have a long introduction on symbolism in ancient art. This was published separately in 1818 and re-edited as late as 1892. The editor there calls Knight 'a man of profound judgement, acuteness and erudition'.

And looking at the collection he left to the British Museum, his judgement and acuteness can indeed not be denied. There's plenty of beauty in it and still more of curious interest – bronze sculptures, coins, implements of all sorts, vessels and so on. Horace Walpole called him in a letter 'the Knight of the Brazen Milkpot'.

Now Walpole was of course the cattiest of letter-writers but he had special reasons to loathe Knight. The two were on opposite sides in the most ferocious artistic battle of the day, the 'Battle of the Improvers'. You know how the improvers and picturesque landscape gardeners of about 1770–1800 were ridiculed by Peacock and Dr Syntax when the war was over. But they fought their war more savagely all the same, with pamphlets, poems and letters. You remember Peacock's Marmaduke Milestone, the champion of large-scale picturesque gardening, and probably know that he is a skit on Capability Brown, the most successful of all gardeners. Brown transformed square mile after square mile of formal parks with straight avenues and trimmed hedges into a beau ideal of unadorned nature with winding paths, serpentine lakes and clumps of trees loosely dotted over smooth lawns.

Now Walpole called Brown when he died 'Dame Nature's Second Husband' and his own Strawberry Hill had a landscaped garden embracing, with gentle undulations, his Rococo Gothic villa. Knight, on the other hand, wrote a poem called 'The Landscape' and published it in 1794, specially to attack Brown. And he improved the grounds of his own seat, Downton Castle near Ludlow, in a spirit utterly opposed to Brown.

We must look at Knight's house before we wander through the grounds. The showpiece of the house is its circular dining room, a noble room with tall columns on the pattern of the Pantheon in Rome. Outside, however, this room appears as part of a battlemented round tower, one of several varied shapes which Knight arranged in a picturesque, wholly asymmetrical fashion. It's deliberately reminiscent of the enchanted castles in the backgrounds of Claude Lorraine. Knight also had a splendid collection of Lorraine drawings.

There are two things specially remarkable about Downton: the purposely contrived, sharp contrast between interior and exterior of the house and the wildness of the scenery around. Obviously Payne Knight relished stronger visual effects than Walpole and Capability Brown. Strawberry Hill is Gothic inside and out, of a playful and flippant Rococo brand of mediaeval revival. Downton, in comparison, looks sombre and forceful. And the grounds at Downton on the steep banks of the rushing river Teme are left wild and rude with little to soften the nature of the country – a strong protest against the Brownian taste, a taste Knight says in 'The Landscape':

> Sprawling o'er all its unprolific spawn
> In never-ending sheets of vapid lawn.

Against Brown's 'Nature shaven and defaced' and against Brown's 'eternal undulating sweeps' and Brown's 'unnatural even serpentiness', Knight sets his ideas of a nature rough and rugged, with

> ... native plants
> In wild obscurity and rude neglect,

with

> ... weeds that creep
> Along the shore or overhang the steep,

with crags and cascades and country lanes with deep cart-ruts and tumbledown cottages.

Now that was an entirely new conception of the Picturesque, a decisive step away from the polite affection for nature in Thomson's *Seasons* and a step away from Richard Wilson and Gainsborough towards the sublime and grandiose natural forces unchained by Wordsworth and Constable. Knight wasn't alone in taking this step. In fact 'The Landscape' is essentially a translation into mediocre rhyme of thoughts conceived by a greater man, by Uvedale Price. But I can't talk of him today. However, neither Price nor Knight in spite of their new appreciation of contrast, roughness, accident and neglect ever penetrated to the true romantic conception of nature. They 'could not catch the hare', as Shelley wrote to Peacock, for they both remained improvers – that is, they thought in terms of correcting nature instead of abandoning themselves to her. So they belong after all to the Age of Reason and not to the age of romantic imagination and observation.

Once that has been understood, it will be recognised at once that Knight's attitude to Greek and Roman antiquity was also the rationalist's and not the romantic's. And a very remarkable attitude it was. I am afraid I can't find a better word for it than psycho-analytical. Knight worked chiefly on religious symbolism. In doing so he discovered the enormous significance of basic sexual symbols. With astonishing instinct he found his way there through a wholly uncharted territory. You can read in his little book on the *Worship of Priapus* of the sexual meaning of fire as against water, of bull and lion and serpent and obelisk as against, for instance, the shell. Nor did Knight consider antiquity only. In the detached way of the eighteenth-century agnostic, he placed, for example, the Early Christian T-shaped Cross alongside the obelisk as a symbol. He relished the daring of such parallels, no doubt, just as he relished his defence of the sexual ceremonies of antiquity as 'a very natural symbol of a very natural religion'. The monks of the Middle Ages, on the other hand, were to him the vessels of 'rankling passions and foul desires' and dogmatic theology he calls 'one of the greatest curses that ever afflicted the human race'. Was he then a fellow fighter of

Rousseau? No, he wasn't. Again he stopped short of the final assault. Listen to this passage, to its crisp and cool style and its elegant touch of the Rococo, written *à propos* Corinthian temple prostitution:

> When there were such seminaries for female education . . . we need not wonder that the ladies of antiquity should be extremely well instructed in all the practical duties of their religion. The stories told of Julia and Messalina show us that the Roman ladies were in no way deficient [either] . . .

That is again the Age of Reason and not of Rousseau.

A curious man, evidently quite undaunted by cherished tradition, by respect or prejudice. Take, in conclusion, his work on aesthetics and you'll find the same intellectual courage and the same pleasure in *épater le bourgeois*. In his 'Analytical Essay on the Principles of Taste', Knight proved conclusively how little of our pleasures in things seen – pictures, buildings, landscapes – is really due to visual perception. While we think we admire form and colour, we're really all the time guided by associations caused by what we know of the objects we look at. A man, Knight writes, may think he admires the 'heavenly form of a lovely bosom'. But is it really the form that thrills him? Let him make a mould from it and

> cast a plum pudding in it (an object by no means disgusting to most men's appetites) and I think he will no longer be in raptures with the form.

If, he goes on to say, we really admired the beauty of a face *qua* beauty and interest of surface, that is aesthetically, then

> a pimpled face would have the same superiority over a smooth one as a variegated tulip over a plain one, or a column of jasper over one of common red.

On the other hand, if you call Rembrandt's picture of the carcase of an ox ugly, as the eighteenth century did, then you should be conscious of the fact that you are not affected by art but by the repellent qualities of the subject depicted.

All that had never before been said so precisely. The whole theory of Art for Art's Sake in the nineteenth century, the whole quarrel of Whistler and Ruskin, is in Knight's remark on the plum pudding.

But – and that brings me back to the Elgin Marbles – a man who reacts to art in such a way, elucidating contents and emphasising their importance, could scarcely be one easily bowled over by beauty in art as such. So we shouldn't really be shocked at Knight's obtuseness when he was faced with Athenian sculpture of the fifth century. We should rather learn from it never to ask an analytical philosopher or the most resourceful antiquarian for a judgement on great art.

1   Pevsner's talk was broadcast in the new Third Programme series 'The Visual Arts', introduced by the novelist Anthony West. It followed another talk by a sculptor, Leon Underwood, recently returned from West Africa, on the occasion of two exhibitions of 'Primitive Art' at the Berkeley Galleries and at Australia House in London.

The architecture of Washington

Third Programme
THURSDAY 10 JULY 1947
Producer: Basil Taylor

To travel from New York to Washington is a change of dimension, not of scale.[1] Both cities are equally grandiose, both will knock you over the first time you see them. But whereas in New York you gaze up and then see in your guidebook that this particular skyscraper (atrocious in its detail) is 950 feet high while Big Ben is only 300, in Washington you gaze along an interminable frontage of giant columns and then see in your book that this building, say the Department of Agriculture, is 950 feet long, as against the humble 350 of the front of the British Museum.

Now you know very well that nobody can take in the nobility of the British Museum façade because you can't step back sufficiently to see it. In Washington you can everywhere step back all right. The spaciousness of the layout is stunning and ten times as stunning if you realise that it was conceived a hundred and fifty years ago when Major L'Enfant, a Frenchman brought up to admire the Place de la

Concorde and the Champs Elysées, designed Washington as the Federal City. He was a bold man to put forward an absolutely patternised plan, miles across each way, with a gridiron broken up by plenty of *ronds points* with wide radiating avenues. The Capitol was to be the centre; along its west axis far away was to stand the national monument to Washington in the exact spot where that axis would intersect the axis due south from the White House.

It was a magnificent plan, probably the most magnificent the Baroque ever conceived, and it was wonderfully mad – or visionary – considering that in 1800 the federal staff from the President down to the most lowly clerk numbered 117 and there was no reason for anyone else to live in Washington.

So what seemed bound to happen happened. Along the avenues grew red brick houses and terraces, nice, friendly, homely houses of two or three storeys and also weatherboarded cottages of all shapes. The population was 8,000 in 1810, 23,000 in 1840. That was when Dickens saw it. He was not amused. He wrote this:

> It is sometimes called the City of Magnificent Distances but it might with greater propriety be termed the City of Magnificent Intentions; for it is only on taking a bird's eye view of it ... that one can at all comprehend the vast designs of its projector ... spacious avenues, that begin in nothing, and lead nowhere; streets mile-long that only want houses, roads and inhabitants, and public buildings that need but a public to be complete ... are its leading features.
>
> Take the worst parts of the City Road and Pentonville, or the straggling outskirts of Paris, where the houses are smallest, preserving all their oddities ... Burn the whole down; build it up again in wood and plaster; widen it a little; throw in part of St. John's Wood; ... plough up all the roads, plant a great deal of coarse turf in all the places where it ought not to be; erect three handsome buildings in stone and marble anywhere, but the more entirely out of everybody's way the better ... leave a brick-field without the bricks, in all central places where a street may naturally be expected: and that's Washington.
>
> Such as it is it is likely to remain ... [for] it has not trade or commerce of its own, having little or no population beyond the President.

After 1850 growth was faster, but from L'Enfant's point of view it went all wrong all to the west of the Capitol – there was not much reason for an East End – so that the Capitol was right out of the city centre. Nobody cared for the plan anyway. It was not outright spoiled because it was too ubiquitous and powerful but it was not followed either. The Mall, L'Enfant's chief west avenue, a quarter of a mile wide, was landscaped with clumps of trees, of all things, and the Washington Monument, that glorious, absolutely sheer obelisk, 550 feet high, was erected about 200 feet off the point of intersection of the two axes.

So when you are impressed by Washington now, don't forget that its monumentality is that of the Baroque only in plan, not in elevation. Even the Capitol is so vast and dominating only because of Walter's additions – 1851–1865 – to which belong the dome (180 feet high and ninety-six feet in diameter) and the wings. And the White House owes its immaculate colonial appearance, the joy of any revivalist, chiefly to what McKim did to it in 1902.

That precisely was the time when L'Enfant's monumentality was rediscovered, so to speak. The 1893 Exhibition at Chicago had been the spectacular victory of a Classical re-Revival over all the splendid American efforts towards a truly contemporary style. Burnham, the chief architect of the exhibition, and McKim were on a 'Committee for the Improvement of Washington' set up in 1901. The Committee emphatically reverted to L'Enfant and now at last buildings began to go up in a style as formal and lavish in their colonnades as any in eighteenth-century Paris. Burnham, after all, was the architect chiefly responsible for the design of Selfridges in Oxford Street, London.

The new buildings with their giant columns came slowly, only three or four before 1925. Then, however, something happened, a regrettable coincidence of this imperialist, optimist, as it were Burnham-and-Bailey style with a fast-growing federal initiative calling for more and more office space in the capital.

So – and this is the main thing I want to tell you – the Washington you see today is what the years from 1925 to Pearl Harbor made it. It owes its Parisian axes to L'Enfant but recent growth has vastly outparised Paris. What in Paris would emulate the two miles from the Capitol to the Lincoln Monument and the mile and a half from the White House to the Jefferson Monument, the one all Doric, the other all Ionic, and the group of three government buildings at the west end of the so-called Triangle, one symmetrical colonnaded composition of ninety-two bays, i.e., well over 2,000 feet frontage? That lot is Roman Doric, the Department of Agriculture is Corinthian. So are the Supreme Court and the Federal Archives. The National Gallery of Art is Ionic – all vast detached or attached porticoes with pediments, very impressive and as dead as so many huge door nails.

Now that is what one cannot get away from in wandering through this city of wonders – wonders of academism, wonders of well-meaning triteness embellished by mottoes telling you, for instance, in the case of the Department of Commerce, something of trade 'stimulating the progress of America upon land and sea and in the air and thereby speeding the nation in the march of mankind'; or, in the case of the Railway Station about 'fire, greatest of discoveries, enabling man to live in various climates, to use many foods and to compel the forces of nature to do his work'. On Constitution Hill it says: 'Let our object be our country, our whole country and nothing but our country.' And on the Archives building: 'The Glory and Romance of our history are here preserved in the chronicles of those who conceived and builded the structure of our nation.'

The Glory and Romance – don't you hear the commentator in the movies? Well, it is easy to be facetious at the expense of this kind of triteness. But the point about it is that it does the trick, just as the shiploads of giant columns for the monumental buildings of Washington do. Tears well up in the eyes of those whom the subtler patriotism of Trollope and the subtler scale of the Erechtheum would leave unmoved.

And they after all are the vast majority and does not democracy build for the many? Here we have to step very gently. For there is first of all the American brand of democracy and there is ours and there is the Russian – which do we mean? Now the interesting and no doubt a little perturbing fact is that from the point of view of architectural monumentality it doesn't matter a brass farthing which you mean or whether you mean democracy at all.

Hitler built in that style – only a little more severe – his large new government building and *Kultur* buildings at Munich, Berlin and Nuremberg. We do it in our deplorable Civic Centres. And as for the

Russians, we have lately heard a lot of their colossal plans for a new Stalingrad, a new Leningrad, and dozens of others.[2] We have seen sketch plans and perspectives with civic and administrative buildings galore and huge monuments to heroes and martyrs. I have always wanted to know what these cities will actually look like.

I think I know it now – exactly like Washington, with its Washington Monument, its Lincoln Monument, its Jefferson Monument and its acres of borrowed monumentality which I have so ineptly tried to conjure up before your startled and pained eyes.

Borrowed monumentality – that is where our problem lies. Younger architects and critics are arguing a lot just now about whether monumentality is possible in our day and whether it is desirable. The answer to the first question is Washington. This is monumentality whether you like it or not. It takes your breath away all right, even if you may feel something like hit below the belt.

That in itself is of course not desirable. Yet monumentality, I would say, is. I would say that against the opposition of those who preach that monumental architecture has no place in our functional world. Let me reply that Mankind had a right to ask from the architect more than the fulfilment of material functions. There is an ideal function of architecture as well. Church buildings served it in the Middle Ages. Now it is no good denying that the Church today has no longer the universal ideal function it then had. What has taken its place? Civic pride, perhaps – the sort of pride that shows itself in buildings for national museums, national theatres, academies of science and so on. All such buildings demand monumentality – that is, a show of their more-than-workaday function.

Yet whether they are put up at Munich or Leningrad or Washington, they all do not seem able to do better than re-hash the glories of Greece and Rome. Why are large, representational buildings in the true style of today so rare? I would answer that the Monumental is bound to turn towards the most permanent, immutable-looking; and a new style, a style as unprecedented as ours of this century, cannot yet look immutable. There is – I am quite ready to say 'Thank Heavens' – there is still too much of the experiment in it. Now the Experimental is *per se* excluded from the Monumental. However, not all our modern buildings have that peculiar experimental look, though some of the most interesting ones have. Take Asplund's Stockholm Crematorium or indeed some of the Italian Civic Centres of about 1930. They look fresh and adventurous but are monumental all the same.

So it is possible. But why does it happen so rarely? There is, of course, a deplorable reason first of all. The Nazis called Modern Architecture 'Bolshevik', the Russians call it 'the Last Gasp of the Bourgeois', Mussolini called it 'Fascist', the Swedes call it 'democratic', the American Government 'undemocratic' or at least 'highbrow'.

It is an awful muddle. But what transpires from it is that a new, progressive style cannot be the style of a whole people or its majority. If democracy in architecture is simply following the taste of the majority as it is, then you get the Russian Beaux Arts stuff and the new Washington: 'Beaux Arts in the purity of death' as Elbert Peets said of the new Washington National Gallery. But if democracy means a public duty of helping people on to develop their faculties – mental and spiritual and also aesthetic – then we can ask for the official monumental architecture of our country and the States to be as fresh and bold as indeed some of the new municipal plans in Britain visualise.

And what a dazzling vision is a capital on the scale of Washington, laid out as generously as Washington, put up as lavishly as Washington, with the best materials – but put up by an Asplund or his opposite number in America.

1 'The Architecture of Washington' was broadcast in the series 'The Visual Arts' in a programme that included contributions from Mary Potter, Tom Monnington R.A., and Leonard Rosoman.

2 Pevsner refers here to Stalin's retrograde Neo-Classical architecture, not the revolutionary 'Constructivist' Soviet architecture of the early 1920s.

★

The Adoration of the Kings

Third Programme
MONDAY 26 JANUARY 1948
Producer: Basil Taylor

> And when they were come into the house, they saw the young child with
> Mary his mother, and fell down, and worshipped him: and when they had
> opened their treasures, they presented unto him gifts of gold and
> frankincense and myrrh.

Now that scene is familiar to all of us from the works of many
painters.[1] Just imagine for a moment how a painter like Gerard David
would have painted it round about 1510 or 1520. I'm thinking of the
picture in the National Gallery. The Virgin seated on the left right in
front of us, the Kings coming along with pious awe. One kneels stiffly,
his folded hands slightly raised, the others hold their gifts. The Virgin
is young, with a pretty, innocent, pink face. At the back is the most
meticulously drawn townscape with dozens and dozens of tiny houses
and a few little people – a scene of serene peace.

The Adoration of the Kings[2] by Bruegel was painted about fifty years
after Gerard David's – in 1564 to be exact – but by a man of different
character, of different calibre and working in a different historic
setting.

Let me try to describe it to you. The Virgin sits in the middle of the
picture but not in the foreground. Behind her is a solid wall of upright
figures – I count sixteen of them. On the left and right she's also
hemmed in by figures. We ourselves, standing in front of the picture,
complete this narrow circle. So there's no way for mother and infant
to get out of the nightmarishly close ring of big, heavy, towering
bodies. It's as if they are at the bottom of a pit or perhaps rather like
small children in a rush-hour crowd, helplessly pinned in from all sides
with not enough air to breathe. I'm sure it's not over-interpreting this
nightmarish effect. Why else should Bruegel have introduced the
heavy felty cloak which half-covers the Virgin's curiously small head?
There can be no question Bruegel wanted to create this feeling of
oppression, the oppression of the holy figures by lumpy obtuse flesh
all around. There's no relief anywhere. The black king on the right

looks at us out of his gleaming white eyes over his fantastic white, wide mantle, a fearsome apparition. The old king creeps forward with hair and beard hanging down like moss from a fir tree. And the third king stares with a taciturn face, peeved, pinched – like an old cobbler.

Yes – that's what it is. All the types which Bruegel painted are types he could see every day in the narrow streets of Antwerp. They are rendered without embellishment, the soldiers in the background, one young with a blank stare, another fat, middle-aged and jolly like Sir John Falstaff. And then Joseph behind his wife, a broad foursquare old carpenter, not without dignity, as he listens to a gossipy creature on his right, one of a group of three sceptical, callous inquisitive burgesses.

Now there's a very remarkable thing. If this painting moves us (and to me at least it's one of the most moving pictures in the National Gallery) it moves us not as a painting by van der Goes or Hans Memling, by sheer power of devotion or sheer finesse of precious painting. Bruegel doesn't make you happy in the way they do. He doesn't leave you alone, he doesn't give you peace. He's violent, he's critical of many things, he's obscure in his message.

Let's try then to understand what made his mind take that turn – what his message ultimately is. To understand it, we must first look for a minute at the years in which Bruegel painted and their events and significance, and then at Bruegel's character and personal experiences. 1564 – what does that year mean in Brabant, Flanders and Holland? Ever since about 1500, doubts of the truth of Roman Catholic dogma had grown, sometimes in the form of a more immediate personal devotion, sometimes as scepticism and rationalism. In 1512 one Herman Rijswijk was burnt at the Hague because he had called Christ a fantasy and the Christian creed so many fairy tales. In 1525 men from Antwerp said to Luther that the Holy Ghost was really identical with human reason. Sebastian Franck wrote that the world is a pig sty and can only be ruled by the authority of a pope, whether he is a Catholic or a Protestant pope, and that what really matters is the divine inner light as Plato, Orpheus and the Sibyls had possessed it, as much as any Christian saints. The logical contradiction in the dogmas of Trinity, of Original Sin, of Christ's Redemption of our Sins, was exposed. Social revolt joined religious revolt, Anabaptists and Adamites were about. When Bruegel was a child in the 1530s, the

Anabaptists coming from Holland had set up their government at Munster.

Then the phase of revolution changed into one of establishment. The Catholic Church started putting its house in order and gathered at Trent to enforce rigid conformity, the Lutheran Church made its peace with the state and Calvin with French logic organised a new reformed church. The tolerance of Erasmus and Melanchthon was suppressed. More and Fisher were executed, the inquisition was reintroduced, the Jesuit Order founded and when Servet fled from Rome to Geneva on account of his anti-trinitarian views, he was arrested there and executed.

In France, things were moving towards the Massacre of St Bartholomew and in Brabant, to which Bruegel's Antwerp belonged, the Emperors were also determined to stamp out heresy. Charles V and even more his successor Philip II were sincere Catholic believers but they were also convinced of the political need of conformity in their vast state. So they insisted on persecution, first of Anabaptists only, then, after 1550, of the Calvinists too. And there were thousands of them, chiefly among the working classes in the Belgian towns, just as among the aristocracy there were leaders such as William of Orange and Egmont ready to fight for Netherlandish independence. In 1561 rioting began seriously. The Spanish suppressed it and burnt the ringleaders. They died on the stake singing psalms and Philip wrote an indignant billet to his half-sister, the Regent. He advised that in future, heretics should be burnt with a gag in their mouths so as to silence them.

But force did not succeed. In 1566, image-breaking started on a large scale and so in 1567 Alba arrived with his tercios. The rest of the story is known. It ended with freedom for Holland but the South remained Catholic and Spanish throughout the age of Rubens and Van Dyck.

Now Bruegel's *Adoration of the Kings* was painted in the very years of the most violent religious and national strife. Can we see from the picture where Bruegel stood? We certainly can't see it from his life. Little is known of it and next to nothing of his views. There's no reason to believe that he left the faith of his fathers. For the rest we have to go to his paintings and first of all again to *The Adoration of the Kings*.

If it's Catholic to make a religious picture a glittering showpiece, then Bruegel was not a Catholic. And if to take a passionate interest in the people was Protestant in Bruegel's time, then he was a Protestant. But passionate as his interest appears to have been, was he really in sympathy with the people? He made his kings look exactly like artisans and peasants, it's true, but these artisans and peasants are in no way idealised. Although Bruegel used to be called the Peasant-Bruegel, he was not a champion of the common man in a political or social sense. He studied him, just as the most advanced psychological writers of his day did, men such as Vivés and Cardano. But he did not like him. That comes out forcibly in paintings of his which portray peasant life and nothing else, for instance the famous *Wedding Feast* in the Vienna Gallery.

If it can be said that by the seventeenth century, the peasant had become as accepted a character in painting as any other class of people, if there were then as many masters specialising in sympathetic pictures of peasant life as there were portrait or landscape painters, Bruegel did obviously not belong to the seventeenth century more than he does, as we have seen, to the Gothic and Catholic world of the past. He appears torn, we can say, between distrust of the old world of van Eyck and van der Goes and the new somewhat pedestrian world of Ostade and Steen. He stands between them – precariously, proudly and unhappily.

But in terms of art, more narrowly speaking, that in-between position must be formulated differently. The world of the fifteenth century and Bruegel's world are really separated by an event of the greatest aesthetic importance, the invasion of the Italian Renaissance. Renaissance ornament appears for the first time in the Netherlands immediately before 1500. Renaissance figures and compositions become known about 1517 when Raphael's famous cartoons were woven as tapestries at Brussels. Then artists like Scorel, Coxie and Lambert Lombard began to study for themselves in Italy. By 1550 the Italian style had conquered all church and official arts. Frans Floris painted his *Fall of the Angels* in 1554, his *Last Judgement* in 1565 – consciously in the style of Michelangelo and his Mannerist successors.

Bruegel also had gone to Italy; he was then about twenty-five or a
little older. There are dated landscape drawings of his which he did in
the Alps and in Naples in 1552 and 1553. Drawings of Italianate
figures or compositions don't exist. Yet although it is perhaps safe to
say that landscape impressed Bruegel on his journey more deeply or at
least more unreservedly than art, *The Adoration of the Kings* would not
be what it is if Bruegel had not been in Italy. Its composition, with
diagonals leading from the front corners into the middle distance
towards the Virgin, is completely un-Netherlandish. It belongs wholly
to Italy and was developed chiefly by Correggio and Bruegel must
have seen and absorbed Correggio's *Virgin with Saints* and his
Nativities in this highly personal way.

Then there is the colour of the Virgin. The combination of slate
blue and mauve is typical of the Italian Mannerists as you can see in
the National Gallery, for example Parmigiano's large *Madonna with St
John*.

And then the infant Christ. Try to remember the little figure
exactly and compare it at the National Gallery with the mighty body
of Lazarus in Sebastiano del Piombo's painting done for St Peter's in
Rome. The position of the legs, the position of the arm, the cloth
across the head – all are identical. The connection has not so far, I
think, been noticed. No wonder. For Bruegel makes a poor little
maggot out of Sebastiano's heroic superman. There is, one feels,
almost a sneer in these Italian borrowings of Bruegel. A *Peasant's
Wedding* composed like Tintoretto's *Marriage at Cana* – it is a challenge
to all the Renaissance stood for. For the Renaissance means clarity, a
rational order, a lucid grounding of figures, beauty of man
and woman, pride in the freely active body, vigorous limbs and noble
features. In Bruegel, on the other hand, nothing is more characteristic
than the savage way in which he deprives the whole human body of
its freedom of action. Time and again you see figures shaped like
sacks, lumpy, lifeless, with enormous sausage-shaped limbs, with hats
or caps or bonnets or helmets which make handsome faces – that is,
the seat of what is most human in man – invisible, and thus reduce the
likes of us to dolls or clods without command over our their destinies.

Remember Bruegel's most terrible paintings – *The Five Maimed*,
hobbling along on their stumps, and *The Blind leading the Blind into*

Disaster and Death. The gloom and fear which hovers over the *Adoration of the Kings* is present in these paintings in an even more concentrated form. They are incontrovertible proof of Bruegel's scepticism, pessimism, misanthropy. The mood of the Renaissance was not unknown to him but he had seen through it. Living in Antwerp in the 1550s–60s he had had enough of pride and hypocrisy. He went for inspiration to the Gothic Netherlands rather than Italy, to Jerome Bosch especially, whose *Crowning with Thorns* in the National Gallery shows clearly how much Bruegel owes him. Now Bosch had been dead fifty years when *The Adoration of the Kings* was painted. So Bruegel cannot be regarded as the end of the Middle Ages. He, as so many others of the painters of this age of Counter-Reformation and the Wars of Religion, consciously returned to their ideas of human bondage, away from the Renaissance illusion of freedom and self-determination.

Only when he painted landscape did his terrors leave him. That is why such pictures as the *Occupation of the Months* at Vienna strike us as so much happier and healthier. But *The Adoration of the Kings* has no landscape. The wall of soldiers with their spiky lances shuts it out and there is no release from oppression, the oppression imposed on goodness and guilelessness in this world.

1   'The Adoration of the Kings' was broadcast in a series called 'Paintings', in which the BBC invited speakers, singly or in pairs, to explain and animate pictures from Britain's national art collection. Pevsner's talk was followed in the same programme by another by Raymond Coxon, who argued that the subject matter of Bruegel's art was more influenced by conventions and technique than by the dialectics of religion.
2   Also known as *The Adoration of the Magi.*

The Dukeries

Third Programme
SUNDAY 7 NOVEMBER 1948
Producer: Basil Taylor

It is surprising how few people know what the Dukeries are.[1] I asked four people in one day so that I could tell you their answers. They all knew the term had something to do with Nottingham and Sherwood Forest. Beyond that, one knew nothing at all, the second started talking about Chatsworth, the third about Belvoir – although Chatsworth is in Derbyshire thirty miles west of the Dukeries and Belvoir in Lincolnshire thirty miles south-east. The fourth was accurate. He said the name stood for that part of Sherwood Forest where at one time a number of dukes had their houses; but he was a history don at Cambridge. Anyway, what he said was more than I knew when I first went to visit the Dukeries. I had in my mind foremost a vision of gnarled oak trees and a number of jingling rhymes about

> Robin Hood, that most lusty outlaw
> As ever yet lived in this land;
> His equal, I'm sure, you never yet saw
> So valiant was he of his hand.

And then Robin Hood goes to Mass at Nottingham, is betrayed by a monk, arrested by the sheriff and escapes with the help of Little John. Another time he gives money to a poor knight, or he outdoes Guy of Gisborne in a shooting match with his good yew bow, or he is beaten up by a beggar – and finally he dies, and so

> Christ have mercy on his soul
> That die-ed in the wood,
> For he was a good outlaw
> And did poor men much good.

Of Robin Hood's Sherwood Forest not much is left. It stretched from close to Nottingham, up to Mansfield and Worksop and east to the river Trent. It was a Royal Forest with its keeper and its foresters-atfee (there is a lovely early fourteenth-century tombstone to the memory of one of them, with a hunting horn, at Skegby). It had its regular forest courts or eyres where pleas of venison and pleas of vert were heard – that is, cases of poaching and cases of stealing timber (a green oak was worth sixpence). The king gave timber to monasteries and cathedrals as a handsome present in kind and also had them used for building such wartime machinery as springalds or giant catapults. And of deer there were still over a thousand in the sixteenth and seventeenth centuries.

Then the decline set in, as the dukes arrived: 1,270 acres were bought by the Duke of Kingston in 1683 and enclosed to form Thoresby Park, about 3,000 acres were bought a few years later by the Duke of Newcastle to form Clumber Park, and so on. In 1800 the Royal Forest was reduced to less than 1,500 acres (Epping Forest has still today more than 5,000). You can still see magnificent oak trees (the Greendale Oak with the archway cut through in 1724, the Mayor Oak, Robin Hood's Larder, and so on) but they are mostly venerable wrecks, delightful to the picturesque traveller with his Gilpin in his pocket but rather more *objets trouvés* than part of a healthy forest.

So the Dukeries as they were before the dukes have rather receded. The dukes themselves were of all kinds. There was the first Duke of Newcastle of the Cavendish family at Welbeck, preceptor of Charles I, friend of Hobbes, minor author and ardent admirer of van Dyck. He writes to van Dyck of 'the blessing of your company and sweetness of your conversation', praises his painting and signs himself 'passionately your humble servant'. The first Duke's wife was Charles Lamb's 'thrice noble, chaste and virtuous, but somewhat fantastical and original-brained Margaret Newcastle' of whom you can read more in one of Virginia Woolf's essays. Then there is the first Duke of Newcastle of the Pelham-Holles family, the opponent of Robert Walpole, an able opportunist politician; and, of the same generation, the first Duke of Kingston, of Thoresby Park, leader of fashion, member of the Kit-Cat Club and father of Lady Mary Wortley Montagu; and finally that paragon of the Dukeries' dukes, the fifth Duke of Portland, whose ghost has pretty well replaced that of Robin Hood.

The fifth Duke of Portland was a handsome man but shy. At

Welbeck Abbey he lived only in a suite of four or five rooms and communicated with the outer world by means of double letter-boxes in the doors: one for messages and mail in, the other for outward communications. Messages might be about a shooting party which was to arrive and be entertained without ever setting eyes on the Duke, or about clothes to be packed away, or about food (a chicken was always kept roasting in the kitchen ready against the moment when the Duke wanted something to eat), or perhaps a message about a journey to London. Such journeys the Duke would make in a carriage which was loaded into a special railway truck at Worksop; the carriage had its green silk blinds drawn while going through the streets. Through the estate the Duke would drive unseen, thanks to the underground tunnel which had been built, a mile and a quarter long and wide enough for two carriages to pass.

That tunnel is only one of the many underground building enterprises of the Duke. He spent £113,000 on building in the course of ten years. Some of the money went into normal building above ground. His riding school is supposed to be the second largest in the world. It is 400 feet long. And his kitchen gardens cover twenty-two acres. They have, for example, a peach-wall 1,000 feet long which could be heated by braziers so as to hasten the growth of the fruit. (I have garnered these facts from Professor Turberville's admirable two-volume book on *Welbeck Abbey and its Owners*.) But these structures, in spite of their size, seem small when compared with the underground ballroom and picture gallery and conservatory. The largest of the rooms is 160 by sixty-three feet and when the Duke died in 1879 excavations were going on for a yet larger Bachelors' Hall.

There have been many surmises as to the psychological causes of this weird burrowing and perhaps one day a suitably equipped psycho-analyst will tell us all about the Duke's inhibitions and repressions. The Duke would have called it a 'merciless dissection'. Some people say the Duke simply intended to enlarge the house without interfering with its eighteenth-century appearance. That is unlikely because it was by no means a house of impressive frontages. Others suggest that his wish was to provide labour at a time of slump. That sounds more probable, for it is known that while the doctor and the vicar were requested to ignore the Duke when he had the misfortune to meet them on the estate, he did not mind at all spending his time with the workmen. And did he not present every one of them, when they began to work for him, with a donkey to ride on and an umbrella? And he favoured skating on the lake for the housemaids.

There is no doubt a lot of hidden interest in his catacombical mentality and his urge to be unseen. I myself know one or two people who have similar desires but they have not the means to satisfy them. It is the scale on which the fifth Duke of Portland could indulge his eccentricities that makes him the worthy successor of Robin Hood in the tales of the Dukeries. If my account of some of these has been rather colourful, I can plead that it is largely based on Lady Ottoline Morrell's account. And Lady Ottoline Morrell, herself a colourful character and a member of the so-called Bloomsbury set, was the sixth Duke's stepsister.

After any description of Welbeck Abbey, the house and its appendages above and below ground are rather disappointing when one actually sees them. The underground rooms are not at all cavernous. They have got ample skylights and are as light as the Crystal Palace. At night they were illuminated by sumptuous gas chandeliers. Above ground the so-called Gothic Hall must have been enchanting when it was new, about 1750. It is an early example of Rococo-Gothic or Strawberry Hill Gothic. The Chapel and Library are late nineteenth-century at its very best – Art Nouveau if you will, or, rather, Arts and Crafts – begun by Sedding and carried on by his brilliant assistant Harry Wilson. So much for Welbeck Abbey. It is the only house in the Dukeries still in the possession of a Duke.

And the other mansions? Thoresby is not an ancient monument. The former house, by the architect of Chatsworth, was replaced in 1864–71 by a spectacular neo-Elizabethan mansion designed by Salvin who was immensely successful in that sort of style. It is a block 180 by 180 feet with a Great Hall which runs up through three storeys and ends in a hammerbeam roof, an impressive monument to Victorian self-confidence, prosperity and solidity and one that is, to one's great satisfaction and pleasure, still lived in by Lord and Lady Manvers in the way in which such big houses were meant to be lived in. The church over at Pearlthorpe is also a living thing.

As for Worksop Manor, the present house is certainly in use, a commodious, comfortable, extremely pleasant home. But with the exception of one room it makes use only of what was once one half of the stables and courtyard. The Duke of Norfolk's mansion proper was built by James Paine in a noble and uncommonly pure Palladian style after 1761. That house, only part of a still more ambitious project, was pulled down less than a century later by the Duke of Newcastle when he had decided to build at Clumber instead. What remains now of Paine's house is only the front of the ground floor with rusticated stonework and arched window niches and nothing behind it – it is just a wall (with the exception of the one room which I mentioned before) – with a beautifully kept garden behind it.

And Clumber? Clumber was rough heath until about 1750. Then Stephen Wright, the architect of the building of the Schools at Cambridge which appears so effectively between King's Chapel and the Senate House, built a medium-sized house for the Duke of Newcastle. That house was replaced by a princely mansion in the Victorian Italianate style by Charles Barry, who is known for the Houses of Parliament, the Reform Club and Bridgewater House. It was much enlarged in the 1880s by Barry's son and must then have looked even grander than Thoresby, overlooking its new Italian terraces and gardens and beyond them the eighteenth-century landscaped grounds. In addition, the Duke spent another £30,000 in 1886–89 for a church close to the house, one of Bodley's masterpieces.

The effect now is eerie. The grounds belong to the National Trust. The house was pulled down just before the war, completely, and hardly a trace remains. And the church stands lonely and magnificent without any services being held in it. It is of good sound stone, grey and red, with a red spire, and it is richly decorated inside. As it stands there by the lake, amidst magnificently grown cedar and oak trees, it is a romantic artist's dream of his ideal church, infinitely more eloquent than Bodley can ever have expected. What is going to happen to it, miles from anywhere? Will they make it a Nottinghamshire war memorial for the whole county, or perhaps sell it, lock, stock and barrel, to some suburb in need of a church? And what is going to happen to the other houses? To Welbeck, for instance, when it is left by the Army College which is now in it and uses it sympathetically?

Or, to look a little further afield, to Rufford Abbey, empty and gloomy and neglected?

These questions are part and parcel of a larger one. Newstead Abbey was given to the City of Nottingham by Sir Julian Cahn and is now the Byron Museum, ideally looked after, with its picturesque grounds as smooth and smiling as ever and with the two miniature fortresses preserved which Mad Jack Byron, in about 1740, had built by the lake to play at naval warfare. His battleship of thirty guns has unfortunately disappeared. Cities can absorb some such mansions, the National Trust takes care of others, the National Coal or Electricity or Hospital Boards of more. Some will no doubt go to America. Then there are schools and convalescent homes and lunatic asylums, for all of which, however, one would wish they could have more modern buildings. And otherwise, there are pick and shovel waiting.

The Palladian Worksop has gone, the Victorian Clumber has gone. What will go next? Will the forest in the end close over the Dukeries again? Alas, it does not seem probable that it will become a forest to the liking of either Robin Hood or the National Trust and the National Park experts. For although you can still, as Washington Irving did more than a hundred years ago, wander 'through natural valleys and greenwood glades, carpeted with grass and shaded by lofty beeches and veteran oaks, sheltered hollow and moss-grown', there are large areas, and celebrated ones too, where you now find yourself surrounded by notices: 'Keep out!' 'Danger!' 'Ammunition!' 'At your own risk!' and so on – although the three-mile Clumber drive with its four lines of lime trees is still there and the long avenues of slim upright Lombardy poplars, just outside the forest, leading to the Mausoleum of the Dukes of Newcastle.

I suppose that is the pattern of the twentieth century: empty and superfluous mansions, a disused church, working-class suburbs approaching the fringes of the forests from Nottingham and Worksop and Mansfield, and ammunition dumps in the National Park. Sometimes one is tempted to speculate whether the thriving monasteries and even the outlaws with their honest yew bows and broadswords were not better suited to the spirit of the Dukeries than anything our century is putting into their place.

1   'The Dukeries' was the third broadcast in the series 'Buildings and Places'.

Danish art

Third Programme
SATURDAY 13 NOVEMBER 1948
Producer: Basil Taylor

A Danish painter, according to the catalogue of the Danish Exhibition,[1] is credited with a wonderful and profound remark. This is what he is supposed to have said: 'All good art is national. All national art is bad.' Isn't it brilliant? And besides, I'd call it eminently Danish. I mean, it's crisp, it's ironical or sceptical and it's very neat. We use such qualifications referring to art or literature or philosophy of nations but we often forget how young the whole notion of national character is.

In a way, the most exciting part of the exhibition is its first few rooms in which prehistory and the Viking Age are displayed. Well, these vessels with their scrolls and vortexes, this processional chariot carrying a sun-disk, these houses in the shape of boats, with outcurving sides and keel-like roofs – who would venture to say that they are nationally Danish? They came so close in character to Norwegian and indeed to some British things. But then the Angles and the Jutes came from Denmark and Saxons from an area just south of Denmark and the Danes – well, but they of course came partly from Norway. It is a bit confusing, like the Plots and the Scots in *1066 and All That*.

Anyway, with Canute ruling over Norway and so much of England, one can say by and large that up to the eleventh century there was a North Sea Style in which regions on the East and West seaboards participated.

Again, the Romanesque art of Denmark is not yet strictly Danish, in spite of the speciality of their splendid Golden Altars. But there is in the sculptures of the twelfth and thirteenth centuries, for instance, the several figures of the *Crucifixus*, so much that links them with Germany and northern France that one can hardly draw a boundary line. The development from the most hieratic, almost fetish-like Christ of the eleventh century to the majestic and yet human heads of the thirteenth century with the silence on their gaunt, exhausted features is exactly the same as you would find, say, in Lower Saxony or the Rhineland.

In addition, there is – although not on show – that curious case of a tympanum with the *Deposition of Christ* on which the style and even the inscription tallies with one at Silos in northern Spain. That of course can be explained by trade routes and even more the pilgrimage routes controlled by the internationally established monastic orders. Again, fonts of granite of the same period are sometimes in style and details surprisingly like fonts in Cornwall and in this case the identity of material is sufficient as an explanation.

It is even more difficult to distinguish between Denmark, Sweden and Norway in the Middle Ages although on the whole, Denmark comes closer to Germany than the others, which is geographically and later on even politically understandable. Denmark was a mighty country in the Middle Ages. It ruled over South Sweden, Gotland and so on. With the rest of Sweden there was a permanent war right down to the eighteenth century. Norway was completely ruled by the Danes from the fourteenth century to 1814.

The centre for the whole area in the art of the later Middle Ages was, however, apparently not in Denmark nor in Scandinavia. It was in Lübeck, just as the centre of late mediaeval English painting and sculpture was Flanders. The style of Lübeck is as apparent in Swedish sculpture as it is in such Danish pictures as the life-size figure of the Virgin painted on cloth. Also, the magnificent, tall, stepped gables of Danish fifteenth-century brick churches have their nearest parallel in Prussia. Just there, and there perhaps for the first time, I would be inclined to see a nationally Danish spirit at work. The sheerness, the tall, slender, organ-pipe-like reeding and fluting of these brick pilaster-strips, or whatever you care to call them, has peculiarities which I think one can recognise as Danish to the present day.

The greatest sculptor in the Denmark of the late Middle Ages, on the other hand, Claus Berg, was again a German, probably from South Germany. His *Crucifixion* in the exhibition has all the Baroque sweep of which the latest Gothic German sculpture was capable. And the fact that it has been repainted in Baroque colours, white and gold, probably in the eighteenth century, stresses that very forcibly. The heads are thrown back in frantic grief and the billowy, screwed-up draperies are vehemently whirling around – not at all Danish in these emotional excesses.

And the contrast between this *Crucifixion* or Berg's *Coronation of the Virgin* and the measured, restrained action of the great *St George with the Dragon* by Hans Brüggemann is also not only a contrast between Late Gothic and Early Renaissance but also between German Gothic and German Renaissance.

In emphasising this I have of course already implied that by then, national character existed, even if in Denmark the specifically Danish element was still overlaid with alien styles. But did not the same happen in many other countries?

Take England: Lincoln Cathedral in the thirteenth century was strikingly different from, say, Amiens Cathedral – that is, strikingly English – and English Perpendicular was so English that it had no parallel anywhere on the Continent. Yet when the Renaissance came from abroad, imported from Italy and later from France and the Netherlands, England in art (not in architecture) retired to a provincial – one is almost tempted to say colonial – existence. Holbein came from Germany via Switzerland, Euworts, Gheeraerts van Somers, Honthorst, Mytens and of course van Dyck and Lely came from the Netherlands, Kneller again came from Germany.

Well, it is the same in Denmark. The dominance of the Netherlands is most remarkable. The most spectacular buildings, the towering brick castles of Kronborg and Fredricksborg were built by Dutchmen; the best drawings of the sixteenth century – every bit as thrilling as Bruegel drawings – are by a German, Lorck; the best of the seventeenth-century portraits in the exhibition is by Wuchters, a Dutchman; the best miniatures are by Alexander Cooper from England and by Paul Prieur from France or rather Geneva; the best seventeenth-century sculpture is by Dieussart from southern Belgium, active in London, Holland, Paris, Prussia, and by Quellinus from Antwerp, brother of the English Quellin; and the magnificent set of tapestries from Kronborg was designed by a Fleming, though made at Elsinore. Their long inscriptions are in German – a curious fact worth remembering. Is it due to the fact that the dynasty came from Oldenburg in North Germany, I wonder?

Where Danes themselves appear most impressively is in wood

carving. The madly Mannerist altar from Naestved could not be brought over to London but the four-poster bed from Clausholm is a splendid substitute, carved with an extravagant welter of religious and allegorical figure-work and of gristly ornament – just the thing to be fruitful in and merrily to multiply.

But although these pieces of Mannerist artistry are the work of Danes, their style once more is in no essential way different from that of such North German Mannerists as Gudewerdt. Now that begins to change at last in the course of the eighteenth century. The Danish Court Painter of the Rococo, it is true, was still a Swede and the first sculptor a Frenchman but among architects some of the leading ones – Krieger, Thura and Eigtved – were Danes. And to my way of looking at Danish art, a piece of furniture such as the walnut wardrobe number 314 in the catalogue is Danish in spirit too: simple, solid, comfortable and yet not without a slightly provincial, honest elegance.

Now at last I can take you into the nineteenth century and present you Danish art as against art in Denmark – a national art in the good, not yet the bad, sense. Curiously enough, the most famous of all Danish artists does not form part of that national style, the sculptor Thorvaldsen. For he lived most of his life in Rome and believed in the international style of the Classical Revival as fervently as any abstract artist in New York nowadays would believe in the international validity of his patterns. And Thorvaldsen's works were indeed bought by collectors all over Europe and especially by the rich English milords who then proceeded in the course of the last thirty or forty years to sell them freely to Denmark and the Thorvaldsen Museum.

The Museum building itself – the building of the Thorvaldsen Museum – is another story. Bindesböll, its architect, wanted to build truly classically but could not help being highly original. His colour sketches for the interiors of the Museum, with their broad, bold, flat washes, are among the memorable discoveries at the exhibition and so incidentally is his design for a Zoological Museum at Copenhagen of 1884 with its Romanesque forms and its wild use of coloured materials. It beats our William Butterfield of the contemporary All Saints, Margaret Street, in sheer brutal force and it foreshadows in the most uncanny way the great H.H. Richardson of Boston.

Bindesböll studied at the Copenhagen Academy which by then had become an institution of international reputation. Its main teachers, Wiedewelt and Abildgaard, had spent years in Rome, Wiedewelt as a friend of the great Winckelmann himself, Abildgaard at the same time as Fuseli. Neither of them is really adequately represented at the exhibition. Especially, it would have made a lot of difference if one could have seen something to appreciate how close Abildgaard in some of his paintings could come to Fuseli. They are sometimes nearly in a *Sturm und Drang* spirit – for instance the *Ossian* at the Copenhagen Museum.

Copenhagen under such teachers attracted students from across the German border too and the three greatest North German romantic painters, Carstens, Runge and Friedrich, all studied for a while at that time at Copenhagen.

The academic Roman taste and the taste for Ossian existed side by side in Abildgaard. As a rule, they appear in different people. The emotional, mystical, romantic side culminated in Kierkegaard and it might interest you to hear that Grundtvig, that famous educational reformer, was at the same time the first translator into a modern language of *Beowulf*.

The clear as against the misty side of Danish art and sentiment, the observant as against the introspective eye, appears in what is perhaps the most characteristic group in the whole exhibition, the paintings of the early nineteenth century, epitomised in Eckersberg. What a curious and engaging picture – those two young girls of his with their parrot in its handsome cage. The one girl dead frontal, the other dead profile, flat, smooth colours, prim and accurate draughtsmanship. And yet somehow, in an overwhelmingly petit-bourgeois way, a humble relation of the clan to which Piero della Francesca belongs – and incidentally, Stubbs.

Eckersberg's *View of Rome* through the arches of the Colosseum has the same smooth, precise, strictly axial quality and Købke's large, odd, flat landscapes behind the church roofs and church towers also. Købke was a more powerful painter though. His portraits have more body, in a robust, untutored way. He died young, as so many painters and poets of the Romantic Movement did. What does this obscure relation between style and biology mean? It has always puzzled me. You need only think of Keats and Shelley and Byron and Girtin and

Mortimer and Bonington and Géricault and Pforr and Fohr. Well, it does apply to Denmark too. And those who lived on usually lose what is best in their art as soon as 1830 or 1840 is reached. You can see it among the Danes with Roed and Lundbye. The standard case in England is, of course, Samuel Palmer.

Young Palmer with his daring on a small scale is in more than one way the British parallel to these minor Danes. On the other hand, if you think of Constable and Turner, who could afford to grow old, Denmark appears at once very provincial, provincial in a quiet, lovable way, so small, so neat, so tidy but also so fresh. The feeling one knows so well from stays in Denmark. It returns at once as you approach the exhibition. There are these clean, white flagstaffs and the Danish flags, their healthy, bracing red and white. Flags can be nationally so very characteristic. Just think of the yellow and red of Spain. The Swiss flag, you know, has the same colouring as Denmark and indeed both countries tend towards the clean and clear, the sceptical, not easily taken-in, the phlegmatic, contemplative, pains-taking.

That side of the Danish character culminates in Hans Andersen, in the architect Arne Jacobsen too and certainly in Peter Nansen, much too little known over here. In the visual arts, I'd say it culminates in today's furniture. There is nothing dashing and daring about it. But it is thoughtfully proportioned, detailed with care, just a little thin and very sparingly decorated in a way rather reminiscent of 1800. The modern architecture of the Danes also does not mind quotations from the Classical Revival, sometimes in actual motifs, more often only in its character. Convincing traditions, native or foreign, are not taboo even among the best modern designers and architects of Denmark.

The other day, Steen Eiler Rasmussen, author of the best book in existence on the building history and the architectural character of London and a distinguished architect himself, gave a lantern lecture here on Modern Danish design. He started with a lantern slide of a chair and kept it on the screen for a minute without saying a word. Everybody was delighted with its delicacy and crispness and architec-tural students started sketching furiously when at last he broke the silence and said: 'This is English of the period of Sheraton.'

I think, on the whole, the Hans-Andersen/Modern-Furniture side of Danish art is pretty clear to people here, especially those who have visited Denmark. But there is again the other, the Bindesböll-Abildgaard-Kirkegaard side, of which less is known, and even Rasmussen himself may tend to underestimate its importance. Bindesböll's son was a designer and a potter. His vases and plates of the 1880s and 1890s are badly, crudely made and crudely designed too but they have an atrocious, gloomy directness, rare in those days of Art Nouveau and the Arts and Crafts. Altogether, Denmark's contribution to Art Nouveau is memorable, more so than the exhibition would make you think. Of the two Skovgaards with their Neo-Runic monuments and symbolic paintings and of Willumsen, one does not get a sufficient idea, really, and Klint's Grundvig Memorial church with its fantastic Neo-Brick-Gothic or Super-Brick-Gothic also must be seen in the flesh to be believed. It is more impressive without any doubt than any of our genteel Comperish brand of Neo-Gothic[2] today.

Maybe those responsible for the exhibition are themselves not terribly sympathetic to that side of the Danish character. Maybe it comes too near to the Nordic of the Nazi years. Well, those who believe so exclusively in what is neat and sensible in Danish art and character should perhaps take a warning – not from me but from Jens Peter Jacobsen, himself so exquisitely civilised a writer. He once jotted down a note which begins like this: 'Poetry of the North should be like Dolmens.' Personally I must confess that I like the Dolmen rudeness in Bindesböll Junior and Skovgaard and especially where it appears in that brilliant sculptor Kai Nielsen.

1   Towards the end of 1948, the Victoria and Albert Museum in London held an exhibition of Danish Art from the Stone Age to the twentieth century.
2   A sideswipe at the architect Ninian Comper.

*

From William Morris to Walter Gropius

Third Programme
SUNDAY 6 MARCH 1949
Producer: Basil Taylor

I wonder how many listeners to these programmes know of Gropius and his career from Weimar to Harvard.[1] I saw him last at Harvard two or three years ago, very much the grand old man of international architecture, very much admired and inspiring everywhere the greatest respect and a good deal of awe. This mixture of respect and awe is not a specifically American reaction. I remember going to see him once nearly twenty years ago in Berlin. I was well under thirty and he about forty-five. He seemed somewhat formidable to *me* then. Besides he wore a fringe – which was slightly disconcerting.

I talked of my work and plans and in connection with a book I was then thinking of writing and which I have since written, I was anxious to have his views on William Morris. I showed him a photo – that splendid photo with the high broad forehead and the flowing hair and beard which Emery Walker took – every inch a Viking. 'So that is Morris,' said Gropius. 'I have never seen a picture of him. And yet I owe him so very much.'

Indeed, in the first programmatic summing-up of the Bauhaus ideas, a little-known pamphlet with a wildly designed cover called *Idee und Aufbau des Staatlichen Bauhauses*, he had already in 1932 written this:

> During the second half of the nineteenth century a movement of protest began against the devastations wrought by academies. Ruskin and Morris in England, van de Velde in Belgium, Olbrich, Behrens and others in Germany, and finally the German Werkbund searched for, and found, ways to re-unite the world of work and that of the creative artists.

Now this is really my chapter and verse for today: the re-union of industry and art and the stages by which it was achieved. They are, precisely as Gropius quotes, Ruskin and Morris, then van de Velde – or rather Voysey and Art Nouveau including van de Velde – and then Behrens and the Werkbund. The last stage then was the Bauhaus.

Ruskin and Morris, mind you, would have been disgusted had anyone connected their preachings and work with industry. Ruskin's contribution of exactly 100 years ago – *The Seven Lamps of Architecture* came out in 1849 – was to insist on honesty in art and on the craftsman's pride in the work of his hands. Machine-made ornament was an abomination because ornament to be of value must be the outcome of a man's thought and a man's skill. Morris took that up and with his much greater vehemence knocked it into a whole system of aesthetic socialism or socialist aesthetics. Art, he said, is man's pleasure in work. To be healthy, art must be by the people for the people, a joy to the maker and the user.

All that was new and most inspiring at a time when the artists, as again Morris said, were 'wrapping themselves up in dreams of Greece and Rome' and left the needs of the multitude to look after themselves. But Morris's tenet, which I have quoted, has various aspects. By the people and for the people and a joy to the maker and to the user. That is, first of all: Art must be such that all can share it. That means it must not be high-falutin' pictures for exhibitions but first and foremost the creation of the things we all must needs use: chairs and carpets and curtains and plates and fire-irons. So Morris instead of becoming a painter or an architect, as he had originally intended, settled down to being a craftsman and an employer of craftsmen. Morris & Co. made and sold woven and printed fabrics, stained glass, carpets, wallpapers and in the end even beautifully printed books.

So much for art *for* the people. But *by* the people? Morris was indeed quite ready to employ all and sundry and emphatically distrusted any talk about inspiration. He believed that honest training in the mediaeval way would lead to honest art. And there is probably no question that his makers indeed enjoyed the work of their hands.

But there was one snag about all that. To eliminate the machine – and Morris hated the machine and called it an unmitigated evil because it drives pleasure out of work – to eliminate the machine means to eliminate cheap production. Hand-woven carpets or weaves must be expensive. And so when he was once busy redoing a house in the West End and a friend was asking him what he was doing, his answer was that he was 'serving the swinish luxury of the rich'.

He saw that his products were not for the people but could not get over that contradiction. Even so, the outcome of his manifold activities and his incessant lecturing was great. He did make artists and architects see that it might be worth their while to take an interest in things of everyday use and that crafts were as good as the art of painting or of designing buildings. So Madox Brown and Burne-Jones and the great architect Philip Webb worked for Morris & Co., and of the younger generation Lethaby, for instance, designed furniture and later as the head of the newly founded London Central School of Arts and Crafts introduced workshops for teaching crafts – quite an innovation at that time, the end of the nineteenth century.

But Lethaby differed from Morris in one important way. He had none of the Luddite, the machine-breaking passion, of Morris. He believed that the machine could be tamed and must be tamed and put to the service of the designer if he is to fulfil his social mission, the social mission which Morris had so clearly mapped out for him.

Nor was Lethaby alone in this changed attitude towards machine and industry. There had, in fact, been a few ever since the middle of the nineteenth century – that is, the time of the Crystal Palace and the great iron suspension bridges – who got an immediate impulsive kick out of such structures of industrial architecture. Théophile Gautier, apostle of Art for Art's Sake, of all people, said in 1850 that a 'new style in architecture will be born the very moment when use is made of the means provided by industry' and he referred explicitly to railway stations and iron bridges. Again Sir George Gilbert Scott, the Gothic church restorer and an equally unlikely witness, wrote that it 'would puzzle the most ingenious bungler to render a suspension bridge unpleasing' and that 'the Crystal Palace would open out a perfectly new field for architectural development'.

But there is still a great deal of difference between such an admiration for industrial architecture and the belief that a vase or a weave, if designed specifically for machine production, can be just as beautiful as if designed for and made by hand. That conception came only gradually. The essential practical step was taken by architects of Lethaby's generation and even older than Lethaby. The leader of them was Charles F. Annesley Voysey, a wonderful man – I knew him: as tough as a militant puritan and as gentle as a nursing sister, a most remarkable mixture of sensitivity and determination. His houses designed about 1890 and after are as original as young Frank Lloyd Wright's were in America and yet of a comfort, an ease, a lovableness unparalleled in Wright's work. Now he found time in the midst of a flourishing practice to design carpets for Tomkinson's of Kidderminster, fabrics for Morton's, wallpapers for Essex's, and so on. And he loved designing them and they possessed a freshness and lightness that made Morris's chintzes and rugs appear gloomy and Victorian in their dependence on the Middle Ages and the Orient.

It was these designs of Voysey's more than anyone else's which made artists and architects on the Continent, van de Velde in Brussels especially, aware of how rewarding designing factory production might be. But Voysey, as much a doer as Morris and much less a thinker, just went on designing without reflecting on the why and the wherefore. The theory of designing for the machine, with its obvious justification of designing without unnecessary ornament, does not start with Voysey, nor indeed with van de Velde who in 1894 pleaded for a 'logical structure of products and a proud and frank exhibition of working processes'. The earliest witness I know is again as odd as Gautier – Oscar Wilde who said in 1882: 'All machinery may be beautiful. Do not seek to decorate it.' The other witnesses however came indeed not from the aesthetes but from the most revolutionary architects of those years, the men who evolved the style of our own time: Adolf Loos in Vienna who wrote: 'To find beauty in form instead of making it depend on ornament is the goal towards which humanity is aspiring.' Then Sullivan in Chicago, Frank Lloyd Wright's beloved master: 'It would be greatly for our aesthetic good, if we should refrain entirely from the use of ornament for a period of years.' And finally Wright himself: 'The machine has noble possibilities ... and will in the end discomfit the handicraftsmen and parasitic artists.'

That is a new tone, isn't it, after William Morris's attitude towards the machine. And it is specially interesting to find Frank Lloyd Wright talk like that in 1903 because he was in an indirect way quite a stimulating force in the early history of the Bauhaus although he never designed for factory production himself. (But then Frank Lloyd Wright is far too complex, too contradictory, too exasperating a problem to be more than just mentioned here.)

Meanwhile there was another movement gathering strength in Germany which was to be the strongest contributory power to the Bauhaus. What was happening was this. Men like van de Velde, besides preaching a machine aesthetic, were designing themselves merrily in a style now known as Art Nouveau and indeed utterly and completely *nouveau* when it came. I have tried to trace the origin of its long sinuous curves, its flower-stalk slenderness and tenderness and its fragility. I am sure they are not to be found in Crete, still unknown then, or in Celtic illumination or indeed in anything of the distant past. They are an application to design of the favourite rhythms of the English Pre-Raphaelites, of Beardsley and Mackmurdo, and they are the first set of forms since the Rococo to be wholly independent of Greece or Rome or the Middle Ages. In that lies the immense importance of Art Nouveau, not in the fantastical suicidal and slim somewhat sickly forms which this revolt against the past took. Indeed its best men abandoned these forms after a few years. That was the case with Olbrich from Vienna, of Hoffmann from Vienna and most emphatically of Peter Behrens. Behrens was Gropius's master. He returned from the orgies of Art Nouveau much sobered and henceforth believed in sharp, crisp, hard, North German straightness of line and unmitigated angularity of blocks. He proved that in his buildings from 1904 onwards and even more influentially in his designs for industry. For with him, thanks to an exceptionally enlightened client, the AEG Electricity Company of Berlin, industrial design really became industrial design. In working for carpets or wallpapers, after all, there is not all that much difference between what is needed for hand and for machine-making. But Behrens designed ventilators in fans, street lamps and such like things.

When he began doing that, an association had just been founded, the Deutscher Werkbund, whose explicit aim was to be a rallying-point for all those able and willing to work towards high aesthetic quality in production. From its beginning in 1907–08, this association refused to exclude the machine from its orbit. 'Work of high quality', they said, 'can be created equally with hand-tools or with machines as soon as man has mastered the machine and made it a tool. Mass production and sub-division of labour are not fatal in themselves but only the fact that industry has lost sight of its aim of producing the highest quality.' And a few years later we hear an equally convincing plea for *standardisation*. 'It is only by standardisation,' exclaimed Muthesius who knew the greatness and the shortcomings of the Morris and English Arts and Crafts achievements better than anybody else in Germany, having lived himself for years in England: 'Only by standardisation,' he said, 'can we recover that universal importance which architecture and design possessed in ages of harmonious civilisation.'

You see how near we get here – in a Werkbund speech of thirty-five years ago – to the problems of today. But standardisation cannot be the only remedy for our worries and thank God for that. That it appeared to Muthesius surrounded by such heavenly glory was no doubt due to the preceding vagaries of Art Nouveau. Van de Velde contradicted Muthesius at once and pleaded – it must have seemed a little outmoded at that conference – for the artist as 'a passionate individualist and a spontaneous creator'.

Now van de Velde during those years was director of the flourishing art school at Weimar. When the First World War came, being a Belgian, he had to leave. In his place Gropius was appointed. The Weimar school became *das Bauhaus* and the programme and activity of the Bauhaus are to me – among many other things of which you'll hear in Dr Adler's talk – the most remarkable effort towards combining creative freedom in art and craft with disciplined work for industrial standards.

1   This was the first of three talks about the Bauhaus school, founded in Weimar in 1919 by Walter Gropius. It was based entirely on Pevsner's groundbreaking history *Pioneers of Modern Design* (originally published in 1936 as *Pioneers of the Modern Movement*) and follow-up work that he did while writing for the *Architectural Review*, all of which had grown out of courses he had taught at Göttingen University from 1930–33 on nineteenth-century British design. The second programme in the series was given by Bruno Adler who worked at the Bauhaus from 1919 to 1924 and described the life of the school, its organisation and methods, and its staff.

★

German painting of the Age of Reformation

Third Programme
SATURDAY 16 JULY 1949
Producer: Anna Kallin

You have learnt at school that the Reformation begins with the ninety-five theses and the Diet of Worms.[1] However the Reformation is not an event that can be dated to the year like the Norman Conquest. It is a movement, a spiritual and a social movement which came to a head in 1517 but whose roots are deep in the thought of the whole later Middle Ages – the Friars who preached not about fine points of dogma but appealed to the elementary emotions of the masses and the mystics who called on the individual to abandon himself in the passion and in the mercy of Christ and to live a life of charity. You find a burning concern with sin and redemption in the lives of people of all classes in the decades when Luther was a child and a young friar. Dissatisfaction with the conduct of the priests and bishops and with the commercial handling of indulgences, insistence on the direct communication of the soul with Christ – you read of these not only in pamphlets and books such as Thomas à Kempis's *De Imitatione Christi* but also in personal records of men and women less professionally eloquent, as chance has preserved them for us.

In 1520 Albrecht Dürer was on a visit to the Netherlands. A rumour reached him that Luther had been imprisoned and probably killed. And there suddenly – in a diary which otherwise runs from entries such as 'I bought a little ivory skull for one Gulden and a small turned box for one Weisspfennig' to entries like 'Bosch is a fine town and has a beautiful church' – there suddenly breaks out:

> Oh God of Heaven pity us. Oh Lord Jesus Christ pray for Thy people. Deliver us at the fit time. Call together Thy far-scattered sheep by Thy voice in the Scripture, called Thy godly Word. Help us to know this Thy voice and to follow no other deceiving cry of human error, so that we, Lord Jesus Christ, may not fall away from Thee. Call together again the sheep of Thy pasture, who are still part found in the Roman church and with them also the Indians, Muscovites, Russians, and Greeks who have

been scattered by the oppression and avarice of the Pope and by false appearance of holiness.

Here for once we hear Dürer's passionate faith spoken out which otherwise we can only feel in his works and in the other great painters of his generation. Their ardour and their directness of expression, sometimes gentle, sometimes cruel, singles out the dozen or two small pictures by German painters of about 1500 from among the treasures of the Vienna and Munich exhibitions. They are all small – with the exception of Dürer's *Paumgartner Altar*. And that his is the only large picture is characteristic enough, for Dürer was indeed the only artist strong enough to reach monumentality at least once in terms of religious painting of the Reformation. I'm of course thinking of his last work, the *Four Apostles*, at Munich (but alas not on show in London). They are every bit as grandiose as a Raphael or a Titian and yet possess a tension in the faces and expressions which is utterly un-Italian and un-Renaissance and belongs wholly to Germany and the Reformation. At the exhibition you can study it well in the expression on the face of Oswold Krell. Dürer made a present of the *Four Apostles* to the City of Nuremberg and added to the paintings a long inscription explaining their meaning:

> God will have nothing added to His word and nothing taken away from it. Hear therefore these four excellent men, Peter, John, Paul, Mark; hear their warning.

And then: 'Peter says ... John in his first epistle says. . .' and so on.

But in the case of the *Paumgartner Altar*, its mood, in spite of its size, is not grandiose and representational but sheltered and intimate. The main figures may be composed in a manner grander than any other artist in the North could then – about 1503 – have mastered. But look at the very centre of the composition, the child surrounded by that enchanting ragout of tiny angels culminating in a little chap in light scarlet with scarlet and blue wings. There is a warmth here and an absence of formula which you find on a smaller scale and with an even more exciting naivety in Baldung's *Rest on the Flight to Egypt* with its moss-bearded tree, and then in the same painter's more sophisticated and less happy *Nativity*. Baldung, who as early as 1521 had made a woodcut of Luther with a halo and the dove of the Holy Ghost over his head – Baldung cannot, we feel, have achieved the same certainty of redemption as Dürer. This *Nativity* is a haunting picture with its slaty sky, the sulphur and orange glories and the dead-white, dirtily streaked wall of the uncomfortable corner into which the group is jammed. No wonder Baldung also painted those white unwholesome nudes – like the Munich one with the voluptuous white cat – and sometimes painted them hugged by a figure of death. The new nudity of the Renaissance is here made use of with an acute feeling of sin, maybe even of vice. Dürer's nudes never have that. But Dürer's image of Death can be just as horrible as Baldung's – in fact more so. Just think of his drawing of *Death on the Horse* or the *Four Horsemen of the Apocalypse*. For Dürer – the more you look at his work, the more you are aware of it – Dürer had an insight into all moods. He watched the world around him with scientific absorption and loving care, the grass or the human face or a rabbit or the ageing ugly bodies exposed in a public bath, and at the same time he visualised with amazing truth the stories as told in the Gospels and re-told them in his series of copper engravings for connoisseurs and of woodcuts for the people. Neither so unwieldy a scene as the *Martyrdom of the Ten Thousand* at the Vienna exhibition nor so hopelessly unvisual a scene as those described in the *Revelation of St John* could frighten him. He was as much at home in the most introspective as in the most restless and breathless moods of those years before the Reformation. No other artist was quite so universal but they all shared the feeling of suspense, as they all or nearly all were indeed reformed Christians.

Grünewald – we have not known this for long – actually lost his job as court painter to the Archbishop of Mayence because of his faith and his famous *Isenheim Altar* – not on show in London of course – has a figure of Christ crucified which many of you will know from illustrations, so hideously tortured as only an age of violent religious upheaval could endure. You can see at the Vienna exhibition something similar in a small *Crucifixion* by Cranach. And Cranach also became a staunch Protestant later and indeed a personal friend of Luther. You can see in that small picture at the Tate Gallery how Christ's passion is lived through by this fervent young painter: again, these almost unbearable flogged bodies with their rivulets of blood and the dog gnawing away at human bones. Or Altdorfer's *Resurrection* with clouds lashed across a sky dark blueish-grey above and bloody red below and Christ as a flaming apparition – impossible in any country but Germany during those years between 1500 and 1520.

Now remember, all these pictures are small, Altdorfer's *Resurrection* twenty-seven and a half inches high, Cranach's *Crucifixion* twenty-three. They were painted not for show and church display but for private, intimate, almost secret, secluded devotion and German art has kept right down to Elsheimer about 1600 and Caspar David Friedrich about 1800 this delight in the intimate scale, although in 1500 it was still adopted for religious content while by Friedrich's time the content had become romantic – that is, pantheistic landscape, owing indeed to the very Reformation of which we are speaking. It is not surprising then that among the pictures exhibited there are a few which possess already the hallmarks of Romantic landscape painting, especially Altdorfer's unforgettable little *St George in the Woods*. Here is Tieck's, Brentano's, Eichendorff's poetry anticipated by 300 years. I'll quote a few lines from one of Tieck's poems:

> Birken, Tannen, Eichen
> Stehn wir durchsammen verwirrt.[2]

And then:

> Der streckt die Zweig in die Weite
> Der steht zum Himmel gewandt
> Führt jeder ein Rauchen, sein eigen
> Und schüttelt sich frisch in den Zweigen.[3]

And so on. In Altdorfer, all that appears real again 300 years before Tieck and 350 years before Wagner's *Waldweben*. We see no sky whatever in that picture; it is all leafage: dense, close-knit, in every shade of green, not a bit frightening; on the contrary, it is a wood with whose every tree we are friends so that even the dragon is hardly more than a curious fungus growth. And the saint himself is certainly no longer an image in the tradition of mediaeval or Catholic saints.

So here, if you like, is one way to secularise art, at the time when the Reformation, once it had settled down, once Dürer was dead and once Luther had become the corpulent and competent leader of a national church – at a time when the Reformation no longer called for religious painting except in the odd and abstruse Protestant allegories of old Cranach. Luther himself in any case had never been a man to take a liking to the arts of painting and carving. So the artists had to get ready to specialise in landscape or still-life or genre, as they finally did in the seventeenth century in Protestant Holland. Or else the artists simply died out, as they did in England. Or finally they might limit themselves resolutely to becoming purveyors of portraits and this is what more or less one of the greatest of German artists did – Holbein. I say 'more or less' because I am well enough aware of all the decorative work he did for the court of Henry VIII. But that was mostly sidelines which came easily to him. Where he is most concentrated and competent is in his portraits with their relentless observation and their breathtaking precision of rendering. That is how you no doubt remember him, his Vienna *Jane Seymour*, his National Gallery *Duchess of Milan*, his Windsor drawings.

He painted few religious pictures and he was obviously never tormented by the doubts and self-searchings of the others who, mind you, were all twenty to thirty years older than he. The Reformation was a matter of course to him from his youth, as the Renaissance was a matter of course. He was the man of the future for the Protestant North, not Altdorfer and Baldung and Grünewald.

And it could not be otherwise. There could be no future in their frenzies. There is such a madly high pressure in the *Isenheim Altar*, it could only lead to explosion. It had either to burn itself out or to collapse of sheer exhaustion. Art could not live at that pitch. So the art of the Reformation as a revolutionary event ends at the time when Dürer died, with the mad vortexes of carved altars as those of Breisach and of Odense in Denmark (incidentally, you could see some such things at the Danish exhibition not long ago). And then the religious fervour of the North abandoned visual art. It did not die but it now poured into all music. What Dürer and Grünewald and Altdorfer could still say in terms of paintings of the Crucifixion, the Nativity and the Trinity, now became motets and cantatas and Purcell's Anthems and Handel's Oratorios and Bach's Passions.

I   1949 was celebrated as the four hundred and fiftieth anniversary of the German Reformation and was marked by exhibitions around the world. This talk is based on

an exhibition at the Victoria and Albert Museum in London but Pevsner also makes
reference to other exhibitions in Vienna and Munich.

2 'Birches, fir trees, oak trees, We stand contained together.'

3 'One stretches its branches wide out, Another turns to the sky, Each with its own rush
and rustle, Lustily shaking its branches.' These translations are attached to the script in
Pevsner's handwriting.

Goethe and architecture

Third Programme
SATURDAY 19 NOVEMBER 1949
Producer: Anna Kallin

If you are like myself, you will by now, when you turn on your wireless
and find yourself in the middle of yet another talk in which the name
Goethe occurs twice every minute, hurriedly switch over to some other
feature.[1] You have – in the last few months – heard about Goethe and
Tragedy, Goethe and Art, Goethe and the Novel. And now there am I
supposed to talk to you about Goethe and Architecture.

Surely to justify twenty minutes on that, I would have to prove that
Goethe contributed something to architecture of considerable weight,
even if one leaves out the fact entirely that it happens to be the
contribution of the author of *Werther* and *Faust* and the *Marienbader
Elegie*.

Well – that is exactly the case. Three times in his long life Goethe
made pronouncements on architecture which influenced developments quite decisively and it is these three moments that I want to tell
you about. Act One is Strasburg 1770–72. Goethe was twenty-one
years old and well acquainted already with Winckelmann's new
undertaking of the noble simplicity and calm greatness of Classical art.
But Strasburg to Goethe meant the very opposite. It meant Herder.
Herder, five years older than Goethe, taught him to worship
Shakespeare and to feel the power of folk poetry, including Ossian.
'The more savage, that is, the more alive ... a nation is,' Herder had
written, 'the more savage, that is the more alive, the freer, the more
sensual and lyrically active must its songs be. The further away from

artificial academic manners of thought ... a nation stands, the less will its songs be ... dead letter.' On art and architecture Herder had nothing to give. In architecture all that mattered to him was still 'exact regularity and noble order'. So it was Goethe entirely on his own who suddenly saw that architecture could be something quite different, something Shakespearean, something Ossianic. Strasburg Minster made him discover that and in 1772 he wrote down his experience in the most vehement *Sturm und Drang* language. The essay was published in Herder's magazine in 1773. I am going to quote from it, in the splendid translation which Geoffrey Grigson made for the *Architectural Review* in 1945.

> When for the first time I went towards the Minster, general notions of Taste filled my head. By hearsay ... I was a sworn enemy of the tangled arbitrariness of Gothic ornament. Under the Gothic heading I piled up ... all the ... misunderstandings of the confused, the unregulated, the unnatural, the patched-up, the botched, the overladen ... And so, as I walked towards the Minster, I shuddered in prospect of some malformed curly-bristled ogre. With what unlooked for emotions did the sight surprise me, when I stepped before it. A sensation of wholeness, greatness filled my soul ... How often have I come back to enjoy this sacredly profane bliss, to enjoy the gigantic spirit of our elder brethren.

And so on. So the discovery was Wholeness and Greatness – a beauty, to quote again, 'by necessity to the smallest part like the trees of God' – that is, naturalness, a naturalness no longer like the nature of the eighteenth-century rationalists, no large Newtonian universally regulated nature, but the new nature of the *Sturm und Drang* and the Romantics, vast, intricate and dynamic.

To have seen that for the first time in Gothic architecture is one of Goethe's glories. The Gothic Revival until then had been an English plaything, not much different from *chinoiserie*. As such it had come over to France and to Germany. Gothic hermitages and similar knick-knacks in picturesque gardens, that is as far as anybody went. A few architectural critics had, it is true, given praise to individual mediaeval buildings, but there was nothing anywhere like Goethe's essay.

The title of the essay is *Of German Architecture*. To Goethe, Gothic was a German achievement, 'of strong rough German soul'. Historically speaking that was a mistake, but no worse a mistake than Rickman made forty years later when he invented the term 'Early English'. Goethe's attitude is not only anti-artificial and anti-Classicist – he merrily insults the 'crawlers among mighty fragments/To cadge proportions' – it is also, there at Strasburg, anti-French. 'The light Frenchman', he says, 'makes a patchwork out of Greek columns and German vaults' and paints 'rouged dummies and cherubs' in 'stagey attitudes' with 'lying complexion'. And then Goethe goes on to exclaim: 'Manly Albrecht Dürer, how dearer to me thy most wooden carved form.'

Do realise how Goethe here, in an aside, takes in his stride the whole re-discovery of the Northern primitives. (I shall have to come back to that later.) Meanwhile he had left Strasburg, gone back to Frankfurt, on to Wetzlar and finally in 1775 to Weimar. *Goetz* had come out and *Faust* had been begun, both themes from the world of 'Manly Albrecht Dürer'.

On architecture I have nothing to report until more than ten years later, when in 1786 and 1787 Goethe saw with his own eyes, and no longer in engravings only, the ruins of Rome, and also the buildings of Palladio at Vicenza, which were so much cherished by the eighteenth-century architects of England, and the Greek Temples of Paestum and Sicily.

How did he react? In his own writings – that is, in the prose version of *Iphigenie* – he had already created a world of characters great and simple and calm, as Winckelmann had made him understand the Greek world had been. But Winckelmann, when it came to art, admired the *Apollo Belvedere* and *Laocoön*, – that is, late statuary, somewhat effeminate or somewhat sensational. The sculptures of *Olympia* and the Parthenon, or course, neither Winckelmann nor Goethe could know. But the severe mighty sixth- and fifth-century Doric of Paestum, Girgenti and Segesta they both did know. The humanity of *Iphigenie* is on that scale and in that vein, neither as gentle and delicate as the *Apollo* nor as sensational as the *Laocoön*.

To Flaxman, the *Apollo Belvedere* was still the *ne plus ultra* of sculpture – just as to his generation in English architecture there

seemed nothing to beat the serene Palladio. As regards Flaxman,
Goethe appreciated his purity and innocence but he also recognised
his deficiency in the heroic. Did he recognise the same in architecture
when he was able to compare Palladio with Paestum? The answer is:
he did not.

He described with great candour his experience the day he saw the
first Greek Doric temple at Paestum. This is what he felt:

> The first impression could only arouse surprise. I found myself in an
> entirely alien world. For as the centuries shape themselves from the grace
> to the pleasing, so they shape mankind ... Now our eyes and with them
> our whole being is ... determined by a slenderer architecture, so that
> these obtuse conical closely-set masses of columns appear irksome, even
> terrible. However, soon I pulled myself together, remembered the history
> of art, thought of the age whose spirit considered such an architectural
> style appropriate ... and in less than an hour I felt attracted, nay I praised
> my genius for permitting me to see these well preserved fragments.

This is a remarkable document, isn't it? There is the author of *Iphigenie*
having to force himself by historical considerations to see what classic
Greek architecture meant. Whereas when it comes to Palladio there
was no hesitation. On Palladio he wrote: 'The more one studies
Palladio, the more unbelievable is the genius, the mastery, the wealth,
the versatility and grace of this man.' There is no stinting of praise
here, whereas in the case of Doric, Goethe wrote a year after that he
thought he had succeeded in convincing himself of its greatness: 'It is
true that Doric temples can have a majestic and sometimes even a
charming appearance' but mankind progressed towards the slenderer,
as 'it could thereby express more sublimity and freedom'. So
obviously, in spite of his efforts, Goethe remained happier with the
civilised, delicately proportioned classicism of Palladio than with the
strong rough Greek soul.

You will notice that I use words here which Goethe had used in
1773 to characterise Gothic architecture and it is a provable fact that
Doric at first struck the recalcitrant – say, men such as Sir William
Chambers in England – as barbaric, uncouth, pretty well in the same
way as Gothic. Both were elementary, primitive, unpolished. And one

might like to think that if Goethe had seen Paestum in 1773 instead of in 1786, he'd have reacted with more enthusiasm. However, as it is, he came as a man of nearly forty and one to whom art and architecture were no longer matters of profound, soul-stirring experience but rather a background of pleasing, *sinnlich-harmonische* and poetic qualities.

Goethe as an art critic, to say it in one word, was becoming academic. That comes out regrettably clearly in the competitions held at Weimar from 1799 to 1805 and in Goethe's comments on the prize-winning designs. But they have nothing to do with architecture and so do not concern us here. As regards architecture, we have to go on to 1815 and after to find Goethe once more taking sides in a controversy. What had happened is that a new generation of critics, chiefly Schlegel and Tieck, had taken up, in a most irritating way, Goethe's own youthful enthusiasms for Dürer and Gothic and made of them a sweeping romantic theory of *neudeutsche, religiös-patriotische Kunst* – New Germanic, Religious, Patriotic Art.

This term is Heinrich Meyer's but Goethe published the paper so called in his *Kunst und Altertum* in 1817. Meyer is very fair in his account of the reasons for and the development of this new style and his arguments against it are worth listening to. 'Since in ancient paintings the attractive simplicity, the touching innocence, was not self-conscious art ... but the conviction of the painters and the period in which they lived, imitation (in our time) cannot succeed.' And in architecture also he pointed to 'artistic as well as technical reasons why it is impossible to revert to the spirit of ages past and borrow what is peculiar to them'.

Goethe felt the same. He disliked the Romantics. 'I call the classics the sane, the Romantic the sick.' But the interesting thing is that whereas Goethe was all against art and architecture harking back to a narrow national past, he was all for making the relics of this same past known. He warmly recommended the work of the Boisserée brothers at Cologne in collecting paintings of the German and Flemish primitives and in publishing engravings of Cologne Cathedral. How could that be?

The answer is that Goethe's late comments on architecture are a synthesis of his early enthusiasm and his mature enjoyments, just as *Faust* at the end of his life is a synthesis of all that had grown in him in the sixty years of his working life.

I would like to end with a few late passages on Gothic architecture to show you in what way he could now again say a qualified Yes to the curly-bristled ogres he loved in his youth.

In 1825 he wrote explicitly that he had no reason to be ashamed of his Strasburg essay of fifty years before. For already then he had felt what he now calls the 'inner proportions' of Strasburg and it is true that he had written how everything in the Minster 'is necessary and ... purposes to the whole'. He was now very pleased to discover that Blondel, chief exponent of classic French eighteenth-century architectural theory – that is, a man of the very rationalism which in his early essay he had fought – had found by measuring up Strasburg 'on the whole the same proportions which please us so much in the contemplation of buildings erected in conformity with the rules of good architecture'.

But that was not all. Right proportion, Goethe felt deeply, is only the outer mark of organic rightness, and so he could now say to Eckermann: 'You see in the works of ancient German architecture the flower of an exceptional state. If you are suddenly faced with such a flower, you can but marvel at it, but if you watch how the flower by and by unfolds, then you see the thing with different eyes.'

So here is Goethe's sympathy with all growth, the fundamental tenet of organic metamorphosis, if you like, translated into architectural terms – or should we rather say into historical terms?

For, purely aesthetically, old Goethe felt as uncomfortable about Cologne Cathedral as the younger had felt about Paestum. He speaks of 'a certain apprehension' while standing beneath 'the portentous and incomplete' choir. But – just as he had done at Paestum – he took refuge in history, thanked those, namely the Boisserées, who taught the public to see the Gothic 'in the right way, that is, historically' and had in the end nothing but praise for the Gothic genius, once the change from seeing to a broader but more detached understanding had been made.

In that sense, old Goethe could in the end appreciate both Antique and Gothic – though both, it must be admitted, now with the mind of the historian of evolution rather than with the passionate feeling of the young disciple of Herder. And so here is a final statement: 'Antique temples concentrate God in man, mediaeval churches aspire to a god high up in heaven.' Well, we have learnt a lot since on the history of architecture in detail but we have not got much beyond that, I think, in our understanding of the essence of Greek and Gothic buildings.

1   'Goethe and architecture' was broadcast in the Third Programme series 'Aspects of Goethe'.

Sir Matthew Digby Wyatt

Third Programme
THURSDAY 3 NOVEMBER 1949
Producer: Anna Kallin

Felix Slade[1] had died in 1868. In 1869 Sir Matthew Digby Wyatt was installed as the first Cambridge Slade Professor, Ruskin as the first Oxford Slade Professor. Ruskin was a celebrated writer and journalist, Wyatt was an architect, designing buildings of a rather distressing quality, as I shall have to mention later, but successful in some other ways, highly successful in administration and organisation, Honorary Secretary of the Royal Institute of British Architects, Knight of the Legion of Honour, Honorary M.A., and so on. He had been his elder brother's pupil, travelled on the Continent, taking a special interest in the use of mosaic inside buildings, and published books on this, on architectural polychromy in general, on metalwork, textiles art and other branches of applied art.

The year which decided his career was 1849. In that year he was sent by the Society of Arts to Paris to write a report on an exhibition of French industrial products. He went over with Henry Cole and won the friendship of that remarkable Victorian. Cole was a civil servant but had also been engaged in work for the propaganda of penny postage and wide railway gauges. He had published pictorial railway charts telling passengers of the sights which their trains were passing, the first Christmas card ever issued and several children's books. He had also designed and sold, through a shop, what he called 'art manufactures', things in pottery, silver, etc., which were meant to be exemplary in design.

And he was, what is more, the spiritual originator of the 1851 Exhibition and his journey to Paris with young Wyatt was part of his campaign to convince first Prince Albert and then all England of the glories and advantages of a London exhibition such as he dreamt it.

He visualised a vast building displaying everything from raw materials and machinery to works of sculpture. But art applied to industry (which term incidentally was first introduced by Albert) was going to be the bulk of the show. And there Cole and his friends cannot have been quite so certain of glories to come or even of a very large number of adequate exhibits.

For Cole and his friends – a small band comprising such notable men as Owen Jones, the architect and author of *The Grammar of Ornament* and of a monumental folio on the Alhambra; William Dyce, the Scottish Nazarene and Pre-Raphaelite painter; and Richard Redgrave, another painter later to be Inspector General of Art – this small band was highly critical of the state of industrial art in England even before the Exhibition of 1851 had shown of what atrocities the Early Victorian Age was capable.

We know pretty well how this disintegration of design had come about in the decades before 1850. The re-shuffling of society, which was the inevitable outcome of the Industrial Revolution, had brought on top a class of people who had not enjoyed the aesthetic training of the Age of Taste nor had the leisure to acquire aesthetic appreciation in later life. Therefore we find in painting the success of the anecdotic – Landseer's *High Life and Low Life* – and the withdrawal from public life of all those painters who wished to pursue more aesthetically relevant problems. They made less and less efforts to please the public – a public indeed less and less worth pleasing – and concentrated on aesthetic subtleties. And Art for Art's Sake in its turn made their possibilities of social acceptance less likely and so the vicious circle was complete.

But while a painter, just like a composer, can create in the solitude of his attic and at least keep up a self-delusion of independence of the public, a designer for industry and an architect cannot. That is why, in my opinion, the highest achievements in nineteenth-century art are achievements of music and painting. But as regards architecture and design, a house or a sideboard simply does not take place unless it pleases a layman, be he client or manufacturer or buyer. And what pleased *them* about 1850? Certainly not what was subtle, because to appreciate subtlety in proportion, outline, etc., requires training and leisure. So efforts had to be loud and if appreciation could be conducted along lines of literary association rather than purely aesthetic exposition, so much the better. Here lies one reason for the insistence of nineteenth-century architecture on the imitation of styles of the past. Different styles of the past are more easily recognised than different moods expressed within one and the same style. Also, the archaeological knowledge which an architect could display in imitating the Romanesque of Lombardy or the Third Pointed of East Anglia was a provable quality and thus accessible to the nineteenth-century patron. And besides, why a college should look Gothic, the Athenaeum Club Grecian, a club of liberal merchants and their champions Florentine Renaissance and a rich man's London mansion like a super *hôtel particulier* in Paris could also be understood without straining one's aesthetic perceptions.

Matthew Digby Wyatt's own buildings are a case in point. For the Crystal Palace in 1854 he did with equal zest – the scholar's, the future professor's zest – the Pompeian Court, the Byzantine Court, the Gothic, Renaissance, Elizabethan Courts. He did the inner courtyard of the India Office in Whitehall in a kind of Genoese High Renaissance and an office building for Dublin in Italian Trecento. For the Albert Memorial he submitted one design as a classic temple and another as an Italian Gothic cross. But where he is most original and most embarrassing, as in the interior of Paddington Station and the exterior of Addenbrooke's Hospital at Cambridge, what strikes one as the characteristics of his style are chiefly three: first, all-over covering of a façade with motifs borrowed from anywhere but all rather thick and robust; second, the display of these motifs without any tension; and third, the complete lack of decided accents. This even pitch of oratory is, I think, eminently High Victorian.

But it would certainly not justify exhuming Matthew Digby Wyatt if there were not more to him than appears in his buildings. In fact the buildings are only the foil to his other achievements. They are that he was secretary to the 1851 Exhibition and that he was an uncannily clear-sighted critic and theorist of design and architecture.

His early criticism is mostly found in the *Journal of Design and Manufactures*, a short-lived but very remarkable magazine which was no doubt conceived by Cole and came out from 1848 to 1852, edited by Redgrave. The leading members of the *Journal* were all older than Wyatt but he picked up their principal theses in no time and they were indeed novel and daring enough.

It is commonly assumed that the reform against Early Victorian flamboyancy in decorative art began with William Morris and I have perhaps myself helped to perpetuate this fallacy. But William Morris's lectures started only in 1877 and here are a few passages from the *Journal of Design* and from some other early writings of its contributors. 'Chaos and disorder rule in art today. Everyone elects his own style . . . We all agree only in being wretched imitators.' Yet it must obviously remain a 'vain and foolish attempt to make the art which faithfully represents the wants, the faculties and the feelings of one people, represent those of another people under totally different conditions'. Hence a new style 'in harmony with our institutions and modes of thought' must ultimately arise. To create it, 'the principles and not results' of the past must be heeded. What are these permanent principles of design to which industrial art of the nineteenth century must return? First of all, every object 'to afford perfect pleasure must be fit for the purpose and true in its construction'. Its ornamentation must be related 'to the process by which [it] is to be executed' and to the position in which it is to be seen. Thus a wallpaper made to cover a wall must give an 'impression of flatness' and a carpet should have no 'Louis Quatorze scrolls, or gigantic tropical plants, shewn in high relief'.

In 1852, Digby Wyatt gave a lecture on 'The Principles which should determine Form in the Decorative Arts' and there again we find 'structural fitness', 'due attention to simplicity' and to truth concerning 'material, method of construction, and uses'.

This insistence on truth in architecture had been preached three years before Wyatt's lecture by a man in no way connected with Henry Cole's circle in a book called *The Seven Lamps of Architecture*. One of the seven lamps, as you know, is the Lamp of Truth, and Ruskin, in the enthusiasm of his thirty years – he was just one year older than Wyatt – thundered against 'architectural deceits' consisting of 'a mode of structure or support, other than the true one' and against the endeavour to make surfaces 'represent some other material than that of which they actually consist'.

Wyatt knew the *Seven Lamps* and even reviewed it in the *Journal of Design* in 1849. He was impressed by 'this thoughtful and eloquent book' and its 'denunciation of shams'. But he was critical of other aspects of Ruskin's preaching and here we are watching the beginnings of a conflict which is of high interest in my present context, not only because it happens to be one between the future first Cambridge and the future first Oxford Slade Professors but also because the two positions held by the two men are still of great significance for our own day.

The points of disagreement were chiefly two. One seems at first quite a small point but is psychologically interesting enough: the attitude of Wyatt and Ruskin to their predecessor Augustus Welby Pugin. The other concerns the much wider issue of the possibility of a genuine style of modern architecture in the nineteenth century. As regards Pugin, Wyatt blamed Ruskin for concealing the influence which Pugin had evidently had on him, and it is indeed true that Pugin was the fountainhead of all reform movements in design and architecture during the nineteenth century. In his fanatical writings of 1836 and 1841 we can read already that 'the great test of architectural beauty is the fitness of the design to the purpose for which it is intended', that 'construction ... should vary with the material employed' and that it is absurd in wallpapers to repeat 'a perspective over a large surface' and in carpets to use a 'highly relieved foliage'. Ruskin's only remark on Pugin in *The Seven Lamps* had been to call him 'not a great architect but the smallest conceivable architect', after which he went on to rave against Romanism – 'no treachery as contemptible' etc. Wyatt, equally indebted to Pugin, paid in two of his books 'a humble tribute to the truth and justice' of many of the propositions put forward by that 'most earnest and earliest' among reformers. Wyatt's charge against Ruskin is no doubt justified and to have recognised this questionable personal character of Ruskin at so early a date is a sign of considerable shrewdness. Equally shrewd is Wyatt's criticism of Ruskin's 'half-views' on the problem of architecture and design under nineteenth-century conditions. This is what he writes – and he was the first to recognise this valid objection to Ruskin, as well as later on to William Morris:

> Instead of boldly recognising the tendencies of the age, which are inevitable, he would attempt to bring back the world of art to what its course of action was four centuries ago. Our course in this nineteenth century may be hateful; denounce it, if you please, but as it is our course, wise men should recognise the fact.

The inadequacy of Ruskin's argument, says Wyatt, comes out most clearly in two things: his lack of a 'consistent theory of mechanical repetition as applied to art' – that is, of machine-art; and in his 'very lopsided view of railways and railway-architecture'. And it is true that in the *Seven Lamps* Ruskin lists 'machine-made ornament of any kind' among the architectural deceits and never considers the aesthetic possibilities of machine-shaped forms. And as regards railway-architecture, that is, the new architecture of iron and glass, Ruskin says bluntly that 'the iron roofs and pillars of our railway stations ... are not architecture at all'.

Wyatt in his turn wrote as early as 1850 that bridges such as the tubular Britannia Bridge and the Conway Suspension Bridge are among 'the wonders of the world' and then goes on: from such beginnings 'what glories may be in reserve, when England has systematised a scale of form and proportion – a vocabulary of its own, in which to speak to the world the language of its power, we may trust ourselves to dream, but we dare not predict'. 'Whatever the result may be,' he concludes, 'it is impossible to disregard the fact, that the building for the Exhibition of 1851 is likely to exercise a powerful influence upon national taste.' When Wyatt wrote this manifesto he was already secretary to the Exhibition and Paxton's design for the Crystal Palace had been made, approved and published.

And so we come to the Crystal Palace, the thrill of the common man, including Thackeray, and the *bête noire* of Ruskin. Wyatt in

1851 said that the Crystal Palace 'may be expected to produce, hereafter, important changes in the construction and appearance of many intensive buildings throughout the country' – which is exactly what has happened, though only sixty, seventy years after the event. Ruskin hurried an appendix into his *Stones of Venice*, just in time for its publication in 1851, to state that iron and glass are 'eternally separated from all good and great things by a gulf which not all the tubular bridges nor engineering of ten thousand nineteenth centuries cast into one great bronze-foreheaded century will ever overpass one inch of'. You see, he felt so strongly about it that even his style went wrong. And he did not hesitate to make it clear what specific building had occasioned this outburst: 'The quality of bodily industry which the Crystal Palace expresses, is very great. So far it is good. The quantity of thought it expresses, is, I suppose, a single and admirable thought ... that it might be possible to build a greenhouse larger than ever greenhouse was built before. This thought and some very ordinary algebra are as much as all that glass can represent of human intellect.'

Well, in respect to contemporary architecture and industrial design, Wyatt, I'd say, was right as Ruskin was wrong.

However, it would be unwise to carry much further such comparisons between the first Cambridge and the first Oxford Slade Professor. For Ruskin, though the less acceptable character, was a genius and Wyatt was not. Ruskin was moreover a man of burning eloquence and high sensitivity and in both these qualities Wyatt was somewhat defective. We need only compare a passage or two from their writings. Here is Ruskin on the criteria of good Gothic work:

> See if it looks as if it had been built by strong men; if it has the sort of roughness, and largeness, and nonchalance, mixed in places with the exquisite tenderness which seems always to be a sign-manual of the broad vision and massy power of men who can see past the work they are doing, and betray here and there something like disdain for it. If the building has that character, it has much already in its favour; it will go hard but it is a noble one.

Well, partiality forbids me to match this with a detailed quotation from Wyatt's Slade lectures on the history of architecture with their rare bald remarks about 'a lighter scale of parts' or 'a beauty of refinement in the execution of foliage and mouldings'.

However, perhaps one should not be shocked by this deficiency in our Wyatt. For since all his signal contributions concern the principles of design and the appreciation of a new technological architecture, why should he be expected to have been a man of any special sensibility? Here also lies of course the explanation of the fact how so undeniably remarkable a man can have been so undeniably bad an architect. Such a contrast between theory and performance is, by the way, frequent among Victorian architects. You find it in Pugin and Gilbert Scott, even more blatantly in Viollet-le-Duc, and in many others.

Very generally speaking one can perhaps say that harmony between theory and practice must be rooted in a much deeper harmony between thought and feeling. This harmony was signally absent by the mid-nineteenth century. It returned only in the arts of design with William Morris and Morris owed more to Ruskin than to anybody else. From Ruskin he received his backward-looking enthusiasm for the Middle Ages, from Ruskin his faith in art as 'a joy for the maker and for the user' and from Ruskin his hatred against his own century, its machines, its commerce and its grimy cities. Wyatt would have approved no more of Morris than he did of Ruskin. Wyatt worshipped industry and 'the comparative annihilation of time and space, through the railway and telegraph'. He firmly believed in 'free trade ... free press, free navigation, free education ... comparatively free postal communication' and 'that ruthless destroyer of conventional restrictions – Competition'.

So Morris became a maker of things, Cole (among so many other activities) a designer of art manufactures. Morris revived handicrafts, Cole and his circle became the instigators and first administrators of government schools of design, of exhibitions, of the establishment of museums such as the Victoria and Albert Museum, of state-endowed competitions for artists – and thereby, if you like, the predecessors of our Councils of Industrial Design and Art: councils and all the other governmentally aided means of promoting art. What the Cole circle and Morris, at first sight, seem to agree on is that art – to quote the formidable Whewell, then Master of Trinity College, Cambridge –

'should not only gratify the tastes of the few [but] supply the wants of the many'. The corresponding quotation from Morris is: 'What business have we with art at all, unless all can share it?' But Morris of course meant something utterly different. Morris's one aim was, to say it once more, to make all work and all art a joy for the maker and the user. To Cole and the others the aim is, as Wyatt put it in 1849, to provide 'the enjoyment of taste to the enormous and now all-powerful Bourgeois class'. Consequently Cole, Wyatt and the others were firmly convinced that art, architecture and aesthetic understanding could be re-established within our own society whereas Morris believed that a complete change of heart, if not a complete upheaval of society, would have to precede the re-establishment of an art worth having.

Well, who in this argument is right? We have to ask ourselves this question just as urgently now as they had to in 1851. Who is right: Ruskin and his disciple Morris, or Cole and Matthew Digby Wyatt?

1   This talk is based on Pevsner's inaugural lecture as Slade Professor of Art at Cambridge University on 17 October 1949. Felix Slade was a wealthy Yorkshire art collector specialising in glass, engravings, books and bindings whose legacy in 1868 endowed three Chairs of Fine Art at the universities of Oxford, Cambridge and London.

Villard de Honnecourt

Third Programme
SATURDAY 16 FEBRUARY 1950
Producer: Anna Kallin

If it wasn't for Professor Hahnloser of Berne University, this talk tonight would not take place. His edition of Villard de Honnecourt's writings, published fifteen years ago, is a model of editing and commenting and has made all future work on Villard a pleasure.

Villard de Honnecourt was an architect or, if you like, a master mason, although the term architect does not really apply to the age in which he lived, and the term 'mason', in the meaning we give it, is much too narrow. Villard lived and worked in France about 1230.

The survival of his work is an almost unbelievable piece of good fortune. The book was at Chartres in the sixteenth century, then late in the seventeenth with Falibien, the art critic, and got into the Bibliothèque Nationale in Paris in 1795. It was first published in the 1850s by Lésais in France and by the brilliant and indefatigable Willis in England. Only half of it, alas, survives – pages of drawings with brief notes, written on vellum. The drawings and notes are principally by Villard himself but were continued by two of his successors.

Successors – in what? Well, the book is not a book in our sense at all. It is really a collection of loose leaves filled at various times with records of things seen and read. Villard had these leaves bound together to make of them a compendium for the use of the junior members of his workshop or lodge – that is what the Middle Ages called the master mason's workshops.

On the second page Villard makes it quite clear that he is addressing 'tous ceux qui de ces engins ouvront' – all those who are concerned with such contraptions, meaning by contraptions a good many widely different things. More than once he addresses his pupils in a schoolmasterly manner: Consider well, if you want to make a good tower, you must use buttresses of sufficient thickness – and so on. As for the programme of the book, he formulates it by saying that he is going to give 'grands conseils de la grande force de maçonnerie et des engins de charpentries et . . . la force de la portraiture, les traits, ainsi que l'art de geometrie'. Masonry and carpentry need not much comment but what are portraiture, traits and geometry? We have to take them one by one.

First portraiture. This apparently covers all drawing of things in nature, human beings, animals, plant forms. And indeed, to one's surprise, this thirteenth-century compendium for the use of a masons' lodge contains accurate though boldly simplified drawings of a snail, a crab, an owl and so on, together with a lion proudly marked 'Sachez que ce lion fut contrefait al vif' – was drawn from life. However, side by side with the lion is a porcupine of which – in accordance with the lovely lore of antiquity and the Middle Ages – Villard tells his youngsters that it shoots out its bristles when angered. Also his pelican is by no means al vif but as crisply stylised as the one in Corpus Christi College at Oxford.

Again, Villard's human figures range from a couple of young lovers on a seat, he holding a falcon on his hand, or a pair of wrestlers and a pair of backgammon players (or whatever they play) to Christ Crucified, seated apostles, the Ecclesia or Church Triumphant and so on – that is, allegorical figures and figures from the Bible as they occur frequently in cathedral sculpture of the period. An interesting fact in this connection is, incidentally, that he seems to have copied these figures from illuminated manuscripts rather than from actual sculpture.

But what must have been drawn from a three-dimensional original is the enigmatic picture of a man in a toga high up on a throne with two almost nude figures above and two clothed below and a kind of altar at the bottom, called '*la sepulture d'un sarrazin*', the Tomb of a Saracen which presumably means a Roman tomb. It is a wildly interesting document but does not, as far as one can make out, correspond to any known type of antique funeral monument. I say 'as far as one can make out' because Villard converts to a certain extent everything architectural that he draws. I shall have to come back to that later.

Meanwhile the most bewildering thing about these various figure drawings is that they are in a mason's compendium at all. There existed evidently no dividing line between architect and sculptor. Carvers of architectural detail and of figures were one and the same as they busied themselves in the lodge. We see them in one of the thirteenth-century windows at Chartres, chiselling away at a statue the block for which lies on a bench, and others holding architectural tools such as L-squares and of course beer mugs too.

Of leaf decoration there appears a good deal and, in accordance with the dates of Villard, his foliage is not yet drawn *al vif* – that is, not yet the realistic representation of leaves in nature but of the stylised variety known in England as stiff-leaf. A specially gorgeous example of this type of foliage is a choir stall end with two large symmetrical scrolls on top of each other. There is also a lectern with such decoration in the '*meilleure manière que je sais*', drawn in an odd and very primitive convention, partly in plan and partly in elevation. More accurately informative architectural draughtsmanship was still very primitive right through the Middle Ages and came only with the Renaissance.

'*Iometrie*' is the next item on Villard's list which needs some explanation. The term in Villard refers to figure art – that is, to portraiture and not what we call geometry. What he says in introducing this section of his compendium is: 'Here beginneth the power of the designing of portraiture, as the art of geometry teaches it, to make one's work easier.' What it amounts to is that Villard shows how the main characteristics of human heads, of animals and of whole human figures in action can be constructed on the basis of triangles, rectangles, pentagrams and so on. It looks sometimes surprisingly like the experiments Dürer made some 275 years later and Luca Cambiaso yet another seventy-five years later.

Then the third difficult term in Villard's list: '*traits*'. It is an ambiguous word but he seems to use it simply as tracing or line drawing. It is however specially important in a mason's book, more so perhaps than comes out in Professor Hahnloser's book, for masons' lodges in mediaeval England sometimes appear in documents as tracing houses and master masons are paid for '*trasurum in moldis*' – for the designing of mouldings. '*Voici les molles*,' says Villard's book where fifteen mouldings of ribs, tracery etc. are shown. What apparently happened in the lodge was that the master mason, after having designed the buildings, got down to the essential details and drew the mouldings so that they could then be enlarged, transferred to templates and from these templates drawn on to the blocks which the inferior masons were to carve into ribs and so on. In this, there is little difference between 1230 and today. But another drawing in the '*maçonnerie*' section takes us again back to an age very different from ours. Villard explains how the height of a tower can be measured from the ground. That is of course a surveyor's rather than an architect's job and shows that, just as there was no clear line of demarcation between architect and sculptor, so there is none between architect and surveyor.

And again, the division between mason and carpenter was not yet as rigid as it is today. Villard was apparently equally familiar with both, as the roof constructions in his book show, and he expected his pupils also to be competent in both. The mediaeval mason was really much more of a glorified handyman than an architect in our sense.

And since machinery such as the thirteenth century knew it was chiefly built of timber and not of metal, the carpenter comes very close to the engineer and Villard evidently regards engineering as part of the architect's job too – as of course it was still universally considered in the fifteenth and sixteenth centuries. He shows the workings of a new mill, a windlass (still called *engin* by the French today) and even a crossbow; and in addition such entertaining automata as a lectern eagle of the type you can see so often in English churches but with a head attached in such a way that it can turn to the left and the right.

There are several such ingenious irrelevancies in the book: a hand-warmer in the form of an apple with glowing charcoal to be put inside – suitable, Villard says, for a bishop to hold during High Mass. Mediaeval churches must indeed have been freezing cold in the winter. And of course there is a whole page devoted to a *perpetuum mobile*, a wheel with seven hammers moved by mercury inside – a conception, as Professor Hahnloser points out, which appears long before Villard, in an Arabic manuscript of the early Middle Ages and goes back to Heron of Alexandria and Antiquity. Well, this machine may still be regarded as acceptable in an architect-engineer's manual but what about a recipe for keeping vegetable dyes fresh and one for an ointment to remove superfluous hair? – *'pour poil ôter'*. Evidently, Villard before deciding to bind his loose leaves in the shape of a book for his lodge had used them to note down anything of possible future use that he had come across on his journeys.

On his journeys – for Villard was a travelled man. And so now at last we come to his life and his architecture. He must have lived in north-west France, in Picardy. He may have learnt his job in the lodge of the Cistercian Abbey of Vaucelles, which was begun in 1190 and consecrated in 1235. He knew Cambrai Cathedral well (which does not survive) – so well that he could say: 'See here the ground plan of the chancel as it is going up now'; and also: 'This is how the apsidal chapels at Cambrai ought to be if they are going to be done right.' Cambrai was begun about 1225 and maybe Villard had something to do with the original plans. In any case it is likely that he designed the Collegiate Church of St Quentin, begun about 1235. He was specially interested in plans of Cistercian abbeys, plan-types recognisable in all countries, and illustrates several, in one case stating explicitly that this particular arrangement of ambulatory and chapels – an arrangement derived from Vaucelles – is one which '*Vilars de Honecort trova et Pieres de Corbie*'. Villard's successor adds to this note that the two had worked it out *inter se disputando*. Corbie, by the way, also lived in Picardy.

But Villard did not stick to his native country all his life, as indeed no architect of ambition seems to have done at that time. We tend to underestimate the extent of travel in the thirteenth century. Villard knew the architecture of the Domaine Royal, the heart-piece of France, which was indeed from the middle of the twelfth to the middle of the thirteenth century the fountainhead of all architectural innovation. He knew Chartres where the style of the stained-glass windows seems to have influenced his curious style of drawing faces and draperies and where he drew the rose window of the west façade – with considerable modifications, no doubt intended as the travelling architect's private suggestions for improvements.

Then he knew Laon where he recorded a plan and a part-elevation of one of the west towers with the emphatic comment: 'I have been in many lands, as you can see from this book, but nowhere have I seen such a tower as the one of Laon' – a statement with which I think a good many of you who know France will be ready to agree. Then he comes to Reims and there he needs four pages to record all he wants to remember – an apsidal chapel from outside and inside (the west parts of the Cathedral were consecrated in 1241), the elevation of the nave from outside and inside, sections of some of the main piers and the bar-tracery of the nave windows. (That tracery is particularly remarkable because bar-tracery, as against plate-tracery, had only just been invented at Reims at that particular moment, between 1215 and 1235.) Some of Villard's drawings of Reims must actually have been made from lodge drawings and not from the building itself for they show details not yet carried out when Villard was there. In his comments on Reims he is again generous with his praise. Of the tracery he says: 'I like it best' – or to be more accurate he says: '*J'etais mandé en la terre de Hongrie*' – I was sent to Hungary – 'when I portrayed this, because I liked it best.'

Now that is uncommonly interesting, isn't it? So he went abroad as far as Hungary. But who sent him to Hungary? I would give a lot to know. Meanwhile there is the fact of the French mason working in Hungary or being consulted for something in Hungary. How many more French architects went abroad? For how much thirteenth-century work outside France were they responsible? Well – one has to be very careful there. Take the case of Henry III's master mason at the time when Westminster Abbey was begun, so clearly under the influence of Reims – that is, at about the time when Villard had just finished his book. That master mason was called Henry of Reyns. Was he French then? It is a tempting proposition. But there are certain essential motifs at Westminster Abbey which are clearly English: the ridge-ribs of the vault, for instance, and the large gallery above the chancel aisles instead of the small narrow triforium or wall-passage at Reims. How should they be explained? There are, I think, three answers. They may be a local mason's modifications applied to a preceding Frenchman's masterplan but they are rather major for that. Or they may be features which the English who commissioned the work, or were chiefly interested in it, may have insisted on because they were familiar features. But ridge-ribs don't seem the sort of thing that lay-patrons would be likely to make a lot of fuss about. And finally Henry of Reims may have been an Englishman after all who went to Reims and worked there, just because the lodge there was so clearly about 1240 the centre of European architecture. When he returned after some years, he may well have been called Henry of Reims. We know of similar cases. We also know that foreigners did in fact go to study in the French lodges. There is Bamberg, for instance, which in its sculpture is without any doubt derived from Reims and yet is wholly German in character. And at the same time the towers of Bamberg come straight from Laon.

We are in a difficult position altogether concerning mediaeval masons, their personalities and styles. The Romantics of a hundred years ago had endeavoured to eliminate masons' names. Cathedrals and abbey churches grew to their glorious sizes and shapes by the zest of bishops and abbots and the pious industry of monks and laymen carrying stones and mixing mortar. Only the Renaissance brought the vainglory of individual architecture. In this form, the thesis is of course nonsense and the late G.G. Coulton[1] and his paladins had an easy job of proving it wrong. But they have gone far too far the other way. It is true that the idea – to design a cathedral with an apse at the east end or a straight east end, with or without a gallery, with one or two towers at the west façade, and so on – must have come from one particular person and that all the mouldings, all patterns of window tracery, must also have been devised by individual people. But while to design a moulding is no doubt a skilled mason's job, any interested amateur – say a bishop or a king – could indicate how he wanted the plan of a church in general. Such drawings as Villard's *église décarrée* (that is, a square-sided church for Cistercian use) are by no means more skilful than the famous ideal plan for the church and monastery of St Gall[2] which was drawn about 830 by some high-up ecclesiastic at the Carolingian court. And besides, if Lord Burlington could design houses in 1720 and 1730, why not William of Wykeham in the fourteenth century? Designing, after all, is the graphic conveyance of ideas, no more than that, and if a bishop was susceptible to the effects of architecture, he must at all times have been able to make himself understood to the craftsman or technician.

But admitting the possibility of the decisive initiative for the design of a church to come from an amateur does not mean to deny that, as a rule, the designer was of course the master mason. So if we know who was in charge of the lodge of Ely at one particular moment, we can be fairly certain that work designed at that moment was designed by him. Mr John Harvey has recently collated hundreds of such names and on their strength attributed hundreds of buildings to named architects. In the majority of cases he may be quite right. But what does it help us? The case of the King's Carpenter being called to Ely to advise on the design of the Octagon is well known. So this most ingenious piece of timber construction and architectural design is in all probability due to a consultant from London. If only we had more documents, in how many other cases might we not read: *J'etais mandé en la terre de* somewhere or other.

Well, if this is so and if we know of the existence of such universal masters as Villard, what benefit is there in the names of those who never became a palpable personality or the carrier of a definable style? Should we not be interested in a man's name only if the name stands for a character and a style? Now that is precisely what makes the survival of Villard's compendium so invaluable. Here, after dozens of dim Richards of so and so and Williams of so and so, is a man with his wide and multifarious interests, his superstitions and his faith and wonderful love, an all-round craftsman ready to turn to masonry and engineering, carpentry and sculpture, a character so universal as our modern age with its ever-increasing specialisation can never hope to produce.

1 George Gordon Coulton (1858–1947) was a historian specialising in the Middle Ages. His death pre-dated Pevsner's arrival at St John's College, Cambridge by two years.
2 St Gall, in Switzerland, was named after the itinerant seventh-century Irish monk Gallus. Under the abbacy of Gozbert (816–837), St Gall began a golden age and Gozbert is credited with devising a model plan for monastery premises, perhaps around 820, an earlier dating than Pevsner's.

Revivalisms in architecture

Third Programme
MONDAY 12 JUNE 1950
Producer: Basil Taylor

Gordon Russell once told me that when he was a boy in the Cotswolds no more than forty years ago, you could still go to one of the older masons, ask him to build you a house, leave the detail to him and get Tudor windows with hood moulds over their tops – not because he wanted to build in the Tudor style but because he knew no other. This was how his father and grandfather had built and this was how he was going to build as long as he had stone to build with.

So that was a case of Tudor survival right into the twentieth century. As I am discussing 'Revivals in English Architecture',[1] it may be just as well to make the distinction clear straight away between survival and revival. Oxford was a conservative place in its architecture; it is to this day. When in 1640 a new staircase was to be built to reach the Hall at Christ Church, the staircase itself was more generously spaced than a mediaeval staircase would have been but it had a fan-vault, not as a special feature but as a matter of course, and fan-vaults were put into Oxford college gatehouses, where the fifteenth and sixteenth centuries had liked using them, right down to 1716, the date of the gateway to the Radcliffe Quad at University College. In the distant provinces, where such things happened – I remember for instance the chapel at South Zeal in Central Devon which is entirely Tudor and dated 1713 – that was without any question done completely unselfconsciously. Whether the same can be assumed at so late a date in Oxford is perhaps a little doubtful. For by 1700 the attitude to the Middle Ages was gradually changing.

In Elizabethan and Jacobean times, country mansions were already very occasionally built with romantic, that is self-conscious, reminiscences of a chivalric past: Wollaton of 1580, for instance, and Lulworth of about 1605 and especially Bolsover of 1613. Then, when we come to Christopher Wren – that is, the architecture of two generations later – we find for the first time the problem of survival and revival recognised as such. Wren in his report on Westminster Abbey of 1713 said this of the towers of the Abbey which were then not yet completed: 'I have made a design ... in the Gothick form ... such as I conceive may agree with the original Scheme of the old Architect, without any modern Mixtures to show my own inventions; in like manner as I have among the Parochial Churches of London given some few examples, where I was obliged to deviate from a better style, which appear not ungraceful but ornamental.' This seems to me a remarkable document. It shows three things. That Wren's Gothic steeples, as, for instance, at St Dunstan-in-the-East and the fan-vaults of St Aldermary, were designed in the Gothic style because Wren felt obliged to use that style and also because he felt that to mix two styles would be unreasonable and, finally, that he could appreciate Gothic as graceful and ornamental. This was, at the time, in opposition to the accepted view. Gothic was still used as a general term of vituperation by Shaftesbury, Addison and even William Kent. 'The taste of most of our English Poets', says Addison in *The Spectator*, 'is extremely Gothic.'

Still, at the same time, some were ready to admire mediaeval buildings for their 'magnificence and curious workmanship' and to enjoy 'pleasing reflections' which they may arouse. These quotations come from a memorandum on the preservation of the ruined manor house of Woodstock. It dates from 1709 and was written by Sir John Vanbrugh, architect to Blenheim Palace. With Vanbrugh we reach the beginnings of a serious mediaeval revival. It is an important moment in the history of European architecture; I say 'European', because the Continent followed England in this new attitude. No wonder, perhaps, that England led in historicism – a country more sensuous in its aesthetic creations and less reflective, associative, literary or call it what you will could not have taken it up. On the other hand, it can also be said that it needed Vanbrugh in England to conceive it. Wren, the scientist, was fair but detached to the style of the past. In a report on Salisbury Cathedral he said that he could 'justly commend' the original architect 'for many things', such as the good proportions which he used and the mouldings which he 'decently mixed' with large surfaces without ornament. There is no enthusiasm in this anywhere, just sound judgement. But Vanbrugh, of Flemish descent and a theatrical manager as well as a brilliant playwright and an amateur architect, built for himself a house at Blackheath with battlements and a round turret, surrounded the grounds of large mansions by castellated walls with bastions and recommended to his clients architecture with 'something of the castle Air' because it would make a 'Masculine Show'. And indeed Vanbrugh's country houses are robust and massive. They are more mediaeval in spirit than in detail; he never copied, never used pointed arches or Gothic ornament and he merges his battlements and polygonal angle towers into a general mood of sombre Baroque grandeur.

Now from the Baroque to the Rococo. From Vanbrugh to William Kent, who is usually credited with the invention of Gothicism as with the invention of the English style of picturesque gardening. Both belong closely together because both replace the pompous by the informal and straight axiality by undulation and because both are concerned more with associational than with strictly visual values. The picturesque garden is to produce certain sentiments which usually only an arcadian nature untreated by the human hand would arouse, and the Gothic house is to produce reflections on a romantic past. In fact Kent did not invent either. In gardening Bridgeman seems to have preceded him and in the new Rococo Gothicism Hawksmoor, whose twin towers of All Souls College,

Oxford, of 1720–34 have already some of the playfulness in the handling of Gothic motifs which Kent succeeded in making a widely accepted court fashion. They are neither as unselfconscious as Gothic had been until then in most Oxford college work nor are they as matter-of-fact as Wren's continuation of Wolsey's gatehouse to Christ Church by his Tom Tower in the same style nor are they as convinced of a fundamental mediaeval truth and power as Vanbrugh was. When Kent remodelled a fifteenth-century gatehouse at Esher in 1729, he added such bits as ogee-arched windows and quatrefoil windows for the sheer fun of it. And the same capricious playing with Gothic motifs appears in some minor remodelling of 1732 at Hampton Court, in the former Court of Chancery, on the dais of Westminster Hall and in some other work at Whitehall. Kent's Gothic is everywhere lively and pretty and nowhere correct or, as he would have said, pedantic. It is characteristic that he liked the elegant double curve of the ogee-arch, a curve so similar to those of the contemporary French Rococo. And you can indeed find occasionally in country houses of the middle of the century Gothic and Rococo plasterwork side by side.

In the same houses, incidentally – and that brings me to the next revival, if revival you choose to call it – you can find mirrors and such like small pieces of cabinet work in a Chinese style, nowadays often called Chippendale Chinese. This China fashion goes back to what Europeans from the seventeenth century onwards knew of China, from porcelain more than from any other sources. Versailles possessed its Trianon de Porcelaine as early as 1670. In England it had become a real craze by 1750. 'A few years ago', we can read in the magazine *The World* in 1753, 'everything was Gothic ... according to the present prevailing whim everything is Chinese.' And in the same year Hogarth writes in his *Analysis of Beauty*: 'There is at present such a thirst after variety that even paltry imitations of Chinese buildings have a kind of vogue.'

Variety was no doubt one reason but another was that delight in the exotic which is so characteristic of the Rococo. You get it in Montesquieu's *Lettres Persanes*, in Horace Walpole's *Letter from Xo-Ho*, in Goldsmith's *Citizen of the World*, and so on. The most fantastic piece of Rococo Chinoiserie in English literature is Sir William

Chambers's, the architect's – and he was a very serious classical, academic architect – Chambers's *Dissertation on Oriental Gardening* of 1772 to which is added a second part alleged to be contributed by 'Tan Chet-Qua of Quang-Chew-Fu, Gent., FRSS, MRAAP, also MIAAF, TRA, CGHMW, and ATTQ'. Chambers says of him that he 'had three wives, two of whom he caressed very much; the third but seldom, for she was a virago and had large feet. He dressed well, often in thick satin; wore nine whiskers and four long nails, with silk boots, calico breeches, and every other ornament that Mandarins are wont to wear; equalling therein the prime macarones, and *savoir vivres*, not only of Quang-chew, but even of Kyang-ning, or of Shun-tien-fu.' But these literary entertainments are of less interest in my present context than the fact that Chambers translated into reality his delight in China (which he was the only English architect to know personally) and built the Pagoda at Kew which you can still go and see. That was in 1763.

Just under three miles south-west of the Pagoda on the river at Twickenham lies Strawberry Hill, Horace Walpole's villa, his 'little plaything-house' as he called it when he bought it in 1747. He did not know yet what he was going to do in the way of alterations. But he was already an admirer of the Gothic style. In 1748 he speaks of it very much in the Rococo way as of the 'charming, venerable Gothic', and in 1750 of the 'whimsical air of novelty' which Gothic as well as Chinese bits give to the grounds of country houses. So Gothic was to be the style of his additions at Strawberry Hill and when he mentions them in his letters he still seems to think very lightly of it. The new staircase he calls 'so pretty and so small that I am inclined to wrap it up and send it you'. It was incidentally to have 'lean windows fattened with rich saints'.

But there is one thing new in Walpole's attitude to the Gothic style and that is what matters to us. He did endeavour quite consciously, especially in his later years, to make much of his Gothic detail correct. With his Committee on Taste he pored over Dugdale's tome on St Paul's and Dart's Westminster and so on, with the result that the library bookcases are a copy of the screen of old St Paul's, the doors of the gallery a copy from St Albans and the fireplace in the Holbein

Chamber a copy from the tomb of Archbishop Warham at Canterbury.

It seems all very odd to us. If he wanted to replace the arbitrary by the accurate, how can he have overlooked the impropriety of making a funeral monument in a cathedral into a fireplace for a villa? And indeed the fascination of Strawberry Hill – and I can assure you it is a fascinating house – is the very incongruity of these copied snippets in their frivolous setting.

Now, book-learning was also the new thing in the other equally important revival of exactly the same moment, the Classical Revival. The Classical Revival was really the oldest of all, in so far as it starts with the Italian Renaissance. By 1500, Roman architectural motifs were copied, Vitruvius was printed and commented on, antique statuary was collected and limited excavations begun. Raphael was made superintendent of Roman Antiquities in 1515; of the four books of Palladio's celebrated treatise on architecture, one was dedicated to the *Antichità Romane* and with the growth of philology and archaeology more and more books came out illustrating monuments of classical antiquity. It was a scholar's job first and foremost but architects were quick in making use of the books for their own purposes. Thus, to return to the eighteenth century and to England, Castell published a book on the Villas of the Romans in 1728, Cameron one on the Baths of the Romans in 1772, Robert Adam his folio on the Palace of Diocletian at Spalato in 1763 and Wood went to Asia Minor and published the *Ruins of Palmyra* in 1753.

This extension of archaeological knowledge must largely be attributed to intellectual curiosity but no doubt also to a genuine liking for the aesthetic qualities of the antique style. The curious thing about it is, however, that Greece herself, and especially the classic Greece of the fifth century, remained for very long entirely out of the picture, in spite of the fact that, on the strength of philosophy and literature, people were quite convinced theoretically of the superiority of Greece over not only modern Europe but also Rome. Poussin, for instance, wrote in 1647, '*Nos braves anciens Grecs, inventeurs de toutes les belles choses*' although he probably did not know a single piece of real fifth-century statuary and certainly not a single Greek temple.

Even when the first archaeological expedition to Greece –

Athenian Stuart's expedition – had been carried out at the expense of the Society of Dilettanti and the first volume of the results had come out in 1762, it contained nothing of the severe and robust style of the Classic period – that is, nothing Doric. The Society of Dilettanti is important in the history of the Greek Revival. It had been founded about 1732, four years after the foundation of the more serious, more pedantic and, as it turned out, more vigorous Society of Antiquaries which devoted its activities to the mediaeval as well as the classical past. The early members of the Society of Dilettanti were bright young gentlemen who combined heavy drinking with quite a genuine interest in what was known as *virtù* and has little to do with what we call virtue. The official portrait of one of the founder-members shows him in a Franciscan habit holding up a cup to the Venus de Medici. Their toasts at meetings were '*Viva la Virtù*' and 'Grecian Taste and Roman Spirit'.

Grecian taste: what precisely did that mean? Certainly not the Doric, for the Doric temple with its complete lack of ornamentation and its sturdy columns shorter than any known to the eighteenth century was bound to strike the genteel dilettante not as a revelation of supreme taste but as something quaint, if not barbarian. And indeed, although it is hard for us to believe it today, when Doric Temples, the temples of Paestum in South Italy, were first published in the 1760s, opposition was wild. Sir William Chambers, a convinced classicist although, as we have seen, not averse to some occasional fun in the Chinese style, drafted an academic discourse in which he was going to say that those who were trying to 'cheat us into reverence for Attic deformity . . . might with equal success oppose a Hottentot and a Baboon to the Apollo'.

Now this seems to me most interesting. What made Chambers react so violently? I think the answer is this. Chambers was architect to the King, co-founder of the Royal Academy and soon to be knighted by the King, his special protector. He must have sensed revolution in this bleak Grecian architecture. If he did, he was an uncommonly intelligent and far-seeing man for the earliest actual buildings in the Doric style in England, such as the little temple at Hagley, near Birmingham, built by Athenian Stuart in 1758, are, although correct copies of the Greek fifth century, really garden ornaments not essentially different from Gothic umbrellas, sham ruins and hermitages. But Chambers was right. The first painting heralding the French Revolution, Jacques-Louis David's *Oath of the Horatii*, has two Doric columns in the background, and the young architects of the period of the Revolution, such as Ledoux, also preferred them to any others. Again, England is important in this momentous change from revivals for fun to a revival in earnest. Soane, one of the greatest European architects of his time, three years younger than Goethe, four years younger than David, six years younger than Goya, showed Doric columns prominently in a design of his, done as early as 1776.

And as with Soane one passes abruptly from the Rococo to a revolutionary Romanticism, first in Neo-Greek and later in wholly original forms, so in exactly the same years Goethe took the corresponding step to a Romantic appreciation of Gothic. When Goethe, as a student in 1770, was faced with Strasburg Minster it suddenly dawned upon him that this was not, as polite people thought, 'in a small taste' but that it had a superb 'wholeness and greatness' and conveyed feelings of necessity and nature just as we get out of 'a sublime wide-arching tree'. In England we have nothing as early as this to revaluate the Gothic style. English architects and patrons went on using Gothic forms as a costume worn lightly. The earliest instance of a juster feeling for the character of Gothic is perhaps some remarks in Richard Hurd's *Letters on Chivalry* of 1762; but they do not amount to much. All he says is that Gothic Romance possesses 'something peculiarly suited to the view of a Genius'. But, concurrently, scholarship proceeded, though much less consistently than classical archaeology. Walpole's friend James Essex at Cambridge was working for many years in the 1770s–80s on a history of mediaeval architecture. However, the first building in England which shows something of a real enthusiasm for Gothic as the style of soaring towers and huge vaults was begun no earlier than 1795. It was Fonthill and even this was still lacking in moral truth, designed by a questionable architect for a questionable patron – that is, designed by James Wyatt for William Beckford. But with all its showiness and snobbery and cheap mysteries, it remains a fact that Gothic forms were used at Fonthill for strong emotional effects. The tower was 270 feet high, and the octagonal room at its foot had piers of sixty-five feet.

Still, Fonthill remains a costly extravaganza with nothing like the earnestness of purpose of Soane's work and to the category of extravaganzas belong the other most famous examples of revival architecture round about 1800. The most famous of all is of course the Brighton Pavilion dating in its present form from 1818–27. Its style is Hindoo[2] and it was not the first building to display this style. The Stables behind the Pavilion had introduced the same style as early as 1803. And there is of the same years a weird country house in Gloucestershire, Sezincote, which is about as gaily Indian as the Pavilion. It was all based on the aquatints just then published by the Daniells who had visited India. And even several decades earlier Sir William Chambers had designed for his garden decorations at Kew besides the Pagoda a little Alhambra and a little Mosque, complete with miniature minarets. So the choice of the style for the Brighton Pavilion by the Regent is less original than people often think. But its scale and gusto and flamboyance, especially inside, remain unique and it is good to see that Brighton has at last taken the Pavilion to its heart and is making a thoroughly good job of it.

Earnestness of purpose, I said, is what these enchanting bits of exotic revivals up to 1820 or 1830 are lacking in, whether they are Moorish or Gothic or, after Napoleon's expedition to the Nile, Egyptian or whether they are in imitation of picturesque Italian villas. And it is perhaps their very irresponsibility which we like in them. When reviving was at last taken really seriously, the buildings lost their *élan vital* at once. In this lies the difference between the pretty blunders of church and chapel architecture before 1830 and the correct reproductions designed by the younger generation after that date – that is, by the men of Sir George Gilbert Scott's generation. Scott was born in 1811, one year earlier than Augustus Welby Pugin, who is infinitely the more interesting character and the one to whom England owes the change from insouciant Gothic to Gothic as a Christian duty. 'Indeed', said Pugin in 1841,

> if we view pointed architecture in its true light as Christian art; as the faith itself is perfect, so are the principles on which it is founded. We may improve in mechanical contrivances to expedite its execution, we may even increase its scale and grandeur; but we can never successfully deviate

one tittle from the spirit and principles of pointed architecture. We must rest content to follow, not to lead.

More churches of deadly dullness are due to this sermon of Pugin's than all the remaining mediaeval churches in this country put together. Of course, really good architects went on turning the canons of Neo-Gothic into an original expression of their own character – think of Butterfield's works, of occasional works by Street and Brooks and of many by Pearson – but such architects were few and far between.

However, while Pugin's obstinate insistence on Gothic forms for nineteenth-century buildings was as a whole fatal, some of Pugin's theories have, by penetrating to a deeper understanding of what a mediaeval revival might be, helped to turn revival into revolution, to defeat imitation of the past and create the new style of the present. It came about like this. Pugin was the first to try to explain the greatness of mediaeval architecture by the unity of faith behind it. Carlyle, at the same time, showed the connection between the greatness of the Middle Ages and the structure of mediaeval society. Ruskin followed both and William Morris followed Ruskin. But whereas Ruskin still remains almost entirely on the plane of criticism, Morris moved on from theory to practice. If the Middle Ages were great and sound, because at that time every workman was an artist and all work was pleasurable, then to re-establish such an ideal state of affairs, we must not copy the forms of the Middle Ages but take their conditions of life as an example. So the revival of craft became a demand for social reform. And indeed honesty of craftsmanship led at once to a reconsideration of the fundamentals of form, to an appreciation of the proper use of materials, to the abolition of much thoughtless ornament and thus in the end to the establishment of a completely new style in art and architecture, a style which, although it was (against Morris's expectations) based neither on craft nor on guild organisation, has yet that much in common with the Middle Ages that it is once again a style in which architecture leads the other arts and in which they co-operate on the same problems.

It seems a long way from Vanbrugh's Masculine Show to pre-fabricated houses and machine-produced equipment but it is a way which, I hope I have succeeded in showing you, leads without break and undue meandering from the Baroque to the Rococo, from the Rococo to Romanticism, from Romanticism to archaeological scholarship, from archaeological scholarship to social reform, and so on to the present day.

1 Pevsner's was the ninth programme in a series called 'Aspects of Art in England 1700–1840'.
2 Pevsner wrote later that he tried to pronounce this word in inverted commas, to make clear that he was referring to a nineteenth-century rather than a modern term.

Baroque painting in Italy

Third Programme
SUNDAY 21 JANUARY 1951
Producer: Leonie Cohn for Roger Carey

I often wonder how many people, when they go to Academy exhibitions at Burlington House, think of Burlington House as Lord Burlington's house. Yet, in spite of all the alterations inside and out, the house is still there. Look at the front and forget about the mid-nineteenth-century colonnade and the fussy trim and you still have an extremely restrained, carefully balanced, Classical composition, very disciplined, nobly proportioned – the great Palladio of Vicenza transported to Piccadilly, London, England. Lord Burlington was in fact the prophet of that classic Italian style in England. He was only twenty-one when Burlington House was begun, a monument to his determined opposition to the Baroque grandeur of Christopher Wren, Hawksmoor and Vanbrugh. It is just as well to remember that Burlington House and Vanbrugh's robust, fanciful, original buildings went up at the same time. Without knowing of this polarity of Classicism and Baroque one can't understand the eighteenth century, nor incidentally the seventeenth, of which I am supposed to talk to you tonight.[1]

The catalogue of the present Royal Academy exhibition tells us that Lord Burlington, who when he was in Italy purchased a number of paintings as well as looking at buildings, spent more money on Domenichino's *Madonna della Rosa* than on any other picture. It seems odd to us. Apparently the Seicento appealed most strongly to a man like Lord Burlington where it seems least attractive to us. Look at that even oval of a face, the long nose, the small yet full-lipped mouth, the hard modelling, the all-too-smooth composition, with the parallelism of the heads of the Virgin and the Child and of the arm of the Virgin and the legs of the Child. Her open hand holds roses – a graceful motif, but how lifelessly handled. Yet go to Sir Joshua Reynolds's *Discourses* delivered sixty and seventy years later and they'll confirm Lord Burlington's enthusiasm: 'The Roman, the Florentine, and Bolognese Schools ... these are the three great schools of the world.' Rome and Florence, of course: that is Michelangelo and Raphael – but Bologna? Well, Bologna means Domenichino and his masters, the Carracci and Guido Reni and some others. Who would now mention these painters in the same breath as Raphael and Michelangelo?

But let's go on for another moment with Reynolds. 'Style in painting', he says, 'is power over materials, by which conceptions or sentiments are conveyed. And in this, Lodovico Carracci, in his best works, appears to me to approach the nearest to perfection.' And again: Guido Reni's idea of beauty 'is acknowledged superior to that of any other painter'. Now, in the light of such praise, go and look at the *Crucifixion* by Reni at the Academy exhibition. The trouble with it is, it's so sentimental. The lacrimose looks – all three, Christ, the Virgin and St John, raising plaintive eyes to heaven. Then these glassy colours ... I suppose one can understand what the seventeenth and eighteenth century admired: an even composition and a free yet not offensive flow of feeling; classical balance made less exacting by an effusion of sentiment. No – this is surely not on the same level with Raphael and Michelangelo. The exhibition itself proves the point, for here, for the first time ever after more than ten years, Michelangelo's marble tondo of the Virgin, the precious possession of the Royal Academy, is on show. Compare it with such a good Carracci *Madonna* as that from Hampton Court or with Lord Burlington's Domenichino *Madonna*. You'll see the difference in calibre at once. Michelangelo has a single-mindedness, a tension, an energy which – in terms of very different characters – the other heroes of the High Renaissance, Raphael and Titian, also possess.

Reni has none of that. Take his *St John* from Dulwich – a first-rate example of his mature style. There is no real concentration on the figure. The contours are open – look at the arms and legs – and the body in its diagonal position is relaxed. The gesture is one of operatic eloquence. The face is surrounded by thick, attractive curls of hair, the mouth is open as if to address us. It is all of an easy, accommodating appeal. Now this is precisely what was so admired. The Bolognese school kept some of the formulae of the classic High Renaissance but loosened its reins.

In the whole Italian Seicento, only one man was as single-minded and concentrated as the great masters of a hundred years before – Caravaggio, the founder of the Italian Baroque, who died as early as 1610. Just compare his *St John* with Reni's. You see how firm he has modelled the body of the saint – how solid and self-contained its composition, how sharp, violent, unambiguous the lighting, how sombre the expression; and you can also see how searching the observation must have been to represent flesh or the herbs on the ground as closely as they are represented by Caravaggio. What was so provocatively new in his work to a generation used to the subtle artificialities of the late sixteenth-century Mannerists (the artists between Raphael and Michelangelo at the end of the Cinquecento) was the vehemence of light and dark for the purpose of a determined modelling and the close-upness of the detail. If you don't see these qualities at once at the exhibition, go to the National Gallery and look at Caravaggio's *Christ at Emmäus* as well, or better still go to the Louvre and look at his *Death of the Virgin* and compare it with any of the huge Bolognese altar-paintings there.

For in this one thing the Academy exhibition fails us and is almost bound to fail us – all appreciation of the Seicento needs a large scale; you need pictures twelve feet high and the decoration of whole church vaults or whole saloons in private palaces. The pathos of the Seicento – the century, mind you, which invented opera – called for large surfaces and, what is more, for whole rooms, architecture and all. Proof of that is the only real genius the Seicento has produced, Bernini. Bernini, who was a generation younger than Caravaggio, has of course certain universal Baroque qualities in common with him. Both are naturalists, both are masters in the handling of light and both are unashamedly sensational. But otherwise the difference of date means great differences in style. Caravaggio stands at the beginning of the Early Baroque, Bernini at the beginning of the High Baroque. That is: Caravaggio has wonderfully compact compositions and the hardest, most obtrusively palpable modelling; Bernini is explosive, expansive, reaching out violently in all directions and he is sketchy and fluid in his technique. Of his brilliantly impressionistic technique as a painter, only one portrait bears witness at the exhibition – a portrait good enough to be by Velázquez. But Bernini was a sculptor more than a painter and his sculptural art is alas at the exhibition entirely unrepresented. There is however a series of sketches for fountains and these are immensely important. Few other things are so completely representative of what the Baroque was after. A fountain is not a work of art: is it architecture, is it sculpture? It is decoration – that is, an application of a number of arts, and I shall have a good deal more to say later about the importance of decoration for the Baroque. Nor is Bernini even satisfied with the contribution of the arts alone. He introduces rocks seemingly untouched by man – that is, he tries to convey the impression as if his work were, before our eyes, growing out of the sphere of reality into the sphere of art. And this sense of growth, of a dynamic event, is also reflected in the technique of the sketches – rapid, daring, unfinished. Finally, a fountain of course calls for that very treatment for its job is to be seen in conjunction with shooting-up and running-down water. So a fountain is a *Gesamtkunst-werk*[2] if ever there was one and the *Gesamtkunstwerk* is a characteristic expression of the Baroque. Just remember the opera.

So the greatest Italian representative of the Baroque, Bernini, was a sculptor and a painter and a great architect as well. In his work at St Peter's or the Cornaro Chapel in S. Maria della Vittoria or at S. Andrea al Quirinale, you can hardly sort out what should be called architecture and what sculpture. Nor need it be sorted out for the superordinate category in the Baroque is not one of these arts, as architecture was in the Middle Ages and painting in the nineteenth century, but decoration – a category which comprises them all but to a certain extent devaluates them all too. Take Versailles, that supreme example of the Baroque. It is a masterpiece of decoration, not of architecture or painting or sculpture. Decoration means that no individual piece need ever be taken quite so seriously as in the Renaissance. You can see that very clearly if you look at the other Seicento drawings at the exhibition. Many of the best of them are brilliantly decorative, for instance the lovely, velvety early Guercinos or the Castigliones with their billowing forms, often reminiscent of liquid bubbling over.

Much Italian oil painting of the Seicento has that same quality and it is the painters who went in for this lively boiling technique, for the dynamics of rapid hatching and whirling, and for swelling curves – it is those painters whom we today appreciate most. That, mind you, is a new thing – the very opposite of the taste of Burlington's and Reynolds's time. They wanted their Seicento mildly classical; we want ours fiery, with a lot of gusto, even if it is facile. But there again the exhibition fails us. Sir Gerald Kelly in his very carefully worded preface speaks of serious difficulties preventing some of the Seicento pictures from appearing on the walls of the Academy. That is alas only too true. They were withdrawn. The pictures which could have been shown would have given the Seicento rooms just that kick which they now lack. What a difference a big succulent early Guercino would have made or some big Genoese mid-seventeenth-century paintings or one of those Giovanni Liss pictures which can be almost as good as Rubens. Well – you have superb Rubenses at the exhibition: that enchanting portrait of his young wife especially, so delightfully young, and painted with a proprietary fondness rarely matched even in his own work. With that, nothing of the Italian Seicento can compete. For the truth of the matter is, of course, that among the very greatest painters of the Baroque, not one is Italian. Who are they? Rubens and Velázquez and Rembrandt and Frans Hals. (Among sculptors, I admit, it is different and a Bernini portrait like the so-called *Mr Baker* at the Victoria and Albert Museum or the splendid *Neptune* also at the Victoria and Albert are superior to anything French or Flemish.)

But in Italian painting, while much is highly enjoyable, little or nothing is really sublime or really profound. Now what is enjoyable? Strozzi, I'd say, who is well represented, with his almost Flemish buxom creatures and his juicy handling of paint, and Fetti with his

spirited technique of storytelling on a small scale and his feathery
landscape backgrounds, and Cavallino with his long, slender, elegant,
overbred figures, and certainly Luca Giordano, the most brazen of
decorators. Him of course one should also see in large pictures, but a
small one such as the *Acis and Galathea* from Chatsworth is a substitute
well worth having. As you look at it, your eye is kept on the move all
the time by pleasantly undulating diagonals. Nothing holds you up
except perhaps the very pinkness and attractiveness of the nude. And
that voluptuous element also belongs to the Baroque.

It is, I think, to say it once more, these qualities of the Seicento, its
sensuousness and sensationalism, its *impromptus*, its impertinence and
also its dash and its brio which we are looking for now, not its semi-
classical attitudinising. That can also be done supremely well – but
again, only rarely by the Italians. In this tendency within the Baroque,
which is only Baroque *malgré soi*, the highest genius is met in Poussin
and Claude Lorraine, although the Domenichino landscape from the
Fitzwilliam Museum at Cambridge explains why Poussin admired
Domenichino more than any other Seicento painter. The Carracci
drawings also, with their firm forms, give one an idea of why
Reynolds could rank them so high and why a French connoisseur of
the late Seicento, Roger de Piles, could, as far as draughtsmanship
goes, call the Carracci and Domenichino, together with Raphael,
Michelangelo and Poussin, the greatest of all masters.

But it remains a shame to have to try and judge the Carracci by
drawings only. Large Carracci altarpieces such as the ones in the
Louvre prove that in spite of their more classical allegiances, the
Carracci belong to the Baroque as much as Caravaggio and as much as
Bernini.

Such terms as Baroque are very useful if they are sufficiently
precisely defined. I have mentioned at least a few criteria; now here is
yet another criterion you can try out at the Academy. I said that in a
painting of Luca Giordano's, one thing always flows smoothly into
another. In all Baroque art each motif, each figure, each individual
work points beyond itself. That can be achieved by agitated gestures,
or by a general sketchiness in pictorial technique, or by the deliberate
mixing-up of reality and fiction (as where painted figures in a ceiling
are continued in stucco figures stretching their arms and legs into our

real space) or by painting sculpture naturalistically and giving sculptured figures real hair (as they liked to do in Spain), or by tricks of illusion, by *trompe-l'œils* such as paintings seeming to be stone reliefs, or in architecture by making a vista appear longer than it is, or – and this is of course a much more serious expression of the same desire – by letting all figures merge in a dark yet fully alive atmosphere, as Rembrandt does with his often misunderstood *clair obscur*. This *clair obscur* is meant to represent the infinity of space around us; it lifts the individual out of his physical isolation and makes him part of a greater whole.

Part of a greater whole: that is what Baroque art is intended to be in its decorative as well as its religious aspects. The statue and the painting may be part of the decorative ensemble of a great hall in a palace, or the individual building part of a town-plan, or the tree in a Rubens landscape part of a universal Creative turbulence never at rest, or Rembrandt's late *Family Group* which was recently shown for a while at the National Gallery, part of a mysterious unity of the universe. No wonder the seventeenth century was also the century of Newton, the century which discovered infinity in mathematics and infinity in astronomy.

Such thoughts and speculation take one far away from the reality of Italian Seicento pictures. Something on the plane of Rubens's wisdom or the *élan vital* of Rubens exists in Italy only in certain grandiose ensembles, not in individual easel pictures. I have spoken to many people about this Academy show. They all expressed the same feeling of anticlimax when they reached the Seicento rooms. That feeling is partly due to the absence of some of the most enjoyable pictures but partly also no doubt due to the fact that Holbein as a master of the Renaissance is great and complete in every one of his drawings but that Bernini and all other Seicento artists will always appear fragmentary if they are torn out of the context of church or palace.

1 Pevsner's talk on the origins of the Baroque stems from pioneering work he had done in Germany in his first major book, known in English as *Italian Painting of Mannerism and Baroque* (1928), but never translated.
2 A 'total work of art', one employing many crafts and appealing to many senses.

How to judge Victorian architecture

VICTORIAN ARCHITECTURE (1)

Third Programme
WEDNESDAY 4 JULY 1951
Producer: Anna Kallin

It is now 114 years since Victoria ascended the throne and 111 since she was married to Prince Albert. The Albert Memorial is eighty-five years old and St Pancras Station about eighty. Surely after three or four generations, it should be possible to assess values. Yet, although critics dealing with, say, Dickens or Swinburne or Brahms use a technique of argument not different from that used for Shakespeare or Bach, when it comes to architecture they seem to be unable to find any common ground at all. In my opinion there are two reasons for this: lack of knowledge and lack of accepted criteria.

Let us take lack of knowledge first. Early English and Georgian are much better known than the Victorian style. There are only about a dozen men – or fewer – who have ever devoted close study to Victorian architecture. And those who know most have not yet published, though books are in hand. The three leading Victorian scholars are Mr Goodhart-Rendel, who knows an incredible amount, has an incredible memory and writes the most felicitous style; Professor Russell Hitchcock of Northampton, Massachusetts, who has worked for a number of years on a massive volume which, he tells me, is now complete; and Mr Summerson, who will, one hopes, one day follow his *Georgian London* by a *Victorian London*. In the meantime Mr Hugh Casson has written a highly readable sketch and Mr Reginald Turner a longer book. But Mr Turner unfortunately dislikes Victorian architecture intensely. As for my own research, much of it was burnt during the war and the rest is scattered through articles chiefly in the *Architectural Review* which is, incidentally, altogether the principal medium from which Victorian scholarship and Victorian appreciation can be gathered.

So how should people at large know about the Victorian style? Lack of accepted criteria was my other suggested cause for the general confusion in dealing with Victoriana. This is due not only to lack of distance in time but also to an intrinsic deficiency in all Victorian architecture, a very real collapse in values. Advocates of the Victorian style today try to deny that. But that won't do. By all criteria which make S. Sophia in Constantinople or Maisons-Laffite near Paris or the Belvedere in Vienna or Seaton Delaval architecturally valuable buildings, Paddington Station and the Langham Hotel are valueless. That architectural badness must not be explained away but accepted and interpreted to reach some understanding of the Victorian style.

The Victorian age runs from 1837 to 1901. But Victoria was not really in the centre of the scene though she and her husband stand stoutly for a particular brand of middle-class eagerness and serious-mindedness which was indeed dominant in English architecture and in successful painting. But the dates of Queen Victoria's reign do circumscribe an age, as it happens – the railway age.

Railways were made possible by the use of the steam engine and by progress in metallurgy (for rails and so on) and railways were made necessary by the needs of supply for an ever faster-growing population and an ever faster-growing industry. Food as well as coal had to be transported, and transported quickly to save time and waste. But this need was not new in 1830; it was felt strongly as early as 1760 when Brindley and the Earl of Bridgewater started on their canals, and later when, from 1815 onwards, McAdam improved road surfaces on his new system. In addition, the steam engine had been invented by James Watt in 1765 (or you might prefer to say 1782), the blast furnace in 1766 and the puddling process in 1783. The amazing phenomenon of the sudden increase in population also sets in at about the same time. All this is connected with that great change in Western civilisation which is familiar as the Industrial Revolution. In this change, England was leading everywhere. We are here only concerned with its effect on architecture. This, to my mind, was twofold. The new large population concentrated in the cities needed new types of building. And the new class of patron who paid for the new buildings had new views and new tastes.

I said 'new types of building'. What were they? People do not usually realise sufficiently that up to about 1800, the history of architecture, as you read it in books, consists almost exclusively of churches, castles, palaces and town and country houses. One reads of town halls and guild halls occasionally but, with the exception of an odd dozen, they might just as well be left out of a book on the history of architecture without altering the argument of the book in the slightest. Now imagine a book on the nineteenth century. Church buildings remain important though not as essential as in the Middle Ages. Castles have become fortresses and concern the military engineer and not the architect. Palaces proper are few and far between. Country houses, at least in Britain, have as large a share of the architect's attention as ever, town houses one larger than ever before – yet, I may add, not a large enough share because the numerically biggest addition to town building, the provision of working-class housing, hardly ever went through an architect's office. What else, then, occupied the architect and his staff? Think of any dozen prominent Victorian buildings which you can easily remember: the Government Offices in Whitehall with their self-assured and a little hollow imperial eloquence; Glasgow University, dark, spiky and towering on its hill; the Rylands Library at Manchester with its more sensitive and fanciful interpretation of Gothic; University College Hospital in London, standing big and pigheaded at an angle to the well-mannered frontages of Gower Street; the Natural History Museum, vast, symmetrical and clad in distressingly imperishable materials; Colney Hatch; the Prudential; Charterhouse School; Covent Garden Market; St Pancras Station and so on. And, in addition, large factories, factories of six storeys even before the year 1800; in 1823 the President of the Prussian Board of Trade, travelling in England, called them 'the miracles of our age'. None of all these types of buildings had existed as special jobs for architects before the nineteenth century. That we must always remember. It was bound to change the architect's job and his outlook considerably.

So much, for the moment, about new types of buildings. But I also said, 'new patrons with new tastes'. The chief difference between the Georgian and the Victorian client is that in the eighteenth century, certain rules of taste were accepted pretty universally. All was fair and Palladian in the landscape gardens of Capability Brown. The first ripple of a disturbance came from the sophisticated dilettante who wanted some sharper architectural spice than the Italian porticoes of Lord Burlington and his *protégés* could provide. So Horace Walpole in the course of twenty years built Strawberry Hill in a fanciful, none too ponderous, none too pedantic Gothic. The house was a huge fashionable success, at home and abroad. In England by 1800 or 1810, you can take it that at least one out of five new country houses in a county would be castellated rather than balustraded on top and have a Tudor gatehouse or a Perpendicular porch rather than a portico. The client, according to his tastes, decided for Classical or Gothic and the architect followed, sometimes after having submitted alternate designs in both styles. When Downing College was to be built at Cambridge, the King expressed his special wish 'that it may not be a Gothic building' and it was duly made Greek in the end. In John Claudius Loudon's celebrated *Encyclopaedia of Cottage, Farm and Villa Architecture* a monumental circular stables building with a high clock tower is illustrated. Loudon says that the plan was designed by him but that Sir Charles Barry sketched two elevations for it, one in the Italian style and the other in Tudor Gothic.

The Italian style, incidentally, is something different from the Roman or Greek, and you must not forget that during the period of which we are talking, the period before Queen Victoria, Classical or Gothic were no longer the only alternatives. Already about 1760 in Kew Gardens, a Chinese pagoda had been built and a mosque and an Alhambra. Sir Charles Cockerell had, about 1805, insisted on having a country house in the Cotswolds in the Hindoo style – a style characteristically later called (by Loudon) Indian-Gothic – and the Regent, with the help of Porden, Repton and John Nash, had introduced this Hindoo fancy to Brighton. All that, you may say, was only whims of eccentrics. But while Chinoiserie and so on never became an accepted taste in English architecture, other styles did, especially Neo-Elizabethan and Neo-Jacobean. They were national and they were, thanks chiefly to Sir Walter Scott, Romantic. So when the Palace of Westminster had been consumed by fire in 1834 and the Houses of Parliament were to be rebuilt in its stead, the terms of the competition called for designs in the Gothic or the Elizabethan style. In 1837–40, Richardson's *Observation on the Architecture of England during the reigns of Elizabeth and James I* had already come out and in 1839 Henry Shaw's *Details of Elizabethan Architecture*. Yet a little earlier, in 1833, Loudon in his *Encyclopaedia* had devoted a whole chapter to what he calls 'the Beau Ideal of an English Villa' and that is, as he says, 'in the mixed style of Architecture, called the old English style . . . and in that ornate manner of it, called the Elizabethan'.

In the end, the competition for the Houses of Parliament was won by Charles Barry with a Gothic, a Perpendicular design, managed equally well in the massing, the varied skyline and the extremely carefully designed details. Those details were due to Augustus Welby Northmore Pugin and Pugin was the one man in the 1830s to whom Gothic was not a matter of one acceptable style among several but a matter of faith and conscience. To Barry it certainly was relatively indifferent whether the Houses of Parliament of the British people would be Gothic or Elizabethan. Some of his grandest country houses were in the Elizabethan style anyway – for instance, Highclere of 1837 – and what is nowadays perhaps best known of his work is in yet another style: the Reform Club and its slightly earlier neighbour, the Travellers' Club, designed in 1829 and 1837 in the style of the Italian High Renaissance. I will not entertain you with such books as Richard Brown's *Domestic Architecture* of 1841 in which he proposes for the growing estates in the suburbs – he mentions specially 'such salubrious and bracing Elysian spots' as Herne Hill and Shooter's Hill – villas in the Norman Feudal, Lancastrian Embattled, Morisco-Spanish, Pompeian-Surburban and of course the more familiar styles. I will not speak about that because Mr Brown was obviously a bit of a charlatan. But Charles Barry was a serious man.

How then should one explain the co-existence at the beginning of Queen Victoria's reign of equally accepted and equally respected buildings in three – and, if you add the Neo-Grecian, four – styles of utterly different character? There is only one answer possible: the Victorian choice of style was no longer primarily a matter of aesthetics. That that could be so was due to a change in the architects' clients as much as in the architects themselves. The Victorian client by and large – the manufacturer, the merchant, the banker – had neither received the kind of education which had been enjoyed by the gentlemen of Georgian times and which comprised a good deal of education of the eye, nor had he ever had the leisure in later life to acquire it. A busy man cannot be bothered with the finesses of how to place most elegantly the metopes in a Doric frieze, or – to take an ecclesiastical example – how to reconcile the concept of the west tower with the concept of the antique columnar portico. But he can understand that a club that looks like a Florentine palace evokes thoughts of merchant princes, that a theatre in a debased Louis Quatorze style evokes thoughts of gaiety and frivolity, a house vaguely like Hatfield thoughts of opulence and unquestioning optimism, and a University College in the Grecian style thoughts of Socrates and Plato – and, incidentally, of opposition to monkish obscurantism and any churchy narrowness. Hence University College, London, was Classical because founded to be non-denominational while Oxford and Cambridge remained Neo-Gothic as long as they remained essentially tied to the established church. Downing College, which is Grecian and not Gothic, had only two chairs established by the foundation statute and they were demonstratively secular, one of law and one of medicine.

So here is one reason why the Victorian age became the age of this kind of architectural historicism: a carnival, as Pugin called it. Another is that the visually untrained eye, while it cannot discover what may be aesthetically poor, can check up on archaeological accuracy. Not that the Victorian imitation of past styles was always or indeed usually accurate – there was much more freedom than people as a rule realise – but to distinguish Gothic from Italian and Louis Quatorze from François I is something that anyone can learn and the Victorians always felt safer where they could rely on facts than where sensitivity came in.

Moreover, the architect himself was to a certain extent in the same position. The nineteenth century was making enormous strides in the exploration of the past. One by one in the field of architecture, folios and quartos appeared filled with accurate drawings of buildings of all ages and nations. It had begun with Palmyra and Balbec and Athens and Spalato in the 1750s–60s. But beyond antiquity this scholarly recording did not go until you reach the very threshold of the Victorian age. Even for English Gothic there was nothing correct before Pugin and Wilson's *Specimens of Gothic Architecture* of 1821 and 1825. Then architects began to bring home from their travels sketches suitable to be worked into books on Spanish Gothic, or the Brick and Marble Architecture of North Italy, or Mosaics of the Middle Ages.

Architecture was raised to the safe height of learning. The architect was a professional man in a new sense. The precarious artist-patron relationship of the past was made a good deal securer.

Besides, historicism is in any case the hallmark of Victorian thought. The nineteenth century is not a century of system-building as the eighteenth century had been. It believed in gathering data rather, masses and masses of data, and in leaving a synthesis to the future: excavations and more excavations, huge dictionaries, series of published state papers and mediaeval chronicles, Migne's *Patrologia Latina* in 221 volumes and so on. In the same way the architect was happier if he could go to some published or sketched mouldings for his Gothic pillars than if he had been asked to invent some himself.

Not that there was a lack of inventiveness – far from it. The lack was one of self-confidence. Consider the oddly warped pride in a passage by Pugin on himself, written in 1843: 'Mr Pugin never claimed the least merit on the score of originality; never does he profess to invent new combinations, but simply to revive.' After Pugin, Ruskin (in 1849). One of his *Seven Lamps of Architecture* is the Lamp of Obedience. Ruskin here preaches against 'that treacherous phantom which men call Liberty' and goes on to the dangers of architects wanting to be original. 'The forms of architecture already known are good enough for us,' he says. And, 'A man who has the gift will take up any style that is going . . . and be great in that.' So all that matters in order to have good Victorian architecture is to choose a style and then try to make it universal. According to Ruskin, the choice lies between the Romanesque of Pisa, the Early Gothic of Tuscany and Genoa, the Venetian Gothic and the English Earliest Decorated.

There were very few indeed who would not have agreed with Ruskin – at least as a matter of principle. One of these was that interesting writer and crazy architect Thomas Harris who said that no style 'can re-live its former life' and that a style truly of the Victorian age (as he actually calls it) was necessary and must be founded on such buildings as the Crystal Palace. In an article of 1862, very probably by Harris, we read that at the Crystal Palace, 'a new style of architecture, as remarkable as any of its predecessors, may be considered to have been inaugurated'. That style was new in so far as it was the outcome of the exclusive use of iron and glass: no stone, no brick was apparent in the structure. But it was also new, and in that even more prophetic of the twentieth century, in so far as it was entirely prefabricated. It was designed on a standard grid, and panes of glass and iron columns and beams were reduced to a minimum number of sizes. Only thus could a building more than 1,800 feet long be put up in a few months.

The Crystal Palace was not the design of an architect at all, nor of a professional engineer. It was the design of an amateur inventor, if you like: the distinguished gardener and horticulturalist Joseph Paxton. Pugin and Ruskin disliked it intensely; the public at large loved it. The public – that is, the architects' clients – could admire inventiveness and technical daring. They were qualities as accessible to the layman of 1850 as accuracy of imitation or the evocative properties of Gothic and Jacobean. But to architects and architectural critics, the use of iron and glass was mechanical, vulgar, not high-minded enough. And high-minded one way or another were all the best architects during the High Victorian era. This new ambition was created or at least greatly fostered by the theoretical writings of the two men whose names I have already mentioned more than once: Pugin and Ruskin. Pugin's influence on architects, especially on Sir George Gilbert Scott, and Ruskin's on laymen as well as architects did much to set the pattern for mid-nineteenth-century architecture.

★

Pugin, Ruskin, Scott

VICTORIAN ARCHITECTURE (2)

Third Programme
WEDNESDAY 11 JULY 1951
Producer: Anna Kallin

Pugin, Ruskin, Gilbert Scott: I have told you a few things about them last week, and I want to tell you more of them now. They were all three born between 1810 and 1820 but their writings range from 1836 to 1872. So, whereas the three men belong to the same generation, a comparison of their attitudes to architecture and life takes us from the Early Victorian to the High Victorian.

We must start with Augustus Welby Northmore Pugin. He was born in 1812, the son of the man who had drawn the plates of the *Specimens of Gothic Architecture* to which I referred last week. His father was French and easy-going, his mother from Islington and severely puritanical. The boy designed furniture for Windsor Castle when he was only sixteen and then theatrical décor for romantic plays. He married at nineteen, was a widower at twenty-one, married again at twenty-two and in the same year joined the Roman Catholic church. His all-pervading passions were Catholicism on the one hand and on the other all that had anything to do with ships and life on the sea. He was a brilliant draughtsman and a brilliant polemical writer, he built a large number of churches (most of them a little disappointing if one comes from his books), he designed with incredible facility for church plate, vestments, wallpapers, woven textiles, furniture, tiles and so on, and he died at the age of forty after a period of mental disorder.

Ruskin was born seven years after Pugin. His father was a prosperous sherry-merchant in the City. The parents were of evangelical piety, cultivated, travelled and extremely fond and proud of their only child. Ruskin never knew an hour's worry about money nor about a job. He established himself comfortably as a free-lance writer, made a success of his first book *Modern Painters* which came out in 1843; and with his *Seven Lamps of Architecture* of 1849, his *Stones of Venice* of 1851, and the second volume of *Modern Painters* of 1854–60 he became an authority on art and architecture and their moral nature.

In 1848 he had married Effie Gray; in 1854 their marriage was annulled and in 1855 she married Millais, the Pre-Raphaelite painter, in order to enjoy the pleasure of physical as well as spiritual companionship. The story so far as Ruskin is concerned is rather unsavoury. His later attachment to Rose La Touche is no more gratifying. In the 1870s his mind gave way. His deliria grew worse in the early 1880s. His last ten years were years of almost permanent derangement. He died one year before the old Queen.

They were both queer characters, these two chief thinkers on architecture in the years between 1835 and 1855. I say 1850 for we need not here take Ruskin further than the *Seven Lamps*. Pugin's theory is the outcome of two personal experiences, the conversion to Rome and the visual disgust with the English town of his own youth. (The ugliness of the mills and interminable rows of houses for the workmen must in fact have had a good deal to do with the desire of all Victorian architects to escape into styles distant in time or place.) Pugin's first book is called *Contrasts, or A Parallel between the Architecture of the 15th and 19th centuries*. It is a tremendous piece of visual propaganda, a cautionary tale of the Before and After type, fantastical and unscrupulous. On facing pages you see such things as a splendid Gothic hospital with church, quadrangles and gatehouses, and a star-shaped modern penitentiary with a little marginal picture of a coffin carried away marked For Dissection. Or you see a whole mediaeval town with soaring spires, chapel on the solidly built and break-watered bridge, a tree-lined promenade by the river and so on, and the modern town with 'Jail' in the front, gas works and warehouses by the river, decaying old churches and pagan-looking new ones. Then there is the Gothic conduit and the chained-on Georgian pump with a policeman chasing away a little boy. Another contrast is between Tom Tower, very idealised and called – I must apologise for Pugin – gateway to Christ's College Oxford[1] and on the other side the plain classical gateway to King's College in the Strand. In the same way, funeral monuments are compared and altars, inns, bishops' residences and so on and so forth. The dice are loaded, that is plain enough, but the game is skilfully played all the same. Take as a last example a special page filled entirely with fake advertisements. It's incredible how ingeniously Pugin has caught the spirit of the coming Victorian

Age: a competition for a church, Gothic or Elizabethan, 8,000 sittings to cost no more than £1,500; designing taught in six hours, Gothic, severe Greek, and the Mixed Styles; Gothic chimneys from 10 to 30 shillings; Designs wanted for a Moorish Fish Market with a Literary Room, a Saxon Cigar Divan, a Gin Temple in the Baronial syle; Shortly to be published: *Architecture Made Easy*; Just published: *The Designer's Reckoner* by which the ornaments ... of churches may be regulated; Places and Situations: An errand boy who can design occasionally. A person to do showy foregrounds for competitions drawings ...

It is uncanny, isn't it? But then you read the long introduction to this fireworks of invective and you read Pugin's other books and you'll find a serious, eminently original thinker. I'll try to compress his theories into a few statements, all actual quotations from Pugin: 'In the name of common sense, whilst we profess the creed of Christians, whilst we glory in being Englishmen, let us have an architecture ... which will alike remind us of our faith and our country.' So you see, a good architect must be a good Christian. 'It is only by similar feelings that similar glorious results can be obtained.' Therefore, you see, no pagan style can be tolerated. Incidentally, for another reason as well. All art depends on climate and custom; so again, English architecture cannot be Mediterranean. Gothic is the style of the North. But Gothic – and here we start on quite a different sort of argument – Gothic is also the only functional style. 'It will be readily admitted that the great test of architectural beauty is the fitness of the design to the purpose for which it is intended.' 'In pure architecture the smallest detail should have a meaning or sense of purpose.' That is exemplified by buttresses, pinnacles, mouldings etc. 'Pointed architecture does not conceal her construction, but beautifies it.' So the position of Gothic is trebly fortified. It is the Christian style, it is the national style, it is the functional style. And incidentally – a surprising touch in Pugin – 'With regard to economy, it is impossible to build in any style so cheap as the pointed or Christian.'

Now what emerges from all this and what proved of great importance is this. Architecture must be Christian and architecture must be true to its purpose. In Pugin the two are one. 'The severity of Christian architecture is opposed to all deception,' he says. After

Pugin, they tended to be two and opposed each other. One school of thought accepted from Pugin his unarchitectural criterion, the other his architectural; one the necessity of glorious feelings, the other of sound, frankly-exposed construction. The leader of the first was unquestionably Ruskin; of the other, smaller men, chiefly Matthew Digby Wyatt and a little later Thomas Harris whom we met last week in connection with the Crystal Palace.

The Crystal Palace and the new railway stations were the touchstone: the Crystal Palace is to Pugin the 'glass monster', to Ruskin a super-greenhouse, to Wyatt the beginning of a new style in architecture. Railways stations are accepted by Pugin if treated in a massive way with buttresses and segmental arches, by Ruskin swept away as no architecture at all, by Thomas Harris hailed, where he exclaims, 'We are living in an age of iron.'

Indeed the three great railway stations of North London illustrate to perfection three essential approaches to architecture in Early and High Victorian days. Hardwick at Euston in 1836 built his giant triumphal arch in the severest Doric style. Does it seem absurd to you, however fine the monument itself? It was not absurd then. The completion of the Birmingham–London line was a tremendous achievement, something as grandiose and as masculine as anything the Greeks had done. It deserved the highest rhetoric available – and it got it. At King's Cross in 1851–52, Lewis Cubitt did the reverse. The Euston arch was frankly evocative, Cubitt is just as proud but entirely unromantic. His façade is simply the display of the two arched roofs of the arrival and departure sheds with a clock turret between – as functional as the Crystal Palace though not as ingenious in its construction.

And then St Pancras, which is really two utterly opposed jobs – and in their complete unconcern for each other, eminently Victorian. The train-shed by Barlow is of iron and glass and has the unprecedented span of nearly 250 feet – as against the 137 feet of the dome of St Peter's in Rome and the 142 of the Pantheon. The screen building in front by Sir George Gilbert Scott is, to quote a nineteenth-century writer,

> of palatial beauty. The style of architecture is a combination of various
> medieval features, the inspection of which calls to mind the Lombardic

and Venetian brick Gothic, while the critical eye of the student will
observe touches of Milan interlaced with good reproduction of details
from Winchester, Salisbury, Amiens, Caen and other French edifices.

One could build a whole talk round this one passage. The truth of the
engineer's work, the make-believe of the architect's, the apparent
absurdity of Venetian brick Gothic for a railway station hotel –
'Possibly too good for its purpose,' the architect wrote in his
Recollections.

You know who was responsible for Venetian Gothic in England.
Ruskin of course, and the flaw that runs visibly through St Pancras
Station runs also through the massive edifice of Ruskin's works. It is
sufficient for our purpose to look at his most illuminating architectural
book, *The Seven Lamps of Architecture*. Ruskin's theory depends on
Pugin, although Ruskin denied it, but it is very characteristically
modified. The Christian Romanticism has gone out, as Romanticism
had gone out of all art and poetry by 1850. Morality replaced piety:
'No rascal will ever build a pretty building.' And why? For instance,
because good architecture must be truthful architecture. 'Let us not lie
at all.' And so structure must be shown, materials must be exposed as
what they are, and so on. This is what ethics demand. Yet, on the
other hand, architecture is defined by Ruskin as 'that which ...
impresses on the form [of a building] certain characters venerable or
beautiful, but otherwise unnecessary'. The lower part of architecture,
we read in the Introduction, is the constructive, the higher the
reflective. And so, by degrees, by establishing that beauty is something
added to the building, that 'ornamentation is the principal part of
architecture', Ruskin can in the end arrive at his choice of those
building styles which should be acclaimed by us today as 'Augustan in
their authority'. You heard last week that they were the Pisan
Romanesque, the West Italian Early Gothic, the Venetian Gothic and
the English Earliest Decorated. Of these four, the last two won. The
Oxford Museum is the most celebrated example of Ruskinian
Gothicism but many others all up and down the country followed – a
considerable fillip to secular uses of Gothic at a time when other, more
florid, more bulgy styles made stronger claims.

On secular Gothic, Sir George Gilbert Scott should be read. He
wrote his *Remarks on Secular and Domestic Architecture, Present and Future*

in 1858, as a summing up of the case for Gothic. The book is in so many ways typical of the High Victorian attitude to architecture that it deserves some study. Scott acknowledges his gratitude to Pugin whom he calls 'for all future ages ... the great reformer of architecture' and he mentions Ruskin quite often, chiefly on the question of whether Italian is the better form of Gothic or Scott's own Middle Pointed – that is, the style in the North from the later thirteenth to the early fourteenth century, the style of Amiens and the Angel Choir at Lincoln and a little beyond but stopping short of the more luxurious Decorated. This is how Scott's argument runs: 'I do not advocate the styles of the Middle Ages as such. If we had a distinctive architecture of our own day worthy of the greatness of our age, I should be content to follow it.' But it is 'morally impossible' simply 'to invent a spick-and-span new style'. 'No age has ever deliberately invented a new style.'

And we are specially unlikely to succeed in it because we are the first age which is really familiar with all the styles of the past. This historical knowledge is bound to influence us. Scott never realised that our awareness of the past only came about because the age had lost trust in its own creation. (I have spoken of that before.) History of literature, history of philosophy, history of religion – everywhere history replaced more determined efforts to create new, original systems.

Once we resign ourselves to dependence on the past, what style shall we choose? It must be one style. It is 'manifestly vicious', Scott says, if one architect builds in different styles. Scott's choice is Gothic because this 'was the latest period which possessed a style of its own'. After that came the Renaissance with the imitation of Antiquity. Gothic also, or rather the Middle Pointed, is 'the best period of our national architecture' and it is in addition 'the most free and unfettered of all styles'; 'it embraces every reasonable system of practical construction', it derives all its 'characteristics from utility' and it is 'comprehensive and practical; ready to adapt itself to every change in the habits of society'. It also incidentally does 'not involve additional expense'. We know all that from Pugin. But as in Ruskin, so in Scott, nothing is left of Pugin's religious fervour. Gothic according to Scott is the thing for the nineteenth century for utilitarian as well as aesthetic reasons and not only for churches, where it was fully accepted by the time when Scott wrote – of that I'll have more to tell you next week – but also for public buildings and private houses. Now people objected to secular uses of Gothic just because it was a church style – Scott adroitly answers by comparing the argument with that which keeps churches locked except on Sundays, because 'religious feeling must be limited to Sundays, and even then to the hours of service'. But more important are those passages in which he defends his secular Gothic by analysing how good it would look in town architecture and specially street architecture. It is here at last that we begin to see through all the heavy period disguise what a man like Scott really wanted in architecture. If you wish to see it in the flesh, look at his group of houses in Broad Sanctuary just south-west of the front of Westminster Abbey – that is, where you go under the archway into Westminster School and to Church House.

This is what Scott says: 'Our streets are throughout of dull and heartless ugliness.' We today may agree with that but we would think of Oxford Street or Princes Street but Scott thought of Baker Street and Gower Street – that is, of the uniformity and unobtrusive good manners of the Late Georgians. Their 'utterly intolerant', 'abject insipidity' is what annoys him most. He is at one in this with Ruskin and also for instance with Disraeli's *Tancred* (of 1845). Disraeli calls Marylebone and Belgravia 'insipid and tame'. Instead of their style, Scott recommends 'the individualising of the houses, giving, as far as possible, to each of them its own front, marked out from those of its neighbours' – that is, the breaking up of the unity of the street into innumerable small independent units – the individualism, the lack of a corporative spirit of the Victorian age in its purest visual form. This is how it should be done: Have 'a few houses of one scale, and a few of another, some higher than others – a group of gabled fronts, and another with parapets and dormers ... with some little touch of system, though chiefly arranged with a view to varied wants'. That is clear enough, isn't it? Little system, and a deep draught of picturesque variety. Variety of colours is also recommended, the use of bricks of different colours, of stones in bands, of mosaic, of polished red granite for columns. Can't you see it all? The picture on the title-page of Scott's book is also eminently characteristic of this Victorian attitude of architectural individualism. It shows an imaginary square arch on the right of the Doge's Palace in Venice and behind it the Town Hall of Siena with its tall Campanile, on the left the Cloth Hall at Ypres and some Flemish Town Hall behind – that is the composition of a grand public square. Not a unity like the Capitolo in Rome or the Place Vendôme but made up entirely of individual buildings with no connection to each other.

Scott's last chapter deals with the future. He sees its style, needless to say, as a derivative from the Gothic, but 'a perfectly new phase, differing more from any form that pointed architecture has hitherto assumed than any of those varieties (whether chronological or national) from one another'. It is not easy to follow this vision, although some people may well say that a twentieth-century steel-frame building with all-glass walls meets the case. And the curious thing is that Scott himself must have had an inkling of that for in the middle of all his pleading for Gothic he writes à propos iron and glass roofs and iron bridges: 'Metallic construction is the great development of our age ... It is self-evident that [its] triumph ... opens out a perfectly new field for architectural development.' This is a surprise, isn't it? But we are back with Scott as we know him when he adds at once: 'It speaks ill for the taste of our architects that they have done so little to render it beautiful.' So the architect remains the beautifier. Construction as such does not concern him. The 'great principle' of Gothic architecture – that is, of the best architecture – is indeed to Scott 'to decorate construction'. It is a hideous misconception of what the designers of St Denis or Chartres had been doing but it is the same which Ruskin had sanctioned when he exclaimed right at the beginning of the Seven Lamps with his usual flow of overstatements: 'It would be ... unreasonable to call battlements or machicolations architectural features ... but if these projecting masses be carved beneath with rounded courses, which are useless, and if the headings of the intervals be arched and trefoiled, which is useless, that is architecture.'

The most distressing thing is of course that there is some truth in all that. The dividing line between building and architecture is indeed the introduction of aesthetic values into structure. The Victorian mistake was to see aesthetic values only or chiefly in the decoration of façades and that again is a characteristic mistake. The building was not felt as a unity of plan and exterior, and beauty not as a quality accessible to both but as something superadded. That is in fact the word used by Scott near the end of his book: 'The architecture of the future ...' he says, 'must be pre-eminently practical ... in the best way providing for the object for which the building is erected ... expressing that purpose in its architectural aspect' and 'superadding to this so much of beauty ... as is evidently consistent with its purpose, and as naturally results from the forms which convenience dictates.' All this remains extremely weird if one remembers St Pancras Station and incidentally Scott's other most prominent public building, the Government Offices in Whitehall which are in the Italianate style and not Gothic at all. It seems a strange thing to do for the author of the book from which I have just quoted so much to you, as strange as his sudden profession of faith in iron. But these contradictions between theory and performance are fundamentally Victorian. I've said that before. They come from a lack of courage to take decisions. Prosperous ages shun revolutions even if they can define and describe their necessity.

And Sir George Gilbert Scott is the distinguished architect par excellence of a prosperous age – shockingly prosperous himself. It is a fitting end to what I wanted to talk to you about today if I tell you a little of his career. By the time he established himself as a successful church-builder and church-restorer, he was in his mid-thirties, happily married and the architect already of some fifty-three workhouses, besides a few lunatic asylums for the poor and a big infant orphan asylum. The workhouses were first built in a debased Classical, then in a florid Elizabethan style. There can't have been much of the Gothic crusading spirit in him then. His life also, as against Pugin's, was uneventful. 'My life,' he wrote in his *Recollections* in 1862, looking back to 1846, 'from this time ... seems to have usually run in so smooth a course that I hardly know what to say about it.' In the end he managed to write nearly 400 pages but they are dull and heavy reading. He was a sensible man and a competent architect; that is all. Competence he possessed to a remarkable degree. His restorations – he worked at Ely, Westminster, Chester, Worcester, Oxford, St Albans, Salisbury, Chichester, of course Gloucester Cathedral and at many more – were always based on scholarly surveys of architectural remains and indications even if, in the end, with that astonishing self-assurance which seems to go so oddly with the Victorian faith in the past, he replaced at Oxford a large Perpendicular window by a Norman rose window of his own invention and did innumerable other impertinences of that sort. How many churches he built, no one has ever tried to count. His fame as a Gothicist was made by the Oxford Martyrs' Memorial which he won in competition in 1840 and the church of St Nicholas at Hamburg which he won in the same way in 1844. In both cases he describes how before designing, he learned the appropriate style, by studying the Eleanor Crosses for the Martyrs' Memorial, by travelling to Germany and studying and sketching German Gothic for the Hamburg church. Altogether, architects today can hardly conceive how Scott and his generation travelled, drawing, drawing, drawing – not for fun but for bread and success. 'Then I went to Siena', he writes, 'and had the hardest 3 hours' work in my life, and the pleasantest.' And in Florence, he says, 'I worked violently to the last day, timing myself strictly to the work I was to do every hour of the day.' With all this industry going on in his work, Scott was, it seems, in the end always satisfied that what he had done was fine. Of the big new parish church at Doncaster, he writes: 'It stands very high among the works of the revival'; of the unsuccessful design for a new Town Hall at Hamburg: 'I think it would have been a very noble structure'; of the equally unsuccessful designs for the Law Courts in the Strand: 'I do not know that my general architectural design was of much merit, though I think that it was fully as good as any recent work I know of by any other architect.'

Scott was not a good loser. The account of the Law Courts in his book begins: 'I have now to chronicle a great failure' and the account of the Government Offices in Whitehall is pretty well the centre of the book. The story is well enough known. It figures large in Sir Kenneth Clark's *Gothic Revival* and in Mr Basil Clarke's *Church Builders of the Nineteenth Century*. Yet it is too good and characteristic not to be told again to finish up with today. The competition for the new Government Offices took place in 1856. Scott won third prize for one half of the building. The two winners were men of little distinction. Lord Palmerston waived the decision of the judges and

and appointed Pennethorne who was closely connected with official architecture. Scott was shocked by this irregularity but less worried when the result of his protest turned out to be his own appointment. He made Gothic designs, rather French than Italian, but with 'a few hints of Italy'. 'My details were excellent', he writes, 'and the drawings perhaps the best ever sent in to a competition or nearly so.' But they were not accepted. Wrangling in Parliament followed and painful wrangling with Lord Palmerston who made it clear that 'he could have nothing to do with this Gothic style' and 'must insist on my making a design in the Italian style'. What Palmerston really wanted was to force Scott to resign. But Scott was not easily made to give up a first-class job. (Just think how Pugin would have behaved – or Butterfield, for that matter. But of Butterfield you don't know yet.) Scott retired to Scarborough and then reappeared in Whitehall with a design in the Byzantine style 'turned into a more modern and usable form'. Palmerston – we can feel with him – called it 'a regular mongrel affair' and told Scott that he must either work 'in the ordinary Italian or that his appointment would be cancelled'. What should poor Scott do? Thinking of his family, he says – we have heard that one before – he decided 'to swallow the bitter pill'. He 'bought some costly books on Italian architecture, and set vigorously to brush up' his Italian. The design was a success, thanks to Scott's ambition 'to show myself . . . not behind-hand with the classicists'.

There you have the whole story. Self-praise, ambition, competence – and as for the architectural style, that can be superadded at the last moment. It is a High Victorian story in many respects.

In many but not all. As a matter of fact, I have been told that architects still today sometimes offer clients façades in alternative styles. And you know as well as I that government buildings can to this day choose to appear in period dress. So altogether, when you come to think of it, we can certainly, from this story of government buildings of the 1850s, still learn a few lessons for future government buildings of the 1950s.

1 Tom Tower is, more accurately, the gatehouse of Christ Church, Oxford.

Churches and public buildings and the neglect of the common man

VICTORIAN ARCHITECTURE (3)

Third Programme
THURSDAY 19 JULY 1951
Producer: Anna Kallin

I chiefly talked to you last week about three men: Pugin, George Gilbert Scott and Ruskin. They belonged, you will remember, to the same generation. They were born between 1810 and 1820. But Pugin began to write in 1836, Ruskin in 1849, Scott in 1858. So Pugin is decidedly Early Victorian, Scott decidedly High Victorian. Ruskin is in an interesting in-between position, handing much of the Early Victorian ideals down to William Morris and the Late Victorians. Yet in his overstatements and the thick style of his preachings Ruskin is unmistakably High Victorian himself.

But now having said this and entertained you for half an hour last week with nothing but architectural theories and writings, it is high time for me to go to buildings themselves and see what they can tell us, or rather what they wish to tell us, and then what they tell us against their wish.

The situation was this. Victoria came to the throne in 1837. By then, as you know, Classicism and Gothicism were both accepted for churches as well as houses, and Elizabethan and the Italian Renaissance were just joining the company on equal terms. In addition, the engineers built their bridges. They were outsiders and their works did not count as architecture. In architecture it was the established principle that your first task, when you have to design a building, is to select a style. Once you have chosen, you have to prove yourself competent in the handling of that style. That is at least as much a matter of historical knowledge as of aesthetic sensibility. Now a conflict arose out of this, which goes through much Victorian architecture. The archaeologist in the Victorian Age chooses what his critical sense tells him is evocatively suitable and aesthetically good – Middle Pointed, for instance – but his critical sense was often at loggerheads with his real appetites. There is a terrible lot that was suppressed in the Victorian Age for reasons of respectability or even a deeper, quite genuine, sense of propriety. In church architecture it remains as a rule suppressed but in secular architecture it often comes out much more rampant than the architects knew themselves. That makes the study of secular Victorian a live and in an odd way invigorating study, at least if you can stick a lot of bad taste, and it makes the study of Victorian churches so intolerably dull – except for the work of less than half a dozen men of whom Scott is not one. Everybody knows the typical nineteenth-century church in the suburbs, of an undistinguished mechanical Gothic with nothing to redeem its total lack of fire. Look up one of the rare books which give you names of Victorian architects and you find that they are by Cutts, by Francis, by one of innumerable others who deserve charitable oblivion. Most of them are cheaply built, but buildings no more inspired also appeared in the region of prosperous villas. The most worthwhile Victorian church architects are in my opinion John Loughborough Pearson, James Brooks and of course Butterfield. But Butterfield is a law unto himself. They were born between about 1815 and 1825. No secular architects of equal qualities belong to those same years.

At the beginning of their period stands the break in the handling of Gothic between a free, somewhat fragile and never quite correct use, and archaeological accuracy. The break occurred in the 1840s. It tells of one characteristic quality of the Victorian age: seriousmindedness. Scott wrote in 1855: 'It is now about fifteen years that we took in hand in good earnest the great cause of the revival.' In the same years the Cambridge Camden Society and its journal *The Ecclesiologist* (started in 1841) took in hand in good earnest the cause of liturgical reform in the planning and equipping of churches, and Pugin the cause of revived mediaeval practices in church ritual. They are also the years of Newman and Pusey. There can be no doubt about the honesty of the change of heart. The first correct churches are Scott's at Camberwell, Ealing and some others – Ferrey's St Stephen, Rochester Row, Westminster; Poynter's Christ Church, Broadway, Westminster; and the much more inspired major churches of Pugin's which were not built too cheaply, especially Cheadle in Staffordshire and St Barnabas Cathedral at Nottingham. But in Pugin some Romantic glamour always glitters on whereas Scott and the others were not subject to such Romish temptations.

Now, what among the later generation distinguishes Pearson and Brooks from Scott and his like is that they combined a fine feeling for Gothic proportions with the courage to gather elements of planning from more than one source. Pearson's Truro Cathedral is a noble edifice although totally devoid of any sense of the Cornish or the Truro *genius loci*, with lofty Normandy Gothic towers and an English Gothic interior – and incidentally vaulted throughout, which is a feature always aspired to by Pearson. He felt strongly that his Gothic would be incomplete without the achievement in vaults. That shows a deeper understanding than most of his contemporaries possessed. In London St Augustine's close to Kilburn Park Station should be visited by anybody interested in nineteenth-century architecture. It is one of the best churches of the century. Its tall Normandy Gothic spire can't be missed. Inside it has proportions and a management of space which any thirteenth-century master might have been proud of. Its distinguishing features are tall unbroken buttresses inside the church so that they form side chapels instead of aisles (just as at Albi in France), a gallery above the chapels with doorways through the buttresses, and a transept divided into two aisles by a tall slim pier as at Fountains Abbey. The nave galleries run straight on towards the choir regardless of the transept so that they form bridges cutting off the transepts and making them into spacious separate chapels. It is wholly successful, not at all playful and unmistakably individual.

The same is true of Brooks's best churches, All Hallows Gospel Oak, St Pancras and the Ascension at Lavender Hill, Battersea. Here also elements are taken from various sources, friars' churches on the Continent for instance, and they are handled seriously and individually but without any demonstrative display of originality.

Now, demonstrative originality is just what distinguishes Butterfield's style although he also kept well within the bounds of the Gothic. Take All Saints Margaret Street, St Marylebone, which was begun in 1849, a testimonial to the new High Church aspirations. It is of red brick with bluish-black bands and stone dressings. Its site does not allow it an unimpeded display of its frontages. The tall, slim, rather North-German steeple is more impressive from far away than nearby.

The church is approached from the south side by way of a forecourt. To the left and right are houses connected with the church. They have a mixture of Gothic windows with tall segment-headed – that is, early eighteenth-century – windows, a mixture which is extremely bold and formed an inspiration for the best Late Victorians. The porch stands asymmetrically in a corner crushed rudely against one side which in fact seems to cut off part of it – a remarkable solecism. The centre of the forecourt side of the church is a big broad buttress. The inside is even more perverse and wilful and no more beautiful. *The Ecclesiologist*, in spite of its faith in Butterfield, called it outright ugly. It has frescoes, marble lining, carving, mosaics, incised patterns and polished granite shafts. It is obtrusive and graceless but it is not timid nor dead. On the contrary, it is most violently eager to drum into you the praise of the Lord.

Ostentatious ugliness for the sake of originality or self-assertion was indeed one of the tendencies of churches in the 1850s–60s, though one only rarely permitted to appear. Men like Lamb, Basset Keeling, Peacock and a few others, without possessing the formidable earnestness of Butterfield, shared his thirst for novelty. The results are churches as original as anything Art Nouveau was to do about 1900 and singularly offensive in their clownish motifs, their ostentatious asymmetries and their wildly unprecedented details. The interior of Lamb's St Martin's Gospel Oak must be seen to be believed. Mr Goodhart-Rendel calls these people rogue-architects (an excellent term) and he puts into the same category Alexander Thomson of Glasgow – 'Greek Thomson'. I can't agree there. I think Thomson in his Greco-Egypto-Oriental is much nearer Butterfield's in his Gothic. They were of almost the same age. Thomson's St Vincent's Church was designed only a few years after Butterfield's All Saints and they possessed the same consistency and ruthlessness. As All Saints seems at first glance just another Neo-Gothic church, so St Vincent's just another Grecian one with hexastyle Ionic portico and pediment, though I admit that Grecian was the least common of styles in the 1850s to make use of and that the position of St Vincent against the steep slope of the hill gives it a Piranesian force straight away. But it is the tower more than anything with its crowded, absolutely unprece-dented detail and its domed top of indistinct bulbous shape which

displays Thomson's maniac originality, and the same is found in details
of his other churches such as the Caledonian Road and the Queens
Park East churches. (The latter unfortunately was severely damaged in
the war.) Thomson incidentally was just as important as an architect of
office buildings as of churches and his chief contribution there is the
frank use of iron for his façades. But I can't speak of commercial
architecture yet. We must first see what happened to secular building
in general in the 1840s–50s. What happened there is from our present
point of view – the point of view of the aesthetics of architecture – in
a way even more important than the development of churches. For
the churches, as I said before, as a rule called for suppression of the
natural Victorian appetites. In secular architecture there was less
inhibition, and so, during the same years in which churches turned
archaeological, public buildings turned Baroque. That is the chief
difference between, say, the British Museum and the National Gallery
designed essentially in the 1820s–30s and St George's Hall, Liverpool
or the Fitzwilliam and the Ashmolean Museums, designed in the
1840s. Look at St George's Hall by Elmes, who died at the age of
thirty-two, with its giant porticoes of rich Corinthian columns, look at
Basevi's Fitzwilliam Museum at Cambridge, also of course with giant
columns and with its jerkily projecting pavilions, massive and restless,
or Cockerell's Ashmolean Museum at Oxford, again with huge
columns, each of them carrying a fragment of a jutting-out entablature
with a statue on top, or look at Sir William Tite's Royal Exchange. In
all these buildings the trend towards a Baroque overdoing of Classical
forms is unmistakable. So is a certain boastfulness and a streak of
megalomania.

The High Victorian climax of this sort of thing is Cuthbert
Broderick's Leeds Town Hall with a tower whose cupola goes far
beyond the possibilities of the 1840s in thick decoration and bastard
motifs and whose outer walls are covered with giant columns and
pilasters so that no part of the building may go without full decoration.

In this connection let me quote this: 'A uniform stone front may
look handsome, but will always be wanting in life and spirit.' Now
this quotation is from Scott, not from one of the Baroque groups, so
you see how the principles which guided Broderick at Leeds with his

Italian columns and Scott at St Pancras with his polished granite shafts and gables in the Gothic style are the same.

That is really what I am after at the moment. It isn't enough to describe the development of the Victorian style in terms of the styles of the past whose imitation became fashionable. In fact most of these are already familiar to us. After the Elizabethan and the Italian Renaissance not much came in. The grand Palladian or Christopher Wrenian of the Leeds Town Hall remained an exception before Late Victorian days. Thomson's Greek is even more exceptional. So there is only one more source to be mentioned which we have not come across yet: the French Renaissance. This was enthusiastically revived under Napoleon III at Paris at the time when the Louvre was completed and the Town Hall rebuilt. In London the key buildings are the Paddington Hotel of 1850–52 – the earliest of the big London hotels, shortly to be followed by the gloomy Gothic Langham – and the two monstrous terraces of private houses by Clutton on the north side of Clapham Common. I call them monstrous; what I wish to indicate with this word is the general High Victorian tendency to overdo all effects.

High Victorian is a loud style. Motifs are big and mouldings thick and motifs are crowded all over the surface of a façade. The plain surface as a foil to the principal decorative effect is not wanted. There must be not too dominating a single effect. All-over covering of a front is more desirable. The motifs are generally of one source but the discrimination is not too nice. The style which was known as Renaissance was frankly regarded as a mixed style allowing for much variety – a variety which might range in one design from the Quattrocento to the Louis XV. Where copying is not done too conscientiously the Victorian character comes out at all seams in thick bulgy curves. The style can best be seen in the great competitions of those years, for the Government Offices in Whitehall (won by Scott), for the proposed façade of the National Gallery, and for the Law Courts (won by G.E. Street). But you get it also in plenty of office buildings in the City of London and other cities, in provincial town halls and so on. We call this style debased and that's indeed what it is. It's no use defending it on the grounds of aesthetic judgement. A few people try to argue that its values have only been obscured by the usual generational aversion of those immediately following and consequently violently reacting against it. But it isn't a case like the neo-Classical antipathy against the Rococo or Gauguin's against Impressionism and the sophistication of Paris. Aesthetically these High Victorian designs can't be saved, although their historical significance can be understood and their coarse vitality appreciated.

A fortnight ago I tried to show you how clients without training and without much time for, and patience with, art would be readier to listen to the more elementary distinction between various styles than to the subtler distinction of proportion or the handling of motifs within one style. Now we must add that the same clients, for the same reasons, also preferred plenty of motifs to a selected few and thick, robust motifs to delicate ones. Architects had to make themselves unmistakably audible to impress those clients, and architects knew that and besides were of course Victorian themselves. The general atmosphere of success and prosperity wrapped them up.

What that prosperity was like in architectural terms, very few of you will be able to visualise even in your wildest dreams. Let me help you by introducing to you Professor Robert Kerr who published a book in 1864 which is called *The Gentleman's House or How to Plan English Residences of the Better Sort*. That, he says, does not necessarily mean big houses. Even small houses can be designed so that 'persons who have been accustomed to the best society find themselves at ease' in them. To achieve that, certain minimum requirements must be fulfilled such as two entrances because it would be undesirable if – I'm quoting – '. . . visitors rub shoulders with the tradespeople'. Another necessity is an arrangement by which 'the lines of traffic of the servants and the family respectively [are] kept clear of each other'.

The snobbery of the High Victorian period and the total lack of any social bad conscience were something monumental. They run through all strata. In the big house, for instance, the house in which the Principal Bedroom suite is matched by a Principal Guests' suite 'for married guests of their own rank', Kerr says, there is among dozens of servants' rooms and offices the Steward's Room in which the steward transacts business, but also dinner is served to those – I'm quoting – 'who enjoy the right of dining' (with the steward, that is) '– the valet, the butler, the head cook, the housekeeper, the head lady's maid, and the head nurse, with strangers' servants of equal rank, and some others occasionally, by invitation, not including however any persons of the lower grade'.

The house Kerr is speaking of here is one that would have, apart from the two main bedroom suites of five rooms each, twenty bedrooms and ten dressing rooms. But he speaks of small country houses too, houses which cost only £1,250 to build and have dining room, drawing room, four bedrooms, one dressing room, nursery, one bathroom, one lavatory, kitchen, scullery, larder, pantry, store room, linen closet, knife-house, coal cellar, wine cellar, beer cellar and one servants' bedroom for two maids and a cook. As for the nurseries, incidentally, Kerr says, that 'the mother will require to have a certain facility of access to them'.

Such were the considerations of planning and such was the scale on which High Victorian architects counted. The same gargantuan ambitions appear everywhere in public buildings, town halls, law courts, university buildings and the like. There were in those bountiful days plenty of jobs going, public and private, to keep architects busy.

No wonder then that they totally overlooked what would really have been the most important and urgent problem for them to solve. Their negligence in this respect has left us with an appalling inheritance. These decades, you must not forget, were a phase of maximum growth in the town population of Britain. Take a few examples: Birmingham and Leeds between 1851 and 1881 nearly doubled their populations. And in the outer London suburbs the increases are even more startling: Islington 9,500 in 1851, 216,000 in 1881; Lewisham 18,000 in 1851, 67,000 in 1881.[1]

Now, the bulk of the architectural work that was necessary to cope with this immense growth of towns all over Britain was housing, factories, warehouses and office buildings. The housing was to be cheap and therefore not of much concern to an architect to whom his job was primarily the adornment of façades but in its visual context it posed questions of planning which might have been – and indeed became to some Late Victorians as you'll see next week – highly interesting. Planned working-class housing is a great rarity in High Victorian days; Saltaire near Leeds, the new town built by Sir Titus

Salt for the workers in his famous alpaca mill, is an exception. As a rule, whole boroughs and suburbs filled up with badly-equipped back-to-back houses wherever there was space – streets and streets, miles of them. Nobody planned them, nobody designed them. These are slums today but often less depressingly slummy than the working-class flats which nevertheless were indeed both designed and planned. They began as a charitable gesture in the 1840s shortly after the horrifying Chadwick report *On the Sanitary Conditions of the Labouring Classes* had come out – very much in the same way in which the even more gruesome report on the sanitary conditions of the old London churchyards had led to the creation of Kensal Green and Highgate and Norwood and so on. The earliest of the new model houses for the working classes still exist, some two-storey cottages of 1844 in Cubitt Street near Grays Inn Road. Then, however, it was recognised that flats would be a more useful proposition. Of the earliest ones, the block in Streatham Street near the British Museum survives, quite dignified in design at least towards the outside, and another block in Deal Street, Spitalfields, less acceptable in looks. At the 1851 Exhibition, Prince Albert showed a model house, two-storeyed, with an iron staircase in the middle open towards the front and four tiny flats with one front window each. The idea was, however, that this unit of four could be enlarged in width as well as height to form big blocks of flats. It looks quite pretty as it is with a bit of Jacobean trim – the architect was Henry Roberts who also designed the Streatham Street block and was altogether the leading man for working-class housing – but if you try to fancy it enlarged as intended, you'll get something exactly as grim as were indeed the first high blocks and estates of blocks. The very first were a venture of the Baroness Burdett Coutts, that rich and remarkable lady-friend of Dickens's. It is called Columbia Market and can still be seen at Bethnal Green. In an eminently High Victorian way, the Baroness built a market with a Gothic market hall as splendid-looking as if it were at Ypres, next to the meanest, grimiest blocks of flats. Dickens found the whole idea wonderful and it was soon taken up by two large organisations, the Peabody Trust, the bequest of an American millionaire, and Alderman Waterlow's Improved Industrial Dwellings Company. The Peabody Trust is a charity; the Waterlow company was meant to make handsome profits. The first Peabody estate dates from 1862–64, the first of the Improved Industrial Dwellings from 1863; the City of London built their own first in Farringdon Street in 1865. They are now a familiar sight of the poorer districts but also appear to one's surprise in Westminster and Chelsea. They are big and gaunt and ill-planned, often with open staircases, and they are separated by asphalted courtyards. It took a whole generation to humanise them – that is, it took the change of mind from the High Victorian mood of complacency to the Late Victorian mood of awakened conscience. But we'll talk of Bournville and the Jago next week.

Meanwhile we must see what the architects had to say about factories. The answer is again: very little. The British invention of the fireproof factory with iron columns, iron beans and vaulted hollow-brick ceilings goes back to the late eighteenth century. When Schinkel, the great Prussian architect of the early nineteenth century, visited England in 1826 he was deeply impressed by the mills of Manchester, seven and eight storeys high and absolutely bare in their brick frontages. He drew a grim-looking sketch of them and also of the iron construction inside. For at that time the ironwork was not yet shown outside. To reach a frank display of iron, we have to go forward to 1851 and the Crystal Palace, and that, to say it again, was not the design of an architect but of an amateur. In city offices and warehouses, much light was also needed and so at about the same time, early in the 1850s it seems, whole façades went up in Scotland, and presumably in London too, which were entirely of cast iron and glass. Greek Thomson, of all people, in one of his early designs appears one of the pioneers. The rule however remained in office buildings right into the twentieth century to hide the construction and decorate the façade in whatever style was selected, Gothic or Italianate or French. Factories as a rule were left bare, even in the High Victorian heyday. Only occasionally did manufacturers feel it a proud duty to embellish their premises *ad maiorem gloriam* of whatever product they turned out. Doulton's in Lambeth on the south bank of the Thames is perhaps the most famous example, fairly bristling with Gothic ornament. But on the whole the architect did not touch the factory more than the housing of the people and in this lies his great failure.

Business life was grim (he knew it as well as his client), factory life was grim, office life was grim. So he regarded it as his job to hang an attractive dress over a structure which socially neither attracted nor interested him. The town was grim too, that also he could not overlook. But the nineteenth century is a century of individualism and no one in England could think in bigger terms than the terms of individual houses. No one took in the town or neighbourhood. Go along Oxford Street or Princes Street in Edinburgh; it is a riot of disjointedly conceived buildings. No continuity was wanted, no spirit of co-operation or corporation. That again came only with the end of the Victorian era and was as much a matter of social as of aesthetic change. Both these changes are intimately connected with the varied and fanatical activities of one man, the greatest of the Victorians to concern us here, with William Morris.

1   Pevsner is quoting here from data he would be publishing the following year in his *Buildings of England* volume on London's suburbs (usually known as *London Except*: that is, London except the Cities of London and Westminster).

The Late Victorians and William Morris

VICTORIAN ARCHITECTURE (4)

Third Programme
WEDNESDAY 25 JULY 1951
Producer: Anna Kallin

In my experience, it seems to come hard to people to make themselves realise that *The Importance of Being Earnest* and *Arms and the Man* should be Victorian plays. In the arts it is the same. Whistler for instance with his light delicate colours, his light delicate touch, his wit, his mischievous playfulness of pattern does not seem to belong to the Victorian Age. Yet his style was complete and mature by the mid-1860s: that is, well before the middle of the Queen's reign. The same anachronism is felt by people in the case of William Morris, especially by those who rather read his lectures than look at his designs. Of course you might say that that happens to any pioneer. Posterity sees him more in conjunction with what he achieved than with what surrounded him. But we can't afford doing that here. Morris was born in 1834, his designs begin in 1861, his lectures in 1877. He died in 1896. So he is entirely Victorian and the fault lies in the universal notion that Late Victorian is not Victorian at all.

When you think of the Victorian style in architecture you think of a style which was complete by the 1860s, even if it went on in the work of most of the recognised leaders of the profession through the 1870s and later. But for the historian, William Morris must be the central figure of the Late Victorian style, even for the historian of architecture, although Morris was no architect himself. I say he was no architect but he had in fact received a six-months' training in the office of G.E. Street, the architect of the Law Courts. Morris had grown up in the country near London and the delight in nature, in trees, in fields, in flowers and in roughing it remained with him all through his life.

He went to Oxford to study divinity but gave it up to become an architect. This however he also gave up because office work was odious to him. As his friend, the architect Philip Webb, said later on, the reason was that one 'could not get into close contact with it; it had to be done at second hand'. This, you'll see, is very typical of Morris. He had been guided towards architecture not only by a general delight in art but also by a wish to find work connected with art which would at the same time be of immediate use to the community. For the time being, however, he exchanged architecture for painting and studied for a while under Rossetti. Then he got married and in trying to furnish rooms in London in 1859 and then a house built for him by Philip Webb in 1861, he discovered that furniture and furnishings as they could be bought were nothing but 'tons upon tons of unutterable rubbish', as he wrote on another occasion. So he and his friends began to design furniture. The first pieces were demonstratively plain and inordinately heavy, 'like incubi and succubi', said Rossetti, a table 'as firm and solid as a rock' and chairs such as Barbarossa might have sat in, but it was at least honest furniture.

When Morris had made this discovery of the best taste and the functional fortuitousness of furnishings, he reacted, as you saw, in a way different from that of most artists and architects of 1860. They withdrew from a world hideously changed by the advent of industry. Morris said, 'they wrapped themselves up in dreams of Greece and Italy'. He blamed them for that and decided in his own mind that it was his duty to remedy the atrocious state of design by designing himself, by making others design and also by seeking out why things had gone so bad in the mid-nineteenth-century world. It is typical of Morris that to recognise a wrong and to do something about it himself was one. He was of a tempestuous nature, given to fearful outbursts of temper, restless and of a furious activity. He couldn't sit still at table during meals. When he got into debate and arguing he got so wild that in one case, I was told, he knocked his head against the wall with such a force as to leave a deep dent in the plaster. In another case he bit his tooth into the rim of the table.

So, with this tremendous sense of getting urgent things done at once, in 1861 Morris started not an architect's office, not a painter's studio, but a firm of what he called Fine Art Workmen in Painting, Carving, Furniture, and the Metals. His chief collaborators were Philip Webb, the architect and one of the best architects of the Late Victorian generation, as you'll see later, Ford Madox Brown, who as a matter of fact had himself apparently tried to do something about furniture a little earlier than Morris, and Rossetti. They made tiles, wallpapers, furniture, fire-irons and so on, and glass. The designs in furniture were plain and honest and inspired by seventeenth-century rustic pieces; in wallpapers they were, thanks to Morris himself, strictly two-dimensional and yet at the same time full of life, fresh and precise with none of that 'slobbering and messing' which he disliked so much. No one in the nineteenth century can touch Morris as a designer. A sense of clean, unostentatious comfort goes through all his produc-tions. In his house, later on, meals were served on a plain unvarnished oak table with no tablecloth, only mats – quite a new thing then. He was a connoisseur of cookery too.

When his business expanded and he wanted to embark on new ventures, he went and learnt the art of dyeing, the art of the colourman himself and then the art of weaving. In four months he spent 516 hours at the loom – a five-hour day average for a six-day week. And mind you he wrote, as well, all the time, reams upon reams of poetry as you know and poetry which although of an easy flow is far from facile. It is prodigious.

Morris's thought appears most clearly in the lectures which he began to deliver in 1877, just at the time when the firm started on carpets and the celebrated chintzes. It is through these and the lectures mainly – that is, from 1877 onwards – that Morris became a power in English (and international) thought, in art – and, as you will see, in architecture too.

Why, he asked himself, had design gone to the dogs and why had London became 'mere masses of sordidness, filth and squalor' and why had art in the Middle Ages been so consistently satisfying? Morris's answer was this:

> Time was when ... imagination and fancy mingled with all things made by man; and in those days all handicraftsmen were artists. But the thought of man became more intricate, more difficult to express; and grew a heavier thing to deal with, and its labour was more divided amongst great men, lesser men, and little men ... As the arts sundered with the greater and the lesser, contempt on the one side, carelessness on the other arose ... The artist came out from the handicraftsmen, and left them without hope of elevation, while he himself was left without hope of intelligent industrious sympathy.

This thought he expressed often and in many ways and as they are all of the same penetration and warmth, let me quote you one or two more passages. In the Middle Ages, he says, 'not every day, you may be sure, was a day of slaughter and tumult, though the histories read almost as if it were so; but every day the hammer clinked on the anvil, and the chisel played about the oak beams'.

That was in mediaeval England, and now in Persia, where they have the most perfect rugs ever made, what was it they wanted to say in these stiffly stylised patterns? They did not copy nature but 'in their own way they meant to tell us how the flowers grew in the gardens of Damascus, or how the hunt was up in the plains of Rimmon or how the tulips shone among the grass in the mid-Persian valley'.

Penetration and warmth – aren't I right in saying that that is what makes such passages from Morris unforgettable? Yet, although no one ever denied his penetration, he did not strike his friends as warm, though no doubt frequently as hot and irate. Wilfrid Scawen Blunt has recognised that shrewdly in a note he wrote in his diary immediately after Morris's death. He writes:

> He is the most wonderful man I have ever known, unique in this that he had no thought for any thing or person, including himself, but only for the work he had in hand. He was not selfish in the sense of seeking his own advantage ... but he was too absorbed in his own thoughts to be either openly offensive or actually kind ... I have seen him tender to his daughter Jenny and his wife, but I doubt if he thought of them much, when he did not see them, and his life was not arranged in reference to them. To the rest of the world he seemed part-indifferent. The truth is that he would not give up an hour of his time to anyone, he held it to be too valuable ... Thus ... I doubt whether he had many friends; they got so little in return to continue their affection.

Yet warmth and affection is just what his work seems to radiate. It possesses indeed something of the directness of mediaeval work. The reason is without question that Morris had been the first to understand the secret of mediaeval craft. The objects now preserved in museums of the Middle Ages 'were common things in their own day', the work of 'common fellows', done 'with many a grin of pleasure'. That is what really matters most. No art, according to Morris, can come about without this grin of pleasure. All art is 'the expression of pleasure in labour'. It must, so Morris taught, be made 'by the people for the people, as a joy for the maker and the user'. It is utterly unhealthy, if – as was the case in the nineteenth century and to a large extent still is today – 'the practice of the arts is kept in the hands of a few highly cultivated men who can go often to beautiful places, whose education enables them ... to shut out of their view the everyday squalors that most of men live in'.

So Morris's remedy is – and you saw that he fervently applied it himself – that artists must again become craftsmen. In the prospectus of his firm in 1861 you read: 'The growth of Decorative Art in this country ... has now reached a point at which it seems desirable that Artists of reputation should devote their time to it.' That was his message to artists and you can see for yourself in which way it is applicable to architects.

Meanwhile – and that again has its architectural implications – what can the layman do about it? Here Morris's answer is particularly topical still. He says: Don't cut down trees where new estates are built, don't throw away old paper, don't put up glaring posters; do something against smoke. But of course Morris knew perfectly well that that was not enough. And when it comes to the future, his vision wavered. You know that he was a socialist, although he confessed that reading Karl Marx meant to him 'agonies of confusion of the brain'. Instead, he said: 'The study of history and the love and practice of art forced me into a hatred of the civilisation' of the century. So his socialism was never flattened by that easy faith in universal progress which makes one so often lose patience with the optimistic politician. On the contrary, in his most lucid passages, Morris appears as a grim pessimist and you'll see in a moment why it was bound to be like that. But here first is one of those passages: 'Maybe man may, after some terrible cataclysm, learn to strive towards a healthy animalism, may grow from a tolerable animal into a savage, from a savage into a barbarian, and so on; and some thousand years hence, he may be beginning once more those arts we have now lost.' That is logical and consistent. If art can only be the craftsman's handiwork, if all designing (as against making) is no art – Morris called the designer 'the squinter on paper' – if, as he said, 'the machine is an enemy' then – in exact accordance with the great vision of Spengler – this whole civilisation must first be swept away and barbarism return for the arts to flourish once more.

So far Morris's life and system seem completely consistent. But there is one flaw and Morris for short moments was aware of it. His own work and the work of his artist friends, though it was indeed a joy for the maker and the user, was by no means by the people for the people. By the people – perhaps, in so far as work at the Merton workshops had no doubt for the workmen the same happiness as all honest craft. But for the people? As it was all handmade and as – Morris knew that – 'all art costs time, trouble, and thought, and ... money is a counter to represent these things', the products of Morris & Co. were expensive. When he was once found by a friend working on the decoration in one of Philip Webb's best houses, he said that what he was busy on was 'serving the swinish luxury of the rich'.

This one flaw in the edifice of Morris's work had the consequence that it could inspire different types of people in different ways. That it was inspiring, and inspiring to many, is beyond question. But the artist-craftsman would see one thing in him, the social reformer another. And architects – to return to architecture after this long digression – might see either. His influence on architecture was indeed very great, for particular as well as general reasons. Among the particular reasons is that the young Late Victorian architect could read in his lectures things like this: 'Unless you are resolved to have good and rational architecture, it is ... useless your thinking about art at all' and he could also read that one should understand the past, but never imitate it, that our own age was content to 'have learnt the trick of masquerading in other men's cast-off clothes' and that no style can be 'replanted in a society totally different from that which gave birth to it'. So here was encouragement for the creation of a new style. And Morris's more general message of simplicity, honesty, no shams and – even more – of care for the common man gave a direction to the new style.

But that is a twentieth-century story. Meanwhile we have to see what actually corresponds to Morris in Late Victorian architecture. The answer is: not one man – there was no one architect as big as he – nor even one trend. But in the aggregate, architectural events are quite clearly a parallel to the Morris story. I need not in this connection mention more than three names: Philip Webb, as I told you, one of Morris's closest friends; Norman Shaw; and Edward Godwin. Morris was born in 1834, Webb in 1831, Shaw in 1832 and Godwin in 1833. So you see by the law of generations they belong very closely together. Webb never became really famous. His style has too much grit for that. His buildings are strong, personal and never wholly attractive. Best known are the Red House at Bexley Heath near London, built for Morris, and No. 1 Palace Green in Kensington. They are both of brick, frankly exposed, which in the 1860s was not at all usual for private houses. The material seemed too cheap; it ought to be hidden. Butterfield must have influenced Webb in that – and in other ways. But Webb was not as harsh as Butterfield; he was a more sensitive man, hard in a different more disciplined way. Butterfield, I told you last week, mixes occasionally the slim segment-headed windows of 1700 with his Gothic detail. Webb goes further than that and he succeeds in blending what in Butterfield looks rudely pushed together. The freedom with which Webb assembles elements from divers styles and not just from divers schools of Gothic as Scott & Co. had done was a first step away from the tenets of period imitation altogether.

Norman Shaw's role was similar but he had a far more fertile imagination if perhaps a more facile hand. His influence was enormous. In his best years, the 1870s–80s, he built almost exclusively private houses, the most important ones in London. They are delightful – things like Swan House, Chelsea; his own house in Ellerdale Road, Hampstead, the Royal Geographical Society in Kensington, or No. 11 Melbury Road in Kensington – brick, with free, informal, always unexpected dispositions of windows, little oriels and gables. The motifs are chiefly of the seventeenth and eighteenth centuries, English and Dutch. Again the contrast to High Victorian is startling. Elegance, wit, sensitivity but none of the former robust self-assertion – work of a more sceptical, more sophisticated generation.

That comes out specially clearly in the few little-noticed but important contributions of Godwin. He was a friend of Whistler and in 1878 built for him the White House in Tite Street, Chelsea. Later Whistler married his widow. Godwin as early as 1860 decorated his rooms at Bristol in light plain colours with a few Persian rugs on bare floors and a few Japanese prints on the walls. Godwin was among the pioneers of the Japanese fashion in England and he later on designed furniture also as spindly and fragile as things from the Far East. Godwin's colour schemes – and incidentally Whistler's in the exhibitions of his paintings in London, with walls in lemon-yellow and pale pink – make Webb's furniture and Morris's wallpapers and designs appear gloomy and in their solidity decidedly Victorian. Thus, you see, the various trends interlock.

Among Godwin's most successful London houses is a small number at Bedford Park, Turnham Green. Now Bedford Park, laid out in 1876 by Norman Shaw and provided by him with an excellent church and an excellent inn and bank and also a number of houses, was really the first of the garden suburbs. Here – as Morris recognised in the lecture I quoted before – trees had been left standing and houses were of comfortable smallish size, grouped nicely and picturesquely. The suburb came in for much mockery as being arty. It was called a village 'where men may lead a chaste, correct, Aesthetical existence' or a little hamlet 'where the steam horse is scorned', and Chesterton, after discovering its extravagant roofs and dwarfish trees exclaimed: 'How very oddly shaped the people must be who could fit in to them.'

Still, it was the first attempt at a planned estate for the none-too-wealthy to live in civilised, attractive surroundings and a very successful attempt at that, as anybody can check by going there on the District Line. The next step was taken by Cadbury's of Birmingham at Bournville and Lever Brothers at Port Sunlight, both begun in the 1890s. Here at last was the principle of civilised housing applied to the working class. Parallel with it, the London Country Council under its architect W.E. Riley made a start with estates of working-class flats no longer as grim as the High Victorian ones had been. It was still largely a matter of trimmings – not yet so much of improved plans or the introduction of grass and trees but the trimmings were now as genteel and indeed pretty as those of Kensington or Chelsea flats of the same date. The time lag between housing for one class and for another was being overcome. Go to Arnold Circus and the streets around, just off Shoreditch High Street – the blocks of flats replacing Arthur Morrison's Jago – and you'll see how much more humane that looks than the earlier Peabody estates.

The step after this was the independent garden city but although Ebenezer Howard's epoch-making book came out in 1898, Letchworth, the first of the garden cities, was only begun after the death of Queen Victoria.

But by the time the Queen died, the Shaws and Webbs were nearly seventy. What about the younger architects, the men who had started in the 1880s and were successful in the 1890s? Now, if one tries to survey their work, it has to be done under a different system and that in itself is a remarkable fact. In High Victorian days the leading architects such as Scott were all-round men and if, with others, a division is necessary according to the type of work they did, it would be the division between the ecclesiastical and the secular specialists. Butterfield would be all churches, Waterhouse of the Prudential for instance nearly all secular. Now the division is different. By and large those who followed Morris's ideals concentrated on private houses while others, superficially more successful and more likely to win knighthoods, went in for the large public buildings and large commercial jobs. It is in other words the division which was made in a fighting book by Norman Shaw and his friends and pupils in 1892. The book was called *Architecture – a Profession or an Art*. The artist-architects, inspired by the Morris ideal of the artist-craftsman or the mediaeval master-builder, stood on one side, the architect-professional men on the other, often more businesslike but often also a little less uncompromising in their attitude to clients. I need hardly add to this that the whole conception of architecture as a profession is a Victorian conception and a concomitant of nineteenth-century liberalism. The Royal Institute of British Architects was founded in 1834 and the regulation that only those who had passed an R.I.B.A. examination could become Associates of the Institute dates from 1882.

Norman Shaw was a leader of the revolt against professionalism yet he himself was still an all-rounder and it is in fact his own late style, the style which culminated in the Piccadilly Hotel, which started what one might call the official style of the latest Late Victorian and the Edwardian decade following it. It is a style different from the High Victorian Monumental. Nothing is left of the beefy honest-to-goodness High Victorian stodginess. The new style was Palladian, Christopher Wrenian, imperial in its ambitions, tasteful in its sources and means and magniloquent in a civilised way. It is the style represented, among men born in the 1840s, by Brydon who built the new Government Offices in Whitehall and the Municipal Buildings at Bath, by Sir John Belcher who built the incredible Ashton Monument at Lancaster, the Colchester Town Hall and Electra House in the City, and by Sir Aston Webb, the architect of the new fronts of the Victoria and Albert Museum and of Buckingham Palace. They were followed by architects born in the 1850s–60s, Mountford of the Old Bailey and so on to Lutyens and Sir Herbert Baker.

The sense of adventure and fantasy which had permeated Shaw's earlier private work appeared in only a few of the younger architects who went in for larger buildings. Oxford is lucky in having employed the two best of these, T.G. Jackson and Basil Champneys, rather than the duller and less inventive official people. Jackson's and Champneys's contributions to Oxford are an asset, Waterhouse's to Cambridge a very embarrassing liability.

But the most delightful of these fanciful Late Victorians was a church designer full of enthusiasm for the Arts and Crafts: John Dando Sedding whose Holy Trinity, Sloane Street, with all its colourful and playful furnishings is the most enjoyable church of the 1890s in the whole country.

The antagonism between official Late Victorian and intimate Late Victorian is not confined to architecture. It is the contrast between the art of the Chantrey Bequest and the art of Whistler and the New English Art Club. And it is as complete in painting as in architecture. Look at the leaders of the intimate school, the domestic revival, look at Charles Voysey, at Mackmurdo, at Baillie Scott, at E.S. Prior, at Townsend and at Charles Rennie Mackintosh. They seem to have nothing at all in common with their representational contemporaries of the Herbert Baker type. Voysey was the most influential of them, Mackintosh without any doubt the only real genius. Voysey with his plain roughcast walls, his bands of low horizontal windows, his light, fresh, dainty, sentimental but heartfelt detail, initiates the twentieth century more than he ends the nineteenth. Prior's and Townsend's and Mackintosh's details are Art Nouveau in the European sense – that is, again, a beginning rather than an end, and Mackintosh's exquisite thin uprights and horizontals and tense curves and his ingenious interpenetration of space from room to room are heralds of the style of today.

But oddly enough when 1900 or 1905 was reached, when that style of today in all its structural and formal peculiarities came true in the hands of architects the same age as Mackintosh, not one of them was British. They are Behrens in Germany, and Loos and Hoffmann in Austria, and Perret and Garnier in France, and Frank Lloyd Wright in America and then soon a number of others. Britain shunned the revolution. It led to its very verge and then gave up. The Edwardian decade and the first two decades of the Windsor dynasty were a period of comfortable, utterly uneventful Neo-Georgian housing for the tasteful, of rubbishy spec-built Neo-Tudor housing for the others and of a vast and hollow Imperial-Palladian for official and commercial buildings. It is not a gratifying picture which we see as we look at these years after the death of the Queen and it took two wars and a catharsis of supreme danger and the loss of half an Empire and of much material prosperity for Britain to recover a position in art and architecture as it is now witnessed by the sculpture of Henry Moore, the interior architecture of the Festival Hall, the plans of the new towns and the layout and buildings of the South Bank Exhibition.

Splendeurs et misères

Third Programme
FRIDAY 30 NOVEMBER 1951
Producer: Anna Kallin

In the centre of one of the rooms of the Palais des Beaux Arts in Brussels stands under glass what is left of Claus Sluter's *Christ* from the Charterhouse of Champmol near Dijon. It is without any doubt the most powerful piece of sculpture in the Burgundian Exhibition,[1] grave and quiet, without any of the grimacings of earlier figures of Christ crucified. A face of deep suffering, eyes closed, mouth tight, but a face of infinite majesty. This *Christ* once hung from a cross of stone on a big base against which stand six figures of prophets, Moses in huge, bulging and cascading draperies being the most famous of them. After him the whole base, alone surviving complete of the monument, is known as the *Moses Fountain*. The prophets are individually character-ised with a variety of age, attitude and type, unprecedented in the North or in Italy. The date of the monument is 1395–1406. If you want something to compare it with, think of Donatello. But he is twenty or thirty years later. In sheer sculptural force, Sluter is Donatello's equal but he worked in an atmosphere very different from that of Cosimo Medici's Florence. For he was in the service of the Duke of Burgundy at Dijon.

The splendour of the Burgundian court is something hard for us to visualise, not only because we are not used to seeing much gold and much jewellery these days but also because our tastes have lost the freshness, the naivety or should I say the childishness of that time. Sluter's *Moses Fountain* was painted originally. In fact Jean Malouel, the court painter, received as much for it as Sluter himself. The prophets had red and blue mantles with gold stars and suns, the painstakingly carved leather belts were painted brown and gold, the hems of the mantles have carved embroidery and that also was painted, and one of the figures had spectacles of brass gilt. Do you find that silly and a little vulgar? Well, listen to this. In 1454 a grand entertainment of the Burgundian court was held at Lille. There you could see the Eglise, an allegorical female, in a tower on an elephant led by a Turkish giant and you could listen to an orchestra of twenty-eight, playing inside a pie. In 1468 on another court occasion a tower forty-six feet high appeared with wild boars playing trumpets, wolves playing the flute and four donkeys as soloist singers.

Deplorably bad taste, we would say. Yet, perhaps we have grown too squeamish in distinguishing between the realms of painting, sculpture and what I suppose we should call the mobile. It is known that Jan van Eyck painted pieces of sculpture. Might there not be a sense lost to us by which one could appreciate the carving of a Sluter and at the same time, applied to it, the painting of a Malouel or van Eyck? It has been suggested, and I for one believe it, that the average listener of music in the sixteenth and seventeenth centuries had a better ear for polyphony than we have after the century of Beethoven and Wagner. Had they in the fourteenth and fifteenth century a better eye to see sculptural and pictorial values simultaneously?

However that may be, the Burgundian Exhibition brings home strongly that strange contrast between a world of gross splendour and another of tenderness and an intimacy just a little narrow and confined. There are on the one hand the huge tapestries, which decorated the palaces of the great and on the other hand the altarpieces – say, of Memling. The tapestries are all crowded and coarse in design, the paintings all meticulously carried out with tiny dots of colour like pearls and a smooth enamel-like surface and, though brimful of incident, never crowded and never restless. Their placidity is indeed one of their most remarkable features for it pervades these paintings regardless of what they represent.

At the exhibition you can see, for instance, Dirk Bouts's *Martyrdom of St Erasmus*. His bowels, as you probably know, were torn out of him, a specially ghastly form of execution. Bouts shows it done with a technique of gruesome neatness. A small incision had been made into the saint's belly and he has been placed beneath a capstan with two handles and a horizontal bar. The bowels come out of the body as a kind of white filament – no blood at all is visible – and are wound up on the bar of the capstan very much as if it were an illustration of some process of mechanical spinning. Behind is a group of figures standing as still in the landscape as if nothing were happening near them, and on the wings of the altar – in the same landscape – are two saints, also completely at rest and at ease.

How should one explain such callousness? Certainly not by saying that such tortures were so alien to the painter that he could not give them more probability. On the contrary, don't forget that public executions, public whippings, all kinds of publicly exposed cruelty, were everyday events. You must think of what some of you have seen in the war and read of the concentration camp to realise fully what the artist of the Burgundian Century – for instance when he painted a *Crucifixion* – could do from memories of sufferings seen and heard. That of course makes Bouts's *Martyrdom of St Erasmus* all the more puzzling.

I suggest the answer may be this. It is true that the painters of the fifteenth century were interested in the things around them much more keenly than artists had ever been before. It is true that they regarded it as the most fascinating part of their job to represent as accurately as could possibly be done every item of clothing and furnishing, every wrinkle in a face, every hair of a beard. But this patient observation and patient copying called for calm, calm in the painter and calm in the world around him. If the world wasn't calm – and it certainly wasn't – it had to be given that calm by the artist. The close intimacy of the craftsman's workshop, where to achieve the high-precision results of this kind of painting no outer disturbance can be permitted to interfere, becomes substituted for the world of gruesome events and of jubilant state occasions.

Still, I admit, the painter could not have created this world of stillness out of nothing. But there existed in fact in the spiritual life of the fifteenth century in the Netherlands a tendency towards that quiet. It is the tendency which had led to the establishment of the lay communities of the Brothers of Common Life in Holland late in the fourteenth century and to Thomas à Kempis's *Imitation of Christ*. 'Eschew thou noise and the press of men,' he preaches, and: 'How may he long abide in peace that seeketh occasions outward and seldom gathereth himself within himself.' It is this spirit of the piety of the narrow towns and the craftsmen that we see in the works of the Eycks and of Memling.

But the remarkable thing remains that those for whom so much of that art was made should have been satisfied with so one-sided a view of their world. The answer here is perhaps that the patrons also, say the Dukes of Burgundy themselves, did not want to see in art the violence and the noise of their lives. They were connoisseurs – that is, to say, they appreciated art as art, art as something artificial, not in terms of values as the brothers Goncourt, nor in terms of significant form, as Mr Clive Bell, but in terms of the most accomplished workmanship.

It is one of the most welcome eye-openers of the Burgundian Exhibition to see at least some of the most precious goldsmiths' works of the period. There are chiefly two of which I want to tell you. One is the triptych of *Christ held by an Angel*, with the Virgin and St John, *Angels holding the Instruments of the Passion, St Catherine and St John the Baptist* and the *Coronation of the Virgin* on top. This is of gold and enamel, partly opaque and partly translucent, and it is less than five inches by five inches in size. And you can also see and be duly amazed by the goldsmith Gérard Loyet's gold and enamel *Reliquary of Charles the Bold* showing the pink-faced Duke kneeling and holding a relic of St Lambert and behind him St George doffing his helmet with a gesture of awkward grace. Now this reliquary was given by the Duke in 1471 to the Cathedral of Liège in expiation of the razing of Liège. The rebellious town which, for the sake of its freedom – a freedom of course of the wealthy and powerful only – had resisted the efforts of the Duke to force it into the orbit of his influence, was taken at last in 1468. The infuriated Duke gave orders at once for it to be sacked. So 'this unfortunate town' (I am quoting from Theodore Bouille's *Histoire de la ville et pays de Liège*)

> experienced all the cruelties which soldiers are used to perpetrate in captured places. They were to the number of forty thousand, burning with desire to enrich themselves and knowing that their master had vowed the destruction of this great and opulent city. So like a raging torrent they forced their way into churches and houses, searched from the roof to the deepest cellars, not sparing even the ashes of the dead, and sacrificing men and women to their greed and their cruel brutality without distinction. Girls were raped and then massacred. Older men were forced by a show of unheard-of inhumanity to be the executioners of their children, to strangle them, to trample them to death under their feet or to smash them on pavements or against the walls of churches.

And then, when all this had gone on for four days, then came the time for contrition, and the precious and pretty little golden reliquary was made and presented. It all seems maddening to us but there it is and without this unresolved clash of violent and completely genuine feelings the century cannot be understood. But to return to art, the fact remains that all the violence, even that of piety, stays outside its bounds – with very few exceptions, such as that grandiose early fifteenth-century French Book of Hours known as the *Grandes Heures de Rohan*, and a few of the last works of that great melancholic, Hugo van der Goes, whose *Death of the Virgin*, on show now at Brussels, is one of the most disquieting works of the century. But otherwise the mood of art, to repeat it once more, is placid, not only in the altar-pieces for town churches, but even in the secular stories in the precious picture-books made for the courts. The tales, legendary or topical, told in the illuminated manuscripts certainly called for the representation of action and movement. But even they seem to us nearly always curiously arrested, as if they were no more than highly mannered *tableaux vivants*.

We get much too much of our ideas of the art of the fifteenth century in the North from our picture galleries. Illuminated manuscripts are seen by few and consequently often forgotten in one's assessment of the century and its art. The exhibition has a gorgeous wealth of manuscripts; the secular books are especially interesting.

They show a remarkably wide range of titles. Surviving oil paintings would never make one expect these stories of Aeneas and Charlemagne, these stories from Cicero and Froissart, Valerius Maximus and *The Decameron*. And in all these manuscripts, around the texts in their crabbed, spiky Gothic hands and around the minutely painted pictures of Lucretia stabbing herself or of '*Messire Charles de Blois, comment il fut pris des Anglois*', there are borders of leaf trails with humming birds and lightly scattered flowers.

This patient art of illumination is the source of the brothers van Eyck and the *Ghent Altar* which, after careful and revealing restoration, could be seen for a few weeks at the exhibition and is now back at the church of St Bavon at Ghent. It had rightly been made the centre of the exhibition for Ghent and Bruges, where Eyck lived, and Seeland and the Hainaut and even Amiens all belonged to the Burgundian Dukes in the fifteenth century.

The *Ghent Altar* shows all the various points I have so far made: a craftsmanship more precise than any painter's before, a faith to nature undaunted by conventions even to the hair on the arms and legs of Adam and the pubic hair of Eve, a perfect stillness which can be that of the solemn processions arriving from all sides to worship the lamb, or that of the cool, secluded chamber where the angel greets Mary. He comes from the left and addresses her in golden letters emanating from his slightly opened mouth and written across the room, and her '*Ecce Ancilla Domini*' is written in the same way from her towards him and therefore, most oddly, in mirror image, the wrong way round, to show demonstratively that it is speech from her to him, from right to left. Equally mediaeval is the conception of the prophets and sibyls above the *Annunciation* with their scrolls giving chapter and verse of their prophecies. This unison of untroubled faith in the traditions and conventions of the Christian past with that very search for a scientific truth in nature which was so soon to break up the old Catholic world is indeed the secret of the art of the *Ghent Altar* and the religious painting of the Burgundian century altogether. The *Ghent Altar* is the work of an artist who belonged to Bruges and its close-knit city life yet worked for courts and was appreciated by them, even several times sent by the Duke of Burgundy on secret diplomatic missions – '*certains voyages lointains*', say the documents, '*pour aucunes matières secrètes.*'

In the Louvre in Paris is Eyck's *Virgin with the Chancellor Nicolas Rolin* – to my taste the most lastingly moving picture in that whole collection. On the right the Virgin with one of those very young faces with an entirely detached expression, as only Jan van Eyck could paint them. A little angel who could be her brother carries along a huge, monstrously bejewelled crown to place it on her head. The way the crown is painted, or for that matter the border of the Virgin's mantle or the orb in the hand of the serious and rather ugly little boy in her lap, defeat description. Facing the Virgin on the left kneels the Chancellor, the mightiest man of Burgundy. '*Soloit tout gouverner tout seul,*' writes Chastellain, '*fust de guerre, fust de paix, fust en fait de finances.*' One trusts the truth of this remark as one looks at these hard, sceptical features and these searching eyes.

You can see the same features painted more broadly by Roger van der Weyden in the polyptych which Rolin commissioned for the altar of the hospital which he had founded in 1443 in his town of Beaune in Burgundy. It represents the *Last Judgement* and the chapel where it hung was part of the large long room where lay the sick. They were the sick poor; for on the first floor in one wing there were single rooms for paying patients. The poor however were treated also to some splendour and there could not be anything more characteristic of the anatomies of the fifteenth century than the heavy, soft Burgundy-red tapestries which were woven to serve as bedcovers for the beds of the sick. One of them is at the Brussels Exhibition. They are adorned with the initials of Rolin and his wife, interlaced, with his device, his armorial birds, the turtle-dove and plenty of stars, all the motifs repeated endless times. These tapestries, the huge room with its warm, old timber-work in semi-darkness, the cold features of the Chancellor and Roger's calm figures of Christ and his Saints presiding over the doom of all those little, frightened, naked people below – the Hospital at Beaune is, I assure you, the ideal shrine to speculate on the *splendeurs et misères* of the Burgundian century, once the exhibition at Brussels will be over.

1   This talk was subtitled 'Some Thoughts on the Burgundian Exhibition in Brussels', referring to one of a number of exhibitions of European art sponsored by the Council of Europe during the 1950s.

Lumley Castle, County Durham

ENGLISHMEN'S CASTLES (I)

Home Service
SUNDAY 15 JUNE 1952
Producer: R.E. Keen

In Camden's *Britannia* you can read:

> From thence the river Were passeth by Lumley Castle standing within a
> park, the ancient seat of the Lumeleies who descended from Liulph, a
> man in this tract of right great nobility in the time of King Edward the
> Confessor ... who married Aldgitha, the daughter of Aldred, Earle of
> Northumberland. Of these Lumeleies Marmaduke assumed unto him his
> mother's coat of armes (in whose right he was seized of a goodly
> inheritance of the Thwongs) ... But Ralph sonne to the said Marmaduke
> was the first Baron Lumley, created by King Richard the Second ...
> which honour John the Ninth from him enjoyed in our daies, a man most
> honourable for all the ornament of true nobility.

'In our days,' says Camden: that means at the time of Queen
Elizabeth. And Ralph Lumley, you heard just now, was made a baron
in the time of Richard II. That gives us our *dramatis personae* and our
two principal dates. In 1389 and again in 1392, Sir Ralph Lumley
obtained what's called a licence to crenellate – that is, permission from
the Bishop of Durham and then from the King to build a fortified
house, and about 1580 or so John Lord Lumley made a number of
remarkable alterations.

A fortified house – that is indeed what you see when you approach
Lumley Castle. It rises sand-coloured, broad-towered and foursquare
above the plentiful old trees of what Camden calls the park. Those
thick woods are now what you may connect in your minds with
County Durham but they are characteristic of the valley of the river
Wear and even more of the narrow, steeply cut-in valley of the
smaller becks – what they call locally 'denes'.

So there is the castle, no longer a stockade on a mound as no doubt
Liulph's had been some time before the Norman Conquest, nor any

longer a tall keep with a few buildings scattered around, as the Normans built their castles, but a solid, massive house with ranges of rooms on two floors on the four sides of a quadrangular courtyard. Mind you, it is a fortress as well, and up in that border country it had to be. But even so, there is in the symmetry of the layout a new sense of order and comeliness which had grown in England in the course of the fourteenth century. Harlech, a castle of Edward I, built late in the thirteenth century, had been the first in England designed on a regular symmetrical plan. (Bodiam in Sussex which is contemporary with Lumley is perhaps the example best-known to Southerners of the symmetrical courtyard castle.)

The most impressive thing about Lumley is its mighty angle projections. They are too broad to be called towers although they are heavily buttressed like towers, and raised like towers, and crowned by little turrets yet a little higher. To gain access to the castle you had to pass through a gatehouse, protected by a portcullis. Only after negotiating that would you stand in the courtyard facing the Great Hall, a substantial courtyard measuring about seventy-five foot square. It is now turfed and has some lovely laburnum trees which with their fine leaves and yellow blossom look deliciously dainty against the background of solid masonry on all sides. In the Middle Ages the courtyard was no doubt cobbled or paved otherwise. Nature was not allowed in such a place of common concourse.

The entrance to the Great Hall is right opposite the gatehouse and like the gatehouse accentuated by two turrets, left and right of the rather low doorway. It is low because it leads only into a vaulted undercroft whereas the hall itself lies on the upper floor. The hall, as you know, was the chief apartment in all mediaeval castles and manor houses. It was larger than any other room, had larger windows and contained at one end the high table for the lord and his family and his guests and at the other doorways to the buttery and pantry and the passage to the kitchen. At Lumley the original kitchen is still there, a very large room that goes up through two floors and has three huge fireplaces – a rare survival from so early a date. And a rare survival the hall is as well, though it has been much altered inside. That it is elevated to the first floor – like New College at Oxford and the later

Hampton Court – we don't notice much now because, seen from the outside of the castle, the undercroft becomes a basement and the first floor no more than a raised ground floor, accessible by a Georgian staircase. On that side the windows also are now Georgian and a Georgian doorway has been put in. In Sir Ralph's time the castle had to be cut off entirely from the outer world.

These Georgian alterations are probably due to the greatest of English eighteenth-century architects, Sir John Vanbrugh. We have no documents to prove that but one room altered about 1720 or 1725 and known as the Library bears the hallmark of his inimitable style. Vanbrugh was the great defender of the robust, the masculine, the cyclopic in an age of gentility and rationalism. He loved the Middle Ages and he loved the rough north. In one of his letters, as lively as most of his letters are, he contrasts it with the 'tame sneaking south of England'. Now that letter was written in August 1721 *à propos* of his work in designing and building Seaton Delaval in Northumberland, his most tremendous building, and it is here also that he refers to Lumley Castle as 'a Noble thing'. He would have liked the virile strength of these mediaeval walls and crenellations for he was the first architect to feel a real delight in the Middle Ages and to try and give, I'm quoting from another letter, 'Something of a Castle Air' to houses he designed and to the smaller buildings in their grounds. Now at Lumley, if the attribution of the Library to him is correct, he certainly tried to emulate the Middle Ages even if he didn't imitate them. For the only enrichment of this plain apartment is two rows of square pillars built up of crazily oversized blocks laid in alternating directions and with their angles bevelled or chamfered or canted so as to give the effect of some gargantuan diamond-cutting. It looks oddly primeval and it is as far as I know unique in England.

But now, after this digression, it is time for us to turn to our second principal character, after Sir Ralph Lumley of the late fourteenth century, to John Lord Lumley of the late sixteenth. Lord Lumley was a remarkable man, not so much because of the intrigues over Mary Queen of Scots and the Roman faith in which he was involved as because of a curious romantic penchant he had for the age of chivalry. I said a few minutes ago that Vanbrugh was the first architect to delight in the Middle Ages. That may be so; but my explorations of Elizabethan buildings and documents in the last few years have made it increasingly certain to me that in those years there already existed a kind of mediaevalism. You know it from Elizabethan tournaments and the Queen's Progresses with their pageants. At Kenilworth in 1575 they had a pageant of 'The Lady of the Lake' from the Arthurian story with an *hombre selvagio*, a savage man appearing. At Whitsun in 1581 they played 'Beleaguering the Castle of Perfect Beauty' and among the actors was for instance Philip Sidney, the poet. The Earl of Cumberland, Queen's Challenger from 1587, called himself 'the Knight of Pendragon Castle' and Spenser in the introduction to the *Shepherd's Calendar* is proud of using, as he says, 'ancient solemn words ... long time out of use'. He calls them 'a great ornament', and Camden after all, with whose name I began my talk today, made his journey through England in 1582 and wrote his *Britannia* in exactly the same spirit of tracing the antiquities and the ornaments of old England.

Now Lord Lumley must in just that mood have considered it extremely pleasurable to reminisce about his ancestors and make up a past to fill in the gaps where it did not quite survive. To see proofs of that I must invite you for a few minutes to leave Lumley and walk a mile or two across the river into the little town of Chester-le-Street. Here in the church, filling the left-hand aisle, lie the Lumleys, from Liulph onwards. To fit all the effigies in they have to be content with rather a narrow space. They lie two deep in a long row (like a Tube shelter) and so tight is the space that some had to have their feet cut off. This procrustean discipline was imposed on them by Lord Lumley who placed them there and, in 1557, made an indenture for the future use of this aisle in that way and set some money aside against the 'spoyling and defacing' of the monuments.

Now all this would be well and good and proper if the monuments were the real article. But they are not. Only three of the fourteen are mediaeval and even they do not necessarily belong to Chester-le-Street; for Camden as early as 1586 tells us that Lord Lumley had 'either gotten (them) together out of monasteries, that were subverted, or caused to be made anew'. So those effigies are partly mediaeval –

some for instance are said to have been taken out of the former cemetery along the side of Durham cathedral – and partly Elizabethan in imitation of the Middle Ages. Only that way could Lord Lumley display his whole unbroken lineage, starting with Liulph, going on to Uchtred, to Sir Marmaduke, to Ralph the first Baron and so on to Lord Lumley's father who died in the thirty-sixth year of King Henry VIII.

It is a curious mentality behind this show of faked ancestors, isn't it? It must have been as much a matter of playing at Middle Ages as of genealogical pride. That Lord Lumley had a vast amount of genealogical pride is certain from his chief contribution to Lumley Castle, to which we can now return. The castle itself was there, as hoary and baronial-looking as he could desire. He altered windows to let more light in, put a new fireplace into the hall and a delicious lavabo or hand-wash basin of white marble and touch, that is black marble, and adorned by a pelican, that bird of symbolic meaning which the sculptors made so much more graceful than he really is when you look at him in the zoo. But more than that, he covered the whole sheer space of the outer wall above the entrance to the hall and between the turrets with a display of eighteen shields of arms again to show the venerable age and connections of his family. And a Latin inscription comments 'In the monuments of the distant past, the curious eye is a bad judge' – and so Lord Lumley helped it with his instructive bits of family history. And as our final confirmation we have an inventory of Lord Lumley's belongings at Lumley Castle as well as his London and Surrey houses. It was published by Miss Milner in 1904 and contains again portraits of sixteen ancestors apart from portraits of other curious people whom you may not expect to find up there in the North: Julius II, for instance, the pope for whom Raphael and Michelangelo worked, Dante and Petrarch, Boccaccio and Ariosto, Chaucer and St Ignatius Loyola the founder of the Jesuits, apart from all the furnishings: the ninety-five 'Turkey' carpets, the eighty upholstered stools, the ninety-five livery beds, the five virginals, thirteen violins and twelve violas, the twenty-five tables of walnut and marquetry and so on. In the Hall of Lumley Castle, we hear in another inventory a few years later, there were two long tables, a deer's head that came out of Ireland, nineteen odd emperors' heads of Rome, and a written table called the 'Theatre of the World', whatever that may have been. However no inventory can make the atmosphere of the past come to life again, especially if an atmosphere of the present has superseded it. And at Lumley that atmosphere is full of vitality for the castle is now a residential hostel of the University of Durham and plenty of young and eager people are always about. At Bolsover next week, no flesh and blood of today will disturb our rummagings among the past. For Bolsover is a ruin.

Bolsover Castle, Derbyshire

ENGLISHMEN'S CASTLES (2)

Home Service
SUNDAY 22 JUNE 1952
Producer: R.E. Keen

You had better first of all get the Cavendishes right. The story starts for us with Bess of Hardwick, that able grasping old woman who built Hardwick Hall, bare, big and forbidding. She built it for herself when she was seventy-two and found herself a widow for the fourth time. She was the daughter of a well-to-do squire in Derbyshire and married a rich squire when she was fourteen. He died when she was fifteen and left his estates to her. So when she had reached the age of thirty-one, she married again, Sir William Cavendish who was thirteen years older than she. She soon made him give up his estates in the south-west and buy new ones in her part of the country: Chatsworth, for instance, where they began to build a remarkably vast mansion in 1553. She bore him about a child a year and six of them grew up, three sons and three daughters. Then he died and left her his estates, and she married Sir William St Loe who after a while also died and also left her what he possessed. She was remarkably rich then and cannot have been lacking in attraction either – intellectual no doubt rather than physical. For in 1567, when she was fifty, she landed her great haul and married George Talbot, sixth Earl of Shrewsbury. And to make that connection trebly sure she arranged for one of her Cavendish sons to marry one of his daughters and one of her Cavendish daughters one of his sons. Having settled all this, she soon began to quarrel violently with her husband. She accused him, to the Queen for instance, of adultery with Mary Queen of Scots. But that was only a sideline. On the whole she was busy administering shrewdly and immensely competently her large estates, including building jobs at the big Shrewsbury mansions of Worksop in the Dukeries and of Bolsover.

Bolsover was a Shrewsbury property. It was, when Leland saw it about 1540 or so, 'a great building of an old castle'. In 1553 it came into the hands of the Talbots. After the Earl's death and Bess's own death in 1608, Chatsworth and Hardwick went to Bess's eldest son William Cavendish, Bolsover to the Talbots. Chatsworth is still Cavendish property – that is, the property of the Dukes of Devonshire, for William, son of Sir William, was made Earl of Devonshire and his great grandson in 1694 Duke of Devonshire. But Bolsover was let to Bess's second son, Charles Cavendish, in 1608 and bought by him in 1613. He died in 1617 and his son then became Earl of Newcastle and later Duke of Newcastle – so Bess in her grave might well be satisfied: her descendants in a few generations had collected two dukedoms. Bolsover then by several marriages went to the Bentincks, later Cavendish-Bentincks, and they, the Dukes of Portland, have only recently handed it on to the Ministry of Works. You can't blame them for it is nearly all in ruins.

You usually approach Bolsover from the town but you should try and get your first sight from the south-east, from that desperate Vale of Scarsdale which is now all open-cast mining and smoke and dust. It is as dreary a piece of scenery as you may find anywhere in Derbyshire and there, above it, rises along the ridge of a steep cliff nearly 600 feet up and very prominent indeed, the silhouette of Bolsover Castle, a castle silhouette indeed, with the spreading stone buildings on the right and the sharp accent of the keep on the left. It is the kind of view one is more used to from France than from England. How many hill castles do you really remember in England? Corfe Castle in Dorset. Ludlow perhaps. What else? And at Bolsover – that brings me to where this talk today hitches on to last week's – Bolsover the castle is not a real castle at all. What Leland saw, you see no longer. Sir Charles Cavendish found the keep in ruins and built it afresh on the old foundations. So here is another man, like Lord Lumley up in County Durham, who in the time of Shakespeare thought it would be fun to re-evoke the baronial age. The Cavendishes were an old family but though they could trace their ancestry back into the fourteenth century, they had not been grand enough for castle building. Is that perhaps what tempted Sir Charles? Did he want to build around himself, at least for special occasions, a chivalric past? We can't say.

Anyway, his keep has battlements and angle towers and might deceive anybody, if it were not for a few features: first of all the forecourt towards the edge of the escarpment. This has an embattled wall all right, but also four little embattled buildings of which two are gatehouses and two summer houses. They are quite obviously no more then *plaisances* and the wall – which is anyway within the old castle walls proper – can hardly have guarded more than a little neatly laid-out garden. Well, you pass the two gatehouses, cross the forecourt and then a wide open staircase leads you up to the doorway. Above it, a figure of Atlas carries a balcony framed by two rather peculiar columns which carry a pediment. All that is Classical stuff and contradicts the Norman character of the building. It is, however, no doubt a compliment to the superior comforts of Sir Charles's own age. Inside, on the ground floor, he carries on his little masquerade. The dining room and another room are divided by columns and vaulted – rib-vaulted in fact – again, as if they were in some monastery of Thomas à Becket's time. But the fireplaces are up-to-date, up-to-date in their slopingly projecting overmantels (a French rather than an English treatment) and in their decoration in white and black marble and alabaster with columns and that peculiar kind of ornament known as strapwork which always gives away the Elizabethan and Jacobean Age. It is a very original kind of ornament, not a bit like anything Roman or Renaissance, entirely abstract and consisting of broad bands or straps rolled up at the ends or intertwined – sometimes like fretwork, sometimes like leatherwork or strips of parchment. You must have seen it many times in church monuments. The walls of the rooms in the keep are panelled and two have paintings, one of the Olympian gods, the other of the Instruments of Christ's Passion. The treatment of the Christian and the pagan heavens as on one and the same level is a remarkable thing and shows how much the idea of humanism and the Renaissance had become accepted fact by everybody at the time of Shakespeare. Equally remarkable is the fact that the paintings as paintings are atrocious. It is an experience you may have anywhere in England, that these wealthy patrons about 1600 had no standards at all when it came to painting and to sculpture also. Hundreds of sumptuous and extremely crude Elizabethan and Jacobean funeral monuments prove that and at Bolsover the Venus Fountain in the garden behind the keep is a preposterous nude, standing stiffly with one foot high up on a kind of stool as if she was trying on a shoe and found it uncomfortable. Artists in the Italian sense of the word were yet rare in England, just as architects in the Italian and the modern sense did not yet exist at all. The carvers and the masons were still the honest craftsmen of the mediaeval type who did their best but knew no elegance or subtlety of proportion.

As a rule masons are not known by name in the sixteenth and early seventeenth centuries. But at Bolsover we are lucky. In the church are memorials to two masons, John Smithson and his son Huntington Smithson who died in 1634 and 1648, and the Royal Institute of British Architects owns a collection of about 200 drawings by members of the Smithson family. In addition, at Wollaton in Nottinghamshire in the church, Robert Smithson lies buried. He died in 1614 and is called the architect of Wollaton Hall, which is perhaps the most sumptuous and certainly the grossest of the Elizabethan mansions. In addition at Wollaton the same romantic mediaevalism is apparent as in the castellated keep of Bolsover – angle turrets, Gothic-looking window details and so on. Moreover, in the documents for Longleat in Wiltshire which Mr Hussey has recently published, another one of the grandest Elizabethan houses, Robert Smithson appears as early as 1568. So here we have the unique case of a dynasty of Elizabethan architects, probably three generations of them, busy on at least four major houses – very likely their designers – and, what is more, with quite a taste of their own.

New building at Bolsover did not stop with the keep. Around the outer courtyard of the old castle towards the town there must have been buildings of some sort and they were replaced by new ones about 1630. The owner now was Sir Charles's son William who was made Earl of Newcastle in 1628. He was a great royalist and he entertained Charles I and his queen lavishly, both at Welbeck and Bolsover, on their progress up to the North in 1634. The show is said to have cost him £20,000 – that is, fabulous as it may sound, well over half a million in present-day money.

For the occasion probably the Earl had that grand range of rooms built which faces the crumbling terrace and the plain. It contains a long gallery and a few very large adjacent rooms and has nothing domestic, liveable-in or intimate, but as a showpiece is extremely effective, though the King might well have found it a little provincial; for in London, at that time, Inigo Jones had created an extremely civilised, restrained style of building – the style of the Banqueting House in Whitehall – all developed from the chastest and finest of Italian sixteenth-century palaces and villas. Bolsover is also Italian in its motifs but its designer – perhaps Smithson – probably did not know Italy personally but was satisfied with engravings in books. Among them he chose quite consistently what was most fanciful and showy, doorways thickly surrounded by diamond-cut blocks of stone or stone blocks treated with what is known as 'vermiculated rustication' – that is, with curly worm-like wiggles in all directions, all over the surface of the block – and columns with their shafts crossed at intervals by fat, raised, horizontal bands or by square raised blocks at intervals and pediments on top which are open and broken and thickly decorated with coats of arms. The books Smithson used must have been such as illustrate not so much the portals of palaces of Rome as gateways in gardens where the Italians were ready to be rustic and jolly. Rubens had published a book on the Palaces of Genoa in 1623 and that may have been known to Smithson. The result at Bolsover is a grand display especially as seen from the terrace. Perhaps the fact that it is all in ruins and that it overlooks so grim an industrial scenery makes it all the more moving and there are few places in England known to me which tempt one so much to populate them with courtiers in van Dyck dress and trumpeters and actors and horsemen on ballotading horses. Yes, I said 'ballotading'. The word exists: you can look it up in the Oxford Dictionary and I have taken it straight from the Marquess of Newcastle's *Méthode et invention de dresser les chevaux* which he published in Antwerp in 1658. For he, the Marquess, former Earl, former Sir William Cavendish, was a celebrated horseman and the other building he put up at Bolsover – at an angle to the Gallery range – is the Riding School, also with one of these sumptuous doorways. It leads straight into a room ninety by thirty feet which was the Riding School proper. In 1638 the Earl was made Governor to the Prince of Wales and he prided himself on the prince's horsemanship. When the Civil War came, he fought for the King and then went into exile in 1644, first to Hamburg, then for three years to Paris, then to Holland and then to Antwerp. So you see, men like the Marquess were personally familiar with things abroad. And in matters of architecture at least, to be in the fashion was to be in the foreign fashion.

You may know the name of Vitruvius, a Roman of the Age of Augustus who wrote on the theory and practice of architecture. No other book on the subject was preserved so those who wanted to build in the Italian way and not the old, homespun English way tended to make rather a fetish of him. Well, when Charles I was at Bolsover, the grand new buildings – we may assume – just being got ready in time for him, a Masque was offered him as an entertainment, written specially by Ben Jonson. And who do you think appears in that short masque to conduct the first of the dances? Colonel Vitruvius supervising his mechanics. They are Chesil our curious carver, Master Maul our Free-Mason, Squire Summer our carpenter, Dresser the Plumber, Quarrel the Glazier, Fret the Plasterer – his work alas has gone – and Beater the Mortarman. That sounds rather like Snug the Joiner and Bottom the Weaver. But the author of the *Midsummer Night's Dream* also wrote *Julius Caesar* and *Coriolanus* and so the mechanics at Bolsover had to be directed by Colonel Vitruvius.

★

Strawberry Hill

ENGLISHMEN'S CASTLES (3)

Home Service
SUNDAY 29 JUNE 1952
Producer: R.E. Keen

There was once a Mrs Chenevix in London who for the fun of it ran a chic toy shop. In 1746, when Horace Walpole entertained a visitor from abroad, the Marchese Rinuccini, he took him to Mrs Chenevix's shop, among other things, and when the year after he bought for himself a cottage near Twickenham he thought he could not do better than describe it as 'a little plaything-house that I got out of Mrs Chenevix's shop'. There was as a matter of fact a double meaning in this, for he had in fact bought the cottage from her. It was a plaything too, so small that its front, which you can still distinguish, is less than half the narrow river front of the present Strawberry Hill and yet it was full of capabilities (as they called it) for Horace Walpole and for a long time it became the chief plaything of his life. He liked everything about it, the landscape by the river for which his descriptive word is *riant* – he was never short of the *mot juste* – and he also liked it that Twickenham was a good address. 'Dowagers', he writes somewhere, 'as plenty as flounders inhabit all around', and, in another letter, 'Pope's ghost is just now skimming under my windows.' Dowagers and Pope the poet – there you have his two ambitions, social and intellectual.

The Walpoles had been squires for centuries up in Norfolk and were of no great consequence until in 1721 Horace's father Robert Walpole became Prime Minister and the mightiest man in the country. He had several children. The youngest by eleven years was Horatio or Horace. Horace was sent to Eton and he was sent to King's College, Cambridge. Neither made a scholar of him nor what you might call a useful member of human society. His father, when the boy was twenty, got him some small political jobs – he was Comptroller of the Pipe and Clerk of the Estreats – and then sent him on the Grand Tour. He went to France and Italy with Thomas Gray, the poet, whom he had made friends with at Eton and who was to write the *Elegy in a Country Churchyard* and *The Bard*, while Walpole translated the same sentiments into the reality of stone and mortar at Strawberry Hill – a reality less elegiac and bardic than Gray's; but then Horace Walpole was a different man.

His father had died in 1745 and left him a comfortable £1,000 a year. So Horace settled down to an existence which he would have called busy and you might have called idle. He read, he wrote, he collected, he talked, he visited and received, and he kept up a vast and entertaining correspondence with friends out of London. His innumerable letters show him as he was: witty, flippant, spoiled, inconsequential, quick of observation, easy and to the point in his literary style, and full of catty idiosyncrasies which he was determined to make the most of and which one never tires of re-reading. Settling down to this existence of the virtuoso or dilettante, whichever word you prefer, he felt he must have a country retreat, a villa, not too far from London and that is where our story begins.

No sooner had he bought his bit of land and his cottage than he started improvements. After a year he called the house 'quite a charming villa' and says that it 'sprouts away like any chaste nymph in the *Metamorphoses*'. It was to be his last Grecian allusion in connection with Strawberry Hill. In 1749 for the first time he writes of his 'future battlements' and a year later of his 'Little Gothic Castle'. So here we are back at our recurrent theme, the castle which isn't a castle, the country house made to look like a castle. Now as to Walpole, the change in his idle mind from the Georgian Villa to the Gothic Castle was one that turned out to be of far-reaching consequence to the development of domestic architecture in Europe. It started a fashion in sham castles, Gothic oriel windows and crenellations which reached its climax only about 1800 and after, by which time it had become the craze of the day in Germany and Sweden and Russia and entered France and Italy and America too.

People speak of 'Strawberry Hill Gothic' and think Walpole invented this kind of domesticated mediaevalism. You know that he didn't. I was speaking last week of the imitation keep at Bolsover put up in 1613 and a fortnight ago of Vanbrugh's battlements and the 'Castle Air' he liked to give to his house. Well, Vanbrugh was fifty years older than Walpole and after him it never quite stopped.

William Kent, one of the leading architects of the years when Walpole was a boy, practised a bit of sham Gothic for the King and his other influential clients; Stukeley, the learned antiquarian, built a Gothic bridge in 1740 and so on.

But it is right and proper all the same that Walpole should have received all the credit. For no one was so thorough-going and so plausible a Goth as he was. Even in his writings he made a show of it. His *Castle of Otranto* started a vogue in Gothic novels as virulent as the Strawberry Hill vogue was in country houses.

In 1750, I told you, he began to call Strawberry Hill his Gothic Castle. Then, from that year onwards, he enlarged and enlarged it until it was nearly as big as it is now. Bit after bit was added, in 1753, in 1754, in 1759, in 1763, in 1772, in 1776. He was sixty when he finally stopped. It gradually grew from the east – that is the river front – to the west and ended on that side with two quite convincing round towers.

You enter the house from the back, an untidy back of many divers projections, the proof of so much adding without consistent plan. The ground-floor rooms are nothing special except for the staircase with its coloured glass in the windows, its pretty handrail of Gothic fretwork with little supporter-boasts on the newel posts – all 'so pretty and small', Walpole writes to one of his friends, 'that I am inclined to wrap it up and send it you in my letter'. Go up to the first floor and you'll find yourself soon in what he called the Holbein Chamber. In style nothing could be more distant from Holbein's clarity and precision. The showpieces in the room are the screen across with the most unlikely closely carved Gothic fretwork under gables, the ceiling gently curved and decorated with a kind of Gothic plasterwork and the big fireplace copied from Archbishop Warham's Tomb at Canterbury, as it has been published in engravings. It looks most incongruous in the room.

And then go at once straight into the Gallery, the most absurd and the most delightful apartment, all Gothic panelling and fan-vaulting, but all such toy size and besides so much white and gilt and mirrors that in effect it is wholly Rococo.

Yes – there is no other word to describe it. And the word Rococo brings me to what is the most interesting question about Strawberry

Hill. What did Walpole really feel about all this, about building this setting around himself? Was it just the delight of the Rococo in variety, irregularity and informality and nothing else? There is a letter that seems to bear that out. He writes this to his pet correspondent Horace Mann at Florence: 'I shall speak gently to you, my dear child, though you don't like Gothic architecture. The Grecian is only proper for magnificence and public buildings. Columns and all these beautiful ornaments look ridiculous when crowded into a closet or a cheese-cake house. The variety is little, and admits no charming irregulari-ties.' Or – to suggest a second answer – was it all snobbery with Walpole? Was it all snobbery of one without much ancestry to speak of, who wanted to have about him what he calls in a letter 'the true rust of the barons'? Or, yet another suggestion, was it the shrewdness of one who carries a real passion seemingly lightly to deceive others and himself? 'I pass all my mornings with the thirteenth century,' he writes, and 'I am as grave about my own trifles as I could be at Ratisbon' (where at that time the politicians were negotiating a peace treaty).

But he probably was much graver really than he was ready to admit. For time and again he consulted with his friends – the Committee of Taste, he called it – what books of engravings there were to arrive at a *correct* Gothic. Now Vanbrugh would not have bothered about that, nor does Walpole's pretty Gallery look as if *he* did. But the fact remains that he did. I told you of the chimney piece copied from an archbishop's tomb. For the ceiling of another room he went to the vault of York Chapter House, for his bookcases to the rood screen of Old St Paul's Cathedral.

It is a very curious thing if you come to think about it. Why try to be archaeologically correct if then your tomb becomes a fireplace and your screen bookcases? No – Walpole was far removed from an understanding of what Gothic design means. He was no doubt much too afraid of pedantry to think about it consistently. He could not have lived in a copy of a true Gothic house. It would have been much too earnest for him. You know how the Victorian Age instead of creating an architectural style of its own was content to imitate those of older ages – and in its churches chiefly the Gothic style. Well, that is understandable even if it is deplorable. The Middle Ages were accepted as the age of piety and so to build in their forms was to build piously. Walpole also built a chapel in the grounds of Strawberry Hill. It is still there and it is, needless to say, Gothic, taken from the tomb of Bishop Audley at Salisbury. Coloured glass spreads venerable gloom over the tomb of Capaccio, some mediaeval Roman abbot, I think – Walpole had bought it in Rome – and over the coloured tiles on the floor, tiles of curiously Victorian-looking pattern unforgettable to those who are familiar with them. But of religious sentiments there can have been none when this was built as an ornament to his gardens. Similarly, when he writes of 'lean windows fattened with rich saints' to describe some stained glass in the house, that does not sound too devout.

No, Horace Walpole's Gothic Revival had as little to do with religion as with scholarship and it is a pleasant and satisfying piece of historical irony that those who now own Strawberry Hill and look so conscientiously and intelligently after it should be a Roman Catholic Training College. Their main building is of course quite separate and tactfully screened. They use as their library a ballroom added quite splendidly, also in Gothic, in High Victorian days. But the Walpole rooms and the Walpole house remain quite intact, their charm as irresistible as ever.

You must see the house from the lawn at an angle, that is from the south-east (the Thames is on the east). It is designed to be quite irregular with a little bay window and a little stepped gable on the river side, with the long side originally open in a kind of cloister walk below the gallery and the fat round tower and the thin taller round turret further west to close the picture. That complete lack of symmetry in the design was, in the genteel Georgian setting of Walpole's time, perhaps the most revolutionary thing he did. Houses without symmetry in their façades just did not exist – except for one: that which Vanbrugh had built for himself about 1720, Vanbrugh Castle at Blackheath. But there are plenty of differences between Englishmen's castles, even those which are only make-believe. Vanbrugh wanted what he called 'a manly beauty'; when Horace Walpole speaks of Gothic buildings, of real Gothic buildings like Bristol Cathedral, he calls them 'neat and pretty' and Oxford 'a charming venerable Gothic scene', which all goes to show that no one can escape his own age and its taste. Walpole lived in the Age of the Rococo and his castle – for all its battlements and tracery and stained glass – remains a Rococo castle: the most delightful I know.

Antoni Gaudí

Third Programme
THURSDAY 31 JULY 1952
Producer: Anna Kallin

Few people in England know Antoni Gaudí.[1] Those who have seen one or two of his buildings at Barcelona are inclined to take him as light entertainment, which only goes to show that the English traveller has never really got over that virulent attack of Ruskin which began to infect English taste in High Victorian days. With Ruskin's standards one cannot appreciate him for even Borromini and the Asams are purity itself compared with that phantasmagoria that is Gaudí style. How fantastic he is, it is at most impossible to convey in words alone and even illustrations fail because they don't tell of scale and of colour.

Now the visitor with a well-thumbed Sitwell might be ready to accept such exuberance as Southern, as Spanish, as Baroque – but the oddest fact is that Gaudí was not a Spaniard but a Catalan and that the character of mediaeval Barcelona is about as far from exuberance and fantasy as anything can be. These churches and these spacious civic halls, all of the fourteenth century – a town hall, a hospital, a dockyard for the building of galleons – are clear-cut and bare and sheer and that is characteristic of the churches as well. Tall, almost unmoulded buttresses, immensely tall interiors with thin plain octagonal or circular piers, simple vaults: it is all of supreme clarity and has nothing whatever of that effusive, fanatic filling of every space with thick intricate ornament which one thinks of in speaking of mediaeval Spain – Gothic as well as Moorish.

Yet the frenzy must live somewhere in the people of Barcelona as well, or Gaudí could never have become a popular, a universally liked figure. You see, historically speaking he belongs to the movement known as Art Nouveau. He was born one hundred years ago this year, and he did his best work from about 1898 onwards. That is just the date when Art Nouveau was rampant all over Europe, the date of the Secession in Vienna, and of Mackintosh in Glasgow, of the *métro* stations in Paris and the Turin Exhibition. As a matter of fact, Gaudí did certain madly Art Nouveau contortions already in 1885 and even before, and that rare bird, the art historian interested in Art Nouveau, will have to note him as a lone pioneer earlier even than the earliest English book decorators and earlier also than Louis Sullivan, the architect of the Auditorium at Chicago. But these are minutiae for the connoisseur. The essential fact is that in all countries, Art Nouveau was a rarified fashion, with all the exclusiveness of the aestheticism of Oscar Wilde and Aubrey Beardsley. What pleasure could the hoi polloi take in these swaying stalks and intertwined trails, these fragile glass vessels and pale enamel plaques of wilfully curved outlines? But Gaudí the hoi polloi *do* enjoy – thanks of course to the Iberian mentality but also to a robustness of his which he was the only one to infuse into Art Nouveau.

Art Nouveau in the history of European style represents the final breaking away from period imitation. It proclaims abstract or nature forms or both, strangely mixed together. Gaudí was older than some of the others. He was, what is more, the son of a tinker in a village, and a humble, unquestioning believer in the Catholic church. So he began as an architect by respecting Gothic forms, as all the others did. He studied period precedent carefully though he must have cast his net much wider than the normal Gothicists for in his later work inspiration from Moorish faience is certain, from South and Central American Baroque likely, and from African tombs at least possible, those conical or sugar-loaf tombs, as they stand in weird silent clusters in North African lands. In this open-eyed examination of promising work in many countries and also in his fanaticism, his faith in craft and in doing things himself, and his faith in the Middle Ages, he corresponds, one might say, to our William Morris. In his religious intensity, however, and in the visible results of his efforts, he does not. These results I can here only describe to you in two works, the church of the Sagrada Familia which was placed into his hands in 1884 and which he left no more than a fragment of what he meant it to be when he died in 1927, and the Parque Güell, a planning and building scheme, begun in 1900 and also never completed.

The Sagrada Familia poses the problem of the church building in the twentieth century more enlighteningly than any other church. Here certainly is one answer, even if not an answer applicable to England, because the English are not Iberian. All that stands is an unpicturesque fragment built in an even brown-coloured stone. The screen wall of an apse with polygonal chapels and rather dull window tracery and then, like a fabulous cliff, one transeptal façade. The other was never begun, the crossing tower meant to be over 500 feet high never begun, the nave never begun, the main façade never begun. A model existed and was burnt in the Civil War; sketch models of one pier, some wooden tracery and such like bits are all that there is to guide in a continuation of the work. The existing façade has three portals with steep gables and that may sound to you as if it were the most innocent French Gothic façade. But right from the ground floor a mad incrustation with ornament starts, ornament still mostly naturalistic, as the Art Nouveau liked it. Embedded in this are large sacred figures of a painfully sentimental Père Lachaise style. But as one's eye is raised higher, or, better still, as one climbs higher, a little precariously, up the spiral stairs, looking down into the abysses not railed off and looking up into weird vaulted halls and chambers, sentimentality and naturalism disappear and what takes their place is a frenzy of abstract art, utterly uncompromising and lonely, worked out by Gaudí himself in plaster models of all the details and then on the scaffolding in discussing more or less stone for stone with the craftsman – this stone to stick out, that to recede, completely without any system – an architecture of the individual, if there ever was one. The façade culminates in four narrowly spaced tall conical or sugar-loaf towers in pairs of two and two close together. They rise and taper, first consisting of tall columns, then of taller piers with spirally set horizontals, or transoms if you like, between and finally ending in forms of no architectural precedent whatever, spires of a crustaceous form, details sometimes like the jazzy light-fittings of 1925, sometimes like celestial cacti, sometimes like malignant growths, sometimes like the spikes of bristly dinosaurs. And the whole of these spires above the conical, brown-stone towers is made of glazed faience with an incredible technique. But of that I had better say more later, when we can study it in more detail.

Meanwhile this description may sound to you crazy. Well, of course it is that. It may sound to you also not religious – but there you are wrong because you are English and Protestant, whatever you call it. But it may sound to you vulgar too, and that it also isn't. It has, at least in my opinion, all the ferocious power of conviction which Baroque architecture can possess. It is fabulous, it is miraculous, it hits you hard, it gives you no peace, it does not let go of you and for that very reason it is proper for the church, rousing you to prostrate yourself and to worship. So at least it must have seemed to the Catalans, for the building goes up out of the donations of the people and the people, I can assure you, adore it.

The Parque Güell is quite another story. Count Güell was a rich man, a merchant and a promoter. He was Gaudí's chief patron. A town house of palatial size was built for him by Gaudí as early as 1885. I can't go into details about that house but I can tell you that it is here for the first time that we see the fury of Art Nouveau swamp Gothic convention. And in 1900 the scheme of the park or garden estate was conceived – a Regent's Park conception really, though the area is smaller and the vegetation less lush and also rougher and scraggier. But like Regent's Park, this park was to have scattered villas and lodges and a market and promenades. The villas, except one, were never built but the lodges possess all the crazy flamboyance of the upper crags of the Sagrada Familia long before these were built. There are two lodges, one entirely unlike the other. They have all sorts of windows and faience roofs like gloriously overdressed hats and they have fancy battlements and just one excessively high chimney.

The market is even more remarkable. It is tunnelled into the rock, or seems so, at half the height of the steeply rising ground. It is like a Turkish reservoir or Moorish mosque, except that the columns are of a sturdy Greek Doric order and all the outer columns lean heavily to the inside – a nightmarish expression of their strength to carry, like the strong men of the Guinness posters of the past who propped up whole buildings. The concise discipline of the Doric capitals is made what some might call 'organic' by squashing them into doughy shapes.

But the high-water mark of Gaudí's art is the open-air arena on top of the market and the promenades. The arena is simply a large sandy square surrounded by a long seat all the way round, a wonderful interminable seat waving forward and backward with a back curving upward and downward – and all this again covered with faience. The back is like the back of an immensely long shiny dragon, fascinating and frightening. The faience is of two kinds, old broken bits with gay patterns used any old way, it seems, though in fact all the time supervised bit for bit by Gaudí, and also specially made faience in delicious pale cloudy colours, pinks, lemon-yellows, lime-greens, sky-blues and so on – all these made in larger surfaces, yet systematically broken up into bits like Japanese craquele.

The promenades are at least as astonishing. They are covered arcades, in various tiers along the hillsides, with raw brown stone piers built up of big boulders, with wildly irregular vaults from which large hideously jagged stones stick down like fiendish pendants. In one promenade the walk is suddenly interrupted by a grey old tree growing with its trunk dead across the way. You don't see inside that it is alive with leaves – outside in the heat of the day. Where you stand it seems dead and it enhances the oddly macabre atmosphere which the architect created and his client must have appreciated. Sir William Chambers in his fanciful book on *Chinese Gardening* of 1773 described with much gusto and recommended for European use the Chinese way of making some part of their gardens into places of horror. I had never believed that that might really be done until I walked in the penumbra of the Parque Güell.

And there is something else to intensify one's feeling of suspicion – Gaudí's ironwork. Here and even in the balcony railings of respectable blocks of flats it is treated as directly and vehemently, twisted as passionately, beaten and pinched as roughly and inelegantly, as if the work were Reg Butler's[2] of today, and not Gaudí's of fifty years ago.

Altogether – and that more than anything made me think on my return from Spain that I should tell you something of Gaudí and his impact – altogether it is the treatment of materials and surfaces that makes him unique in his age (I say unique and mean unique). So far I have spoken of him mostly as a giant of Art Nouveau; now we must, to finish with, look at him as a man of the twentieth century, the direct predecessor of that other great Spaniard, Picasso. For you must not forget that Picasso grew up with Gaudí. Picasso left Barcelona for good only in 1903. So he must have watched that very change in Gaudí's style which concerns us here. And if I tell you a little more of Gaudí's use of ceramics you will no doubt realise what I mean. Take this, for instance. The market hall has between its Doric columns little vaults high up. They are there to give glitter and so he has faced them with pottery and glass. But when you look up steadily and screw up your eyes a bit, you suddenly discern that that white disk up there is a cheap saucer and that green, boldly-modelled disk the bottom of a broken old bottle and then looking round the other vaults anxiously you see necks of bottles sticking out and cups with their handles, collages of before the First World War. It is a violent and a delightful shock, for the eye as much as the mind.

One more word. Gaudí died in 1927 and since then the Barcelonese have pondered over the problem what to do with the Sagrada Familia. I told you, no more is up so far than about one eighth. What can be done? It is obvious to me that one can't, not even with all the dedicated lunacy of Spain, continue à la Gaudí. He was, you will now agree, the most personal, inimitable of architects. He kept only the fewest of designs or models. Every detail was decided face to face with block and surface. So there seem to me only two possible answers, one more tempting, the other probably more constructive. You can leave this cliff of a church as a ruin, plant the rest of the site sensitively and enjoy the building in future as the hugest of all *custodias* – that is the Spanish name for these tower-shaped monstrances you see in the cathedrals. Or you can trust in the Spanish genius and make a competition inviting designs not in the style of Gaudí nor in the so-called International Modern Style. Perhaps among the talented young architects of Spain one would come forward, as fervent as Gaudí and as original as he.

1   This talk was delivered on the centenary of Gaudí's birth. It was wrongly introduced by the BBC as coinciding with the centenary of his death.
2   Reg Butler (1913–81) was an English sculptor. It is his Constructivist works that Pevsner refers to here. In the late 1950s, he turned to the female figure, increasingly erotic and mimetic in colouring.

Reflections on not teaching art history

Third Programme
SUNDAY 19 OCTOBER 1952
Producer: Leonie Cohn

You must realise from the beginning that I am speaking to you tonight as a rank outsider.[1] I have not been to a public school, nor to Oxford or Cambridge, although I am now – pro tem – as happy at Cambridge as anyone.

That happiness is partly due to my rooms at St John's College in New Court, the 'Wedding Cake', that delightful folly at the north end of The Backs. I have a Gothic plaster ceiling of the 1820s and a polygonal bathroom with the plumbing twining over the walls like ivy. My happiness is also due to new and old friends inside and outside College and to the wonderful change of being able to walk through a town for a whole mile without being hurt by the sight of a single building. That can happen only in three towns in the whole of England. At Cambridge indeed there are walks where nearly every building is a pleasure to the eye.

It is my job at Cambridge to keep young people's eyes open and to open them if they are still glued up – an extremely gratifying job in many ways. For one thing I find that young people like the operation. They like being talked to about the art and architecture of the past and don't mind if it is done seriously.

Besides, I can be lazy at Cambridge. For so my job decrees it. You see, I am not teaching at Cambridge. That I do in London. At Cambridge I am appointed to stand on a platform and talk about all that fascinates me.

However, in the middle of all these delights, a voice quite often whispers that I should teach, I should get hold of those who are really keenly, vitally interested in my subject and see what I can do *for* them, what I can do *with* them. But that I can't – for my subject, the history of art and architecture, does not exist at Cambridge as an academic subject pursued to attain a degree and start a professional career. Nor does it exist at Oxford.

That may not surprise you. But it surprises anybody who may enter

Britain from Yale or Tucuman in the Argentine or Leiden in Holland or Uppsala in Sweden or Göttingen (where I come from) or Tübingen or Padua or Pisa. Everywhere the History of Art is established as an academic subject; only in Britain it isn't. In Germany, which I know best, there have been chairs for a hundred years and more, and for fifty they have existed at nearly every one of the twenty and more universities.

So the subject has quite a respectable history and a history not without interest even to those over here who still look at it as an alien body. The interest lies, I think, in two facts. One is how closely the history of any one subject reflects much more general trends of development. The other is simply the variety of existing trends, the manifold ways in which one subject can be treated and the manifold kinds of results obtained.

The history of art grew out of the world of *virtù*, the world of the intelligent and sensitive, wealthy amateur. In his purchases of pictures and statuary he was advised by the painter who was supposed to be able to distinguish between an original antique and a fake, and an original Raphael and the work of a pupil or follower. Hogarth cursed this passion for art of the past and of foreign countries.

If, on the other hand, the virtuoso felt more attached to his own country and as a rule especially his own country, then he might well develop into an antiquarian, enthusiastic about the druids or the stained glass of a departed abbey. This antiquarianism, as well as the painter's and collector's connoisseurship in individual cases, developed into erudition on a very high level. You get Waagen's *Treasures of Art in Great Britain* in 1854 or Crowe and Cavalcaselle's *Early Flemish Painters* of 1853 as examples of advanced connoisseurship and even earlier Sir Richard Colt Hoare as an example of the scholarly amateur prehistoric archaeologist and Count Arcisse de Caumont as the scholarly amateur mediaeval archaeologist. Caumont's *Cour d'Antiquités Monumentales* came out in 1838–43.

Nor is the type extinct now. In Britain at least it is still with us – both as the sound and creative amateur scholar in Italian Renaissance and Baroque or English architecture and as the sound amateur local or regional antiquarian. Some of the best work that comes out in this country we owe to this type and the work has qualities which the specialist scholar's work tends to lack. It is as a rule presented with elegance and that is more than one can say of much that the *Art Bulletin* publishes in America or that German learned journals used to publish. Also it has often more vitality because it is based on a man's understanding of literature as well as art and, better still, on a man's experience in some field of practical life. On the other hand, the amateur is more likely to develop a bee in his bonnet because he has no solid foundation and is likely to venture on wild theories in the absence of sufficient information of what has already been ascertained by others, especially abroad.

Abroad, certainly, the amateur in the history of art is more of an anomaly than here – and understandably so, for in most countries on the Continent the amateur has gone the way of the dodo – for once the history of art and architecture has become a subject of university teaching and research, as accepted as botany and bacteriology, the interested young amateur will naturally drift into it.

The first man whom we can call an art historian and who was Professor of the History of Art was Franz Kugler at the Academy of Art in Berlin. He was appointed in 1833 and wrote a *History of Painting* in 1837 and a *Handbook of the History of Art* in 1841–42. At that time Jakob Burckhardt was a student of history at Berlin, under Ranke; and with Burckhardt the history of art in one sense begins. His *Cicerone* of 1855, it is true, has still much of the connoisseur's approach and his famous *Civilisation of the Renaissance* is cultural history enlivened by an exceptional amount of data from art. But his less known *History of the Renaissance in Italy*, a volume of Kugler's *History of Architecture* which came out in 1867, is entirely history of art proper – so much so that it is to this day the best textbook we possess, a record purely of durability.

What is it that makes me call it history of art proper? Perhaps I can better explain that if I move one step forward to the time, about 1890, Burckhardt's last years, when in the hands of his pupil and successor Heinrich Wölfflin the history of art finally discovered itself. Wölfflin was not alone in this. His key books date from 1888 to 1899, his Basel period, those of August Schmarsow at Leipzig from exactly the same time – 1894–99 – and the *Questions of Style* by Alois Riegl of Vienna again from 1893. Questions of Style is indeed what these three men and Burckhardt were concerned with and although such basic divisions of style as Classic and Romantic or Greek and Gothic had been felt and even analysed by the German Romantics, especially Schlegel at the beginning of the nineteenth century, the innovation of the end of the nineteenth century lies in the direction of the analysis of style and it was this innovation which won its independence for the history of art.

Let us take Wölfflin because he has been translated into English and is therefore best known here. What does he teach? Three things, mainly: that the history of art is the history of the human eye, of seeing; that not everything can be seen at every period in history; and that the Greeks see objects in isolation while the Baroque sees things merging into one great ensemble, whether it is Bernini's ensemble of decorative architecture, decorative sculpture and decorative painting or Rembrandt's ensemble of all figures and objects in one unifying *clair obscur*. So Wölfflin rigidly restricts the art historian's job to analysis of form and then, on that basis, reaches out to categories of style. A style is defined by those formal characteristics which all significant works of art of one period have in common. Wölfflin is not closely interested in the individual work nor the individual artist. To know your material is a matter of course; not to be taken in by imitation goes without saying. The job of the art historian as against the connoisseur only starts on a plane above that. Wölfflin chiefly exemplified his thesis from the contrast of Renaissance and Baroque, Riegl from that of Late Antiquity and Early Christianity, Schmarsow's forte was the analysis of architecture in formal terms. It led him to discover that space is the distinguishing medium of the architect, a discovery not fully acclimatised in this country yet.

So by the time of the First World War, the history of art as a subject in its own right and with its own tested methods was established in most countries on the Continent. But there was one snag in the Wölfflin method: the artificiality of isolating the formal aspects of a picture or a building. A building also serves a purpose and is conditioned by that. And a picture represents something. Choice of subject and treatment of subject are surely component parts of the painting. Wölfflin deliberately left out all that – understandably so, you may say; for to establish his criteria they had to be separated and overstressed, just as Roger Fry did here. 'I want to find out what the function of content is,' he wrote in 1913 to Lowes Dickinson. 'I am developing a theory that is merely directive of form.' What happened in the end, I can tell you from experience, is that two ardent students of the history of art could go to a museum and debate wildly over, say, a mediaeval relief and only on the way home realise that neither of them remembered what it actually represented.

So one reaction against the aestheticism of the Wölfflin–Roger Fry approach was a new interest in *iconography*: that is, if you like, *subjectology*. This reaction is forever connected with the name of Aby Warburg, the founder of the Warburg Institute. One of the foremost documents of its approach is the late Fritz Saxl's and Professor Panofsky's volume of 1923 on Dürer's *Melancholia*. What does this mysterious engraving show? What made Dürer do it? How could he do it in this form? All these questions call for research into the history of astrology and of the survival of antiquity in mediaeval Germany. Less profoundly, but equally successfully, iconography was at the same time handled in France by Emile Mâle in his volumes on religious art in France from the twelfth to the seventeenth century.

The results of iconographical research are always interesting but whether they be of deeper significance depends on how wide or narrow the scholar's approach is. It can be fascinating to read, say, how different periods represented Death or Justice but we may in the end still have only a catalogue of species and subspecies instead of something stirring and illuminating if the author of the book or paper is not aware of the fact that all changes in iconography, as all changes in style, are only the signs of far deeper changes in Zeitgeist, the spirit of ages. So at the same time as iconographical history of art was placed on a pedestal by the Warburg circle at Hamburg, Max Dvořák in Vienna established what he called *Kunstgeschichte als Geistesgeschichte*, history of art as history of the mind. He took the word *Geistesgeschichte* from the philosopher Wilhelm Dilthey who had used the term *Geisteswissenschaften* since the 1880s, and Dvořák's work is indeed closely connected with those philosopher-historians like Dilthey, Max Weber and Ernest Tröltsch who had used this approach in their epoch-making books on the history of philosophy, theology and economics. Dvořák's magnum opus, his *Idealism and Naturalism in Gothic Sculpture and Painting*, came out during the First World War and this was followed by his brilliant Bruegel and Greco studies of 1920.

Finally, but so far as hardly more than a sideline of *Geistesgeschichte*, a special interest in the social history of art set in in Gemany just before the Hitler regime started. It took two forms rather parallel to the Warburg and Dvořák attitudes: factual research into history of art as a social activity, art criticism, art education, art collecting and so on; and a socialist form of *Geistesgeschichte* in which the *Geist* was replaced by the working of economics. Of the second kind, a good instance is Dr Antal's recent book on *Florentine Painting of the Fourteenth Century*; of the first kind the French have given examples for a long time, quite unperturbed by deeper changes in the history of art. Henri Focillon in the 1930s was indeed the first in France to take note of Central-European developments and liberate French medi-aeval scholarship from its archaeological limitations. Focillon is a great influence on the United States and for that reason alone deserves mention in my context tonight.

For when the history of art as an academic subject at last made an appearance in this country – as late as 1931, the date of the foundation of the Courtauld Institute of Art in the University of London – it was more an outcome of the rapid spreading of the subject in America than of its well-tested existence on the Continent.

The Courtauld Institute has established itself firmly as a centre of art-historical training; and post-graduate research a little later made the best possible start when the Warburg Institute succeeded in extricating itself from the Nazis and re-opening in London as a school of the University. The Warburg has already done much, especially in Professor Wittkower's publications, to elucidate British art and architecture to the British. The Courtauld training is of a remarkably high standard and I can testify that a Courtauld First in his oral examination has to give proof of a knowledge more detailed and precise than his opposite number in the German universities I have known in my time. The Courtauld does not, however, seem to have found yet a new approach to the subject, different in principle from those which I have tried to outline with German examples; nor is that perhaps needed at this stage in England. My own experience at any rate makes me think so. For my own work, you can take it from me, is entirely eclectic and yet seems to meet a demand. A book on the history of art academies, that is social history of art; papers on the religious and historical foundations of Mannerism and Baroque in Italy, that is *Geistesgeschichte*; a treatment of architectural evolution in terms of space, and so on. Nothing that had not been done before. And in the same way I would be ready, if I had time, to analyse recent work by the dozen or so best art-historical scholars in England – scholars who have produced, I assure you, very much weightier and more valuable work than I as a general practitioner have ever attempted – and show that from the point of view of the general progress of history of art as an independent academic subject, they have not really broken new ground. But is that so relevant? – at least in England, at least now?

For the moment it is perhaps more important, so far as England is concerned, simply to see how and where the history of art is taught: as 'uplift' or as background and parallel to history and modern languages; or as history of art proper, for its own purposes. Uplift is all right, as far as it goes. But is it really good enough as the only recognition of the history of art in the great institutions of Cambridge and Oxford?

Art as background and parallel to history and languages should certainly also be recognised. And, mind you, I don't mean here simply history of costume, or the means of fortification and siege machinery, or portraits of Charles V by Titian and Marat dead in his bath by David, just to show what they looked like. I mean the development and character of the art of one nation at one period as a parallel to history and literature so that the eye should help to enlighten the mind on matters of style as they apply to drama and poetry or even to social history, as much as to painting. There can be, I think, no two opinions on the value to the student who reads French to look at the Cemetery of the Holy Innocents when he concerns himself with François Villon, or at Poussin when he studies Corneille or Descartes, or at Courbet and Manet when he studies Baudelaire. I have done that kind of background lecturing for nearly ten years at Birkbeck College in the University of London and my impression is that it does help students. At Oxford and Cambridge, knowledge of the art and architecture of the country or period in which a man specialises might well be part of a tripos, especially the history tripos – in what way would, of course, have to be seen – and in addition something might be done to encourage for postgraduate theses subjects of some bearing on history of art in its relation to history. These are legitimate subjects. They are as helpful to the student as a subject from political history, and there are after all – thank God for that – some students who are visually gifted and attracted by the visual expression of the history of man's mind.

Should Cambridge and Oxford for the moment go beyond that and recognise the history of art in its own right? There seems to be some feeling that that is sufficiently well looked after by the Courtauld and Warburg Institutes in London. Whether these two are enough and whether they provide for all needs – I am inclined myself to think they do – it is not for me to discuss, but I suppose Professor Waterhouse will have something to say about that.[2]

1   Pevsner was the first Cambridge Slade Professor to be appointed for a second three-year term. This talk coincided with the start of his fourth year.
2   Pevsner's was the first in a pair of talks; the second by Professor Ellis Waterhouse on 'Art History – an Un-English Activity' followed a week later.

Arts and commerce promoted

Home Service
SUNDAY 21 MARCH 1954
Producer: Lorna Moore

On March 22nd, 1754, a small group of noblemen and gentlemen met at a coffee house off Covent Garden.[1] Viscount Folkestone and Lord Romney were among them, and Stephen Hales, the plant physiologist and inventor of artificial ventilation, and a Mr Shipley, a drawing master from Northampton. The idea behind this meeting was his, the idea of forming a society 'for the encouragement of arts, manufactures and commerce'. The society was duly founded. Five years later the membership had passed the 1,200 mark – with a subscription of two guineas and five guineas for Peers. In 1760 a member could say: 'We are now the greatest assembly of men that in any country ever sat in a disinterested manner to the good of its people.' Three years later a copy of the society was formed in Hamburg, another three years later at St Petersburg.

What was the secret of its spectacular success? What did the encouragement of arts, manufactures and commerce involve? How could it be served disinterestedly? The answer was simple for Shipley: it would not be now. It was then the giving of prizes to reward skill and inventiveness. This was a period happily ignorant of our sub-division of labour. A squire might have a laboratory in an out-building, a clergyman might invent a machine. Promise them rewards and they will come forth – with the result that their inventions will become common property. Nothing that was patented qualified for the society's rewards. Moreover, the Industrial Revolution, though it was imminent, had not yet, shall we say, broken out. To quote a poem written by the society's trusty porter and later registrar in 1766, industry still worked largely

> by windy pow'r or wat'ry force,
> or by a circumambulating horse.

Progress for – as it was formulated in the Charter of 1847 – 'the riches and honour of the Kingdom' was still more in terms of agricultural than of industrial improvement. And agriculture was indeed the most important field of the young society. Encouragement in the cultivation of new crops for winter fodder as well as for human consumption, potatoes, swedes, kale, kohlrabi, encouragement of better tools (the scythe instead of the sickle), encouragement of land reclamation and finally encouragement of afforestation. The results here were prodigious. In 1793 awards were made for the planting of 491,000 trees but the total of new trees of which the society was informed in that year was over 800,000. In 1806 the successful candidates alone had planted 1,269,000 trees. Colonel Thomas Johnes of Hafod in Wales who received six gold medals from the society is said to have planted four million trees.

Such activities, you can see that now, would indeed recommend themselves to a society of public-spirited gentlemen ready to spend two guineas a year for the benefit of their country. Yet it does remain surprising how many people were ready. Dr Johnson was a member, and Hogarth and Reynolds, and Robert Adam and Sir William Chambers, the architects, and Gibbon and John Howard, the prison reformer, and Joseph Banks, the botanist, and Benjamin Franklin, and Baskerville and Caslon, the printers, and Garrick and Goldsmith, and so on.

There were incidentally also prizes for children for draughtsmanship. Flaxman got one when he was eleven, and Pater, Landseer and Millais when they were ten. Prizes were also at first offered for designs for textiles, wallpapers and so on, because 'Fancy, Design and Taste are absolutely necessary to all persons concerned in Building, Furniture, Dress, Toys, or any other matters where Elegance and Ornament are required'. But there was very little response to those and by 1778 they had all but dropped out.

So much for the palmy days immediately after the foundation. The membership figures about 1775 were not reached again until about 1855 and that date takes us into a completely different world. The Industrial Revolution had done the riches of the kingdom more good than the riches of the society. The principle of the society, as I told you, was that industry and commerce were to be awarded prizes only where inventions were to be accessible to all. But when large factories sprang up all over wide parts of the country and inventions clearly meant bigger money if they were patented, self-interest almost every time eclipsed any interest in a medal or an honourable mention in a volume of transactions.

So the society receded into the background. In 1763 its income had been £4,600; in 1836 it was down to £1,235 and there was a debt as well. The general feeling must have been that the society had had its day and was superfluous now and that all that was still to be expected was an honourable funeral.

Prince Albert, however, did not think so. He was made President in 1843 and when Prince Albert began to take an interest in something, he was not the man to allow it to vegetate. He analysed the case, he prescribed remedies and he saw to it that they were taken. Mind you, I am probably exaggerating his personal role. Inside the society at the same time men also appeared who were of equal clear-sightedness and tenacity, first and foremost among them Henry Cole – Henry Cole, that remarkable Victorian who, before concentrating on the society had fought for penny postage and the broad railway gauge, had issued the first Christmas card ever printed and charts for railway passengers to tell them of the sights which their train was passing. The diagnosis of Cole and Prince Albert was that the society had been founded for the purpose of a liaison of art with industry and commerce or, to use Prince Albert's words, that 'to wed mechanical skill with high art is ... directly in the path of its duty'.

The outcome of all that was the Great Exhibition, the Great Exhibition of 1851, the first international exhibition of industry and applied art ever held in any country. It is the most famous of all the innumerable children of the Society of Arts. It was a huge success in its displays of machinery and manufacture but it revealed an atrocious state of industrial art and Cole and his friends, chiefly Richard Redgrave and Matthew Digby Wyatt, admitted that openly and criticised it savagely.

But however disappointing that one aspect of the Great Exhibition was, its general success is reflected in the membership graph of the society after 1851 which shot up steeply and steadily until about 1865 it had passed 3,000. Now it is just under 6,000. That is a fine record and yet, in some ways, the position of the society today seems to me once again almost as precarious as before 1851 – not for financial but for functional reasons.

In the wake of the 1851 Exhibition, the society had promoted very many useful objects, far more than I can mention here – the first exhibition of photography ever held, an extensive system of commercial examinations (which is still going strong), early demonstrations of electric lighting and the gramophone (both as early as 1878), drill in schools and the foundation of the Royal College of Music. This had been the society's own National Training School for Music but it proved so successful that eleven years later it became the official Royal College.

There is, however, in nearly all these enterprises an ever-recurring, half-gratifying, half-sad story. Time and again the society promoted something and when it was successful it was handed on to someone else. This is of course connected with the alarming development of specialisation in the nineteenth century. Our society had on its premises the very first exhibition of painting ever undertaken in Britain and then the Royal Academy was founded and took that over. Much later our society established a special section for applied chemistry, until the Institute of Chemistry appeared. Again, our Society of Arts built the first two public lavatories in London, lost heavily on them (the one for gentlemen was used by only fifty-eight people in one month) but then the London County Council saw the point and adopted the idea. The society started examinations in trades and the City & Guilds Institutes carried them on. The society held exhibitions of inventions; now you go to the Patent Office to look up inventions. And so on and so forth. Every time, the self-chosen function of the society – the Royal Society of Arts since 1908 – became the function of other more specialised bodies, often government-run or government-sponsored. You find the story told in detail, both instructively and very entertainingly, in Derek Hudson and Kenneth Luckhurst's new history of the Royal Society of Arts which is going to be published tomorrow.

On the strength of that past and the position of art and of commerce today, we should now, to finish with, ask ourselves what can be the function of the Royal Society of Arts today. The promotion of art in industry? The Council of Industrial Design is doing that. The promotion of new art more contemporary in character than what as a rule goes into the Royal Academy? The Arts Council is doing that. And similarly other functions which would be in harmony with the programme of such an association are safely in the hands of the National Trust, the National Art Collections Fund, the Royal Photographic Society, the Town & Country Planning Association, the National Playing Fields Association and dozens of others.

Can there be any *raison d'être* left for a private society such as the one whose history I have outlined to you, and can there be a future in the mid-twentieth century in terms of work of as much urgency and vigour as had been the work undertaken by the original founders and again by Prince Albert and Henry Cole?

My answer is this. For one thing, to keep 6,000 people informed by lectures and their publication of results in a large number of subjects and not just in one specialised subject is itself an important thing. It holds up a tradition of all-round culture which is in danger of disappearing. Secondly, a society so entirely private can offer a platform for any new idea or new approach or for any criticism of what is inadequate or outmoded. I said 'it can offer' for it does not necessarily do so. Henry Cole and his friends were certainly more outspoken than the society usually is now. But the sense of adventure of 1754 and the ruthless integrity of strong-principled criticism of 1854 must remain the lodestone of the society. If it goes genteel, it is lost.

But I don't think it will. Prince Albert was twenty-four when he became President. He was thirty-one in the year of the Great Exhibition. The Duke of Connaught was sixty-one in 1911 when he became President. He had stipulated that he ought not to be expected to attend council meetings; he was too busy otherwise. He died in 1942 at the age of ninety-two. In 1947, a new President was elected. She was twenty-one. And when the duties of Queenship were laid on her, she handed on to the Duke of Edinburgh. And so the future lies now, as it did a hundred years ago, in the hands of a young President, a man of thirty-two, brought up in a young school and in sympathy with young ideas. This is what I regard as the society's best guarantee for the future.

1   This talk on the two hundredth anniversary of the Royal Society of Arts took its title from the motto on the RSA's medals.

*

Bavarian Rococo – or the eloquent in art

Third Programme
WEDNESDAY 17 NOVEMBER 1954
Producer: Leonie Cohn

In the opinion of Pugin, the monuments by Roubiliac in Westminster Abbey, the monument to the Duke of Argyll, to General Wade and General Hargrave and Mrs Nightingale, were 'incongruous and detestable'. Ruskin called them 'ignoble and incoherent'. William Morris was even more eloquent; he speaks of 'monstrous and ghastly pieces of perversity and bluntness of feeling'.

Now the West German and Bavarian governments have sent to London an unprecedented display of works of the Bavarian Rococo built up round some of the most splendid sculpture of the eighteenth century in all Europe.[1] Very well, but *The Times* says about it that, in it,

> the reckless sophistication of rococo is most apparent. Without a tremor or a qualm the artist has transformed and adapted his Madonnas, saints and archangels to the old fantastic world of the prince-bishops and Electors of the eighteenth century; their postures are those of a great actor at the climax of his performance, their expressions those of courtiers or princes in an absolutist court ... It becomes absurd to ask whether these works are beautiful; as a technical performance they are overwhelming and it would be ludicrous to look for depth of feeling in anything so extreme ...

I find this very interesting – in two respects: a) because those who commissioned, paid for and delighted in the works of Roubiliac were the English – men of the same race and nationality as Ruskin and as *The Times* correspondent, and b) because the passage I have quoted from *The Times* is proof that in referring to our own day we should not speak of Neo-Elizabethans or Neo-Georgians because Victorian prejudices still prevail in so many quarters. Here at least, in the article just quoted, the same fury and abhorrence as Ruskin's has produced the same confusion.

It is easy to refute some of the arguments of *The Times* – though not

all. The easiest to refute of course is that it should be absurd to ask
whether the sculpture of Ignaz Günther is beautiful. It can never be
absurd to ask works of art that question. Although the fact that they
are – and exquisitely so in this case – may not be enough. Some
people say it would be enough – that is the attitude of Art for Art's
Sake or of aesthetic autonomy. But that is not my view. I hold with
those who believe that significant content must join forces with
significant form to create the fulness of art. Thus for instance, if Ignaz
Günther, as *The Times* maintains, represented saints and Madonnas not
acceptable as religious art, he would stand condemned.

But is the Bavarian Rococo not religious? Or are we perhaps
wrong in wanting to represent religion the Protestant way? Let me
make this clear at once. I don't speak here from a Catholic point of
view. My origins are in a part of Germany which is Protestant and in
this country I would certainly be called very low church indeed. But
that is not the point. I don't believe in Buddha either yet I would not
deny that statues of Buddha are pure religious art. So, whether the
church at Rott, on the Inn, built by Johann Michael Fischer in
1759–63 and provided with altars by Ignaz Günther and with frescoes
by Matthaeus Günther and with stucco by one of the Feichtmayrs, is
conducive to communication with God for me personally is really
quite irrelevant. What matters is that these churches have been the
vessels of worship for innumerable simple souls, as you still see them
kneel and fervently pray in them now, and that their festive character
had moreover very good and perfectly legitimate reasons in the minds
of those who commissioned the churches and their decoration – and
they were by no means simple souls.

Let me give you a few examples. Over the entrance to Fischer's
church at Berg am Laim near Munich, you read Psalm number 118:
'This is the Lord's doing and it is marvellous in our eyes.' Over the
entrance to the monastery of Melk in Austria, it says in large letters:
'*Absit gloriari nisi in Christo.*' In the palace of the Prince of Kempten
there are two paintings, the one of the old modest buildings of the
monastery, the other of the lavish new ones, and the captions read:
'*Pietate patrum*' and '*Labore nepotum*'. So that is how one should look at
the buildings: by our labour we have made these buildings glorious to
celebrate God. And indeed the Prior of Diessen wrote to Fischer to

ask whether he would be ready to undertake the building of 'a temple, new, splendid and worthy of the King of Heaven and Earth'.

Now I would like to ask you: What is wrong with that? Palaces for the kings, the princes, the bishops and abbots who were secular rulers also, even if often on a small scale – and the palace of palaces for the Lord. Here you prostrate yourself, here you feel awed by so much vastness and splendour and at the same time elated by the thought of perhaps being allowed to participate in it. You or I may find that a naive reasoning but it is the consistent reasoning of centuries of Catholic design and it seems to me absurd to blame Ignaz Günther for not having written motets rather than carving his saints and virgins.

Unless of course you blame him for a lack of piety in these very saints and virgins, and there again I would deny the charge. Take first such a piece as the *Pietà* from Nenningen. Does it not show respect, does it not show suffering, does it not show grief? You can't deny that it does. But you may point to two things: first to a certain display of these feelings which you would call theatrical and secondly to a certain elegance in the hands and the alabaster-like folds of the draperies. But what is theatrical? If you mean demonstrative or even ostentatious, that is what all Baroque art was intended to be. Possevino, a Jesuit of the late sixteenth century, writes: 'The greatest art is to reproduce the thing itself, their torments in the case of martyrs, their tears in the case of the weeping, their glory in the case of those transported to heaven.' Here then, in Ignaz Günther's *Pietà*, you have torments and tears, and in other statues of his, there is glory.

And as regards elegance, it would be futile to deny that elegance is the all-pervading element of the Rococo. And here let me explain at once that in my opinion Rococo is not a style in opposition to the preceding style of the Baroque but the last, most refined, sublimated phase of the Baroque. Both styles are extrovert and sensational in the original sense of the word – that is, ready to appeal to all our senses in order to convince us of what Possevino calls 'the thing itself' and both styles believe in breaking down boundaries between inner and outer space, that is to say between a building and the nature surrounding it. But the Rococo is light where the Baroque is heavy, in colour as well as weight, and so elegance is a quality wholly of the Rococo and not of the Baroque. Now where elegance appears in religious art of the eighteenth century, is that perhaps its form of expressing the victory of the mind over the body? *The Times* finds it absurd that St Kunigund, the Queen, stands with one bare foot on a red-hot ploughshare and yet looks 'as if she were bestowing an honour on a favourite'. But is that really so absurd? Is it not the triumph of the martyr to remain untouched by physical pain and master of himself? Was it not one of the triumphs of the innocent sufferers in our own days of the concentration camp to raise their heads, look down on their tormentors and say: 'You cannot touch me.' That is my interpretation of the expression of St Kunigund. It may not be your or my idea of religious art. You and I would perhaps rather stick to Rembrandt and his interpretation of Christ and the Holy Family but it was the eighteenth-century line of arguing — as you can see in the saints of Tiepolo as well.

Tiepolo is indeed the only artist with whom Günther can be compared. There was certainly no painter in Germany to touch the heights of Tiepolo's art. The exhibition shows that. On the other hand there is not, as far as I can see, any sculptor in Italy in the eighteenth century as exquisite and as refined as Günther. Let us annoy *The Times* once more and for a moment look at the *Kunigund* and the *Pietà* from Nenningen and the wonderful *Annunciation* from Weyarn purely as art and enjoy the serpentine movement of the angel in the *Annunciation*, the flame-like aplomb of the Queen and the strained screw-turn of the body of Christ to the Pietà.

I have said screw-turn and flame-like and serpentine and that kind of composition is indeed the hall-mark of the Rococo. Rococo compositions move upwards in a slender undulation and move into space and through space as well. You can look at a Watteau or a Tiepolo or a Boucher and you will discover it. You will discover it everywhere in this exhibition and, what is more, you can discover it in the churches themselves for which these pieces of sculpture and these paintings were done. The way in which their ingenious and inspired designers interlock ovals or circles, throw out curved balconies here and retreat into niches and recesses there, it all belongs to this contrapuntal elegance. Ignaz Günther's draperies for the same reason ought to be followed, just for once, in one figure in every detail. Their knife-edge creases, the meetings and departures of thin folds, follow with uncanny mastery that principle.

But just because Günther possesses such a subtle mastery of his art, the most remarkable and really inexplicable thing about him is that, whereas Tiepolo filled the palaces with his works and travelled from Venice to Germany and to Spain, Günther was evidently a little man, a peaceful worker in his workshop in Munich much like a Gothic hand-carver of 250 years before. It is true Günther had travelled at the end of his apprenticeship and been to Salzburg as well as Mannheim when he was about twenty years old and it is true that he had for a short time attended the Academy at Vienna a little later – that is, that he had experienced some of the new academic type of training, training in a socially superior, no longer mediaeval way. It is finally true too that he received the title Sculptor to the Bohemian Court in 1754. But that title did not mean more in his case than that he was exempted from certain guild restrictions just as distinguished craftsmen had been in Germany and in other countries already in the later Middle Ages. Günther certainly was not a courtier and one of the most fascinating piquancies of his art is the contrast between the round, chubby faces of his figures on the one hand, faces which are certainly characteristic of the people in Bavaria, and on the other hand expressions of extreme superiority, sometimes almost arrogant and at other times almost supercilious. *The Guardian Angel* with the little boy from the Bürgersaal at Munich shows that particular aspect to perfection, a work both sophisticated and yet popular, almost in a Hofbräu way. It was indeed used for a lay congregation or fraternity of artisans and merchants. That peculiar combination of folk qualities with courtly practices you would not find in Tiepolo, who was at home in the great world, nor, for instance, in a sculptor such as Willem de Groff, whose delicious silver statue of the kneeling prince Max Joseph is also at the exhibition. De Groff came from Antwerp (as did Rysbrack and Scheemakers) and had studied at Paris (as Roubiliac had). The statue shows the child in accomplished court dress kneeling and performing an elegant gesture of devotion. Now, to harp on the same thing again, if you don't like life-size votive statues of silver in churches, well, then you can say goodbye to the Middle Ages as well, the time when Richard Beauchamp Earl of Warwick bequeathed to the shrines of St Thomas à Becket at St Albans, St John of Bridlington and St Winifred an image of himself in gold.

No – I always have a suspicion that those who insist so much on the superiority of art of the Middle Ages over that of the Baroque forget that mediaeval sculpture was as fully painted as is much in the Rococo exhibition and certainly no more sparing of silver and gold. The colours of course differ. The Middle Ages with their younger, more naive senses and minds, liked blue and red and grass green where the Rococo prefers white and heliotrope and a pale silvery green.

It is a curious thing in the exhibition to see side by side coloured and uncoloured sculpture. We are so used to appreciating sculpture in the monochrome and so ready to call coloured sculpture vulgar and sensational. Yet here the absence of colour certainly makes the lime-wood look naked. That is all the more remarkable because the coloured figures are deprived of their natural equally colourful setting and ought, one would think, to suffer from that.

Here, in my opinion, lies the greatest triumph of the exhibition. Baroque art – that is, its outstanding quality – is art of the ensemble, more so than any art had been before. Architecture, decoration, sculpture and painting all combine to achieve that glorious unison which the Italian and German church of the seventeenth and eighteenth centuries is. You would think that in tearing out of this ensemble some individual statues, you would ruin the effect completely. But you can see at the Victoria and Albert Museum that the small-scale models and also the larger statues turn out to be, by their own ingeniousness or composition and mastery of craftsmanship, quite capable of looking after themselves. So, if you are not planning a very specialised journey through small villages and remote monasteries of Bavaria, you had better go and look at this exhibition carefully now. It offers an opportunity which will not and, as far as I can see, cannot be repeated.

1   Pevsner was discussing an exhibition of Bavarian Rococo at the Victoria and Albert Museum.

The geography of art

REITH LECTURE (I)

Third Programme
SUNDAY 16 OCTOBER 1955
Producer: Donald Boyd

I belong to the happy few who can make a living out of studying the history of art and out of communicating the results of their studies to others. The history of art is not a universally accepted academic subject in this country as it is on the Continent and in America, though its acceptance is clearly growing. Now why should one study art history? There are of course two questions contained in this one: Why should one take an interest in art? And why should one take an interest in history? I suggest that an understanding and appreciation of the work of the artist adds to the truly valuable pleasures and thereby enhances one's life. That poetry or music can do that, no one denies. The revelations which can reach us through the eye are less familiar.

Now you may go to any great museum and just let work of art after work of art speak to you, as it comes. But most intelligent visitors after a time find that they need history to understand and even to appreciate art. They see differences between, say, one statue and another which are not merely personal but must be the result of a distance of several centuries between the two. The historian of art, after having looked at a statue or a picture or a chair purely for its own sake then asks himself what it can tell us of the age that made it. That also can be a thrilling enterprise, for the layman as well. It can be applied also to literature, music, philosophy and even science. So past periods come to life with the various expressions of their ideals and prejudices and in the end we shall understand our own age better by comparing and contrasting it with the past.

Art historians differ of course in their personal preferences. The artist tends to look at the individual work for its aesthetic character and its craftsmanship regardless of its historical setting; the connoisseur for its handwriting and its genuineness regardless of its historical setting. The biographer is interested ultimately not in the individual work but in the man behind it. His question is: How did this unique individual express himself by means of his art? The historian need not underestimate the individual but he tends to neglect the individual. He is more fascinated by what men and works of one age have in common and he watches how one age develops into another. He says that the spirits of ages as he watches them are greater than the individual. He is the generaliser – and I may just as well make it clear right now that I am one of them.

But these lectures are not going to deal with the development of style from period to period – that is, the history of art – but with a different type of generalisation, a type you might call the geography of art. Instead of asking what all works of art (and of course architecture) have in common because they belong to one period, in whatever country within one civilisation, I am going to ask here what all works of art (and of course architecture) of one *people* have in common, at whatever time they may have been made. That means that my subject is really national character as it is expressed in terms of art.

As soon as one poses this question, there will be two objections. First: is it desirable to stress a national point of view so much in appreciating works of art and architecture? Second: is there such a thing as a fixed or almost-fixed national character? Neither of these questions is confined to art. I would, needless to say, answer 'Yes' to both.

Those who are against stressing nationality in art argue that in an age of such rapid communications as ours keeping everyone all the time in touch with all other parts of the world, everything ought to be avoided that glorifies obsolete national divisions. It is bad enough that nationalism has been boosted so much in the last twenty years and that new small national states have appeared and are appearing on the map left and right. Therefore any approach to art or literature is better than the nationalistic. To that I would answer that geography of art is not really nationalism in action, although some very intelligent and sensitive art historians have unquestionably made it appear so. The result of what I am going to spread out before you is not simply: This is English and don't you do anything else. It will on the contrary be, I hope, so complex a tissue of seemingly opposed forms and principles that in the end you ought to emerge with a juster understanding of the art of other peoples and a widened instead of a narrowed sense of this country's national possibilities.

Now the second question – which is, as you will remember, whether there is such a thing as a national character consistent over centuries. Let me give a preliminary answer which is very simple. You know *Romeo and Juliet*? You know the line about the nightingale and not the lark? 'It was the nightingale and not the lark'. Well, here it is in Italian: '*È l'usignol, no è la lodola*'. And here in German: '*Es is die Nachtigall und nicht die Lerche*'. Are these not three national characters speaking, each at once recognisable? Or another example. Do you know what *costoletta* is in English? A 'chop'. So I suggest that as long as one nation says mutton chop and another *costoletta di montone* there will be national characters. *Costoletta di montone* – it sounds like a whole line of poetry in English. And if you retort: Let us therefore have Esperanto, my answer would be: At the end of this series of lectures you will, I hope, be ready to admit that that would deprive us of an infinite variety of valuable things. What of course it will be my job to prove to you is that English art bears out the existence of national qualities represented in the syllable 'chop'. We shall see whether that can be done.

I'd rather at this stage give you a preview of another of the basic and permanent premises of national character: climate. That is one of these premises recognised to a certain extend already by Hippocrates and certainly by Jean Bodin in 1566. The Abbé du Bos in 1719 was the first to apply it to art. Winckelmann much more inspiredly built on it his evocation of the spirit of ancient Greek art. From him the notion went to the Romantics, especially Schlegel, and so into the nineteenth century. And the argument is convincing enough. Art will develop differently in the mists and under clear blue skies, in a moderate or in a hot climate. So perhaps the fact that Turner and Constable are English has something to do with our climate.

Climate may also explain English sympathy with the atmospheric art of the seaboard republic of Venice. English poetry ever since *The Wanderer* and *The Seafarer* has been aware of the sea around the island and perhaps it follows from this that hearts of oak are not only the ships but also the mighty and ingenious roofs of the churches. People from the Continent find it difficult to understand that the English never accepted stone vaulting as the one and only dignified thing for a church of any pretension. A timber vault in imitation of stone such as you have at York Minster in the transept and in the chancel at St Albans seems ignominious to a Frenchman. But then he has nothing like the double hammerbeam roofs of East Anglia. However, let me quickly add a first warning. Problems of national character in art are not as primitive as that. You would think that climate and language are among the most permanent factors that can be, but not even they are permanent. I have just finished reading the proofs of a book by Francesca Wilson.[1] It is called *Strange Island* and it is an anthology of foreigners' impressions of England from Froissart to Maurois. That the 'gloomy fogs', the 'foul smoke ... with which the city is covered eighteen hours of the twenty-four' appear prominently in such an anthology goes without saying. What is remarkable is that they don't come into the book at all before the middle of the eighteenth century. A moist climate may be natural but fog is moisture plus soot and so what one complains of as climate is the combination of climate with such things as the exploitation of coal, a development of industry that calls for vast masses of coal and in the house a system of heating evolved for wood fires and not yet universally adjusted to the use of coal. Perhaps this staunch conservatism in the teeth of the greatest discomforts is English? Perhaps the early and ruthless development of mining and industry is English? We shall see, we shall see.

Anyway, what I wanted to show at this stage is that even climatic conditions are not entirely permanent in the way they affect us. Nor is language really permanent. Not only because Anglo-Saxon is not English and because the Norman court and nobility spoke French and because the literary language of prose was Latin. The Royal Proclamation of the Provisions of Oxford in 1258 is the first major document in English and only in the fourteenth century did English become the accepted official language of England. Yet even Chaucer's English needs the translator. And has it any of the characteristics demonstrated in my comparison of chop and *costoletta*? Chop is undoubtedly typical of today's English. One of Miss Wilson's foreigners, Conte Pecchio, says: 'The great quantity of monosyllables looks like a kind of shorthand.' Here is one example which I heard the other day. It was an anxious question about an unreliable character at an important meeting. 'Will he rat?' Now that, translated, say, into Dr Johnson's English, would be: 'Do you consider it probable that he will desert our cause at this perilous stage?' So that is eighteenth-versus twentieth-century English. And similarly, the English preference for short sentences (as against the long sentences of German or Italian writers) is not permanent. Look at the great seventeenth-century divines like Jeremy Taylor and you will agree.

So one ought to be careful not to take today's character as it has been analysed and lampooned so gracefully by the Czech Čapek and the Dutchman Professor Renier and expect always to find it in the past. For today the qualities are obvious and I will here rattle off only a few. Personal liberty, freedom of expression and wisdom in compromises, the two-party system not shaken by communism or fascism, the democratic system of negotiating in Parliament as well as on boards and committees, the distrust of the sweeping statement (such as mine are) and of the demagogue. Then the eminently civilised faith in honesty and fair play, the patient queuing, the wisdom in letting go of Ireland, of India, of Egypt, a strictly upheld inefficiency in the little business-things of every day such as the workman's job in the house, windows that will never close and heating that will never heat, a certain comfortable wastefulness and sense of a good life and the demonstrative conservatism of the wig in court, the gown in school and university, the obsolete-looking shop-window in St James's Street, the Steward of the Chiltern Hundreds, the Keeper of the Queen's Swans, the Portcullis Poursuivant, the City Companies, and £-s-d and yards and acres and Fahrenheit. All those things seem as eternal as the rock of Gibraltar.

Are they? I'll take two examples from Miss Wilson's book. Here is Erasmus, the great humanist, writing from Cambridge in 1517. 'The rooms are generally so constructed that no draught can be sent through them.' And here is Alexander Herzen, the Russian émigré politician and philosopher who lived in London from 1852 to 1864: 'Nowhere is there a crowd so dense, so terrifying, as in London, yet it never in any circumstances knows how to queue.'

So much for the permanence of national characteristics. And don't say that such little things as queuing and ventilation don't matter compared with the great qualities of a nation's character. For not only has Sterne in his *Sentimental Journey* said very rightly that one 'can see the precise and distinguishing marks of national characters more in these nonsensical minutiae than in the most important matters of state' but the important matters of state have also changed. Where has the Elizabethan privateer-cum-poet gone, the man who takes big risks and knows few scruples and who writes accomplished sonnets at the same time? He was a Renaissance type. And can't one expect him in the twentieth century? Very well – that is just the point I want to make. There is a spirit of an age and there is national character and the two can act in accordance and they can interfere with one another until one seems to black out the other completely. Do our most highly appreciated actors play Shakespeare correctly, the Elizabethan Shakespeare? What Voltaire calls 'these monstrous farces which one calls tragedies', written by 'a genius full of force, of nature and sublimity, without a spark of good taste'? You have to go to Donald Wolfit to see that side, the exuberance, the boisterous virility of the Elizabethan Shakespeare – that is, go to an actor who was not trained in an academy but in the rough-and-tumble of music hall and troupes of strolling players as they still existed until a few decades ago.

Strolling Players is the title of a Hogarth picture of which I shall talk next week and as Shakespeare's England, so Hogarth's England has gone. And with the cock-fighting and the roaring debauchery of Hogarth's England, the England of Chippendale has gone – that is, the England of high, exacting craftsmanship. In Miss Wilson's book we see that, according to César de Saussure about 1725, the English craftsmen 'work to perfection' and 'the perfection of craftwork' is still praised by Grosley in 1765. But gone also is the world replacing that of Chippendale, the world of the pioneers of English industry, of the great iron masters and engineers and inventors, of Darby and Wilkinson, of Boulton and Watt, of Telford and Stephenson. England was leading in the world then: it was the America of the day. Wilkinson went to advise at Le Creusot and in Prussia, Telford built the Göta Canal in Sweden, Aron Manby, Cockerill and others had factories in France and Belgium, the first railway engines in Germany were English.

That does not sound like English conservatism, does it? So where are we with our search for the permanent national qualities? Actually not in quite as desperate a position as it may seem. The mistake one tends to make is to expect national qualities to show up too universally and to be too simple. In all that I am going to demonstrate to you in this series of lectures, you must remember that national character does not only gradually change but is also not at all moments and in all situations equally distinct. The spirit of a moment may reinforce national character or repel it. Moreover, as we are dealing with the visual arts, the national character of one nation may be more likely to seek expression in that particular field than the national character of another nation and the question as to how far England is a visual nation or not, or has been a visual nation and is no longer, will have to engage our attention. Then, in addition to all that, you must remember that the visual arts, even in the most artistic nation, cannot reflect everything. There may be whole important traits to which we can find no equivalent in visual terms. That must make any picture of national character, in terms of art and architecture alone, one-sided.

There is, however, one way in which one can avoid at least the worst one-sidedness. One should never try to arrive at the simple statement: The English are x and not y, the Germans are y and not x. Such statements are bound to be useless. Instead I am going to try to pursue geography of art here in terms of polarities – in pairs of apparently contradictory qualities. English art is at one and the same moment Constable and Turner, it is the formal house and the informal picturesque garden surrounding it. Or if I may now take as my examples the apparent contrast between two consecutive periods, English art is the Decorated and the Perpendicular style in architecture, it is Vanbrugh and Lord Burlington, Hogarth and Reynolds. What we shall have to do is to analyse for each of them individually what is English in them and then see how far the results really contradict each other. For instances, Decorated is the flowing line, Perpendicular is the straight line, but both are line and not body. Constable's aim is truth to Nature, Turner's world is a phantasmagoria, but both are concerned with an atmospheric view of the world, not with the firm physical objects in it – that is, again, not with bodies. I know that in this, Constable and Turner also represent a European and not merely an English development, but their specifically unsculptural, unplastic, cloudy or steamy treatment is English all the same. You'll hear a good deal more about that as the weeks go on.

And besides, now that I have said so much, to show what is not permanent in the national characteristics of England, may I indulge in a few examples of how surprisingly much after all does appear to be permanent. Paul Hentzner already, the German tourist who came to England in 1598, says the English are 'impatient of anything like slavery'. Misson in about 1690 says they 'eat a huge piece of roast beef on Sunday ... and the rest cold the other days of the week'. Their idea of vegetables, says Karl Philip Moritz in 1782, is 'a few cabbage leaves boiled in plain water'. The English don't work too much, says Sorbière in 1653; they believe that 'true living consists in knowing how to live at ease'. And one more example. Antonio Trevisan, Venetian ambassador to Henry VII in 1497, remarks that the English say 'whenever they see a handsome foreigner: he looks like an Englishman'. Saussure, who was a very shrewd observer, says the same: 'I don't think there is a people more prejudiced in its own favour than the British.' And go to Ogden Nash and you'll find this:

> Let us pause to consider the English
> Who when they pause to consider themselves they get all reticently
>   thrilled and tinglish,
> Because every Englishman is convinced on one thing, viz:
> That to be an Englishman is to belong to the most exclusive club
>   there is.

There seems to be pretty well unanimity here. Yet in this particular case, I am not at all sure myself whether they are right, all of them. But then I am never a hundred per cent sure either how far I am not a foreigner and how far I am. Now that brings me to a few personal remarks which I think I ought to add in conclusion. Why should I give this particular series of lectures to you? Why should I, with a never-fully-conquered foreign intonation, I who am not too certain of the difference between a centre forward and a leg volley, stand here to talk to you about the Englishness of English art? My defence is that in order to see clearly what's what in national character, it is perhaps a good thing at one stage to have come in from outside and then to have settled down to become part of it. It is a curious experience, I can assure you, but one worth undergoing. In my own field of research, I came from the German Baroque of Saxony at its most exuberant and had then done some years' work on Italian Baroque painting before – in 1930 – I first visited England. It was a discovery. Very few people on the Continent knew about English art then or had studied it. I was able to travel quite a lot and started teaching history of English art. It was then that I began collecting material on this problem of Englishness. The material grew slowly at first and much faster when I left Germany and settled in London. By 1941 or 1942, for a course of lectures at Birkbeck College, the staff of which I then joined and to which I still happily belong, all this collected material had to take some shape. Immediately after the war, I went back to it and this time with a view to making a book of it. It was then that I came across the only existing book on the subject, a very remarkable book by the Viennese art historian Professor Dagobert Frey. It is called (I am translating the title) *The English Character as Reflected in English Art* and was published in the middle of the war, in 1942. Yet it is absolutely free or any hostile remarks, let alone any Nazi bias – a completely objective and indeed appreciative book, written with great acumen, sensitivity and a remarkably wide knowledge. And it confirmed often to an amazing and almost embarrassing degree my views, the criteria I had worked out, even the examples I had chosen to illustrate them, though Professor Frey runs through the manifestations of the English character in English art chronologically, from epoch to epoch, whereas I shall here take the liberty of jumping about freely in time.

I shall in every one of these lectures start from a well-known figure, fairly close to us in date, analyse a work or two of his and then see how their distinguishing qualities recur in the most unexpected periods or contexts. My next point of departure will be Hogarth, after that Reynolds, then the architects of the Perpendicular style, then Blake, and finally Constable.

---

1   Francesca Wilson was Pevsner's landlady in Edgbaston, Birmingham when he first moved to England.

Hogarth and observed life

REITH LECTURE (2)

Third Programme
SUNDAY 23 OCTOBER 1955
Producer: Donald Boyd

It is almost impossible to talk about art unless we can show illustrations at the same time. Hogarth is to some extent an exception to this rule. One can present many of the salient points about him just by describing a few of his pictures. That is due to one particular trait in his art and that particular trait contributes more than anything else to his outstanding Englishness.

Of the Englishness of Hogarth there can be no doubt. Time and again he has gone out of his way to parade it. He went abroad only once – to France, and a fellow traveller and fellow artist says that 'wherever he went, he was sure to be dissatisfied with all he saw'. He 'was often clamorously rude' in the streets. He signed a letter to the press 'Britophil' and complained in it of 'foreign interlopers' and he dissuaded young artists from travelling to Italy because it would 'seduce the student from Nature'.

Now what did Hogarth call Nature? He is most famous for his series of paintings and engravings such as the *Marriage à la Mode* or the *Four Stages of Cruelty*. But he began as a painter of what are called conversation-pieces, small groups of people joined together in conversation or some other action. Among his early paintings there is also one of a parliamentary commission sitting in judgement over a jailer who had ill-treated prisoners in Newgate Prison. That is a kind of pictorial newspaper report – and a very early case of that sort of topical illustration in paint. But Hogarth saw that he could not make enough money out of conversation pieces without employing assistants and thereby reducing the quality of his work. So he tried his hand at – I am quoting him – 'what the puffers in books call the great style of History Painting'. But he did not succeed in 'this grand business' and so – I am going on quoting – 'I turned my mind to a novel trade, the painting and engraving modern moral subjects, a field not broken up in any country or any age'. Such subjects, he wrote, would 'both entertain and improve the mind' and 'bid fair to be of the greatest public utility'. And so, at the age of thirty-six, he came out with *The Harlot's Progress*, soon to be followed by *The Rake's Progress* and then all the other series – *The Four Stages of Cruelty*, *Beer Street* and *Gin Lane*, *The Election Entertainment* and so on, and also with amusing and improving single paintings and prints such as *The Roast-Beef of Old England*, *Credulity, Superstition and Fanaticism*, the *Strolling Players in a Barn* and so on.

Now this decision of Hogarth has several aspects of special interest to us. One is the almost complete absence in all English art of that so-called Grand Manner, the large, monumental, rhetorical painting of religious or mythological subjects which plays so predominant a part in the art of the Baroque – that is, the seventeenth and early eighteenth centuries in Italy or France or Southern Germany. As for the Baroque style in religious art, Hogarth knew the reason for its absence in England very well. He says: 'Religion, the great promoter of this style, rejected it in England' – that is, England is a Protestant country and there was no demand for much painting in churches. But the character of the English was against it too. That should not surprise you, for understatement or reticence or whatever you choose to call it is nowadays universally regarded as typically English. But there is yet more to it. The distrust of the Grand Manner is based on common sense, on reason. Lord Shaftesbury, the great philosopher who died when Hogarth was sixteen, had written: 'You cannot successfully evoke, if you don't believe.' And Hogarth's father-in-law Sir James Thornhill, by far the most Baroque and grandest of native English painters, in an extremely interesting drawing published some years ago by Professor Wind has argued most reasonably the case for and against the Grand Manner and a truthful representation of what actually happened.

The event he was going to paint is the landing of George I in England in 1714. For reasons we don't know, he tried to represent it truthfully as it happened. That, it seems, is what he wanted to do or was asked to do. However, he annotated his sketch with the artistic objections to such truthfulness: 'First of all,' he starts 'it was night.' So that he could not keep to anyway. And then people would have to appear who were by that time in disgrace, the dress the King wore was 'not graceful or enough worthy of him' and so on. But in the end,

Thornhill reached a decision in favour of a moderate realism and not the Grand Manner.

His son-in-law, Hogarth, would probably not have hesitated to banish the Britannias, the Father-Thameses, the Tyrannic-Powers-trampled-under and so on – all stock allegories of Thornhill himself and his contemporaries. Hogarth agreed with Dr Johnson who once said: 'I had rather see the portrait of a dog I know than all the allegories you can show me.' To me this is as irritating as most things the old bully said but I'm afraid it is crushingly English. Fuseli, the brilliant, somewhat sensational, Swiss painter who lived in England from his twenty-third year to his death and knew Reynolds as well as Blake, said: There is 'little hope of Poetical painting finding encouragement in England. The People are not prepared for it. Portrait with them is everything. Their taste and feelings all go to realities.' So Hogarth painted his Newgate newspaper report with the Portrait of Bembridge the jailer looking, as Horace Walpole wrote, as if Salvator Rosa had painted Iago, and so he took his decision and started his series of 'modern moral subjects' 'to improve his mind'. Of course I know that such a decision is very much what the Age of Enlightenment might have led to in any country yet I suggest that there is something specifically English again in the cool self-consciousness of the decision. 'I determined to have a brush at it,' he writes. That is not the way a German or an Italian artist would express himself. This oddly detached attitude to his own creation, this seeming lack of compulsion, is English – and of that aspect I'll talk to you at greater length next week.

Today what matters is what he painted and how he painted it. Take just one single painting and one episode from one series. First, the painting called *Strolling Players in a Barn* which was published as an engraving in 1738. The action seems at first complete chaos. The barn is crowded with people and the most heterogeneous things. Jupiter and Cupid, both fully dressed up, are taking down a pair of stockings hanging from a washing line. Juno is rehearsing her part while the Goddess of Night is mending her stocking. A woman impersonating Jupiter's eagle is feeding a baby with gruel; the saucepan stands on a royal crown. And in the middle stands Chaste Diana, also rehearsing.

She has only a chemise on and allows you to see her very attractively rounded bosom and her plump thighs.

Now we turn to the *Marriage à la Mode*. The series is in the National Gallery. In No. 1, the marriage contract between the son of the earl and the daughter of the city merchant is signed. The two fathers are busy, one with his family tree, the other with financial documents. The young people do not care for one another. The viscount is looking away from his fiancée and taking snuff; the girl is engrossed in a conversation with the young and ardent lawyer Councillor Silvertongue. In the foreground a dog and a bitch are tied together by an iron chain and don't seem to enjoy it. Scene 2 is the morning after a party at the house of the young couple. The viscount had not been present. He has come back from gaming and whoring: you see him sitting in a chair, exhausted and also depressed by his losses. A cap and ribbon hang out of his pocket taken in the night from his female companion. Her ladyship is *en déshabillé*, also in a chair, stretching idly. Playing cards and musical instruments lie on the floor. In the adjoining dining room, a servant shuffles about respectlessly yawning and the old steward is leaving with his ledger and a packet of unpaid bills in his hand, looking desperately worried.

And so the story goes on. Even the pictures on the walls take part. In the scene of the *Levée*, a picture of Ganymede appears above the Italian castrato singer, Correggio's *Jupiter embracing Io* above the group of the viscountess attended by Councillor Silvertongue. In front of this group incidentally, a black servant boy holds grinningly a statuette of Actaeon – that is, a man with horns on his head.

Here again, from my particular point of view, I have to make several comments. Hogarth was a brilliant painter, one of the naturally most highly endowed painters of eighteenth-century England. The technique in which he tells his stories is sumptuous fluidity, unhesitating and exuberant. But to him the story mattered more than the art. The purpose of painting is not painting but the telling of stories with all the incidents which an observant eye can discover any day. They are not embellished. On the contrary – see the *Strolling Players* – Hogarth has a mischievous pleasure in debunking. And he is never without an eye on the moral to be culled from the stories. In *Beer Street*, 'all is joyous and thriving'; in *Gin Lane* you see the horrors of drunkenness – a woman, her legs covered with ulcers, dropping in her stupor her baby who crashes to its death in the area in front of the gin-shop. 'Drunk for a penny, dead drunk for twopence.' In *The Four Stages of Cruelty* you have Tom Nero as a little boy torturing animals and at the end murdering a girl and being himself dissected. Well – of these engravings, Hogarth wrote: 'If they have in some degree checked the progress of cruelty, I am more proud of having been the author, than I should be of having painted Raphael's cartoons.'

A stupid statement, although Hogarth's sincerity in his efforts to help the suffering is beyond doubt, whether they are infants or the prisoners in the indescribable jails and so on. What it does establish once again is that to Hogarth, art is a medium for preaching and that the most effective sermon is the recounting of what the observant eye sees around. Both are English attitudes. The first is naturally entirely post-mediaeval, for in the Middle Ages most art was there to preach anyway; the second is eternally English. So my further examples of preaching by means of painting will be from the centuries after Hogarth, my examples of the English as observers also from the centuries before him. As regards the English tendency to preach and to reform by art, I need only remind you of the flourishing of political caricature in England in Gillray's day – that is, about 1800 – quite some time before Daumier in France. Caricature of course is also connected with English liberty, but that aspect will come our way later in these lectures. Regarding preaching, I can also remind you of the pre-Raphaelites, of Millais's *Accepted* or his *Retribution*, of Holman Hunt's *The Awakened Conscience*, or of Ford Madox Brown's picture *Work* with the honest navvies, the rich girl distributing edifying pamphlets, the children in rags, advertisements of the Working Men's College and in the foreground Carlyle and F.D. Maurice out for a walk. Or might I mention Ruskin's theory that: 'The art of any country is an exact exponent of its ethical life' and that painters cannot be great, if 'they are not (in the broad human and ethical sense) Good'.

But the other aspect of Hogarth's art, the vivid rendering of observed life, is even more universally English. You are first of all no doubt aware of the fact that nearly all the greatest painting of the British school is either portrait or landscape, Constable and Turner, and the watercolourists from Cozens to Cotman, Gainsborough and Reynolds and Romney and Raeburn and so on. You are also aware of Frith's *Derby Day* and *Paddington Station* and *Ramsgate Sands* and perhaps even of such pictures as *An Experiment with an Air Pump* painted by Joseph Wright of Derby in 1768.

But it is not only in the eighteenth and nineteenth centuries that we find the English as the keenest observers. We can go back to the Middle Ages and find the same qualities in the English art there.

You have probably at some time or other been surprised by a strange habit of the illuminators of manuscripts for church use in the late Middle Ages. They may put Jesus Christ into the middle of the page but the margins are covered with birds and beasts and little scenes from everyday life and grotesque caricatures. The Middle Ages called them babwyneries – that is, babooneries or monkey-business. They are beloved by the artists of all countries and to tolerate them is undeniably mediaeval rather than English – the naivety which allows the immediate neighbourhood of tragedy and laughter. But if you try to trace the baboonery to its source, you will find that it originated in England. Here it appears already at the height of Gothic nobility, in the middle of the thirteenth century, and by 1300 it had become a universal English fashion – just at the moment when the religious representations on the same pages had become more exquisite, sophisticated and often most exacting in their emotional intensity. But don't forget the doctrine of polarities of which I spoke last time. So that aspect of English art will come into the open later. As regards the marginal grotesques, you find them in the Bible of William of Devon at the British Museum, written as early as about 1250, and in the Psalter of Alfonzo of 1284, and then in the more famous Ormesby and Gorleston Psalters. The margins of the immensely copiously illustrated Queen Mary's Psalter show you a ploughman and wrestlers, a man beating down acorns for his pigs, a windmill, hounds chasing hares and a mock funeral conducted by rabbits – with no more respect and decorum than Hogarth.

And once you have spotted this English keenness on the everyday world observed, you will notice it also in the misericords or pity-seats of choir stalls carved from the thirteenth to the sixteenth century and in the delightful little scene on the capitals or bosses of thirteenth-century cathedrals at Wells, at Lincoln and so on; or go yet further back to about 1140 and you come to such details of English Norman sculpture as the grave-diggers on one of the two big reliefs at Chichester Cathedral which once belonged to a chancel screen. And finally, back another sixty years, and you reach the Bayeux Tapestry, now recognised as an English work of about 1080. Here the story itself is told with an amazing wealth of incident – soldiers wading in the water, their surcoats tucked up high, a sailor looking out from the top of a mast, the roast served on long spits – and on top and bottom margins of the long strip which tells the story, you find a ploughman again and what seems to be an act of indecent assault and a huntsman blowing his horn. No Continental country, I assure you, has anything like these riches of observed life in mediaeval art.

Incidentally, a friend of mine, a German scholar, has just after nearly twenty years of research started publishing a five-volume collection of the evidence on English mediaeval art as found in chronicles and so on, and he tells me this (I am reading from his letter): The English sources, especially in the twelfth century as against those of other countries, 'are characterised by a far more vivid description with occasional criticism and even an occasional joke'. He stresses specially Abbot Ingulf's description of the Fire at Croyland Abbey in 1109, Gervase's famous story of the fire and rebuilding at Canterbury Cathedral in the 1170s and Jocelyn de Brakelonde's description of monastic life at Bury St Edmunds.

And if I might now widen our field for a moment, any history of philosophy will show you the firm and lasting concern of the English with realities and facts rather than ideals and systems. That starts with Roger Bacon right back in the thirteenth century who wrote that nothing can be sufficiently known without experience. It goes on to Francis Bacon in the Elizabethan Age whom Voltaire called the father of experimental philosophy. He wrote this: 'Those who determine not to conjecture and guess but to find out and know must consult only things themselves.' Only things themselves. And so it goes on to the utilitarian philosophers of the nineteenth century.

However I must not give way to the temptation of talking about Englishness in other fields than art. But as regards art, one thing I want to stress which you may already have gathered: art to me emphatically includes architecture. Any separation of the two as it is usual in England seems to me dangerous nonsense. Now you may think that the particular aspect of Englishness which we are dealing with today would not be applicable to architecture. But it is.

For instance, England was the first country to develop an architecture of industry and engineering. That is of course connected with the unparalleled precocity of the Industrial Revolution in England and the reasons for this are outside art and certainly outside my subject today. But the fact remains that the architecture of the spinning mill – that most matter-of-fact, most utilitarian, most workaday architecture – is originally English and so is the architecture of the iron bridge and the iron-and-glass architecture of the Crystal Palace. In both, I think, the practical direct approach of the Englishman, the unconcern with the Grand Manner, can be detected.

Another architectural aspect is subtler. England was the first country in the eighteenth century to do consistently what the nineteenth century did everywhere – namely, to break the unity of interior and exterior and wrap buildings up in clothes not made for them but for buildings of other ages and purposes. Your country house might be Grecian or Gothic, a summer house in a garden even Chinese or Moorish. After 1830 a club would be like the palace of a princely merchant in Italy, a grammar school would be Gothic and so on. Now I know full well that this historicism, as we call it, is universal in the nineteenth century. Yet England was the pioneer country – for better or worse – and in England it seems to me that there was a national disposition in favour of that kind of thing because the costume tells a story; it is an evocative, not a strictly aesthetic, quality. The architect, like Hogarth as a painter, is not driven to express himself in one style and one style only (his own or that of his age); he chooses a style for what you might call literary reasons, just as the landscape gardener – and the landscape garden is again an English invention – places and designs his seats and temples and urns on pedestals to create certain moods.

Well – I suppose it is time now to sum up. Making England responsible for the fancy-dress ball of architecture in the Victorian Age is not complimentary to the aesthetic genius of the nation. Nor is it perhaps complimentary to stress the concern of the English with narrative. But you must not forget two things. First, that the discovery of reality in the Middle Ages was a great and constructive effort, even if England – as so often – in the end refused to go the whole hog and left the final achievement of realism to painters like Jan van Eyck.

And secondly painting, because it tells a contemporary story, need not be bad painting. Why should it be worse than painting telling about Venus or Neptune or St Jerome? This brings me back finally to Hogarth. Hogarth was in fact a born painter. His stories are dashed off with vehemence and his paint is creamy and runs in juicy curves and scrolls and whirlpools. This sensuousness of handling and this brio and also Hogarth's delight in the feminine body half-exposed and in equivocal situations – all this was something quite new in English art. On the Continent, this free and open technique and exuberant sensuality had been created by Titian 200 years earlier and developed by Rubens and many of the great and small painters of the Baroque. Hogarth in his succulent paint and also in the robust directness of his portraits represents this international Baroque in England. When we come to mediaeval architecture in England, you will see that the style of the fifteenth century had been robust too but it was hard and angular; and you'll also see that the architectural style of about 1300 had been curvy and scrolly too but it was not expansive – it was thin and almost disembodied.

So in this particular respect, Hogarth represents first of all of course himself, his personal style and genius, but secondly he represents the spirit of the age interfering with his Englishness. These cases do happen. You see the same interaction of International Baroque and Englishness in the two greatest architects of England during the years when Hogarth painted: Vanbrugh and Hawksmoor. Both strike one at first as more Baroque than English yet there is Englishness in them too. In their Baroque massing both remain angular and in their motifs they remain Classical – and angularity and classicity, as we shall see later, are English. Besides, Vanbrugh at least was not of English descent. His family was Flemish. However, Hawksmoor's remains without a doubt a case like Hogarth's: Continental qualities modifying English.

And as for Hogarth, the spirit of the age appears in yet another interesting way in his work. In 1753, he brought out a book, a book on the theory of art. He called it *The Analysis of Beauty* and its essence was the praise of what he calls 'the line of beauty' – a shallow, elegant, undulating double curve. Now the fondness for these double curves is actually (and that, Hogarth could not know at all) a profound English tradition, one that runs from the style of 1300 to Blake and beyond. But the double curve is also an international principle of the Late Baroque and Rococo and you will find it without any effort in individual figures and even whole compositions of Watteau in France, of Tiepolo in Venice, of Ignaz Günther, the greatest German sculptor of the century, of Roubiliac, the Frenchman who was the great sculptor of that time in England, of early Dresden china and of Rococo plasterwork on ceilings, woodwork surrounding mirrors and so on.

So here then, an English quality in Hogarth and an international quality of Hogarth's age work hand-in-hand. Hogarth's moralising is another case of such combined operations. It is English, as I have tried to show you, but it is also a general tendency of an age which we call the Age of Reason and Enlightenment.

You see at the end of this half-hour that the structure of the web of any country's art at any one moment is highly complicated. And I can only warn you that if you listen again next week, when I shall introduce Sir Joshua Reynolds into the eighteenth-century picture, you will find it yet more complicated. But then historical reality always is complicated.

★

Reynolds and detachment

REITH LECTURE (3)

Third Programme
SUNDAY 30 OCTOBER 1955
Producer: Donald Boyd

Last time I talked to you about William Hogarth. Sir Joshua Reynolds
was not a friend of Hogarth. It is true that when he was sixty-five he
was ready to grant Hogarth within his own field of 'familiar scenes
from common life' a mastery 'in which probably he will never be
equalled'. Eighteen years earlier, when Hogarth had been dead only
six years, Reynolds was less tolerant. Hogarth, he then said, expressed
'with precision the various shades of passion as they are exhibited by
vulgar minds' and those, he added, who employ their pencil only on
such 'low and confined subjects' can never 'enter into competition
with the universal presiding idea of the art'.

These passages come from *Discourses* delivered by Reynolds at the
prize-givings of the Royal Academy of which he was president.
Hogarth, only a few years before the foundation of the academy, had
expressed himself with his usual outspokenness against 'the foolish
parade' of an official academy on the French example. He was, as I
told you last week, virulently anti-foreign even to the extent of
wanting to exclude travels of students to Italy. Reynolds had been in
Rome for over two years and in his *Discourses* reiterated the necessity
of such journeys for students. According to him, they could not
develop their art without a knowledge of Classical Antiquity.
Hogarth's comment on the many books of orders, English, French
and Italian which were current among students and architects and
which contained the five orders of columns of Classical architecture
(Doric, Tuscan, Ionic, Corinthian and Composite) was his *The Five
Orders of Periwigs*, a brilliant skit published in 1761. The Royal
Academy was founded in 1768.

To feel to the full the contrast between Reynolds and Hogarth, you
need only look at two self-portraits, Hogarth's at the Tate Gallery,
Reynolds's at the Royal Academy, the one round-faced, with
sensuous lips, looking you straight in the face and accompanied by a

pug-dog licking his lip and looking very much like his master. The dog sits in front of the painted oval frame in which the portrait appears – that is the Baroque trick of a picture within a picture. Reynolds scorns such tricks. His official self-portrait shows him in an elegant pose with his glove in his hand, the body fitting nicely into the clear and noble triangular outline which Raphael and Titian had liked, and behind him on the right appears a bust of Michelangelo.

This portrait is clearly as programmatic as Hogarth's. We know Reynolds's doctrines in great detail. He gave altogether fifteen discourses and they were all printed. And whereas Hogarth's *Analysis of Beauty* was admired by a few and neglected by most – a crotchety book with touches of genius in surprising places – Reynolds's *Discourses* were international reading, owned for instance by Queen Marie Antoinette and the Empress Catherine the Great of Russia.

What did Reynolds plead for? It is on the whole a consistent theory (I am now quoting all the time). 'Study the great masters ... who have stood the test of ages' and especially 'study the works of the ancient sculptors'. Copy 'those choice parts' from them 'which have recommended the work to notice' for 'it is by being conversant with the invention of others that we learn to invent'. Don't be 'a mere copier of Nature', don't 'amuse mankind with the minute neatness of your imitations', 'endeavour to impress them by the grandeur of ... ideas'. That is what the Italians call *gusto grande* and the French *beau idéal*. Don't strive for 'dazzling elegancies' of brushwork either; form is superior to colour as idea is to ornament. The history painter is the painter of the highest order for a subject ought to be 'generally interesting'. It is his right and duty to 'deviate from vulgar and strict historical truth'. So Reynolds would not have been tempted by the reporter's attitude to the painting of important contemporary events as Thornhill had been. With such views on vulgar truth and general ideas, the portrait painter is *ipso facto* inferior to the history painter. Genre (as we have seen à *propos* Hogarth) and landscape and still-life rank even lower. The student ought to keep his 'principal attention fixed upon the higher excellencies. If you compass them, and compass nothing more, you are still in the first class ... You may be very important, but still you are an imperfect artist of the highest order.'

Well, as I said, that is a consistent theory and it is that of the Italian and even more the French seventeenth century, of Dufresnoy and *Félibien*. There is nothing specifically English in what I have so far told you. But what is eminently English about Reynolds and his *Discourses* is the far-reaching contrast between them and him – between what he preached and what he did. History painting and the Grand Manner, he told the students, is what they ought to aim at but he was a portrait painter almost exclusively and an extremely successful one. The great Roman painters, Raphael, Michelangelo, and Annibale Carracci ought to be the English painter's examples but his are the Venetian Titian and the Dutchman Rembrandt, though he blames Rembrandt for 'taking individual nature just as he finds it'.

How can one understand it? Is it hypocrisy or cant, as the French and the German would no doubt without hesitation call it? We'll go into that later. Whatever it is, Reynolds was aware of the clash between his art and his teaching. Already in 1770 he said: 'A man is not weak, though he may not be able to wield the club of Hercules; nor does a man always practise that which he esteems the best, but does that which he can do best.' I need hardly stress how much this statement contradicts his advice to the students. At the end of his life, in his last *Discourse*, he is more melancholy. He ends a long passage on the exalted perfection of Michelangelo by saying: 'I have taken another course, one more suited to my abilities, and to the taste of the times in which I live … Yet were I now to begin the world again, I would tread in the steps of that great master.'

Now what is all this if it is not hypocrisy? Compromise, that familiar English ideal? I think on the whole I would call it compromise for Reynolds's official portraits themselves are a blatant compromise. He recommended that to raise portraiture to the higher excellencies of art, the artist ought to enlarge the subject 'to a general idea', e.g. by changing 'the dress from a temporary fashion to one more permanent or by ennobling the character of a countenance' even at the expense of likeness. That is the explanation of such portraits as *Miss Morris as Hope Nursing Love*, his *Mary Mayer as Hebe*, *Mrs Crewe as Ste Geneviève* or *Lady Sarah Bunbury sacrificing to the Graces* and also of borrowing the composition of *Mrs Hartley as a Bacchante* from Michelangelo's *Doni Madonna*.

The theory does not satisfy us. We are inclined to think that an understanding of what is individual in a person if coupled with 'dazzling elegancies' of the brush is more profitable than such a general idea as Hebe. We may respect Reynolds's *Mrs Siddons as the Tragic Muse* and intellectually appreciate its subtle dependence on the sibyls of Michelangelo's paintings in the Sistine Chapel but when we look at Gainsborough's portrait we are thrilled by Mrs Siddons the actress as she must have been in life, just as we are thrilled by Hogarth's portrait of Captain Coram as he must have been in life or of the Arnolds, father and daughter, at the Fitzwilliam Museum in Cambridge, though we know nothing much of who they were.

And don't think that Reynolds's low estimate of splendour and elegance of painting as such has anything to do with sour grapes. You need only look at such a portrait as that of *Nelly O'Brien* at the Wallace Collection to see that Reynolds was every bit as accomplished and subtle a painter as Gainsborough – the delicious striped skirt, pale blue and white, the play of light over her throat, the shaded pinks of her face. But it was *Lady Blake as Juno receiving the girdle from Venus* and such like portraits that he sent in to the newly founded Academy.

Now I would not have spent so much time over this curious case of Reynolds if I did not see something profoundly English in it. There is anyway plenty that is English in the fact that he painted portraits and not mythology or saints as they did for instance in Italy and also in the fact that his portraits are so remarkably reticent and not a bit showy. But to that I shall revert later. For the moment I still want to go on with this peculiar problem of cant or compromise. It is by no means always easy to see where the border runs. If, as G.M. Young tells us, a manufacturer in the Bleak Age kept children of nine at work for nine hours at a temperature of ninety-eight degrees and let them sing hymns, that is cant at its worst. If in the famous Voysey case of 1871, the Judicial Committee of the Privy Council decided that clergymen 'may follow any interpretations of the Thirty-Nine Articles, which, by any reasonable allowance for the variety of human opinion, can be reconciled with their language', that is not cant but compromise, even if compromise entering a field where I personally would not expect it. However, perhaps English is right. Perhaps this is indeed wisdom – the wisdom that made Pope write:

> For forms of government let fools contest
> That which is best administered is best.

It is admittedly practical wisdom, worldly-wise wisdom; it is also admittedly illogical – and in action it can indeed look like double-facedness but it can on the other hand also be tolerance. 'Every case on its own merit' is in my opinion one of the greatest blessings of English civilisation, whether you are dealing with the higher walks of administration or with some detail of daily life. If for my research in connection with the *Buildings of England* (the county inventories of buildings on which I am always busy) I find I can without any forewarning knock at the door of pretty well any country house and be, after some explanation, allowed to examine the inside as well as the outside, I feel ready to forsake French logicality without a murmur of regret – a logicality which shows itself in the irrevocable *C'est interdit* or *C'est impossible*, when one tries, out of the blue, to see not even a private house but say a school housed in a former monastery. No – give me reasonable and tolerant illogicality every time.

But I must return to Reynolds; for we have not exhausted yet the important aspects of the problem in hand. Reynolds, who praises Raphael and Michelangelo so highly, knew their work in Rome. But what was his reaction to Raphael's immortal *School of Athens*, so noble, so calm? He painted a parody of it with caricatured English visitors instead of the Greek philosophers. He even admitted in his last *Discourse* that the first sight of the great art of Renaissance Rome is a disappointment to the young English painter and recommended that we ought 'to feign a relish till we find a relish come'. That is the hypocritical end. The tolerant end is that Reynolds did not only paint *Mrs Crewe as Ste Geneviève*, but also *Master Crewe as Henry VIII* – a sturdy pink-cheeked little boy of four dressed up as Henry VIII and standing legs wide apart in the famous pose of Holbein's portrait of the King. That also is parody, parody of the painter, parody of pomposity of pose, parody of the sitter – in short, the ability not to take oneself too seriously.

The detachment which this implies is, I think, of profound significance in English art. I'll show you one unexpected way in which it makes an appearance. In my last lecture I mentioned the historicism of Victorian architecture and its early appearance in the

English eighteenth century. I was then interested in it in so far as it showed a literary rather than a visual approach to architectural style. Now I want to suggest that detachment is another cause of the pioneer position of England in the history of architectural revivals. The earliest case known to me was mentioned in the *Eagle* without aesthetic comment – no, not the *Eagle* you are thinking of;[1] I mean the magazine of St John's College, Cambridge, in 1896 – and I have commented on it in the Cambridgeshire volume of my *Buildings of England*. As early as 1624 when the new Library of the College was built, Gothic windows instead of the Jacobean ones one would expect were chosen deliberately because, as the document says, 'some men of judgement like the best the old fashion of church windows, holding it most meet for such a building' as a college library. Surely here, at an amazingly early date, the whole detached attitude of the Gothic Revival is complete. Sir Christopher Wren, in spite of St Paul's Cathedral and Hampton Court, had exactly the same attitude. To some of his City churches he gave Gothic spires and towers and was of the opinion that they were 'not ungraceful but ornamental'. And for the completion of Westminster Abbey, he strongly urged a continuation of the forms of the ancient building; for 'to deviate from the old Form, would be to run into a disagreeable Mixture'.

Now what do you call that? Detachment? Conservatism? Or is it scepticism, as was so much leading English philosophy of the eighteenth century? You could call Reynolds's *Master Crewe* scepticism and certainly much of Horace Walpole's attitude to the Gothic Revival. As you know, he built his own country house, Strawberry Hill, in the shape of a Gothic castle, very pretty, very Rococo, yet with much care for the correct imitation of details. But in his letters he studiously avoids taking his own Gothicism too seriously – a civilised, detached, if perhaps somewhat pale attitude.

But that is not what one would say of the extraordinary case of a self-conscious detached choice of style in England as early as the fourteenth century. Henry Yevele, Master Mason of the King's Works, built the nave of Westminster Abbey from 1362 onwards, essentially in accordance with the system of elevation laid down a hundred years before by the first masons. He was ready to waive the Perpendicular style of his own generation for the sake of this conformity. And at Beverley Minster the same thing had happened about 1320–50, again in continuation of work designed a century earlier. I would be interested in parallels to this from other countries.

Of course, as we have already seen, once historicism in architecture was established in Europe early in the nineteenth century, the attitude was the same in all countries. Yet it seems to me that England went further than the others. We would call it shameless to submit to a client church elevations in three different styles to the same plan. Yet something of that kind was done in England even by Sir John Soane, the most original, uncompromising, idiosyncratic of English architects of the early nineteenth century. Soane of course never completely fits into any category or system, as Hawksmoor does not in the eighteenth and Butterfield in the later nineteenth century. They are to a certain extent laws unto themselves and the only way in which I would feel inclined to link them to something peculiarly English is their very eccentricity. 'Spleen' is the term used on the Continent for this English quality, the quality that has made England the land of follies! I mean what we call follies in architecture, odd look-out towers or eye-catchers or such like structures, built for no utilitarian purpose whatever.

However, that is only by the way – introduced at this particular moment to remind you of my fundamental tenet of the polarities. We were talking of detachment so let me make one more point to carry us over to next week. Detachment is not only the attitude of Reynolds to his art (as it was – please remember – of Hogarth in his cool decision to start a new genre in art) but detachment appears also in the attitudes of the sitters themselves. It is the very thing that distinguishes the English portrait, whether Reynolds's or Gainsborough's, from those of France and Italy. The English portrait speaks in a lower voice, as the Englishman does today, and as indeed the muffled sound of the English language seems to demand. The English portrait conceals more than it reveals and when it reveals, it reveals with studied understatement. These men and women seem to be intent on doing what Jane Austen in *Emma* calls 'the true English style': 'burying under a calmness that seems all but indifference, the real attachment'.

Nobody shows passions in Reynolds and Gainsborough and if there is more than one person on a canvas there is no heated argument.

There is perhaps also not much fire. May I connect this for a moment with something unexpected: The landscape of England, of which you will hear much more later. It is a moderate landscape. Do you know William Morris's wonderful description of his beloved England? 'Not much space for swelling into hugeness; ... no great wastes overwhelming in their dreariness, no great solitudes of forests, no terrible untrodden mountain walls; all is measured, mingled, varied, gliding easily one thing into another, little rivers, little plains ... little hills, little mountains ... neither prison, nor palace, but a decent home.'

A decent home – yes, that moderation is indeed deeply English. No Michelangelo, no Rembrandt, no Grünewald, no Greco, no grand painting and sculpture, no vast machines in church and palace, but beautifully carved bosses and capitals in the churches and water-colour and miniature, all things on a small scale. And also the amateur painters from aunts to Prime Ministers, nowhere a violent compulsion at single-minded self-expression to which a lifetime must be devoted – the amateur altogether and not the specialist. In the art of the mid-nineteenth century, naturalism is not as obtrusive as in Courbet and Zola. It is that of the Pre-Raphaelites. And in the architecture of about 1900 there is the fresh yet friendly and human style of Voysey, not the whole-hog throwing-overboard of all traditions as in Frank Lloyd Wright in America, in Garnier in France, in Behrens and Loos in Germany and Austria.

The revolution which led to the establishment of modern architecture was prepared step by step in England, first by William Morris in theory and design, then by such architects as Voysey; but the revolution itself had to be made abroad. Revolutions in England are unbloody, as that of 1688 and that of the last twenty years. Everything changes; only names, formulas, the outer demonstrative signs don't change. There are two causes for this, both equally English. One is reasonableness and of that I'll have to say more in my next lecture, à propos the architecture of the Perpendicular style. The other is conservatism and with a few words on that, I want to finish today. I have already in a previous lecture rattled off for you a whole list of some of the venerable and ridiculous phenomena of conserva-tism in today's England – I hope with sufficiently audible sympathy –

the Judge's wig, the Cinque Ports and so on.[2] Now I will argue that the instinct which made Henry Yevele, the mason of Chaucer's time, choose a thirteenth-century style for his abbey; the instinct which made Wren and Vanbrugh interested in mediaeval forms, was not only detachment but also conservatism. But whichever of the two, it was in all of them an English instinct.

To clinch this argument, I'll invite you to consider three more examples, one each from architecture, painting and sculpture. Wren intended to give St Paul's a shape on the monumental central plan of Rome and Paris. The clergy would not have it. Compared with Baroque cathedrals abroad, the plan as it is today when you see it on paper is, I assure you, surprisingly like that of an English Norman cathedral – length of nave, of choir, of transepts and so on. And Wren even gave St Paul's flying buttresses, although they are hidden by high screen walls.

That is one case of conservatism. The second takes you back many centuries further. Canterbury owned a famous manuscript written about 830 in France under strong oriental influences – the so-called Utrecht Psalter. It was usual for monastic scribes to copy motifs from manuscripts in the possession of their libraries. But it is highly unusual that in England, that particular manuscript was copied in the early eleventh century, again in the mid-twelfth century and again – though now much transformed – about 1200. That is a striking sign of conservatism.

And finally the Perpendicular style. England created it about 1330. It was an utter break-away from what had gone before. But once it had been established universally in the country, say by 1370–80, it remained virtually unchanged for 150 years, so much so that it is not at all easy even for the specialist to date Perpendicular window tracery or other details. Even sculpture does not help, for that also, in total contrast to e.g. Germany, remained without a firm progressive direction for about a century – a specially interesting fact, I think, because the Perpendicular style is about the most English creation in architecture. So I am going to devote to it a good deal of my next lecture.

1   A popular boys' comic of the 1950s.

2 These examples were deleted from the broadcast version of the talk. When the lectures were published in book form in 1956, they were reinstated and the list expanded: 'They are without doubt immensely characteristic of twentieth-century England and one cannot be proud of them at all – not of obsolete railway stations with unspeakably shabby and dreary waiting rooms, nor of antediluvian dust-carts scattering more garbage than they collect, nor of museums in provincial towns – to return to art – where stuffed birds live side by side with paintings of some value and the snuff-box of some defunct citizen of the town. Here conservatism comes dangerously near inertia and the Americans and Germans take it to be a sign of old age and tiredness. Whether there is some truth in this or not, there is certainly a warning in it and it may be unwise to stress, as will be done here, that conservatism can have positive qualities.'

Perpendicular England

REITH LECTURE (4)

Third Programme
SUNDAY 6 NOVEMBER 1955
Producer: Donald Boyd

If you go into one of the big English parish churches of the late Middle Ages, the age of Henry V, Henry VI, Henry VII, what will you find? I'll take as my example Newark in Nottinghamshire, nave fifteenth century, chancel 1487–98, transepts after 1500. Tall nave, thin sinewy, very emphatically perpendicular piers. Large aisle windows, large upper windows, their tracery hard and impressively if monotonously repetitive. Timber roof of low pitch (not a vault). Chancel and transepts long, angular, and square-ended, not with rounded ends or rounded or polygonal chapels. Vast end-windows in the chancel and the transepts of seven lights each running up to immediately below the roof. It makes the east parts of the church a veritable glasshouse – clear, light, vast and not a bit mysterious. It must always have been like that for figured glass at that time was confined to selected areas. There was plenty of white – that is, transparent – glass.

What qualities stand out from this description? – which would be much the same if we took others of the great English Perpendicular parish churches: Lavenham or Long Melford in Suffolk, or Chipping Camden or Cirencester in Gloucestershire, or Kings Lynn or Walpole St Peter in Norfolk. Large size, simple plan, flat chancel end, general angularity, hard separation of parts, repetitiveness, boldness of the very large openings and in the end a generally rational, surveyable, unmysterious character.

Mind you, in enumerating these qualities, I must once more refer to my fundamental tenet of the polarities. The description I have given is not a hundred per cent true. For these churches were originally full of screens and chantry chapels and so looked less bare and square than they do now, even if those screens and chantries were often, compared especially with contemporary German work, very repetitive in their details too. Where there are stone vaults also, it is a little different (as in St Mary Redcliffe at Bristol). But even there, the innumerable ribs and subsidiary ribs themselves are again straight and angular and hard. At Bath Abbey, on the other hand, the vaults are fan-vaults and indeed introduce a note of exotic luxuriousness quite in contrast to the angularity of the forms of the church otherwise.

But the fact remains that, almost without exception, the English of the later Middle Ages did not believe in the stone vault. This is in total contrast to the French and the Germans and that fact is in itself highly characteristic. It proves positively the English faith in oak of which I spoke briefly some time ago. But it also proves negatively a peculiarly English neglect of moulding space − you might even say of pulling things together. One wall, another wall and beams across. Parts can be left as parts. We'll hear a lot about that today and later.

But there is one proviso. The tendency towards large, easily surveyable, wide-open spaces in parish churches belongs to all Europe in the fifteenth century, not only to England. The orders of friars had introduced everywhere plainly and unimaginatively planned large preaching spaces. They influenced the parish churches a great deal everywhere: and parish churches are the most typical churches of the late Middle Ages because they are the churches of the burghers, the merchants, the bankers and the manufacturers who had the money, the greatest ambitions and also perhaps the greatest need for redemption. So some of that pride and squareness and matter-of-factness is typical of the period more than of England.

But it is very much of England all the same, so much so that the Perpendicular style has in its details not even a remote parallel abroad and so much so that it lasted unchanged for nearly 200 years once it had been created. So we can with some confidence start now looking for the qualities of the Perpendicular in other periods of English art and architecture.

Angularity first. The flat chancel of the Perpendicular church has its immediate parallel in the flat-topped tower of the Perpendicular parish church – something extremely rare on the Continent but something that to the foreigner is part and parcel of the English landscape. There are spires of course also, especially of between 1300 and 1350, and especially in such counties as Northamptonshire and Lincolnshire but the square-topped tower remains England at its most English all the same. And incidentally, the almost-flat roof with parapet or battlements instead of the high-pitched roof of, for instance, German or Dutch churches of the fifteenth century is equally typical.

Now the square-ended chancel itself. This is, except for the churches of the reforming order of the Cistercians in the twelfth century, very unusual in France and Germany. They prefer the rounded end with or without a passageway like an aisle around – what we call an ambulatory. That gives a sense of moulded space, of plasticity, of pulling together. England prefers that the walls should meet at right angles and remain separate from each other and that the enclosed space should be a box, or cube, or block. The English cathedrals of the classic High Gothic style, to go back for a moment to the thirteenth century (Lincoln or Salisbury), have a square end, Wells had one, Ely and Worcester acquired one in that century and so on. If Westminster Abbey has a rounded chancel end and polygonal chapels radiating from that, that only proves how close Henry III wished to keep to the precedent of Reims and other great French cathedrals.

Even in the Norman style of the twelfth century, England occasionally voted for this straightness. The Normans had brought the Norman style from the Continent of course and at the beginning their cathedrals and monasteries therefore had rounded ends and often chapels radiating from them. But at Southwell and in modified forms at Romsey, at Old Sarum, at Hereford and at others, the chancels end straight and at Holy Island in Northumberland they replaced as early as about 1140 a chancel on the French pattern by a flat one.

In point of fact, this preference in Norman times was a direct reflection of an Anglo-Saxon preference. In Anglo-Saxon churches, rounded ends occur mostly in Kent, close to France. In all other parts of England, straight ends are usual. And may I say that in perfect accordance with this idiosyncracy, the Anglo-Saxon designers had a liking for an area which is not an arch but an open triangle – that is, with straight shanks instead of the rounded, plastic, moulded form of the arch proper. And may I point out that even that mannerism occurs again occasionally in mid-Gothic, especially in the north transept of Hereford Cathedral.

Now that angularity seems to me to be closely related to an English habit of rather adding part to part than of – how shall I put it? – kneading them together. The Anglo-Saxon church builders, for instance, had a curious way in planning. Instead of building aisles left and right of the nave, they added separate closed chambers, the so-called *porticus*, opening to the nave only in narrow arches. This is to my mind the forerunner of the way in which the thirteenth-century church transepts in England stick far out to left and right, often two pairs of transepts – all straight-ended. Here again, part is added to part instead of the sculptural pulling-together in France, where transepts get short and keep close to the unified composition of the centre.

Also, the main entrance to the French thirteenth-century cathedral is from the west by three portals which funnel you into the nave and the two aisles. The English way is to have a large north porch instead as a completely separate cube or block. The west front on the other hand tends to be a kind of screen, wider than nave and aisles with insignificant portals and without any structural logic placed in front of them – a separate wall with its own laws of design, not subordinated to the layout of nave and aisles. I see in this an important principle: the principle of insubordination. Well, this principle also dictates what the English designer does with his screen façade, say at Salisbury or Wells and especially at Lincoln. He covers it with an even grid or net of blank arches or niches – and he did that already in Norman times: see for instance the façade of Castle Acre in Norfolk. The English loved these long rows of blank arches, running on apparently interminably and wholly uniformly. They are also found often inside aisles on the walls below the windows: uniformity and repetition, and – this I want to add – also a great desire to stress the surface as a flat surface by such patterning.

That is why the English are also so fond of other flat surface patterning, diapers in the thirteenth century, the close and repetitive tracery of the Perpendicular windows and the panelling of the walls around them with blank panels always the same, the reredos – that is, a stone wall behind the high altar – with row upon row of images in more or less identical niches, the close and repetitive patterns of ribs and subordinate ribs in fourteenth- and fifteenth-century vaults, the spectacular very close patterning of the exterior of Henry VII's Chapel in Westminster Abbey and even, if you follow me, in the mid-nineteenth century, its reflection in the never-ending terraces of Kensington and Bayswater. On a higher level, in the same nineteenth century you can see the same even patterning in the façades of the Houses of Parliament by Sir Charles Barry and by the great Pugin, the fanatic of the Gothic revival and the most fertile of designers of Gothic detail.

Finally, it seems to me that William Morris was destined to become the best designer of the nineteenth century in all Europe, at least where flat surfaces are concerned – that is, in chintzes, wallpapers and the like – just because he was English and had grown up with a sensitive and intelligent appreciation of the English traditions in design.

The tradition I am speaking of is that of close all-over repetition of decorative motifs on a surface. Now, the term all-over implies that the motifs ought to look as if they could be and might be continued interminably in length as well as in height – again, I think, a contrast to the plastic sense of other nations which shapes and rounds and thereby confines. The façade of Lincoln could go on for ever to the left and right. It could also go on for ever upwards, by more tiers of the same arches.

You can in fact separate these two directions and show that in English design, excessive horizontalism as well as excessive verticalism occurs and sometimes a grid of both.

We'll start with horizontal extremes and the curious proportions of Anglo-Saxon churches – Monkwearmouth nave, sixty-five feet long but only nineteen feet wide; Escomb, forty-three and a half by fourteen and a half; All Hallows Barking-by-the-Tower, apparently seventy by twenty-four feet and so on. We can then go on to Norman cathedrals. In France, if a nave has twelve bays – that is, twelve arches of the arcade between nave and aisles – it is very long. (Cluny Abbey e.g. or St Sernin in Toulouse.) St Étienne in Caen has only eight, Vézelay ten. But Ely and St Albans have thirteen, Winchester and Norwich even fourteen. That lengthening makes a lot of difference to the eye. Similarly, if Germany in her wonderful late-mediaeval parish churches gave the aisles the same height as the nave, that meant that one unified space could flow through the whole breadth of the triple room. England kept to lower aisles – that is, kept the three streams of canalised space from portal to altar more separate and went on emphasising their individual parallel lengths. Is it too far-fetched, finally, to think in this connexion of the Long Galleries of Tudor and Jacobean houses? – so long, sometimes, that again you feel they might go on for ever.

It may at first seem surprising that this horizontal stress is not in the least contradictory to the vertical or perpendicular stress which has given the Perpendicular style its name. But it is not: the conception of the grid united them, as you will see presently.

Perpendicularism is indeed exactly as frequent in English art as horizontalism. There are so many examples, I don't know where to start: the gaunt proportions of Anglo-Saxon churches (Monkwear-mouth with its nineteen-foot width is thirty-one feet tall); the overstressed verticalism at Ely of the mast-like shafts all up the long nave walls; the preference of the English in the thirteenth century for the long, slender lancet window over the broader traceried window. Again, the French type of window tracery with a circle or rose above the two or four lights of the window is a tribute to rounding, to moulding, just like the rounded east ends with their radiating chapels. Then also in the thirteenth century, the delightful alternation of buff stone shafts and shafts of black Purbeck marble, again vertically dividing a composite pier into its components, all to be seen in their separate perpendicularity. Or finally, the timber-framing of Perpendicular and Elizabethan houses in England with narrowly set perpendicular studs between the main posts – so different from the broader and sculpturally richer composition in the timber-framed fronts of Hildesheim and Brunswick or Rouen and Lisieux.

Nor is the perpendicular preference of the English noticeable in architecture only. Professor Frey, whose excellent book I have referred to before, insists that there are more whole-length portraits in England than anywhere else, from Holbein (for the English had not created the type) to van Dyck and on to Reynolds and Gainsborough. I don't know if one can really say that – in Venice and Bergano they certainly always liked the whole-length too – but the innumerable slender, very erect young noblemen and ladies on the walls of country mansion and galleries are indeed a striking experience when one first travels in England.

We are on safer ground with sculpture of the thirteenth century. There, in the façade of Wells with its more than a hundred statues or with the *Annunciation* in the Chapter House of Westminster Abbey, you have extremely elongated figures and draperies stressing this verticalism by their long, sharply cut, perpendicular folds. Contemporary French sculpture is fuller and again somehow more kneaded, if you see what I mean; less cut. And this perpendicularism pleased the English so much that they went on with it and in their most national branch of late mediaeval carving (their alabaster altars and panels), the figures are long, lean, thin-faced and sparing in their movements – unmistakably types you see about in town and country in England.

The favourite type of figure of the first Anglo-Norman school of manuscript illumination is in fact no less than a caricature of this English type. In the Psalter of St Alban and related manuscripts, they stand in groups – gaunt, stiff and with motionless features, extraordinarily and oddly similar to some of the Elizabethan funeral monuments where husband and wife or two wives lie similarly long and stiff and motionless side by side. The Elizabethan style in architecture also concerns us here – a style wholly English, however much inspiration from France and the Netherlands may at first have got it going. The Elizabethan style – as illustrated by, say, Longleat or Burghley – has a good solid hard core of Perpendicular tradition. The façades are a rigid grid of uprights and horizontals, windows are tall and wide and of many lights with many upright and horizontal stone bars. They have lost the last vestiges of curves which still existed in Perpendicular tracery. In the end, in the most characteristically English houses of about 1600 – at Hardwick, for instance – there is nothing but square and oblong blocks, flat roof, square-topped towers at the angles, square and oblong windows leaving little of solid wall – a rigid, rational grid.

Blocks added to blocks – and façades designed as grids. You can go on with this English system through the centuries after Elizabeth I and you'll find styles changing but this attitude remaining. What else, for instance, is the Circus at Bath – that round square, if I may say so? John Wood designed it in 1754. The architecture is Classical, columns superimposed on each other in three tiers – but the columns and the friezes which they carry are a grid all the same. So is, of course, the exterior of the Houses of Parliament (I have referred to that before) but so is also, say, Gower Street near the British Museum – the long stretches of completely unadorned terraces of Georgian brick houses with nothing but evenly cut-in, unmoulded, unenriched window openings.

And if the English liked to build their country houses and palaces in the taste of Palladio's mid-sixteenth century villas round Vicenza and Padua rather than in that of the Baroque and Rococo, can we not now state a reason – one of many, of course? These restrained houses[1] with their porticoes with tall columns, are they not also a new post-Renaissance version of the English ideal of the square block, the verticals and horizontals – to say it again, of rationalism?

For this is where we have arrived at the end of this lecture. Rationalism or, if you prefer it, reasonableness is the quality behind the Perpendicular and the Palladian. It is a middle-class ideal rather than a feudal one and the Perpendicular world was in fact predominantly one of merchants and the nobility which built in the English eighteenth and early nineteenth century was not a feudal nobility but one largely of recent creation, more often than not on a claim of wealth. Voltaire already commented on the fact that younger sons in England go into trade. The custom lives on, happily and sanely, to this day. In what other country could the uncle of the Queen be an active director of a private bank, travelling home on, shall we say, the 5.50 every night? If you take Whitaker's *Almanack* and check on the dates of creation of the English titles today, you'll find – at least I found, errors and omissions excluded – that of about 390 dukes, marquesses, earls and viscounts, only about twenty date from before 1600 but over 200 from after 1800. Of about 500 baronetcies, over 400 date from after 1800, about thirty from before 1600. That gives you some idea of the fact that aristocracy and middle classes have never been a hard contrast at any time in the last 600 years in Britain.

So if reasonableness is primarily a middle-class ideal and so much English art and English culture in general and on all class levels is so eminently reasonable, that is not a contradiction. It is a shame I can't go on for a bit with culture. This is the country of government by Parliament at an early date, of few political parties, of Queen Elizabeth's and William Cecil's policy of reasonableness and so on. But that is outside my subject. So to return to art again, let me quote you three first pages of English essays or books dealing with art or architecture.

Francis Bacon's *Essay of Building* has as its first sentence: 'Houses are built to live in and not to look on; therefore let use be preferred before uniformity, except when both may be had. Leave the fabric of houses for beauty only to the enchanted palaces of the poets, who build them with small cost.' And Hogarth's *Analysis of Beauty*, in spite of the flamboyance of his paint and his enthusiasm for the serpentine – that is, the Rococo line – starts like this: 'Fitness of the parts to the design for which every individual thing is formed, either by art of nature, is first to be considered, as it is of the greatest consequence to the beauty of the whole.' He then goes on to illustrate this by the size and shape of chairs, of pillars and arches, and in a few sentences he arrives at this: 'In shipbuilding, the dimensions of every part are confined and regulated by fitness for sailing. When a vessel sails well, the sailors . . . call her a beauty; the two ideas have such a connexion.'

And even if you take Pugin, in spite of his neo-Gothic and his Catholic fanaticism, you read on the first page of his *True Principles of Pointed or Christian Architecture*: 'The two great rules for design are these: First that there should be no features about a building which are not necessary for convenience, construction, or propriety; second that all ornament should consist of enrichment of the essential construction of the building.' Pugin hated all Classical design. To him it was pagan and therefore unworthy. Yet if you want to find the best illustration of Pugin's sound rules of good design, where would you go? To English eighteenth-century chairs – so functional in their elegance and so much less arbitrary than those of the French Rococo, and to the shapes of Wedgwood dinner and tea sets. These really are of an eternal rightness, undated in their clean and pleasing shapes. We use them still exactly as you can see them illustrated in Wedgwood's catalogues as far back as 1800.

Two pages from a catalogue of 1816 are illustrated in a book in which you would least expect to find them: Mr Geoffrey Keynes's *Blake Studies* of 1949. For William Blake, of all artists, engraved these pages – Blake, the arch-enemy in English art of all those qualities which I have so far placed in the foreground, of Rationalism on the one hand, of Observation on the other. With Blake, and with the Decorated style in mediaeval architecture, I shall next time try to explore the other pole – the irrational element in British art.

1   An earlier version of his script shows that Pevsner was thinking of Wentworth Woodhouse in Yorkshire (1735), Prior Park in Bath (1740) and Croome Court in Worcestershire (1750s), among others.

Blake and the flaming line

REITH LECTURE (5)

Third Programme
SUNDAY 13 NOVEMBER 1955
Producer: Donald Boyd

I said at the beginning of this series that such phenomena as national character in art can only be defined in terms of polarities. William Blake called them Contraries: 'Without Contraries is no progression. Attraction and Repulsion, Reason and Energy, Love and Hate, are necessary to Human existence.'

Today I want to start not with Blake (I prefer to lead up to him gradually) but with what to my mind is the outstanding example in England of progression by Contraries – the development of architecture from about 1290 to about 1350. What 1350 stands for I told you in detail last time. The Perpendicular style is reasonable, angular, matter-of-fact, repetitive and impressive by its spaciousness and clarity. The style that went before – the Decorated style, as we call it – seems in every respect the opposite of the Perpendicular. Yet it is as utterly English as the Perpendicular. It has no contemporary parallels whatsoever on the Continent – though, oddly enough, it has parallels (or repercussions) especially in Germany, starting fifty years later. But that does not concern us now. What concerns us is the distinctive qualities of English architecture of 1290–1350 as exhibited in such buildings as Bristol Cathedral, the Octagon and the Lady Chapel at Ely, the east end of Wells Cathedral and innumerable funeral monuments, none more fascinating than the tomb of Edward II at Gloucester and the Percy Tomb at Beverley.

Now 'fascinating' is the last word one would use to describe Perpendicular architecture. 'Admiration', yes; 'respect', yes – but 'fascination' is a term just slightly ambiguous, slightly questionable. And Decorated architecture is indeed capricious, wilful, unreasonable (where Perpendicular is reasonable), illogical, unpredictable even perverse if you like.

The Decorated Style must be understood as a reaction against the noble clarity of the Early English, the style of the thirteenth century, the style of Lincoln and Salisbury. There, as in Perpendicular later but without any of its hardness and thinness, part had been clearly added to part, each carrying on its free yet measured existence – the nave, the aisles, the crossing, the transepts, the chancel. Arches were resiliently rising to the point where they achieve themselves, capitals were either moulded in clearly defined parts or enriched by that springy kind of stylised foliage which we call stiff-leaf. It had been as superb in its own way as Chartres and Reims.

Now all this was abandoned, for reasons, it seems, of a strange nausea of perfection. Windows, instead of being noble groups of lancets or, if they had tracery, just circles with inscribed quatrefoils or cinquefoils above the lancet lights as at Westminster Abbey, develop the weirdest tracery – shapes like the leaves of trees, like daggers, like kidneys, like bladders, bounded by lines like flames or like waves. Flowing tracery is indeed what we call this type of decoration. It is specially fanatical in the parish churches of East Anglia and Lincoln-shire. The foliage of capitals instead of being stiff-leaf or crisply naturalistic as it had become here and there between 1250 and 1300 turns away from Nature and the resulting forms are vaguely reminiscent of seaweed (but definitely not imitations of it) – bossy, knobbly and, again in their surfaces, undulating.

And now take the great art of English illumination of the same years, about 1290 to 1350 – the Arundel Psalter, Queen Mary's Psalter, the Ormesby and Gorleston Psalters and so on. So far we have only looked at them marginally – literally marginally: at the babwyneries in their margins, these amazingly lively little scenes of everyday life or caricature or grotesque. Now we must examine the centres of the pages, the scenes from Holy Writ. They were as much admired on the Continent as the babooneries and had, so it seems, some influence on French and German manuscripts. They are indeed exquisite, very much in the sense in which Decorated architecture is exquisite. The actors in these scenes are long slender figures, their heads exceedingly small, their bodies attenuated and swaying, their outlines sinuous. There are no real backgrounds, just a diapering perhaps, and no clearly directed actions. This is a world of disembodied bodies, almost spectres, visions, moving weightlessly, or shall I say with Blake: 'silently, invisibly', with inscrutable expressions in their oddly boneless faces. Yet these figures can express passion – a passion not displayed in action but rather suffered, a passion distorting body and face in those very curves which at other times seem to express no more than a sophisticated courtly elegance. The line of the Decorated style, you might say, can be flowing or flaming, elegant or tense. We are face to face here with a phenomenon with which you may be more familiar in the paintings of El Greco or other Mannerist painters. There, also, one can seldom escape a disquieting ambiguity between what seems the self-effacing experience of the mystic and what may be no more than a highly self-conscious kind of ritual ballet.

I know it is not easy for you to check up on what I am saying about manuscripts; for in the museums you can usually see only two pages opened for you in a showcase. However, English embroidery of the same years represents exactly the same style and of that the Victoria and Albert Museum possesses such delicious masterpieces as the Syon Cope. This English embroidery was called internationally *Opus*

Anglicanum, so much was it considered specifically English. It was famous all over Europe.

Now that we have got as far as this, we have reached the point for the first time where you can see my notion of polarities in action. So far, I have presented the Decorated style as in everything a contrast to the Perpendicular. But it is not – and for a complete picture of Englishness in art, you need both and you have to watch what they have in common. Both are, shall I say, anti-corporeal or disembodied in the sense of a negation of the swelling rotundity of the body. Perpendicular denies it with the angular plans, angular towers, long thin wiry sinewy lines; Decorated also with long, also with thin, but with flaming, flowing lines. But both are unfleshly, incorporeal.

Other phases of English art in the Middle Ages deny the body by yet other means. Professor Wormald and others have in the last years drawn attention to the characteristics of English illumination in the tenth and eleventh centuries. What are they? A 'scintillating' line, Professor Wormald says; a denial of the frame so that 'figures can escape where they will, on the page', or – and this is incidentally what Reynolds says of Gainsborough – 'odd scratches and marks'. Colour in these English manuscripts is used for linework only instead of the solid body colour of contemporary Germany. The source of this inspired draughtsmanship is Continental of an earlier age and initially Oriental, as I have said before. But that does not matter. All I am saying is that it became an English speciality. Again, at Winchester, where from about 970 onwards illumination flourished, the draperies are drawn in wild lightning zigzags and the thick lush frames in flaming, scalloped leaf shape. The Normans did away with all that. Their style of stiff bolt-upright figures is a kind of 'Perpendicular' reaction to these 'Decorated' excesses. But it in its turn was immediately followed by a milder, gentler style of illumination about 1150 and after, and there the figures are slender and bounded by shallow tender curves. What goes through all these transformations of English mediaeval painting is an unconcern with the solid body and a watchful interest in the life of line instead – the zigzag at first, undulating later; violent at first, tender later – but always line, not body.

Once that has been established, you might even go as far as Professor Dagobert Frey went and connect this tendency with the art of the Celtic Britons in England in the Iron Age, the spiral scrolls decorating the Birdlip Mirror at the Gloucester Museum and the shield from the Thames at the British Museum. And you certainly could connect it with Irish illumination of the seventh and eighth centuries with its fabulous interlacing of bands and scrolls and its distortion of the human body into a flat board to place a diaper pattern on or a pattern of intertwined bands.

The English are not a sculptural nation. Most Norman decoration is abstract, not figural. Most large-scale English sculpture of the thirteenth century is inferior to that of France, most large-scale English sculpture of the fourteenth and fifteenth inferior to that of Germany, even allowing for the ruthless destruction of so many images by Puritans in the ages of Henry VIII and Cromwell, which in itself of course was an anti-sculptural demonstration. Remember also that for funeral monuments of the later Middle Ages, the English developed an enthusiasm for brasses – that is, not sculpture at all but engraved linework. Then Elizabethan and Jacobean sculpture. Most of that is amazingly poor. And yet later, who is the most famous English sculptor of the last 300 years? It is natural that you hesitate before answering. I suppose Flaxman must be the answer. He, as the *Gentleman's Magazine* said at his death in 1826, 'acquired a higher reputation than any artist of our country excepting Sir C. Wren and Sir J. Reynolds'. Well – I submit he was not really a great sculptor. His fame rests not on his monuments, though the more intimate of them are indeed extremely attractive, but on his outline drawings to Homer, Dante and others. Nothing could be more characteristic.

Incidentally, if at this juncture you try to defeat me with the name of Henry Moore, I at once declare myself defeated. In fact his art – and I do think he is the greatest sculptor now alive – contradicts everything I have said. Well, let it and let us remember that the great individual may at any moment widen the possibilities of a country. Over centuries and centuries, England has not produced real, three-dimensional, solid sculpture of the highest European order. This fact remains, but Henry Moore's sculpture – English mid-twentieth-century sculpture – also remains and in future we have to puzzle over a new polarity. The case is not unique. Turner, I think to a certain extent, is such a – may I say? – lucky freak and Shakespeare of course would not wholly fit into any scheme either of historical period or of national style. But that is at the moment only by the way.

The English have, I would still insist, nothing of the Italian, the Mediterranean confidence in the body. Maybe Puritanism has driven it out – but Puritanism is English and its persistence in Victorian guise is English. The nude, for instance, in spite of William Etty, has been a rarity in English painting over centuries – and is now. Just compare in your mind the Royal Academy and the Paris Salon. This is also why England has not produced Baroque art. I have given you other reasons before. But you can also say that Baroque, as practised in Italy and later in Southern Germany and Austria, is so impregnated with a sense of body that you can never get away from it: curving interiors, curving façades, crowds of painted and stucco bodies in the ceilings, vast muscular gesticulating saints in the altars, half-naked hermaphrodite angels exposing their long limbs. England has little of that. Even Vanbrugh's Baroque is not moulded, kneaded but angular masses, of cyclopic cubes. And even if you take Hogarth with all his liking of a fetching semi-nudity and of rich, fluid Baroque paint – what is it he proclaimed as his panacea of beauty? I told you it is The Line of Beauty, the elegant double-curved line, the ogee of the Decorated style, the *linea serpentinata* of the Italian Mannerists – that is the very thing I am talking to you about tonight.

We have so far only followed it in mediaeval art. But now, with your eyes sharpened, you will discover it without effort in the graceful stance and the elegant frailty of van Dyck's English portraits and even more in both Reynolds's and Gainsborough's portraits – no obtrusively physical presence (understatement if you look at it from another angle), no gorgeous colourings.

Exactly the same you could say of Robert Adam's interiors – delicate, transparent, pastel-shaded and here let me say for a moment that I cannot for the life of me see any peculiarly Scottish qualities in Robert Adam. Of the Scottishness of other Scottish architects, there can be no question. Thus, for example, Charles Rennie Mackintosh of Glasgow at the end of the nineteenth century seems indeed in his tense and predictable curves to draw on an obscure store of Celtic fantasy and magic; and Basil Spence, working in the completely different architectural idiom of today, seems to do the same in his designs for Coventry Cathedral.

But to return to the gentle curves of Gainsborough, Reynolds and Adam, take a Wedgwood vase and compare it for a moment with a Greek fifth-century vase. (Do you know that Wedgwood called his factory Etruria because it was believed then that Greek vases were Etruscan and he wanted to emulate them?) Well, compare a Wedgwood vase with an Athenian original and the contrast will be not only between red and black and Wedgwood's soft duck-egg blue but also between every form and outline, full-bodied in Greece, attenuated in England. Flaxman worked for Wedgwood and his delicious outline drawings to Homer, compared with Greek scenes painted on the vases, show just the same contrast.

Mind you, the shallower, more elongated curve does not necessarily mean a lack of tension. I had warned about that when we talked about illumination in 1300. Now you need only compare Flaxman and Fuseli, both inspired by Homer and Dante, to see the difference. Fuseli also stretches his bodies and bounds them by long curves and he also, in spite of hysterically exaggerated muscular displays, does not really work in the round. But his lines have an excessive tension unique in the England of his time, the ferocity of his stretched-out arms and of legs set widely apart. But then Fuseli had originally been Füssli. He was Swiss and Benjamin Haydon shrewdly observed about Fuseli's *Ghost of Hamlet's Father* that it is 'A German ghost', alluding no doubt to the savagery of Fuseli's style.

What English tension in terms of English line looks like, no one can tell you better than Blake and so I have at last reached Blake – whom I have had in my mind all the time while we were speaking of flowing tracery and the Arundel Psalter. 'Mental things are alone real, what is called corporeal ... is ... an Imposture.' 'Imagination is My World; this world of Dross is beneath my notice.'

Such were his convictions, such his theories. I can of course not here enlarge on them, on his obscure private mythology, on his passionate hatred of political oppression and of the oppression by the iron master and mill-owner. But we have to remember all that and remember the reality of his visions – 'After dinner I asked Isaiah' – and the uncomfortable closeness of some of his graphic work to the art of the insane, the way he covers all the free spaces on his engraving of the group of *Laocoön* (which he calls *Jehovah and his sons Satan and Adam*) with oracular sayings in all directions.

All that we must remember. Yet when we then see among these sayings the sentence 'Where any view of Money exists, Art cannot be carried on', then we are right back in our problem of polarities, Reynolds's and Gainsborough's prosperous practices and Hogarth's frank admission that he turned to his new field of 'modern moral subjects' because what he had done until then 'was not sufficiently profitable to pay the expenses my family required'.

Blake never was able to pay the expenses his household required. His poetry, his prophecies, his painting remained unprofitable and were acclaimed by few. They – Thomas Butts and later John Linnell of Wyldes, North End – kept him alive. However, we are concerned here not with his life but with his art. Now, no one can fail to recognise a Blake. There, whether the scene is one of bliss or terror, are his long, attentuated bodies, boneless almost, one feels, so little does he articulate the nude body, so ready is he to bound the joints of an up-stretched arm within gliding curves. There are his small, strangely impersonal heads and his flowing beards, his garments also flowing gently or falling loosely and evenly in perpendicular curves. They are of light, immaterial stuff. The curves, however, according to the character of the scene can be tense or tender, the lines flaming or flowing – that is, inspired by or sometimes rather in harmony with Fuseli or Flaxman, who were both his friends. Fuseli certainly inspired him much. He was sixteen years Blake's elder and his style as developed in Rome in the 1770s was complete when Blake began as an engraver in Basire's workshop. Another equally important inspiration in the same years was Gothic sculpture and that also is very telling. 'Grecian,' he once wrote, 'is mathematical form, Gothic is living form.'

Gothic sculpture he knew from Westminster Abbey where he had drawn for Basire but he must also have seen Gothic illuminated manuscripts for his printed books, written, drawn and printed by him, are a renewal of the unity of the book page as it had been a matter of course in the Middle Ages. It is eminently characteristic of Blake that on the pages of *The Songs of Innocence*, or *America*, or any of the others of his books, figures, trees and script are all drawn together and all of a piece. Now that means in his case that the figures are not body but part of an overall calligraphy. It is equally characteristic that Blake places his figures so often in a row with many long, parallel, vertical curves of drapery folds and gestures, much as the illuminators of 1120 had done in hard, and the illuminators of 1300 in sinuous, uprights. He also, surprisingly often, shows his figures floating in a cloud and becoming part of it or in a stream and becoming part of it or rising in a flame and becoming part of it. In other cases, where energy rather than abandon is intended, he forces figures into an imposed abstract geometry. Think of *The Ancient of Days*, kneeling in the clouds within a perfect circle, his hair and beard blown perfectly horizontally, his one leg standing perfectly vertically, the other a triangle, his arms stretched down to set 'his compass upon the face of the depth' – and the compass makes a perfect right angle. In a similar sense you find the rainbow used and the crescent and the gigantic posts and lintel of the druidic monument.

Now this imposition of an abstract geometry allows me for a moment to introduce the greatest English architect of Blake's day, Sir John Soane, a contemporary of Blake, only four years older. It is apt that he should appear here for what characterises his entirely personal, highly idiosyncratic and often eccentric style is that he also likes the incised line as an ornament instead of anything more bodily and swelling and that he builds in an overwhelmingly English way with surfaces which appear like membranes and with shallow curved vaults which seem to hover over the rooms. The Greek Revival in other countries tended to emphasise mass and solidity; only English Soane contrived to disembody it.

And to return to Blake and his imposed geometry, he applied it even to his portraits, if you think you can use that term for Blake. It certainly applies to his visionary portraits such as the strange *The Man who built the Pyramids*, the even stranger *Ghost of a Flea* and even, though of course much softened, to the straightforward portrait head of John Varley, the astrologer for whom he drew *The Man who built the Pyramids*.

It needs hardly saying that Blake was not a portrait painter – could not be one. Portrait in the accepted sense for him stood for all that was evil, debased, mechanical in England. It belonged to what he called 'the sordid drudgery of fac-simile reproductions of merely moral ... substances' yet was the only art 'applauded, and rewarded by the Rich and Great'. Fuseli said the same. I have already some weeks ago quoted him as saying: 'There is little hope of poetical painting ... in England ... The People are not prepared for it. Portrait with them is everything.'

And curiously enough Gainsborough also agreed with these remarks, though less emphatically and for very different reasons. You probably know him mainly for his portraits and I have certainly not so far mentioned anything else of his.

But he could write to a friend: 'I am sick of Portraits and wish very much to take my viol-de-gamba and walk off to some sweet village where I can paint landscape.' So with him it was not poetical painting, imaginative painting versus portrait, but landscape versus portrait – and that also is an eminently English problem in the eighteenth century. It is the one I want to talk to you about next time. But, meanwhile, as a parting thought, perhaps you might care to ponder over this. The landscape garden, the English garden as the French and Germans call the landscape garden, was one of the greatest creations of England in the eighteenth century. It stood for many things – liberty, the golden Arcadia, romantic dreams of grottoes and cascades – but it also stands for what I have just been talking about: the line of beauty, the undulating line. For what are the ingredients of the landscape garden? – the winding path, not the straight avenue; the serpentine lake, not the straight canal. Please remember that also for my next talk.

★

Constable and the pursuit of nature

REITH LECTURE (6)

Third Programme
SUNDAY 20 NOVEMBER 1955
Producer: Donald Boyd

Constable never visited Italy. Nor did he visit Paris. Neither did Blake, neither did Gainsborough, neither did Hogarth. I don't think Constable seriously wanted to know Italy. There is a letter written when he was twenty-six about someone's 'mind and talent mouldering away at Rome'. In an address to students of the Royal Academy, he warned them 'not to be in too great haste to [seek] instruction in the schools of France, Germany or Italy'. Yet he was an ardent worshipper of Claude Lorraine's Italian landscapes and once wrote to his friend Archdeacon Fisher that he feared he might be doomed – these are his words – 'doomed never to see the living scenes that inspired the landscapes of . . . Claude'. That seems to contradict what I said just now. However this passage immediately goes on like this: 'But I was born to paint a happier land, my own dear old England; and when I cease to love her, may I, as Wordsworth says, "never more hear her green leaves rustle, and her torrents roar".'

Constable loved his country and if such love can be taken as an indication of frank naive Englishness, then Constable ought to be as promising a case for my purpose in these lectures as Hogarth, who signed himself 'Britophil' and Blake who called himself 'English Blake'. Blake and Constable are contemporaries and they are what Blake called Contraries. They have indeed hardly anything in common. Constable and Hogarth can more easily be compared. 'Nature is simple, plain and true in all her works.' Constable could have said that but Hogarth did. 'By a close observation of Nature [the artist] discovers qualities . . . which have never been portrayed before.' Hogarth could have said that but Constable did. And who, would you guess, said at the beginning of his career: 'There is room enough for a natural *peinture*'? Actually it was Constable. Blake on the other hand said: 'Natural objects always . . . do weaken, deaden, and obliterate Imagination in me.'

But now to return to their Englishness as it appears in their art: Blake's Britain is a dim druidical Albion, Hogarth's is the noise and bustle of London, Constable's is the English countryside and more specifically the Suffolk countryside where he grew up, the son of a miller. There his art, as he said so truly, 'is to be found under every hedge, and in every lane'. So is of course Hogarth's under every pub-sign and in every alleyway of London.

But there the comparison ends. For Hogarth is a storyteller and Constable is emphatically not and Hogarth wants, as Garrick put it, to 'charm the mind and through the eye correct the heart' whereas Constable had no such extraneous programme. He contradicts thereby what I put before you as specially English four weeks ago, namely the English artist's literary leaning. But the contradiction is only on the surface and it can largely be solved by a look at the change in the whole of Europe between the Age of Reason and the age of Romanticism. Observation remained but it was no longer the observation of man in his actions but the observation of Nature. Nor was it any longer so much the observations of man simply in his likeness – that is, portrait went on of course but painters of the highest talent who had concentrated on portrait in the eighteenth century now went into landscape. The years between just before 1800 and about 1840 saw a prodigious flowering of landscape painting in England, unparalleled in any one country on the Continent.

The development starts of course in the mid-eighteenth century when Richard Wilson came back from Italy and turned from the idyllic landscapes of the south to English and Welsh landscape. Gainsborough, I told you last week preferred painting landscape to painting portraits and his landscapes have indeed the happiest insouciance of handling and the most enchanting tenderness of sentiment. Even bolder is the handling of Alexander Cozens's landscapes. For their groundwork they have ink-blots crossed by an accidental network of lines which is created by crumpling the paper and smoothing it out again before the blots are made. The result has a breadth of vision, a weightlessness and a sense of atmosphere prophetic of the nineteenth century. Alexander Cozens even made special cloud studies as Constable was going to do later.

But there is yet a fundamental difference between Constable on the one hand and Wilson, Gainsborough and Cozens on the other hand – even Alexander's son John Robert Cozens whom Constable once called 'the greatest genius that ever touched landscape'. The masters of the eighteenth century have in their compositions and their stylish handling of the brush still a self-consciousness which reflects the century's sense of superiority over Nature. Nature must be composed, Nature must be improved – in this the landscape painters agreed with Reynolds and incidentally with the 'improvers' par excellence, the eighteenth-century landscapers to whom I shall come presently.

All that changed with Thomas Girtin who died young in 1802 and then with Crome and Constable. Their world is the English everyday world, their theme is atmosphere, the technique they used to interpret an ever-changing nature is open and sketchy.

Now this pre-eminently painterly technique was not created at that time nor in England. It is the direct descendant of Venetian sixteenth-century painting and then of Baroque painting especially in Holland. In England it appeared out of the blue with Hogarth – but he, as you know, did not want to be a painter primarily; he wanted to be a teacher of morality as Reynolds wanted to be a teacher of Classical culture. Hence both wrote on the theory of art as well. Gainsborough was not interested in theory and general ideas and that is why Reynolds blamed him, in spite of his respect and a sensitive appreciation of his technique. The wording of his reproof is that Gainsborough saw Nature 'with the eye of a painter' and not a poet. It seems absurd to us to blame a painter for seeing with the eye of a painter – but we have been through the experience of Constable and the nineteenth century with its climax in the French Impressionists. That has changed our views.

It is time now to say something of the character of Constable's landscape. The motifs are humble: Dedham Vale, Hampstead Heath, Willy Lott's Cottage, Boat-building near Flatford Mill. As C.R. Leslie, his early biographer, writes: he worked 'within the narrowest limits in which, perhaps, the studies of an artist ever were confined' but his aim could 'be best attained by a constant study of the same objects under every change of the seasons, and of the times of day'. The sky Constable called indeed 'the keynote' of all classes of landscape. Fancy Poussin saying that or Courbet or Cézanne. And clouds were Constable's delight and obsession. In one of his letters to C.R. Leslie, he suddenly breaks off and puts in the exclamation: 'I can hardly write for looking at the silvery clouds.' On his cloud studies you find entries such as this: 'September 5, 1822, ten o'clock, morning, looking South-East, brisk wind at West, Very bright and fresh, grey clouds running far over a yellow bed, about half way in the sky.' And we have an analysis of a painting by Ruisdael from him which is a masterpiece of analysis not of composition but of the weather conditions prevailing at the moment when Ruisdael painted. The adjectives with which Constable describes his own pictures are very telling too: 'Sparkle and repose' are the two extremes he wanted to combine. 'Silvery, windy, and delicious ... all health ... [nothing] stagnant,' he says of his painting *A Lock*. He knew no false modesty about his achievement. He knew that his peculiar, dewy, breezy bloom had never before him been 'perfected on the Canvas of any painter in the world'.

Fuseli, who belonged to the eighteenth century and the world of Blake, said of Constable: 'He makes me call for my greatcoat and umbrella.' But Blake himself, when he saw Constable drawings said: 'Why, this is not drawing but inspiration.' Constable, incidentally, answered: 'I meant it for drawing.' Even so, however, he did call himself a visionary to excuse being irritable with clients and dealers – the very word Blake used with so much more justification. I suppose to Constable, the word must have had an undertone of vision in the optical sense. It is in any case very remarkable, I think, that the last sentences of the last of a course of lectures he gave at the Royal Institution nine months before he died are: 'Painting is a science, and should be pursued as an enquiry into the laws of nature. Why, then, may not landscape painting be considered as a branch of natural philosophy, of which pictures are but the experiments.'

Well, there we are back with a bang in our subject of Englishness: the rational approach, even in Constable where one would least expect it. And the atmospheric approach is just as English and so is of course Constable's primary choice of landscape as his exclusive subject too. Just as Hogarth spoke of 'what the puffers in books call the great style of history painting', so Constable in a letter of 1828 wrote: 'I have heard so much of the higher walks of art, that I am quite sick.'

Hogarth's art, Constable's art and, please note, also Reynolds's art have indeed this in common – that they are all based on close observation of what is around us, whether the behaviour of people or the features of a man or of a sky and trees. That, we have seen, is England's eternal contribution.

But we have also seen *à propos* Blake and equally *à propos* mediaeval architecture that England is ill-at-ease in the world of bodies, self-consciously displaying their fleshly presence, and so, when it came to landscape, in the Romantic Age, it was England that led Europe away from the landscape arranged of carefully disposed masses and towards the atmospheric landscape. That Claude Lorraine in Rome and such Dutchmen as Cuyp had done much the same in the seventeenth century need not detain us here. The fact remains that Constable's searching naturalism is devoted to air and that Turner's anti-naturalism carried him away into phantasmagorias of nothing but air. 'Golden Visions', wrote Constable, 'but only visions' and Hazlitt is suggested to have spoken less respectfully of 'tinted steam'.

English landscape painting of between 1800 and 1840 is immensely varied in character and personalities. Blake's few landscapes range from the completely disembodied *God moving on the Face of the Waters* to the small, wonderfully compact woodcuts for Thornton's Virgil, which almost at once released Samuel Palmer's youthful genius and gave us the landscapes of his visionary years (as Geoffrey Grigson has called them). Many years later Palmer spoke of the 'Raving mad splendour of orange twilight glow' in these landscapes. While he painted them, he wrote: 'I will, Gold help me, never be a naturalist by profession.' The surface of a Palmer landscape is, to quote him again, all 'sprinkled and showered with a thousand pretty eyes, and buds ... and blossoms, gemm'd with dew'. Both Henry Moore and John Piper owe much to this exciting dapple.

Cotman, with the heavenly peace of his smooth, flatly and coolly coloured landscapes, is the very reverse of Palmer. Yet what they have in common is the intensity of feeling for Nature combined with an unreal coherence of the surface, independent of the corporeal shapes lying as it were behind. A look at any Bonington landscape will show what draws Cotman and Palmer together. Bonington on the other hand belongs to Constable. He has the bold open brush strokes of

Constable, the sense of breeze and never-once-arrested change. To explain what distinguishes the two would need more time than I could give to it here. Bonington died as early as 1828. Constable died in 1887. With David Cox and plenty of good minor painters in water-colour, this broad English achievement carried on beyond the middle of the century.

Incidentally, the watercolour as such is of course also an English phenomenon. For one thing it is small in scale, as are for instance the small-in-scale bosses and capitals and marginal little people in the Middle Ages and as are also the wonderful sixteenth-century miniature portraits by Hilliard and Isaac Oliver. But the watercolour as such, as a technical medium so much thinner and less full-bodied than oil, is English too.

And side by side with the pure landscapes, there are such English specialities as the sporting picture. It is characteristic enough that it is a speciality but how it is handled when it is at its best is equally characteristic. Mr Basil Taylor has recently written a Pelican Book on *Animal Painting in England*. The title of the book is significant for it deals little with the popular sporting picture of the Alken and Leech kind,[1] which may be skilful reporting or boisterous cartooning but does not reach higher. Where animal painting is at its best, where even the racing picture is at its best, there is no exciting action but a curious stillness. There is no one in England to compare with Rubens in the Netherlands or Delacroix in France except perhaps James Ward. Stubbs, the greatest animal painter in England, was a scholarly student of anatomy. His compositions are, as Mr Taylor says, 'very still, very fastidious' and he went to Italy in 1754 'to convince himself that Nature ... is always superior to Art, whether Greek or Roman'.

Another English speciality is the open-air portrait: other countries – at least before the Impressionists of the 1860s–70s – have nothing like it. I am thinking of such delightful pieces as Gainsborough's *Morning Walk* or Zoffany's *The Garricks Taking Tea* on the lawn by the River Thames at Hampton; or of a later date and therefore in a more romantic mood, of Joseph Wright of Derby's portrait of *Brooke Boothby* lying somewhere in his grounds and dreaming over a book he has been reading; or Raeburn's *Sir John and Lady Clark* walking through their possessions and discussing no doubt improvements.

For that is really the setting in which the open-air portrait and the sporting picture must be seen – the passion of the eighteenth-century English for gardens and park and the passion of the present-day English for gardening which is the latter-day poor relation of landscaping. The landscape garden as I said last week is the most influential of all English innovations in art. Its effects can be studied all over the Continent and from the United States to Russia.[2]

Now the master-key, I suggest, to landscape gardening and landscape painting and the open-air portrait and the sporting picture is the English climate. Climate is indeed, as I mentioned in the introductory lecture to this series, one of the fundamental premises of character. The English climate has been discussed so often and ridiculed so often that it may be just as well to quote to you here a very different view. It was Charles II's and you must realise that he had been brought up in France and so knew what he was talking about. He said that 'he lik'd that country best, which might be enjoy'd the most hours of the Day, and the most Days in the Year, which he was sure was to be done in England'. You think that is a King's blatant flattery of his country? Well, don't forget two things. First that Rochester, who was not what you would call a kind man in his judgement of others, said once that Charles 'never said a foolish thing';[3] and secondly that no man in the seventeenth century would have called scorching sunshine something to be enjoyed outdoors. So outdoor life at that time and right to the nineteenth century required moderate weather – too warm not to want to be outdoors, too cool to be idle outdoors. Hence sports, hence gardening. And surely such weather turns up for some time on nearly every day in England, however much moisture there may be in the atmosphere lying in wait to condense into rain and drip off your sandwiches, taken to enjoy the sunshine on top of Bowfell or the Gogmagogs or Porlock Hill.

That moisture steams out of Turner's canvases as well, it makes Constable's so uncannily clear and fresh, and it lays a haze over man and building in England which dissolves their bodily solidity. All that is equally true but is not my business at the moment. It rather links up with what I have described as the Incorporeal in English art. At the moment I want to introduce you to English gardening and a conceit which is in my opinion of fundamental importance in the Englishness of art in the eighteenth century as well as today: the Picturesque. The English Garden, as you know, the *jardin anglais*, the *englischer Garten*, is asymmetrical, informal, varied and made of such parts as the serpentine lake, the winding drive and winding path, the trees grouped in clumps and smooth lawn (mown or cropped by sheep) everywhere and reaching right up to the French windows of the house.

Now I suggest that the English garden is English in a number of ways, all profoundly significant. We'll take the simplest way first. Formally, the winding path and the serpentine lake are the equivalent of Hogarth's Line of Beauty and the ogee curves of the Decorated style in architecture. When, on the other hand, Hogarth himself uses these motifs of the garden to illustrate his point, he says that they 'lead the eye a wanton kind of chase'.

Now that is something a little different. It introduces such elements as surprise in the composition of the English garden, and surprise was indeed one of the elements consciously aimed at:

> Let not each beauty everywhere be spied
> When half the skill is decently to hide.
> He gains all points who pleasingly confounds,
> Surprises, varies, and conceals the bounds.

That is Alexander Pope and though Pope was a teacher of reason and a friend of Lord Burlington who, as you will remember, established in eighteenth-century England the clarity and the cubic simplicity of Palladian architecture, Pope designed for himself at Twickenham (on a very small scale, I admit) one of the first picturesque gardens of England. That was about 1718.

But surprise is not all that Pope demands of a garden. There is also 'the amiable simplicity of unadorned nature'. Both take us back to the early eighteenth century and even back into the seventeenth. On the Continent, neither of these trends in gardening appeared before the great cultural English invasion of the mid-eighteenth century. Sir Henry Wotton, the first coherent writer on architecture in the English language, wrote in 1624: 'As Fabriques should be regular, so Gardens should be irregular.' Then Sir William Temple, in his *Gardens of Epicure* of 1685, wrote more explicitly, after some pages on the formal gardens of his time: 'There may be other forms wholly irregular, that may, for ought I know, have more beauty ... that they must owe it ... to some great race of fancy or judgement in the contrivance.' Such, he says, are the gardens of the Chinese. But to attempt that kind of beauty in England would be an adventure 'of too hard achievement for any common hands'.

If the adventure was yet embarked on, that was due to yet another train of thought. And it is this train of thought with which I shall now end. Lord Shaftesbury, the philosopher of the early years of the eighteenth century, praised wild Nature 'where neither Art, nor the Conceit or Caprice of Man, has spoil'd [her] genuine order by breaking upon [her] primitive state'. To him 'the verdure of the Field' and 'even the rude Rocks, the mossy Caverns ... and broken Falls of Waters' represent that natural, unartificial world which roused his enthusiasm.

Addison in *The Spectator* wrote the same more quietly. 'For my own part, I would rather look upon a tree in all its luxuriance and diffusion of boughs and branches than when it is ... trimmed into a mathematical figure.' That refers of course to the Dutch and French Gardens with their formal parterres and their cut hedges. Shaftesbury refers to the same when he says that his rocks, caves and waterfalls are 'Nature more truly than the formal Mockery of princely Gardens'.

Now with 'the formal rockery of princely Gardens', politics come in. England is liberty, France is suppressed by her rulers. James Thomson in the long poem which he called *Liberty* and in which he sings of Britain 'These haughty tyrants ne'er shall tame' also speaks of 'sylvan scenes' in picturesque gardens 'Such as a Pope in miniature has shown'. And George Mason in his *Essay on Design in Gardening* of 1768 explains the creation of landscape gardening in England by the English sense of 'Independency ... in matters of taste and in religion and government'. There you have the link between liberty and the Picturesque clearly expressed. But there is also a link between both liberty and the Picturesque and certain problems of planning which press hard on us today. I shall try to show in my final lecture how they bear upon each other and how the English character bears upon them.

1   Henry Thomas Alken (1785–1851) and John Leech (1817–64) specialised in archetypal scenes of foxhunting and horsemanship, often as social satires about 'Mr Jorrocks' and his milieu and captioned with comic dialogue.
2   The published version of Pevsner's Reith Lectures brings Lecture Six to an end here. The material that follows appears at the start of a seventh talk, retitled as 'Picturesque England'.
3   But added: 'nor ever did a wise one', as Pevsner acknowledged in the published version of this talk.

The genius of the place

REITH LECTURE (7)

Third Programme
SUNDAY 27 NOVEMBER 1955
Producer: Donald Boyd

You will have asked yourself more than once in the course of these lectures and you have a right to ask me at the beginning of this last[1] of the series: What is the good of all this? Where does it lead us to? I have presented to you a number of qualities and shown where they appear in English art and occasionally in other fields of English life. I hope I have convinced you that they are English and in what way they are English. But so many of them seem to contradict each other. What does it add up to then?

My answer is very briefly – much too briefly – this. First of all you must expect polarities, as I warned you at the very outset. National character much more than individual character is bound to be composed of seeming contradictions. I have analysed in greater detail those between Decorated and Perpendicular. You may now ask why Decorated appeared when it did and why Perpendicular appeared when it did. It is not too difficult to give one sort of answer to this question. Overriding all national differences, each period and each phase in the whole of European or Western history of the last thousand years has its own spirit. That spirit in each country calls up certain national qualities at any given moment and has no use for others. So Decorated in 1300 and Perpendicular in 1400–1500 are the specifically English expressions of European situations.

But I trust you will grant me that I have gone one step further. I have tried to show that the seeming contradictions between Decorated and Perpendicular are not really contradictions. In spite of appearances, the two styles have certain basic things in common, just as Blake and Constable have, or Hogarth and Reynolds. Among such basic qualities, I have referred to the curiously negative attitude of the English to the display of the body, to the grand gesture and the Grand Manner, to the kneading, as I called it, of mass or space. I have also tried to show how the forms in which English art expresses itself can be associated with such ubiquitous yet impalpable qualities as illogicality, detachment, rationalism and finally tolerance.

I call them ubiquitous because they pervade English expression in the arts. Now they may be ubiquitous today but have they always been? This is a curious problem which I have touched on in my first talk. Some of the English qualities which are now considered permanent are quite recent, the work in fact of Dr Arnold and Ruskin and of Queen Victoria and Prince Albert's exemplary domestic life. The cruelty of the eighteenth century – to children, to the insane, to the poor if they broke the law – is beyond belief now. The grossness, the jollity and public corruption of the eighteenth century are equally uncomfortable reminders of how recent our standards of ethics in small as well as large things really are.

Yet there exist, on the other hand, the many instances I have quoted in these lectures of typically English traits of today which occur as early as the Anglo-Saxon, the Norman, the Plantagenet age – the lively reporting of observed facts, angularity, thinness, a distrust of extremes and so on.

There is nothing conclusive here. You cannot expect in dealing with a nation to find permanently fixed qualities appearing and reappearing at permanently fixed moments and if I have succeeded in proving that to you, I have certainly fulfilled one task I had set myself.

But perhaps you are entitled to expect a little more than that, some attempt at answering the question as to what particular aspects of Englishness in my opinion are to the fore today and what, by their means, England might achieve for her own benefit and perhaps for that of other nations as well.

To do that means that we must go back to what I have told you about landscape gardens and the theory behind them – the theory of the flowing line, the more general aesthetic theory of surprise and concealment, the way the Picturesque is tied up with English outdoor life and ultimately the even more general British philosophy of liberalism and liberty.

But there is yet one more aspect of the Picturesque which has to come in at this stage. I'll introduce you to it by another passage from Pope. It follows immediately after the lines I quoted last time. This is how Pope continues:

> Consult the genius of the place in all
> That tells the waters or to rise or fall
> Or helps th'ambitious hill the heavens to scale
> Or scoops in circling theatres the vale,
> Calls in the country, catches opening glades,
> Joins willing woods, and varies shades from shades.

There you have an extensive programme of improvements typical of what eighteenth-century landowners did indeed do. Now, as you see from the details which Pope enumerates, all they did and nearly all that contemporary theory is about concerns the garden and the grounds. You find, in addition, the occasional eighteenth-century model village, an old village rebuilt because it had been in the way of some picturesque vista, and the occasional remark in the books on village design. On the town, there is for all intents and purposes nothing.

Yet to us today, the problem of improvements in towns – including the metropolis and the laying out (or as we call it, planning) of new towns or new parts of towns – matters much; planning in private grounds little. Now it is my contention that the English theory of the Picturesque, or as you may just as well call it 'the traditional national English planning theory', has an extremely important message. To appreciate it to the full, I would ask you to remember the first words of Pope's passage just read to you: 'Consult the genius of the place'. The genius of the place, the *genius loci*, is a mythological person taken over from Antiquity and given a new meaning. The *genius loci*, if you put it in modern planning terms, is the character of the site and the character of the site in a town or city is not only the geographical but also the historical, social and especially the aesthetic character. You want to plan for the City of London? What is the visual character of the City? Or of the centre of Cambridge or of Blandford?

Now this kind of consideration is to me something profoundly English: it is to treat each place 'on its own merit', just as each political situation is taken on its own merit or each case at the Ministry of Pensions (or so we hope). To cast our net yet wider, 'each case on its own merit' is the application of the principle of tolerance, a principle firmly established in England by the unbloody revolution of 1688 and by John Locke. Locke's first Letter of Tolerance came out in 1689. Twelve years later, Queen Anne gave one of the principal beams for the building of the still-surviving synagogue in Bevis Marks and the architect, a Quaker, gave his fees to the congregation. That is English and that is why the first of Voltaire's *Letters on the English* is about the Quakers. In a later letter he says a little less kindly: 'All denominations meet on the Exchange, and the only ones called infidels are those who go bankrupt.'

In planning and architecture today, 'each case on its own merit' is the functional approach. And mind you, I don't understand that term 'functional' to apply to utilitarian needs only but to include ideal needs as well. And if, in this sense, present-day urban situations are treated functionally, taking into consideration what is practical for the walker as well as the driver, for the man in a hurry as well as the man with leisure to stand and stare, for the shopper on foot and from the car and also for those who want to enjoy the looks and the feel of where they live or work – the result would not look like Versailles, with symmetry enforced on streets and buildings. The informal – it is a better term than 'the irregular', for the *regulae*, the rules, are not absent, they are only of a subtler kind – the informal is at the same time the practical and the English. Listen to Voltaire once more and this time *à propos* Shakespeare:

> It seems that up to now the English have only produced irregular beauties ... Their poetical genius resembles a closely-grown tree planted by nature, throwing out a thousand branches here and there and growing

lustily and without rules. It dies if you try to force its nature and trim it like the gardens of Marly.

Nature, said Voltaire's Scottish contemporary, the sceptical philosopher David Hume, 'Nature is always too strong for principle.'

Finally a passage from another eighteenth-century writer, Sir Joshua Reynolds. It will be a surprise to those of you who remember what I said and quoted of Reynolds some time ago. So far he has only appeared to you as the rationalist and the purveyor of academic doctrine. Now here he is in his thirteenth *Discourse* on architecture:

> It may not be amiss for the Architect to take advantage some times of ... accidents, to follow where they lead, and to improve them, rather than always to trust to a regular plan ... The forms and turnings of the streets of London and other old towns are produced by accident, without any original plan or design, but they are not always the less pleasant to the walker or spectator on that account. On the contrary, if the City had been built on the regular plan of Sir Christopher Wren, the effect might have been, as we know it in some new parts of the town, rather unpleasing; the uniformity might have produced weariness.

These new parts of London of which Reynolds speaks in 1786 must be the West End from Portland Place to Portman Square. We do not find them wearisome, or we wouldn't, if Londoners had left them alone instead of interfering with them by incongruous additions. On the other hand, what other term than wearisome uniformity would the visually sensitive choose for the High Victorian terraces of South Kensington and of nearly all the inner suburbs of London, let alone the slums of the industrial North. Yet both are the outcome of Liberty – and that shows how careful we must be in this juggle with terms. The planning of Bath is liberty in the sense of the most imaginative Irregularity; South Kensington and the terraces of back-to-back houses is liberty in the sense of *laissez faire* – that is, an equally typically English refusal to interfere even with those set upon blighting acres upon acres of the town with their unimaginative regularity.

England suffered from this blight earlier than other European countries because she had undergone the Industrial Revolution earlier than others and her faith in tolerance and in individualism had prevented her from checking the fatal effects on the appearance of towns of the rapid growth of industry and urban population. When the reaction came – and it came earlier than on the Continent too – it took, characteristically enough, the form of a return to the principles of the informal. The results are the garden suburb and the garden city. They succeeded in the blending of small-size housing with nature and the application of the principle of variety to the layout of streets, the provision of footpaths and so on. But they failed in not being garden cities in so far as they neither were nor wanted to be truly urban.

Yet Bath under the two John Woods had already shown how with the material of terraces of tall as well as small houses, of squares and crescents and circuses, varied planning in urban terms could be achieved and variety and surprise, those visual blessings, obtained. John Nash in his ingenious and again informal procession (if an informal procession can be conceived) of Regent Street and Regent's Park succeeded even better. Here again was urban scale, variety and surprise in the bends and turns and well-placed accents of the street, combination of grand terraces and lush park, an area of picturesque cottages behind called 'Park Village' and so on.

So here is plenty of precedent to make use of in our situation today – not by copying but by applying the same principles, the same great English principles.

The situation in planning in all countries today calls for two things in particular, both totally neglected by the nineteenth century: the replanning of city centres to make them efficient as well as agreeable places to work in and the planning of new balanced towns, satellite towns, New Towns, which really are towns. For a town is a unity *sui generis* and not an accumulation of garden suburbs with an occasional shopping centre as an urban enclave and a trading estate along the railway. Now planning is of course largely a matter of economics, sociology, traffic engineering and traffic organisation and so on but it is also a visual matter and if, in the end, the city centre or New Town does not make you visually happy – I don't mean only in its buildings but as an urban whole – it is a failure.

As you see I am getting carried away into a bit of propaganda but I am in fact quite close to my subject. The New Town built – and the obsolete centre of the old town rebuilt – are urgent problems for all countries but what I have said about English character shows that no country is aesthetically better provided than England to solve it and thereby leave its imprint on other countries. If English planners forget about the straight axes and the artificially symmetrical façades of the academy and really set out to design functionally – that is, Englishly – they will succeed. There are in fact promising omens in many places already, the consistent policy of the *Architectural Review* over the last twelve years and more, resulting in sketch plans for the City, the area round the Houses of Parliament and several small towns; Sir Hugh Casson's and Mr Misha Black's layout of the 1951 Exhibition on the South Bank of the Thames; then the Holden and Holford plans for the City of London; the new City Corporation and Holford plans for the Barbican area in the north part of the City; Sir Hugh Casson's plans for the Faculty of Art precinct of Cambridge University; and – in the flesh as it were – certain parts of Harlow New Town by Mr Frederick Gibberd and some of the new housing estates of the London County Council by Dr Leslie Martin and his department.

These are the things eagerly studied by architects from abroad but they are also things that still need support, support from the very highest quarters as well as from you, against ignorance and shortsight-edness and against the stupid prejudice that such newfangled ideas as would give London a modern and worthy centre must be outlandish. You see now, I hope, how thoroughly inlandish they are.

But can the same be said of the twentieth-century style in architecture as distinct from planning? Isn't it true that this style came to England from abroad? – even if its prehistory, as I have mentioned before, is partly English, thanks to William Morris and then architects such as Voysey. The new style could only be reached by a revolution and, once again, England dislikes and distrusts revolutions. So England was not only inactive in bringing the new style about but also slow in accepting it when it had been created by such men as Gropius in Germany and Le Corbusier in France. That of course can also be called conservatism.

You see here how one can get tangled up in one's own categories. I have tried elaborately to prove to you that distrust of novelty, sensible hesitation and conservatism are English qualities. What reason can there be, then, to grumble over imitation-Tudor suburban houses, Neo-Georgian villas and the dead, dull, inert Classical Revival and re-revival of the new Government Offices off Whitehall? Conservatism can have two causes and one is inertia or tiredness while the other may well be reasonableness and the wish to see a thing tried out before one commits oneself to it. And besides, England (as I told you at the beginning of these lectures) has not always been conservative. She was not at the time of Elizabeth I and she was not in the Industrial Revolution. Ralph Waldo Emerson still in 1856 treated the English as the leaders of inventiveness and enterprise in the world. 'It is England', he wrote, 'whose opinion is waited for on the merit of a new invention.' Who would say that so categorically now? Not that the practical capabilities and the stamina of the nation have decayed. I may have mentioned them too little in these lectures – but then my subject was art and this particular English trait does not often get opportunities of manifesting itself in art. In fact it manifests itself every so often in anti-art – I mean, in an attitude hostile to the imaginative element in art. But today, this is my point, the traditional English practical soundness has once more a great chance. I have shown you how Englishness might benefit the whole urban scene. Now I want to suggest that Englishness could also contribute to humanising a rational, very intellectual style of designing buildings. I say 'humanising', not prettifying or watering down. However, that can only be so if the conservatism of inertia does not get the better of another, more constructive conservatism which insists on carrying on from the Crystal Palace, from the suspension bridges, from Wedgwood's eighteenth-century dinner ware and from Hardwick Hall.

Is that special pleading? It may well be and I don't mind for the moment if it is. For what you will, I hope, take home from these lectures is that categories worked out honestly by the historian are neither meant to provide, nor to be capable of providing, a divining rod for the future. It would be fatal to exclude exploration and experiment just because this-that-and-the-other has not been English in the past. Perhaps what has been the plight of the modern architect in England, and still is, is the conflict between the sense of adventure in the individual and the sturdy resistance to adventure in the multitude represented by councils and committees.

But what is the plight of the modern painter and sculptor? There the case is different. It is first of all an international plight, that of a man without an accepted function and hence without a public. The rootlessness of fine art today has often been commented on and complained of. Remedies do not to my mind lie within purely national capabilities. They have to be ideological and don't concern us here. But it can perhaps be said that if English painting today does not seem to have too much to offer to the world at large, the reason is that the moment is once again – as we have come across them in the past – one of a conflict between the spirit of the age and Englishness. Painting is all the expression of conflict now, of extreme dissatisfaction, of violent revolt. The Englishman's conflicts are still handled politely between a ruling party and Her Majesty's opposition. There is – thank heavens – no desperate dissatisfaction, no risk of revolt. That benefits us all but it does not benefit the artist who in this century, if he is a true artist, is driven to see that Western civilisation and indeed survival are both in utter peril.

Yet – and this takes me back again to the problems which we have met in these lectures – yet there is Mr Henry Moore and with him England can boast the greatest living sculptor. The greatest living sculptor, as the product of the most unsculptural nation. I made this point before. I have to make it again because it underlines the impossibility of prophesying by means of historically discovered data. But after all, Henry Moore was not a more improbable thing to happen than William Blake coming between Gainsborough and Constable or the Decorated style between the Early English and the Perpendicular. The irrational element is there in England, more often latent than patent and more often patent in poetry than in painting and architecture – but it may re-appear any day and throw up a man of genius.

And now at last, as time is getting on, many of you will ask whether this whole series of lectures has no other message than this one in the field of visual planning. But a historian's lectures cannot have much of a message or else they cease to be historiography. However, in thinking over what else in the nature of a message you might be able to distil out of what I have told you, I thought it could perhaps be this:

Please get to know the history of English art and if I say that I include the Middle Ages and I include architecture. Get to know them because knowing them would not reduce but increase your estimate of English capabilities. You will agree your estimate is very low now. England has a veritable inferiority complex about her art in the past as well as her prospects in art. I feel sure Englishmen are more likely to make a pilgrimage to Vézelay than to Durham, to Amiens than to Lincoln. Well, go to Durham, go to Lincoln, go to Ely. That much for the eye. And for the mind, remember that England was far ahead of the rest of Europe at the time of the Venerable Bede, in illumination as well as the sculpture of the High Crosses; that the art and civilisation of Charlemagne's court accepted inspiration from Britain; that Norman architecture in England was, if not ahead, certainly not behind the principal French schools; that the creation of Gothic structure in Royal France received its greatest stimulus, even if indirect stimulus, from Durham; that the Early English style of the thirteenth century was very different from the French High Gothic but architecturally (at least in its best works such as Lincoln) not inferior; that English Decorated architecture of about 1300 was far more brilliant than any contemporary architecture anywhere else and English illumination of the same time at least as fine as anywhere else; that English Perpendicular architecture was an eminently original and telling creation; that Elizabethan architecture also was as original and as telling as that of France, the Netherlands and Germany; and so on to Constable and Turner.

When Constable's pictures were on the point of leaving for the exhibition of 1824 in Paris, his friend Archdeacon Fisher wrote: 'English boobies who dare not trust their own eyes will discover your merits when they find you admired in Paris.' That is true to this day and although English painting has not since been in the vanguard in Europe, Roger Fry had in my opinion no right to call the English school 'a minor school'. He was admittedly talking of painting only and of the last two centuries at that, but then that was just the mistake. To get a fair notion of what English art is capable of, everything from the illuminated manuscripts of the Early Middle Ages to William

Morris's designs and the planning of precincts and buildings today must be included.

These lectures of mine were an invitation to you to do so and to consider what you have seen and read about, not only historically – that is, as so many examples of so many styles – but also nationally – that is, as the examples of a national art and architecture which is all your own. Or will you give me leave to say: 'our' own?

1   In the published version of these lectures, the seventh lecture was renamed 'Picturesque England' and was followed by an additional concluding chapter.

A setting for St Paul's

Home Service
SUNDAY 6 MAY 1956
Producer: Leonie Cohn

The Minister of Housing and Local Government, Mr Duncan Sandys, had asked for a 'worthy setting'.[1] Those were his words. As most of you will know, a controversy has arisen as to whether Sir William Holford's scheme is a worthy setting. In order to be fair to both sides and to show the honesty and justification of both points of view, I want to start by taking the problem right out of its topical context and showing it to you in its quintessence. The problem is this. There are two possibilities of achieving a masterly design of the highest value for an area so packed with traditions and affections as that round St Paul's. Let me illustrate them by describing two of the most admired and most beloved town-planning gems in the world, St Peter's Square in Rome and the Piazzetta in Venice.

St Peter's Square is something grandiose. Its depth is over an eighth of a mile. It lies in front of St Peter's which, as you know, was the largest church in Christianity up to its time and the church where you may expect to see the Pope. The square is really a forecourt. It has as its prime function the gathering of the masses who come to visit the shrine of St Peter and perhaps to receive the blessing of the Pope. It holds 50,000 comfortably. Bernini, its designer, surrounded it all the way with colonnades 100 feet high but the façade of the church itself is high enough for the colonnades not to compete with it and there are no real buildings, usable buildings, anywhere in the composition, or at least there were not until a few years ago.

The Piazzetta in Venice is quite a different story. It is a square which extends from the water to the church of St Mark's, the most magnificent church of Venice, and is there continued by a second square at right angles. I'll speak of the first, although the two make one composition. If you stand at the water's edge looking towards St Mark's you see this: to the right is the Doge's Palace, to the left the Library. They run away from you into the distance: the one Gothic, the other in the Renaissance style; the palace of brick, lovely pale buff and pale orange brick, the Library of stone; the one almost flush, the other richly decorated. They are in contrast to one another except for the height which relates them. Now the façade of the Doge's Palace is continued by that of St Mark's which therefore, from where you stand, you would not see at all if it weren't for the ingenious device of the designers of the Doge's Palace to keep the façade of that building back by sixty feet in relation to the church. So while you get its full impact only from the other square it concerns you also from where you look, by means of this sixty-foot projection. What you see is of course not the façade but the side of the façade. But that is just enough to realise that *there*, something miraculous sticks out that you must hurry to see.

In addition there is the tower of St Mark's, the Campanile. This stands, in the Italian fashion, isolated from the church. It stands in one corner of the other square and would be hidden from you, standing by the water, if the architect had not repeated on an infinitely smaller scale the same effect as in the case of the church – namely, to let something project just enough to whet the appetite. He added to the tower a small, low, but very richly decorated loggia; it is a guardroom really – and that again juts out just enough to be seen from your vantage point and to focus your attention on the point where in a moment, round the corner, you'll see the whole Gothic bell-tower rise with its sheer brick walls.

Now you must not think that these effects I have tried to describe are just accident, as so many of the (sometimes happy, sometimes unhappy) effects in our cities are; for the two squares in Venice are surrounded entirely by public buildings and so any other scheme might have been chosen. They might for instance have been made into one large one, or the campanile might have been put squarely in the middle of the composition, or what you will. But no, this is planning just as much as St Peter's Square.

If in Rome you admire majestic monumentality, in Venice you admire a subtly balanced complexity. If the Roman piazza is grasped at one look and the shock is there at once, the Venetian piazza is taken in, in time, in many smaller shocks of delight. Both principles are of equal value and, as you see, of equally distinguished ancestry. France on the whole followed Rome, England followed Venice. France has created monumental squares and long straight vistas wherever possible, England prides herself on the intricacies of the Oxford and Cambridge colleges with their contrasts of style, scale and detail within nearly every one of them, and on the complexity of the planning of Bath with its sequence of Circus, climbing terraces and Crescent, and its contrasts of stone and greenery.

But Bath and Cambridge are one thing, London is another. In a great capital city – even an English one – there must be focal points which cry out for monumentality. Such a one is no doubt Sir Christopher Wren's St Paul's Cathedral – a grand, majestic, monu-mental building, designed at the most monumental moment in English architectural history. If you want to see what Wren meant by a monumental composition, go to Greenwich, and there you see the magnificent axis from the older Queen's House down to the river, a quarter of a mile in length with long processions of columns, left and right (to hide the pensioners' quarters) and with the symmetry of the two domes of Hall and Chapel. For St Paul's itself, we possess indeed one Wren drawing in a similar vein; it shows symmetrically disposed five-storeyed buildings all round the church, starting with two quadrants facing the front, and Wren's immediate successors – Hawksmoor in his projects for Cambridge and Vanbrugh in his monumental country palaces such as Blenheim and Castle Howard –

also designed on a monumental scale and with a formal symmetry of wings and outbuildings.

So it is palaces outside cities, of Greenwich and Blenheim, one ought to think of to visualise monumentality and formality in English planning and those who regard a monumental and formal setting for St Paul's as the only 'worthy setting' turn to them for their historical justification. Their artistic justification lies in two arguments. One is that a setting must be in harmony with the style and character of the centrepiece. The other and closely related argument is that to pay respect to a great building of the past one ought to isolate it. This is in fact what the nineteenth century has done to so many cathedrals on the Continent – to remove accretions.

If you now try to visualise a St Paul's surrounded by a wide symmetrical open area, with a forecourt like Bernini's, the effect would no doubt be splendid; it might be breathtaking. Is it then not our duty to aim at such an effect and to turn down Sir William Holford's informal, asymmetrical, unmonumental scheme? My answer is No, in spite of all these arguments. No, because such a scheme cannot be carried out and, what is more, because it is not desirable that it should be carried out.

Let me start my explanation by saying emphatically that St Paul's is not St Peter's. St Peter's is the focus of all Roman Catholic Christianity; it is the goal of thousands of pilgrimages every year. St Paul's is one of many venerable cathedrals in England; it is also very much the major church of the City of London. It belongs intimately to the City. It lies in a busy quarter; thousands work close to it and many of them every day go in for a few minutes to pray. For that reason alone the Cathedral does not call for splendid isolation. That is the ideal argument but there is also a practical argument. A forecourt like Bernini's would extend to somewhere very close to Ludgate Circus. To do what Bernini has done, all that area would have to be evacuated. Let us be realistic and admit that surely, surely, that would not be done. But then I am perhaps exaggerating the scale and I should perhaps not take the colonnades of St Peter's as my text all the time but take my clue from Wren and examine the possibilities of usable five-storeyed buildings arranged monumentally.

To show you that that would not give us anything really satisfactory, I want to mention a plan for the setting of St Paul's which was worked out in 1941–42 by the Royal Academy under Sir Edwin Lutyens. There you have exactly what I was just suggesting. It has a wide symmetrical area cleared around St Paul's, it keeps Wren's Deanery and Wren's Chapter House but as they are not placed symmetrically or in positions that suited the plan, they are duplicated and, since they stand fairly close to St Paul's, these four small buildings are scattered over the new open space. Ludgate Hill is closed and instead a new, straight, tree-lined avenue taken up towards the façade from New Bridge Street, the street which runs from Ludgate Circus to Blackfriars Bridge. This street and Ludgate Circus are joined into one large and wide turfed oblong square. The railway has disappeared. The entry from the new square to the avenue is flanked by two identical office buildings twenty-two windows wide each and with giant columns. So much for the Lutyens plan. That it cannot be regarded as the answer is perhaps best illustrated by the fact that, as far as I can see, no one in the present controversy has gone back to it and recommended it.

As a matter of fact, to my mind, any such plan must fall down on three counts. One is this. Lutyens's new avenue is not long; it stops at the new Ludgate Square. That is fatal, for such monumental axial schemes must be re-echoed in the layout of a whole town or town centre. Bernini's is a different type. A forecourt helps to isolate. It takes a building out of the workaday world. An avenue links it with that world and, as I said before, St Paul's ought not to be isolated but linked.

There is indeed a monumentality of linkage as there is one of isolation. The finest example of that in the world is Paris. Just think of the Place de la Concorde and the way you look down a street, between two identical monumental and elegant buildings, straight towards the portico of the church of the Magdalen. And then, when you turn round, that vista is answered by the portico of the House of the Deputies, away across the river. The grandeur and the ruthless formality of the whole are dazzling. To make the straight axial approach to St Paul's visually the thrill one would want it to be, one

ought to straighten Fleet Street and the Strand as well and get Nelson's
Column in Trafalgar Square into focus. I am not joking. That is how
it is done in Washington where axiality dominates the plan. The dome
of the Capitol, a descendant of that of St Paul's, dominates ten or
twelve straight vistas from all directions and the Washington obelisk
answers at a distance of a mile and a half – half an hour's walk.

If you want to be monumental you can't be cheese-paring.
Monumentality on a moderate scale is a contradiction.

But even if London were to spend the many millions on all these
conversions – and you need a Louis XIV for that as in Paris or a virgin
site as at Washington – I still doubt very much whether the result
would be the worthiest setting for St Paul's. And that brings me to my
last two arguments.

One is that the sketch of the Lutyens plan shows that such five-
storeyed monumentality and such gigantic columns – which anyway
are a fancy dress for normal workaday buildings – would not exalt the
Cathedral, they would dwarf it. That is what has happened in Rome.
Under Mussolini, the isolation of the forecourt of St Peter's was given
up and a road of monumental façades built to link it with the Tiber.
Any postcard you buy will prove to you that I am right. One is
surprised that the front of St Peter's does not appear larger. It is an
error to think that monumentality helps monumentality. You don't
set a ruby in rubies. The majesty of a building benefits by the contrast
with frankly different buildings around. Just think of the intimate and
varied buildings along such a cathedral close as that of Wells.

And finally, my last argument. But there I am very hesitant; for
there – for the first time, I hope – I am introducing something which
is no more than my own feeling. It seems to me that this twentieth
century of ours, wherever it tries to go monumental and formal, goes
dead. That may be due to the fact that ours is not a formal century,
that it is a democratic century, in fact a century so informal that no
one but a historian can imagine the formalities and conventions of the
Wren period. Or it may be due to the fact that this century as against
Wren's and Bernini's possesses an architectural idiom completely its
own. It need no longer make shift with Gothic arches or Roman
columns as even the Victorians still had to. And so perhaps, in the

possession of our own idiom, we have lost the natural ease of Wren's period in handling materials of past ages.

Here is to my mind a very strong reason why, formal or informal layout, the architectural idiom round St Paul's should not be of an imitation-Wren kind but should be ours, as it is in Sir William Holford's plan.

And so, at last, I have arrived at Sir William's plan. I have said earlier, and I hope I have proved in my Reith Lectures, that there exists in England a strong tradition of informal, picturesque planning, the tradition of Oxford and Cambridge, of Bath and of John Nash's Regent Street and Regent's Park. Sir William stands in that tradition. His approach, the traditional English approach, must be judged according to its own categories and not those of Bernini and Louis XIV. Sir William knew the City inside out when he started. He had, with Dr Holden, been responsible for the general City plan of 1947 and he is in sympathy with those who spend half their lives in it. Whatever he was going to do was intended to be a delight to them as much as to the sightseer or the person who comes for a ceremony. Moreover, Sir William is an eminently competent, clear-headed, sincere man. So he accepted that any scheme that would not function was out of the question. And for a scheme to function in the twentieth century there is much more to be worked out than in the seventeenth. Traffic must work and it must fit in with the wider traffic schemes not even finally decided on, and parking must be possible and out of sight in the precincts. Access and exit to those underground parking spaces must be worked out. You and I, that is the people planners call pedestrians, must be able to walk at leisure without risking their necks. The mood to admire the Cathedral must be safeguarded, the mood to enter it created. There must also be space for a large number of people to gather, there must even be shops and there must be – whether we like it or not – approximately the same tenancy as before. Wholesale evacuation, once again, won't do. So there was Sir William's jig-saw puzzle. And all the time, while these problems were turned over in his head, he had to keep in his heart the vision untarnished of the delight, the manifold delights to the eye he wanted to create. It required prodigious concentration and a great sensitivity. Well – I am here only concerned with the aesthetic side, with the worthy setting, and so let me say now that to my mind, Sir William's plan, judged quite independent of its practical ingenuity, is worthy of Venice.

There will be the approach up Ludgate Hill – at an angle as it always has been – so that the façade reveals itself gradually. Then you enter a paved court with buildings in the modern style arranged to achieve a loose balance. The traffic which now rushes along the right flank of the church is deflected to the line of Carter Lane. On this right side, instead, one building comes close to the façade and then, as one walks towards the back, space widens into a lawn and with that lawn we are taken round to the altar end; here, Wren's little tower of the parish church of St Augustine's remains to give scale to the mighty wall of the Cathedral and a new, low building for the choir school nestles against it. This especially seems to me a stroke of genius, humanly, visually, also traditionally. Choristers have a right to be close to their Cathedral and there couldn't be a better foil for the Cathedral than this light, low, little building.

Now we go back to the front of the Cathedral and start exploring along to the left. Here from the paved forecourt we can turn up a flight of steps on to a terrace, which, incidentally, is the roof of a two-storeyed garage. The terrace is flanked by two identical office buildings, higher now than anything close to the Cathedral, but placed at right angles to the vistas so as not to interfere with them. From the terrace, again reserved for the walker and gazer, one can admire a different – much like that of St Mark's from the Piazzetta – cunningly calculated view of the Cathedral, and the terrace can also be used, tucked away from the immediate cathedral mood, for displays, exhibitions or the like. Then, walking on, even more tucked away, behind Wren's chapter house and an office building, are the shops. And after that the old trees start which you all know and which surely must remain where they are. So walking under these trees you reach the altar end again and the lawn round the choir school. Finally, behind the shops, further away from the Cathedral, more office buildings of varying shapes and heights until we are in Newgate Street and outside the precinct.

Can I hope that this conducted tour has given you an inkling of the variety of pleasures which the Holford Plan has lavished over this complex area? And mind you, not one of these pleasures is not devised in relation to Wren's building, to lead the eye to it, at the best moments and in the best ways, to increase its scale, to provide a foil now for the rotundity of the dome, now for the crowded columns, volutes, bulgy curves of the tops of the front towers.

Sir William's plan is not monumental, for all the reasons I have tried to put to you as fairly as I could, but what it loses in monumentality it has gained in subtlety, in intricacy, in the variety of vistas and also in warmth.

Several of the best men in the profession have backed Sir William enthusiastically; so has the House of Lords, so have some M.P.s. Others have voiced disapproval, so have (preliminarily) some of the most respected newspapers. The decision now rests first with the City and then with the Minister. They chose Sir William and for that I personally shall always remain profoundly grateful to them. Are they now going to trust him?

1   Controversy over the rebuilding of the bombed precinct of St Paul's Cathedral led Pevsner to be invited to give his view of a new plan by Sir William Holford. At the time, the *Architectural Review* was the mouthpiece for a new informal approach to modern urban design. The spirit of this was represented visually in the enticing line drawings of the architect and town planner Gordon Cullen, who designed Peterborough city centre. Cullen's pictures, partly influenced by those of John Piper, with their dramatic shadows, their contrasting surfaces and textures, their views through archways, and their counterbalancing of volumes and spaces provided architects with a visual code that made the severe rectangularity of 1950s architecture seem more artistic than it really was. Pevsner's function in this was to show that the *AR*'s approach was justified by the historical English antecedent of Uvedale Price and the 'Picturesque' movement of around 1800. His subsequent talk about St Paul's was an illustration of how that theory might work in practice and while its contemporary appeal was persuasive, especially to architects, it was a red rag to conservative opponents. One in particular, the Cambridge Classicist Hugh Plommer, who had already crossed swords with Pevsner over his Reith Lectures six months earlier, fired off a letter to *The Listener* accusing Pevsner of wanting to sway 'the rawer members of the public' against 'simplicity and modest symmetry'. Pevsner's choice of comparisons – St Peter's in Rome and St Mark's in Venice – were less relevant than Sta Maria Maggiore or Florence Cathedral, he said, because both were large churches in busy surroundings, and he showed that Pevsner had exaggerated to an unacceptable degree when quoting sizes, since Bernini's colonnades were only half to two-thirds the height that Pevsner had claimed. His larger complaint, however, lay with the validity of the *AR*'s policy of 'English Picturesqueness' and the likelihood that what 'five centuries of slow planning and piecemeal addition' had done for the centre of Venice could be

imitated instantly. Another correspondent the following week argued that Pevsner had failed to tackle the impact that Holford's twin office towers would have on the silhouette of St Paul's and that his comparison with Venice was unfortunate because 'St Mark's is badly dwarfed by the Campanile, and that is exactly what we do *not* want in the case of St Paul's'. Holford's project would be too high and would compete with Wren's dome, he went on. 'No slab-skyscraper ought to be allowed within a mile of St Paul's.' Pevsner's views carried the day and the Holford buildings went ahead. They were never popular, however, and have now been demolished and Pevsner's talk is a test case of him being utterly wrong for the most plausible of reasons.

Some thoughts on German painting

Third Programme
SUNDAY 13 MAY 1956
Producer: Leonie Cohn

Albrecht Dürer is not only the most famous of German artists, he is also the greatest German artist, not because his genius purely in the field of painting emulates that of Grünewald – it doesn't; not because his draughtsmanship has the perfection of Holbein's – it hasn't; but because his range is wider than that of any other artist.[1] It comprises in fact absolutely everything that is most German in German art. Take three or four works of his all from the same two or three years – my years are 1503–05 – and you'll find the piece of turf in its breathtaking truth to nature, its meticulous and yet respectful accuracy, the figure of Death riding on a mare, with its shrill uncompromising horror, and the warm, loving intimacy of the engraved *Nativity* and the engraved figures of Adam and Eve, two model nudes, of canonical proportions and in Italian attitudes.

I was reminded of all that and of Grünewald and Holbein and also of Altdorfer and the Romantics such as Runge and Friedrich – and furthermore of the great German sculptors of the fourteenth, the fifteenth and the eighteenth centuries – in the first ten minutes of my first exploratory saunter through the exhibition of German painting of the last hundred years. There they were again, the same qualities, only spread out through three or four generations of artists and their works – mostly exceedingly well-chosen works, I may say straight away.

You start with a man like Menzel who was born in 1815 and lived to the age of ninety, a dwarf and a bachelor and an eminently talented man whose early paintings have a direct, sunny, airy freshness which is the belated German equivalent to Constable but who forsook all that almost at once for the sake of a minute, precisely and sometimes rather cruel rendering of observed scenes – something like Frith, though with a superior painterly competence behind it which he possessed from the beginning and developed during a stay in Paris, when he was forty. Similar is the case of Wilhelm Leibl, a generation younger, working in Paris in 1869–70 and capable of a broad realism and an impressionism, the outcome of the experience of Courbet first and Manet afterwards. But he also turned away from the superficiality (in the literal sense of the word) of Impressionism towards the exacting draughtsmanship of Holbein and Dürer. At the exhibition, his *Women in the Pew at a Church Service* is a monument of this respect of his for every detail of features and clothes, far superior in unity and ultimate truth to Ford Madox Brown, let alone Frith. Leibl's most ambitious painting, *The Poachers*, occupied him for four years but after an indifferent reception in Paris in 1888, he cut it up.

Paris of course was the focus of all European painting in the late nineteenth century. It was what Rome had been in the centuries before; and to Paris also the generation of the German Impressionists proper went for longer or shorter periods: Liebermann, the most competent of them, very Berlinish in his cool, assured, unhesitating handling; Corinth whose strong and somewhat brutal vitality in the end burst Impressionism and resulted in a position which might tentatively be compared with that of Jack Yeats; and Max Slevogt, the most elegant, witty, lively of them. Liebermann went for the first time to Paris in 1873, Corinth in 1884, Slevogt in 1889.

But the Goethe tradition of Italian nostalgia, indeed the Dürer tradition (for Dürer went twice to Italy at the age of twenty-three and thirty-five) was not abandoned in Germany either and there was a group of painters in those very years who went for their inspiration to Italy and indeed chose to live there. Böcklin is the most ostentatious of them but Hans von Marées infinitely the greatest. He is a lonely figure but without doubt a figure of European stature. This, to the best of my knowledge, has never been realised in England before. The triptych at the exhibition, *St Martin, St Herbert, St George*, is not Marées's best work but it introduces him well to a public which can hardly know him. It is not superficially Italian and it is technically as tentative, indeed as ignorant, as the early work of Cézanne. The comparison with Cézanne is true at least as far as their concern with pictorial construction and their never-ceasing experimenting and doubting goes. But Marées's palette is sombre, the mood of his scenes hushed, the figures seem to exist rather than to act. England has nothing like Marées. In France he might be compared with Puvis de Chavannes but he is a far more serious, searching artist. And unlike Puvis but like Cézanne, his art leads one from the nineteenth to the twentieth century.

The years 1905–25 are the climax of the exhibition and they were, I think, a climax in German art. The break from Impressionism to Post-Impressionism or as the Germans call it – rightly in their case – to Expressionism is represented at the exhibition by outstanding works of a large number of painters. The source of Expressionism, it is true, was again Paris: chiefly Cézanne and Gauguin although artists of other countries, Van Gogh and Munch, played a part as well but this initial inspiration set free a most powerful set of reactions and the results were most emphatically German – strident colours, angular, distorted bodies, a violent simplification of features. There were various groups, the Brücke at Dresden, the Blauer Reiter at Munich, the Bauhaus later, but there were also artists who remained single and there were plenty of them. It must indeed be said that for an understanding of the changes in European art before and immediately after the First World War, a knowledge of events in Germany is imperative, which cannot be said of English events (except for the one Mr Wyndham Lewis). German painting admittedly at this stage includes the Swiss Klee and the Russian Kandinksy but it was Germany undoubtedly that aesthetically they belonged to in those crucial years.

You must not expect me to try and characterise these painters individually although most of them deserve prolonged individual attention. The new mood includes Kokoschka's prodigious alpine phantasmagoria with its nervous lines, some of them scratched in, and its fabulous sky; it includes the gentler, more unsophisticated harmonies of Franz Marc's peaceful *Horse in a Landscape*, a hymn to the unity of animate and inanimate nature; it includes Klee's whimsical, crafty comments on a strange world – small in scale like Dürer's best work – and with such delightful titles as *The Revolt of the Viaduct*. You must go and see the picture yourself to understand it.

I think that Emil Nolde who died a few weeks ago was the painter of the greatest calibre. His *Family* gives you some idea of that with its glowing intensity of relations, human as well as aesthetic. But Nolde is at his most moving and most German in his religious paintings and of them no first-class example is on show.

That is one serious gap; the other is the artists of political and social criticism, George Grosz and Otto Dix. Were they deliberately left out as too left-wing? They certainly are an indispensable part of that violent whole, German Expressionism, specially indispensable because Beckmann, another of the best, is only represented by later, more accommodating, more colourful and more international work. What would have been needed is something like his *Trapeze* of 1923. But I must not go on in this vein, throwing out names of painters who must be unknown to a good many of you. And yet I have not by any means mentioned half yet of the Europeanly important of the German Expressionists, not Kirchner nor Schmidt-Rottluff, nor Feininger nor Rohlfs – enough!

Here in point of fact lies to my mind the difficult problem of such an exhibition as the one of which I am talking and the difficult problem of such a talk as mine to you tonight. To me, many of these pictures are old friends and the painters are those with whose names I grew up. Some of them I used to know; many of the controversies I remember vividly; in a few I was mixed up to the extreme degree of physical violence. To you, the impact of the exhibition must be different. I know only too well that when one is faced with so complete a display of the art of a relatively unknown country, one usually reacts by noticing similarities with the great painters of more familiar countries, and influences from them, and leaving it at that. The original contribution is easily overlooked, attention to so many new individuals one after the other tires and the label 'provincial' is quickly attached to anything outside Paris. This sort of thing ought not to happen in the case of the German exhibition. The exhibition is, as far as I can see, extremely well chosen. Germans tell me that it is more representative of their art, especially of the early twentieth century, than any museum in Germany is at present and it is in addition – as I said right at the beginning – quite uncommonly representative of German qualities in art.

Expressionism surely could not have become the movement it became in any other country but Germany. You find in twentieth-century terms the violence of German fourteenth-century sculpture and of Grünewald's *Crucifixion* and also of Dürer. You find, for instance in Klee, Beckmann and early Kokoschka the graphic sense of Dürer. You find Grünewald's ecstatic and excessive reaching out for the unattainable in Nolde and also in Kokoschka and you find the direct outpouring of feelings which is often so uncomfortable to English observers of German art in nearly all the early twentieth-century Expressionist painters represented. In this lies the profound difference between Gauguin and Nolde.

Finally, and this is perhaps the most noticeable, there is the all-pervading concern with subject matter. Dürer was primarily an illustrator: he was right through his life illustrating the Passion of Christ and other sacred stories. Klee is nearly always an illustrator – the sense that one must know the titles of his drawings and paintings to understand them. Grosz of course was an illustrator almost entirely. And even the painters of the Brücke can very often not be appreciated independent of their illustrative subject matter. The concentration on the purely aesthetic aspects of art which you get in contemporary Picasso, Braque, Léger and Matisse rarely find parallels in Germany. But while there are such fundamental differences, they are certainly not differences of high and low qualities nor of central and provincial. They are the differences between one country's contribution and another country's contribution, both equal partners in the artistic revolution of the early twentieth century.

1   This broadcast appears to have been a review of a travelling exhibition organised by Volkswagenwerk entitled: 'Deutsche Malerei: Ausgewählten Meistern seit Kaspar David Friedrich'.

King Ramiro's churches

Third Programme
THURSDAY 13 MARCH 1958
Producer: Leonie Cohn

I can't imagine why so few people visit the north of Spain. Instead of exploring that mountainous strip that runs along from Santander to Santiago, the businessmen go to Madrid and visit Toledo, the lazy go to the Costa Brava and the romantically inclined go to Seville and Cordova. Admittedly, *we* were after something special when we toured parts of northern Spain rather intensely some months ago. We were with friends in a comfortable and roomy car – theirs, not ours – and if the gear-lever every now and then got so hot that you burnt your fingers when you touched it, what can you expect of a countryside where you never go from one place to another without climbing 3,000 feet or more somewhere? This obstruction is in fact what accounts for the historical mission of Asturias, the centrepiece of the northern strip, and for the survival of these buildings which we travelled all the way to see. It was worth the trouble – a trouble including many hotels with no water between 5 pm and 9 am, queer hotels with hair-pins as light switches and some hotels with really rather revoltingly greasy food.

But perhaps you should not ask for luxury on a journey through time, back to the eighth and ninth centuries. For the historically minded, the Spain of that period has a great thrill. You must remember that the Moors had occupied Spain in the years after 711 and had only been held up in 735 right in the middle of France. By then revolt had also started in Asturias. It started with the battle of Covadonga below the snow-capped peaks of Europa, east of Oviedo. Oviedo is the capital of Asturias, a big modern city, much damaged in the fierce fighting in the Civil War and now undecided between industrial shabbiness and flashy new building. The hero of the battle was Pelayo, a nobleman of Visigothic descent. When the Moors came, the Visigoths had ruled Spain for nearly 300 years. Their capital had been Toledo and they had built some remarkable things. However, little of that survives. But when the Asturian revolt spread, when first the north-west with its venerable spiritual centre Santiago de Compostela and then territories south of the Asturian mountains were captured, the Asturian liberators could choose for their own buildings between Visigothic and Moorish models.

These buildings which I shall try to describe to you belong to the ninth century – that is, in European terms, the time from Charlemagne's glorious empire and his Renaissance of Roman beauty and splendour to the collapse of that empire, or in English terms to the time of the Danish invasions and the settlement under Alfred the Great. The King of Asturias who is of central interest to us is Ramiro I, a man of whom little is known. He is said to have been 'hard and just'. He made several sallies against the Infidels and during one of them, the legend tells us that Santiago himself – that is, the apostle St James Major – appeared to him on horseback and guided him to victory. Santiago also told him that Christ had made over to him, Santiago, as his special province, the whole of Spain.

But while history is silent about King Ramiro, he means much to the history of Western architecture – much more than most people know. The buildings which were designed during the short eight years of his reign and happen to have survived in their improbable situations are among the most important and the most rewarding of their time in Europe. They are not as grand and noble and civilised as Charlemagne's own palace church of Aachen but they are far more powerful than smaller Carolingian churches. They are also more interesting, I think, than any of their date in France and they are as interesting as the Anglo-Saxon churches of England and without doubt architecturally much more exciting. But they have more in common with the English churches than with any on the Continent and that makes them specially worthwhile from our insular point of view.

They are small, that must be said at once, but so are Bradwell-on-Sea, Bradford-on-Avon and nearly all the others in England. That does not mean that there were no bigger churches in Spain or England. The Cathedral of Oviedo in the ninth century had twelve altars. York Minster at the same time had thirty and the cathedral church of Tours in France in the fifth century had fifty-two windows and 120 columns. But these major buildings have all been swept away.

Where we are lucky, we have such small fragments of them as the catacomb-like crypt at Hexham or the cavernous two-storeyed vaulted chamber of the Camara Santa at Oviedo. It is very likely that these major churches of England and Spain and of France and Germany were like those of Ravenna and Rome – that is, buildings with a relatively long nave and aisles, and a uniform procession of columns accompanying the worshipper from the entrance to the apse with its high altar.

But the surviving Asturian churches are quite different and, what is more, they are entirely different one from the other, not at all standardised in plan or in elevation – although all are of one unmistakable character. Their naves are short. Some have one apse but most have three in a row, all straight-ended, not rounded. Straight-ended like those of Bradford-on-Avon, Barton-on-Humber, Escomb and so many other Anglo-Saxon ones. And they have, again exactly like the Anglo-Saxon churches, curious chambers attached in all directions: *porticus* was the contemporary name for them in England. It may be a west porch, one- or two-storeyed, like at Monwearmouth, or it may be square side chambers, transept-like but not open to the body of the church like at Bradford-on-Avon, as transepts usually are, or it may be – and this is especially odd – a two-storeyed chancel. So these Asturian churches consist of a number of separate apartments, composed in a variety of ways. This strange method of agglomerating began in England at Bradwell and Bradford earlier than the year 700. So it did in Spain.

The most impressive monument of this early date is San Pedro de Nave some fifteen miles west of Zamora – that is, not far from the Portuguese frontier. You reach San Pedro on a dusty lane and find it in a hot dusty village, as African as any I have seen. But it was not originally on this site. It was removed to it when the big reservoir was built nearby and flooded its original leafier site. That church, although well over 100 years before our King Ramiro, has all its architectural essentials in common with Ramiro's churches – except for one thing, the principal innovation of this particular group and indeed an innovation of great European moment, even if done on such a small scale. These later Asturian churches are vaulted throughout. You may not realise what an innovation that was but you must remember that vaulting in stone is a technical problem and that the science of it, in which the Romans excelled, was all but lost in these centuries. Aesthetically, the difference between vaulted and not vaulted is enormous. You can see that in any comparison with the Anglo-Saxon churches which are all unvaulted. The Asturian vaults are what we call tunnel- or barrel-vaults and they occur low and high, small and less small, short and long, and they make you feel as if you were in some cave or sombre shrine. Stone all around you, small windows only, and the weirdest decoration, little columns like twisted rope, capitals with barbaric foliage or even more barbaric figure work, pairs of beasts and pairs of birds facing each other or even scenes with human figures. And the side rooms appear mysteriously through low little arcadings.

The principal buildings are Santa Cristina de Lena, San Salvador de Valdedios, San Julián de los Prados, San Miguel de Lillo and Santa María de Naranco. Lena lies on a hill, off the main road from León to Oviedo where the scenery turns from the mountainous wild to the blackness of the steel mills. You can reach it only on foot and there is only one service a year in it. Like all the others it has no tower and its attraction is the various shapes and heights of the core and the attachments and, of course, the beauty of the warm-coloured stone. While we were trudging up, they were just burning the shrubs along the path and it became a bit of a jumping procession.

San Julián de los Prados is no longer in the Prados – that is, the meadows – just as St Germain des Prés in Paris is no longer in the Prés and St Martin in the Fields no longer in the fields. San Julián in fact lies rather bleakly in a suburb of Toledo and once formed part of a suburban villa of the King. We know that King Ramiro built baths and a *triclinium* – that is a dining hall – as well, and the church, bigger than the others, seems in fact to have adjoined domestic buildings. Wouldn't one give a lot to know what such a palace was like 1,100 years ago? Well, one can conjure it up to a certain extent – thanks to San Miguel de Lillo and Santa María de Naranco. Two miles outside Oviedo, the chronicles tell us, halfway up the refreshing coolness of Monte Naranco which rises 3,000 feet above the town, Ramiro – so the chronicles tell us – built '*palatia et balnea pulchra adque decora*', palaces and baths, beautiful and splendid, and they were built '*cum pluribus centris forniciis*' with various vaults, 'the likes of which', the chronicle adds, 'do not exist anywhere in Spain' – which means in

Saracen Spain, the Spain of the rich and highly civilised Saracen rulers, builders of the Mosque of Cordova. San Miguel and Santa María lie some five minutes' walk from one another, halfway up the mountain. They are surrounded by trees, tall pines and acacias, I remember, and they belonged no doubt to the same precinct. But whereas San Miguel is a church, Santa María de Naranco is not, or at least was not originally. It was built as the royal hall, the *triclinium*, of this villa of King Ramiro's. Kings had their *aula regia*. You know the one in *Beowulf*, timber-built, and the plans at least are known of Charlemagne's great halls at Ingelheim and Aachen. They were focal points in large symmetrical plans with atria and colonnades, and the hall at Aachen, of which walling still stands high, was over 160 feet long. Naranco is not like that. It is no more than sixty-five feet in length. But it is complete and it is delicious, with many surprises.

The Hall itself lies on the upper floor and is accessible by an outer staircase. It is as sombre inside as the churches, oblong and tunnel-vaulted. But at both its ends the sun streams in, at one end in the morning, at the other in the evening. For here, the walls open in three tall arches upon terraces or loggias and in the middle of the side facing the entrance there was a third such loggia. The view over Oviedo is spectacular. And in the undercroft below the hall is a bath, just as the chronicles tell us, even if not one equipped with the luxury of contemporary Oriental baths.

What other buildings belonged to the villa? And how was life lived in it by the King, by the court, by the meaner orders? We don't know, though we could perhaps risk reconstructing a little from Einhard's *Life of Charlemagne* and Asser's *Life of Alfred the Great*. But while that would remain hypothetical, the buildings are there in solid stone, well buttressed and well vaulted, intricate in plan and cunning in decoration, and that, I suggest, is enough and plenty to be thankful for.

★

The ingratiating chaos

Third Programme
TUESDAY 11 NOVEMBER 1958
Producer: Anna Kallin

To me, the most striking thing about New Zealand is the complete contrast between the landscape and the life and houses of the people. There is this thrilling exotic landscape, rain forests with tree-ferns and innumerable parasites, mosses, lichens, lianas, the rugged fjords with dark and dense trees growing right up to the snow-line, the immensely wide shingle beds of rivers, the bare-brown rocks and tawny tussock on which the sheep feed and the sinister geothermal regions where steam rises from ominous cracks, where mud boils in pools with a hideous blub-blub and where one feels the foul fiend to be within calling distance. And yet, wherever one comes across houses – I say houses, not whole suburbs for they are as chaotic as the raw forest and as alternating as the furthermost regions – all identical houses and gardens, perfect tidiness everywhere. You'll see no misery or poverty, no picturesque neglect and no pleasing decay. You'll find lanes far out in the vast countryside labelled with street names as if they were in subtopia. You may find the occasional old hotel of the 1860s built during the gold rush in Central Otago but it is newly painted and the town has lost all the fascinating ghost-town character which is familiar in Colorado.

I confess it was a bit of a disappointment to me. For I travelled less to enjoy the landscape than to study buildings and towns of the past and the present. Buildings of the past in New Zealand are either Maori or Victorian. Of Maori art and architecture I knew nothing when I arrived and know little now. So my impressions are a tourist's and not worth bothering you with – except perhaps for one thing. The crafts of the Maoris are gone. Maoris have had access to schools, university and all jobs for a very long time and so their natural skills have disappeared. Now the whites are trying to develop a revival. Some of the vanished crafts happen to attract us today and efforts concentrate on them. I was, for example, impressed by the tuku-tuku, a weaving of a wall-covering with split or, rather, halved bamboo as the warp. It creates very decorative simple patterns and seems ideally suited for a modern setting. Perhaps the new New Zealand House in London could somewhere take notice of it. What is sold of wood carving and greenstone carving in the traditional Maori style is terrible – the greenstone idols incidentally being carved in Germany.

But souvenirs shops not specialising in Maori stuff are equally terrible. The taste of the common man in New Zealand, I think I can safely say, is very raw. You recognise it in the furnishing stores and in women's clothes and men's ties as well. It poses a problem for the modern architect who can, for the furnishing of a house, often not get what he would like to or has to buy one particular Danish chair for use everywhere because it happens to be the only one imported and even these imports have now come to an end owing to the restrictions introduced recently by the Government. The public at large does not worry about them as it does not worry about visual subtleties anyway.

I found that particularly distressing with regard to one aspect of architectural history and its implications for today, an aspect which happens to be specially close to my heart. You can call it the *genius loci* – that is, the appreciation of the individual qualities of one particular site and the buildings on it and the endeavour in any development to take these qualities into consideration.

Now I found the *genius loci* in the four main towns of New Zealand very strong, very different one from the other and not without lessons even for us, let alone the New Zealanders. My technique for discovering *genius loci* is to walk extensively and at leisure. It is a technique trained over years, in work on the volumes of my *Buildings of England*. The people in New Zealand were very puzzled by it for their natural way of moving about is, just like in America, the car. While they are in the car they watch the road. Once they are out of it, they watch the shops. They never watch townscape. There are four main towns which I had to walk: Auckland and Wellington on the North Island, Christchurch and Dunedin on the South Island. Auckland has fewer inhabitants than Bristol; Christchurch and Wellington about as many as Coventry or Leicester; Dunedin about as many as Northampton. The two South Island towns have their major old buildings of stone, the two North Island towns often of timber. The two South Island towns are examples of Victorian planning – a rare thing anyway – and in some ways of Victorian planning at its most remarkable.

Christchurch is in the flat though there are volcanic hills close by and the Southern Alps in the distance. The town is laid out on a grid plan but the small river Avon winds its way through it and its banks are planted with lawn and English trees. That adds a delightful touch of the informal and the picturesque. Moreover, a large park lies immediately next to the town centre. So in spite of the imposed colonial grid, the landscaping tradition of the old country reasserts itself successfully. Dunedin is surrounded by hills and the houses rise up them. Here again, right from the beginning, the British love of greenery has left its mark and the town possesses a Green Belt designed fifty years ahead of schedule. For Green Belts are supposed to have originated in America at the end of the nineteenth century.

The principal buildings of both towns are in the Gothic style. The Cathedral of Christchurch stands in the middle of the central square, a remarkably ambitious building considering that it was begun when the town had a mere 8,000 inhabitants. For the design, the authorities had gone to George Gilbert Scott, again an ambitious thing to do. Altogether, in assessing the work and style of the Victorian architects, one tends to forget their colonial jobs. For instance there is a very fine late church by Pearson at Auckland and Sir Ernest George built a big Jacobean house at Dunedin. Similarly the Roman Catholic cathedral at Christchurch is the work of an Englishman, though a less-known one, F.W. Petre, a member of the family of the Lords Petre and the building is of a size hardly equalled by more than one or two Catholic churches in England and at least internally, with its two superimposed colonnades all along the apse, very monumental. Externally, admittedly, it is awkward and behind the times. Time lags indeed have to be expected and they can be shockingly large. For instance, in a smaller town, Palmerston North, I found in one street a little Congregational church which, even to the lettering on it, looked a pretty 1845 but was begun in 1900 and another church looking like a somewhat ill-informed 1850 was begun in 1924. The best parts of the buildings of one of the most distinguished public schools in New Zealand, Christ's College, Christchurch, are in a very charming Arts and Craft style and I dated them about 1905. But they are of 1921 and the work of Cecil Wood who was a nephew by marriage of Norman Shaw and trained in England by, among others, Leonard Stokes.

But there can't be a rule about time lags and New Zealand has occasionally been up-to-date to the last minute – not only where English architects provided the design. The great Council Chamber at Christchurch of the 1860s, for example, might be just as well inside the Northampton Town Hall and the Grafton Bridge at Auckland, a single-span three-hinged concrete bridge of 1908–12, was the largest of its kind in the world when it was built by an Australian firm and as progressive stylistically as any concrete structure at the time anywhere.

The centre of Auckland has not much else that would be as thrilling though the suburbs are punctuated in a surprising way by bumps which are extinguished craters with grass growing and sheep grazing on them. If there were possibilities for the planner in this, they have certainly not been taken notice of and as for the centre of Auckland, it is a grid without a square or open spaces. The grid is moreover applied to a site which slopes down to the harbour like a trough – that is, natural contours are completely disregarded. So Auckland would need desperate action to endow its centre with any *genius loci*.

Wellington has plenty of it. The sides round the beautiful harbour rise steeply, houses seem to stand upon houses, and a cable car takes you from the bottom to tier after tier of streets. The principal Government offices are a building of four storeys, twenty-three windows wide and all of timber, a tour de force, even if completely in imitation of stone. But the cathedral of the 1860s is also of timber and this has a lovable, homely exterior and an interior with timber piers and an ingenious timber roof which I would certainly try to illustrate in my *Buildings of England* if I came across it in an English town.

Yet the church authorities, including the Archbishop and the Dean, have decided to pull it down to save upkeep, sell the site and add it to the fund for building a large new cathedral on another site. Mind you: on another site. Surely that kind of ecclesiastical vandalism would by now be impossible in England. The same fate befell some Wren churches in the City but that was over two generations ago. But in New Zealand, they think buildings cannot be worth preservation because they are not old enough – a fatal error. Age is relative and can determine neither architectural nor historical interest. In New

Zealand, as in the Middle West of the United States, the oldest buildings are no more than 100 years old. So the 1860s are a venerable age and the cathedral at Wellington is the principal building of the date in the capital, and moreover it is a cathedral. I was very shocked by this callousness. On the other hand, I was of course not alone in being shocked by it. But the common man, I assure you, is not shocked.

The bugbear is of course what you might call the pioneer attitude of New Zealanders. Wooden buildings have always been put up when and as needed and have been added to or replaced easily and without much thought. So preservation seems against the grain, especially so in the case of buildings for use: farmhouses, warehouses, office buildings. Only the oldest stone houses and stone churches round Auckland are accepted as ancient monuments but hardly anything else, however pretty the cast-iron verandas of houses on the North Island and the fret-saw verandas of houses on the South Island may be. And if I told people at Dunedin that the interior of their railway station of 1904 with its Art Nouveau maiolica facing would be very good of its date anywhere in England and ought not to disappear, they just laughed.

Well – perhaps you laugh too. That is, of course, why the preservation of certain Victorian buildings does not enjoy yet the backing of public opinion in England. But then *we* worry about preservation of buildings of 2,000 years; they in New Zealand are concerned with only 100 and so the not-too-many best buildings ought to be specially precious.

Now at this point I come to a personal difficulty which I found myself up against. When I told this to a normal businessman, he took it that I was against modern architecture. What is one to do about that? In fact, my interest was, of course, evenly divided between old and new. So let me now tell you something of the state of modern architecture in New Zealand. The first important fact is this: there are very few big jobs going. You must remember that the whole population of New Zealand is no more than that of Warwickshire. Secondly, the biggest jobs – that is, I think, an interesting point – are nearly all in the hands of the Government Architect, Mr Gordon Wilson, an enlightened man in sympathy with recent development. And so a point block of Government offices is now going up at

Wellington with a very interesting earthquake-proof concrete core and other high-rise slabs for offices and flats. Also, at least connected with the Government, is the new Hermitage Lodge, an extremely pretty holiday hotel of timber right below Mount Cook, which is as high as Mont Blanc. This hotel belongs to the New Zealand Tourist Corporation, a Government-sponsored body, and is designed and finished as well as any such hotel anywhere. It lies on a slope with entrance hall, lounges, dining rooms, bars etc. on ground floor level; and then at their back, a staircase leading straight up and out, rising under cover in three laps to a separate bedroom block, behind which lies, higher up, identical bedroom and shower units in two storeys. The style is comparable perhaps with Cortina. The architects are Hall & Mackenzie of Christchurch.

As for the rest of what I have seen, it was mostly the work of young architects and it was – worse luck for them – almost always on a very small scale. The standard job is the timber house for an enlightened and appreciative client, done with little money. New Zealand is not a country of very rich as it is not one of very poor. So intelligence goes into planning, the way a staircase is placed and surrounded by space or the way a house is set across the whole of a narrow, deep plot with front garden and back garden of varied shapes instead of sitting in the middle of the plot with inadequate equal spaces left and right. The timber detailing, on the other hand, seems to me not quite so satisfactory, rather minimum and a little coarse. But there, one of the best younger architects argued with me and from what he said it transpired that he regarded the European architect's fuss over mouldings and profiles a little as an old man's game. A young nation might well, he implied, be a bit impatient about it and be ready to call a spade a spade and a four-inch timber post a four-inch timber post. So perhaps what seemed raw to me is in fact robust and vital.

The same doubt crept into my mind with regard to what is the real visual horror of New Zealand, the suburb which is subtopia to a degree I had hardly believed in my worst dreams. There are miles of timber bungalows, all neatly built and neatly painted in gay, boiled-sweet colours. Slums don't exist. What they call a slum is simply bungalows spaced too tightly but still neat. It is complete chaos but the most ingratiating chaos one can imagine. There are no attempts at planning except that Government estates use the winding roads of the English garden suburb. But that can't help much and terrace housing is taboo because of shades of Victorian terraces way back home and flats are taboo too. So mixed development on the lines of the London County Council has never once been attempted yet. And without that, these vast areas of small houses just defeat you.

On the other hand, if you look at the individual houses provided mostly by builders and not architects, the depression gets less and a ray of hope illuminates this suburban chaos. The thing is this. Admittedly, many of these builder-built houses are awful but they are without any hesitation in the modern style and only distinguished from the houses of the young architects by being ignorant or jazzy in details and generally lacking in sensitivity or planning intelligence. But, for better or worse, they are contemporary all right, which is more than one can say of the spec builders' post-war efforts in English suburbs. And the common man who buys them or has them built doesn't object to the style, doesn't call it modernistic or futuristic or what have you. He has never developed prejudices against what is new. He knows no snobbery about the upper class's Georgian setting. And so, after this journey, in one way I believe more in a healthy future of twentieth-century architecture out of the New Zealand chaos than out of our planning over here.

★

Dark gold

Third Programme
MONDAY 16 JANUARY 1961
Producer: Leonie Cohn

There must be something inherent in Baroque architecture which makes all reactions to it violent. It either infuriates you blindly, as it did Ruskin, or it sends you. I think that what makes indifference impossible is the claim of the Baroque to dominate all, first not only the building strictly speaking but also its decoration, its sculpture and painting and ultimately its setting as well, a whole area, a whole town, and if possible – in Versailles for instance – a whole region. But the Baroque enthusiast eager to make converts must distinguish. It is not always the sweep of the Baroque which annoys, it is often its scale. I hadn't realised that distinction fully until some months ago, in Brazil, I found myself in a perfect Baroque town where all was on an intimate scale. I got into an argument with someone who, like ourselves, had just come from Brasilia, the new capital, and attacked its plan (ready-made for half a million people) as grand, axial, blustering – in short, he said with all signs of disgust, Baroque.

My answer was simple in defence of the Baroque, not so simple in equally convinced defence of Brasilia. But Brasilia is not my story today. For the defence of the Baroque, all that was needed was to point from the terrace of the hotel where we had lunch over Ouro Preto, the town of which I am going to tell you, and say: 'This is Baroque, not only in its architecture but in its sense of an all-embracing unity, undisturbed by any pre-Baroque buildings and nearly undisturbed by any later ones. Is it grand? Is it blustering? Is it totalitarian? It obviously isn't.'

The reason why Ouro Preto is so completely Baroque and has stayed in its Baroque shape is simple and yet remarkable. Ouro Preto is a gold-rush town. But for heaven's sake, don't think of the ghost-towns of Colorado. Here, the gold-rush belonged to the eighteenth century and the result is a superb little place, its many hills crowned with delightful churches. The first gold was discovered in some black granite with glittering spots which a mulatto had found and sold just before the end of the seventeenth century. The rush pioneers fought each other. A more serious revolt against the government, trying to run the finds, ended in its leader being drawn and quartered and the four quarters being sent to four places nearby. That was as late as 1720 and it is just as well to remember it in today's peace in the steep cobbled streets of this town of many hills.

We went up to Ouro Preto by car from Belo Horizonte, a rich upstart city of half a million inhabitants. Pampulha is a kind of suburb of it. You may remember the name Pampulha; it was here that Oscar Niemeyer[1] did his trial runs in 1941–42 with buildings so curiously shaped and in their details so unfunctional or anti-rational that they caused as much irritation as argument. Yet they started – one can say – an international fashion for canopies curling up, for raking walls and parabolic curves which is still very much with us. Niemeyer has grown wonderfully from this dare-devil naughtiness to the maturity of the President's Palace at Brasilia.

As one leaves Belo Horizonte and its untidy skyscrapers and climbs up to Ouro Preto, a variety of landscapes passes by. Little farms, large virgin woods, bush – we might say – of dense but short growth, red earth, yellow earth, banana palms and the glorious yellow Ype which has its flowers before its leaves, just like the lilac Jacaranda.

Ouro Preto appears quite suddenly after a drive of nearly two hours. It has 9,000 inhabitants and thirteen proper churches, quite apart from a lot of small wayside chapels and, as we drove in it, looked twice as many: churches on the hills, churches in the dips, churches in all directions. Yes, in all directions – that is, not at all orientated. This is an odd thing that applies to South America in general and I have never yet found a satisfactory explanation of it.

The churches are all of the eighteenth century and they combine a unit of type with a great variety in detail. Building started seriously in the 1720s but most of what one visits is of the later eighteenth century and about 1770 or 1780 the whole town must have been in a cloud of building dust, just like Brasilia today. Some churches went up quickly, others took a generation, and the Ouro Preto style, emphatically still Baroque and not yet neo-Classical (nor even yet Louis Seize or Robert Adam) kept going to about 1830 or 1840, a remarkably obstinate survival, due to the fact that by then Ouro Preto's boom was over. Auguste de St Hilaire in 1816 called the town melancholy and deserted.

What is fascinating about the churches, at least to the scholar – provided he is as inveterate a Baroque enthusiast as I am – is that they are all clearly of one family and yet all individually different, not in accidental decorative ways but different in a deliberate, strictly architectural way – variations on a theme as, admittedly more subtly, are the churches of Neumann[2] or the Dientzenhofers.[3] What they have in common is this. They are all of rubble, whitewashed a really white white and with ample stone dressings, either a stone of Pentelic beige or of grey soapstone. The major churches have two towers at the ritual west end, smaller ones one tower. But here the differentiation starts. Between the two towers, one church comes forward with a canted centre, another in a bow, a third in an elegant double curve. Not one of the churches has aisles but the naves again vary from the plain oblong to the longitudinally placed oval or the oblong with canted corners or convex canted corners or an elongated, longitudinal decagon. This experimenting with possibilities of spatial variation strikes one as more akin to what one knows in Austria and South Germany than to Spanish or Portuguese Baroque and the religious orders in the Colonies such as the Jesuits, the Franciscans and so on were indeed completely international.

The layman may be taken by the decoration more than by the architecture. The altars are rich and intricate, brown and gold or white and gold, and as crowded with ornament as they are in Spain, though not as frantically encrusted with carving and gilding as at Bahia or Rio. The centres of the altars are flanked by twisted columns or pilasters with odd scrolls in all directions, by angels as supporters and cherubs playing in the foliage. Some of the soapstone sculpture is just as rich and most of it is more accomplished.

The hero of the Ouro Preto story is El Aleijadinho, that is Antonio Francisco Lisboa. He was born in 1738 and died in 1814. He was the natural son of a Portuguese master mason and a mulatto girl, was short, dark, strong, with thick curly hair and always ready for girls, wine and pranks. But then a terrible disease got hold of him and he became the Aleijadinho, 'the little cripple' – 'little' referring only to stature and certainly not used as an endearing term. Lisboa was formidable in his revolting distorted body, a fanatic worker, chasing away anyone who wanted to watch him while he carved and chiselled. His disease is not identified with any certainty. It deformed him, his eyes were inflamed, he lost his teeth and in the end his toes fell off and most of his fingers fell off. No wonder he went early in the morning to his churches in a dark cloak and on horseback and locked himself up inside. Aleijadinho carved some of the best pieces at Ouro Preto. His portal surrounds and lavabos in sacristies are exuberant and full of life. The ornament is Rococo. The style is rustic rather than accomplished. With Günther or some others of the best Germans he must not be compared. Yet, the standard of carving at Ouro Preto, by the Aleijadinho and others, is far superior to the standard of painting, which is really poor.

It is easy to visit the churches. They have time-tables of opening varied so as to offer one or two at all hours. We would have missed some if it had not been for the happy chance of a procession which filled the streets with its single file of followers, now here, now there. The canopy of Cardinal purple led the way and we could take advantage of it. It was a modest procession, nothing like the memorable one of 1733 when the relics were returned to the newly rebuilt church of the Pilar. There had been the four Winds then, the seven Planets, Fame and pages and cherubs and nymphs and even Turkish dancers.

Walking through Ouro Preto is arduous and you need strong shoes. Many of the streets are extremely steep and the cobbles as well as the setts tend to be slippery in the dryness of a sunny day. The town is entirely protected by the Ancient Monuments Commission. You may find that it looks a little neglected all the same. In any case, it is not a bit dolled up. The smoothness which our Ministry of Works can't help leaving as their mark when they have excavated or secured old buildings is quite absent here. Donkeys graze peacefully in a churchyard, whitewash flakes off, painted doors look pale and washed out. But on the other hand, the town is convincingly a live little town. John Luccock about 1815 says it then had about 2,000 houses. That may still be the same now. There is little new building and it is tucked away – except for the regrettable new Grand Hotel which, though low and by Niemeyer, jars painfully. Still, lunch there is welcome and if one eats the lunch courageously, leaving out the main dish, one may still feel able afterwards to go on climbing.

The centre is the oblong square with the governor's palace at one end, the town hall at the other. The palace is inconspicuous, the town hall with its tower over the remarkably incorrect frontispiece fits in with the churches. Some private houses of the later eighteenth century are quite lavish too, especially the one that is now the Post Office. But the charm is not in the individual houses, it's in the ensemble. There are really hardly any houses which don't fit, and a large number are of the time when the churches were built. They are all two-storeyed with windows and doors ending in shallow arches. On the ground floor is a door and two or four openings identical with it and leading to one or two shops. Above are the windows – French windows as we would call them – with iron balconies or parapets and occasionally oddly Mahometan-looking wooden shutters. And then there are the fountains of soapstone, large or small, richly ornamented or humble, with dates: 1753, 1757, 58, 59, 60, 61, 1763 – the great years of building at Ouro Preto – and occasionally with inscriptions. Richard Francis Burton who visited the town a hundred years later commented on them: 'the water is better than the latinity'. The water is indeed beautifully pure.

'Exceptionally pure' Burton also calls the girls of Ouro Preto. Of this I have no experience but I can support him in his contention that they are at their most exquisite between thirteen and sixteen. You see them everywhere on the balconies, always in pairs or threes, looking down on the boys and the general bustle, girls, fair, brown, black. Ouro Preto is a perfect mixture of races, though the black, the Negro blood, dominates. And there seems no cleavage between the colours. Black youths, very slender and erect, broad shoulders, narrow hips, sauntering with inimitable grace by the side of small lively Spanish-looking girls. Prematurely old men with creased, permanent-looking faces, stand in the bars and mothers sun themselves outside their houses quite impassive and unmoved by their five, six, seven children playing about them.

But then suddenly the strolling groups all fall in with one another.

The brassy blare of a band approaches and gets louder and louder. I suppose they are on their way to join the procession. For the time being they play something military and suddenly it comes back into one's memory that it must be the national anthem. And with it come back late evenings in the black-out and the series of anthems of the allies, played faithfully by the BBC. The series was short at first and grew only longer after Pearl Harbor. Brazil joined the war early, shortly after Pearl Harbor, and the sense of alliance with Europe and the West has never faltered since. Ouro Preto shows how right it is. What makes us Europeans so happy there is the feeling that this is, in spite of the colours of skins, something Portuguese – not quite, Spanish – not quite, South Italian – not quite, but something generally Mediterranean that is in the prime European tradition without any doubt.

1   Chief architect of Brasilia.
2   Johann Balthasar Neumann, 1687–1753, Germany's leading Rococo architect.
3   The Dientzenhofer family, Georg, his sons Johann, Leonhard and Christian (or Christoph), and Christian's son Kilian Ignaz, were leading Baroque architects working in Bavaria and Prague between around 1680 and 1750.

The return of historicism

Third Programme
SATURDAY 11 FEBRUARY 1961
Producer: Prudence Smith

Queer things are happening in architecture today, none queerer than what made me call this talk 'The return of historicism'.[1] Let me explain what I mean by this title. Historicism is the outcome of such a dominating faith in history that it chokes original action and the action which replaces it is inspired by the past. In architecture the nineteenth century was the period of universal historicism. The architect and the architectural historian were as a rule the same man. As a historian he would travel, look at buildings of the past, draw them and measure them and then he would return and, as an architect, design his building in their image or at least exclusively with their motifs.

But then, about 1900 to 1910, a race of giants arose and created a new style for a new century, a style which was completely independent of the past. It was a tremendous thing to do and we have grown much too blasé to appreciate that any longer to the full. The courage, the force of imagination and also the intellectual effort were truly gigantic. For there were not only new forms involved but also a new attitude to architecture. The new conception was that architecture, besides being an art, is also a service to the community. This new sense of social responsibility expressed itself in the principle of functionalism – that is, the principle that form follows function in the sense that a building must function first of all and nothing on its exterior – or inside either – must reduce its well-functioning; or, the other way round, that the beauties of the exterior must be developed after the assurance of the fullest functional fulfilment and never at the expense of it.

These new principles did not establish themselves at once, of course. The development of the years 1890–1930 is a straight line only in so far as novelty of forms goes, but regarding the social side it is a development in which functional and anti-functional tendencies alternate. The first emergence of new forms, nothing to do with function, was about 1890 to 1905 in what was called Art Nouveau in England and France, *Jugendstil* in Germany, *Stile Liberty* in Italy. It was mostly a matter of decoration and the crafts but culminated in a few architects, the greatest of them Gaudí of Barcelona. They broke up historicism and introduced unprecedented, sinuous or crustaceous, abstract or naturalistic forms. Their courage was great, their ornamental inventiveness uninhibited, but their works often make those of the historicists preceding them look very sensible and serviceable indeed.

Then came my giants, Frank Lloyd Wright, Perret and Garnier, Loos and Hoffmann, Behrens and Gropius and the principles of functionalism – and at the same time, the straight unrelieved forms of the twentieth century were established in opposition to Art Nouveau. By 1914 that style was complete. But in the turmoil of the First World War which destroyed the universal faith in progress and rationality, a reaction appeared: Expressionism with forms as fantastic as Art Nouveau, but now sharp, violent and aggressive and with as little interest in function as Art Nouveau. It was an episode confined chiefly to Germany and Holland but even Gropius and that noblest of purists Mies van der Rohe lost themselves for a while in that undergrowth. And then, by 1924 I would say, the functionalism of 1910 returned and for a while all seemed well to us young people.

But we were deceiving ourselves. The style was too exacting, too perfectionist, too puritanical and perhaps also too inflexible to be a popular success. It was never wholly accepted – certainly not in England or France, in the United States or Italy; and in Germany, where more than anywhere it was accepted, Hitler suppressed it. It had really become an internationally welcome style only by 1945–50; but by then, a vigorous opposition against it had started, an opposition not from the diehards but from the young – young in mind if not always in body. That opposition is not strictly speaking my subject tonight. But the return of historicism is one aspect of it and its most unattractive aspect.

The fact of the matter is this. While there are still some of the old Neo-Georgians about, building for the financiers and the farmers – the *Financial Times* and the Farmers' Union – there are also among us, some in this country, many in Italy, those who go in for brand-new Neo-Isms. There is Neo-Liberty in Italy, there is quite a lot of Neo-Gaudí and there is Neo-Expressionism. I'll try and give you some examples. Gaudí's Casa Mila at Barcelona has a curved front with heavily rounded details as though it were scooped into by surf. It seems inimitable when you see it, bold and crazy. But years later, there is John Johansen's design for the American Embassy at Dublin doing the same thing and Messrs Howell, Killick and Partridge's Science Building at Birmingham University also, though comparatively moderately. Well, since 1955, seven books on Gaudí have come out in Barcelona and very recently two in America and England. One of the Barcelona ones has a foreword by Le Corbusier who – we all know – is always so anxious to prove that he has been there before or that he told you so. Well, in that foreword he says that he discovered Gaudí for himself in 1928, a remarkably early date considering his own development, to which I shall revert later. What matters for the moment is only that Le Corbusier in 1960 wants to display himself in the line of descent of Gaudí rather than of Perret.

Now a second example of the return of historicism. There is the famous furniture made by Rietveld in Holland about 1917–18, very square, very chunky, with every part clearly and demonstratively separated from the other. A forceful statement in favour of the return to the elementary and of course part of the Cubist movement as well. Now look at some recent furniture, again by Howell, Killick and Partridge and also by others and the dependence will not be denied by anybody. Then there were the similar, chunky, arbitrarily projecting bits in the façades designed by the members of the School of Amsterdam – de Klerk and Piet Kramer – just before 1920 and there they are again, for instance in buildings designed about thirty years later by Messrs Stirling and Gowan. The School of Amsterdam also went in for weird bits of brick decoration and fancy window shapes: if you thumb the Italian architectural magazines, you will find them revived in buildings by little-known but also some very well-known Italian architects. And again, the same magazines carry fully illustrated articles on the leaders of Art Nouveau, on Horta, on van de Velde, on Mackintosh, on Sommaruga – in fact, the lot.

But here I must stop for a moment in self-defence. I myself wrote a book in 1936 on the development from 1890 to 1914 and it must have been the first for many people in this country to present to them Art Nouveau. Expressionism of course was outside my field. Well, it came out and it sold slowly. Then, in 1949, the Museum of Modern Art in New York took it over and its prospects began to look up. And now it is a Pelican. I am therefore undeniably a beneficiary from the return to historicism. But am I also a culprit? Is it not us, the historians, who have presented to these architects what tempted them into imitation or even inspired them? It is probably us, yet I deny that any historicist intention guided at least *my* hand. My motives were quite different. I was an ardent modern in the 1930s and I still am – that is, an old-fashioned modern who goes on believing in the soundness of the principles of functionalism. But as a historian I was not going to be swayed by that. My curiosity was roused by this new style I was experiencing: how did it come about? What happened between the period inspiration of the nineteenth century and this new style? So out came William Morris, out came the Arts and Crafts, out came Art Nouveau – and in the end I was satisfied that the various trends had been recognised, described and set against each other and that the task was fulfilled. But to recognise Art Nouveau for what it was and to define the part it played in history does not necessarily mean to recommend it, least of all for imitation. On the contrary, I wish architects and especially students would always understand that the historian presents styles as eloquently and evocatively as he can, not as examples to be followed but as examples to prove that each period and each phase have to create their own expression and that therefore our day is under the same obligation. The historian deals with the uniqueness of each style and is in this respect the very opposite of the partisan journalist who presents bits from the past because they will please certain people today.

I do apologise for this bit of apology. What really matters much more than to allocate guilt is to ask in all seriousness how this return to historicism can be happening? Now my answer would be this: it is part of something much wider. I have already said that in the Second World War and immediately after, a violent reaction set in against the rationalism of the style of the twentieth century, if we can still call it that. Historically speaking, it started with young Oscar Niemeyer in Brazil in 1942 and 1943. It broke into full virulence with Le Corbusier's Maisons Jaoul and his Unité d'Habitation at Marseilles – nearly twenty years after 1928 – and it culminated in his Pilgrimage Chapel at Ronchamp. And now roofs like collapsed tents are with us, roofs like the tops of mushrooms, porch canopies curling up or doing a Hitler salute or snaking left and right, windows in a wall of all shapes and sizes as if the wall were a complicatedly punched card, walls also with an applied chequerboard pattern, either by imposing it on formal fenestration – as for instance in the gilt-edged windows in Grosvenor Square – or by setting the windows themselves chequerboard-wise.

You can easily imagine that behind such a wall, planning must be either bad or adjusted with veritable acrobatics; 'acrobatics' in fact is the word which that great imaginative engineer-architect Nervi uses to describe many of the fashionable and exciting new roof configurations. Nervi actually used it for the sail- or shell-shaped roofs of the future Sydney Opera House. Of course, you can argue that for an Opera House in such a glorious position, you want something exciting rather than something rational. But we must be clear all the same that this new style of the 1950s is an anti-rational style. It has been called neo-sculptural, neo-plastic, neo-formalist – anyway, it is anti-rational. And with that it is anti-functionalist. The controls of function as established in the first third of the twentieth century – and in this immensely important process we can forget the Expressionist episode – these controls are now relaxed. How fatally relaxed they can be you can see in the exhibitions of students' work from the most go-ahead schools. I remember particularly vividly the so-called Show-rooms for the Furniture Manufacturers' Association by a student who was certainly not lacking in initiative. This building was abstract sculpture of a doughy, rooty, bony or gristly kind, not the functionally best solution nor an economically justifiable solution nor acceptable in terms of townscape. And the design was most certainly influenced by Gaudí.

It is the undisciplined individualism of such designs that worries me. I have been told that I shouldn't worry. Let architects do what they like. Why shouldn't they have fun? If the situation looks chaotic, as it did *not* twenty years ago, well then – and it is Philip Johnson of New York who is reported to have said this at a lecture in London a month or two ago – well, then let us have a nice juicy chaos. No: that isn't good enough. Surely, if the historian of architecture does not take style dead seriously, then he stops being a historian. If, by definition, style is the visual expression of an age, then style must matter. The style of 1900–50 was the visual expression of an age. That is what makes it so thrilling to me, both as a person belonging to that age and as a historian. The forms created, the planning solutions found, represented faithfully what the age was up to. Leadership of science and technology, industrial production of parts, catering for mass needs in housing, factories and also of course schools, hospitals, hotels and so on; anonymous clients not only as tenants, pupils, patients, but often even as building committees approving designs, *firms* of architects designing for these committees instead of working as lonely geniuses in their studios. These conditions were recognised and accepted. The outcome was the attitude of the architect as the provider for material and spiritual needs that had been intelligently analysed.

Spiritual needs? Perhaps in the rigidity of the style of before the Second World War, spiritual needs were not sufficiently taken care of. Yes, there is something in that, and if Le Corbusier is so lucky as to be commissioned to design a pilgrimage chapel, by all means give free play to his genius. As you have seen, I am ready, reluctantly, to concede this freedom to the Sydney Opera House as well. But to the secretariat by Le Corbusier at Chandigarh, which is an office building, or to a science block for a university? To showrooms for furniture manufacturers? Who wants to be excited by them?

And in the end, even the admission of two fundamentally different approaches to two different types of building worries me as a historian. An age ought to be capable of creating a unified style and I am not convinced that the Stockholm Crematorium and the Gothenburg Concert Hall are emotionally less effective because they are neither Art Nouveau nor Expressionist but display a noble unaffected simplicity. Yet I admit the frequent failing of the style of the 1930s when it came to building for spiritual needs, and I admit the necessity of more variety than the rigid parallel lines of rational housing in the 1930s provided. But I believe that siting, grouping, landscaping and a sensitive selection of materials should take the place of the fashionable funny turns – that is, I believe that architecture can remain rational and functional without having to be dull and barren. That conviction of mine has nothing to do with historicism although if it had been universally accepted, there would have been no return to historicism.

The reason for the return of historicism is in my opinion simply this: when the great ones start doing funny turns or, to be more polite, to be original at all costs, then the less great ones will imitate them and repeat their funny turns or try to achieve an easier originality with less obvious imitation by borrowing from sources of the past not yet familiar from past borrowers. To borrow from the eighteenth century or the Neo-Classicism of the Regency would be too blatant; but it seems that to borrow from Art Nouveau or Expressionism is almost to be original.

1   This programme is based on a talk given at the Royal Institute of British Architects
in London by Pevsner in January 1961. Pevsner's use of the word 'historicism' has
been much discussed and appears to be all his own. He means the (improper) use of
artistic and architectural forms developed in and associated with past ages, and in this
sense the word always carries a negative connotation. This differs from its usage by
Hegel, Marx, St-Simon, Comte, Spencer, Spengler and Toynbee for whom it means a
law of history that reveals an inevitable sequence of cultural changes to which every
age must conform, including future ages.

Mannerism and Elizabethan architecture (PART I)

Third Programme
FRIDAY 21 FEBRUARY 1964
Producer: Anna Kallin

I have recently had a very entertaining experience. In a volume of the
Oxford History of English Art which came out a year ago, Mr Eric
Mercer writes of my views on Elizabethan architecture that they are
conditioned by my Prussian Junker background. This is priceless, as
anyone who knows me and my background will see straight away, but
it is also based on so much misunderstanding and misinterpretation of
my views that it made me wonder whether it was not at least to a
small extent my fault and whether I should not take the trouble to
formulate a little more fully what I think of Elizabethan architecture.
The problem – and this is what may make it interesting to some of
you – is very closely bound up with that of Mannerism and that term
has been much used and misused in the last few years. Moreover, Mr
Mercer rather regrettably throws my pronouncements together with
those of a younger German scholar, Dr Wüsten, who has written a
whole book – a bad book in my opinion – on Mannerism in English
architecture. Mr Mercer's attacks on him are entertaining again
because Dr Wüsten is an East German and Mr Mercer appears from
his book to hold solid Marxist views of history. You see it is all rather
involved.

Now I am not a Marxist and this must have been clear ever since I
first wrote on Mannerism in 1925. It was a paper on Mannerism and
the Counter-Reformation and it linked the most important facts of

Italian sixteenth-century painting and sculpture with the spiritual situation of the same decades – 1520 about to 1590 or 1600. I might even be blamed by non-Marxists that that paper did not contain enough of material, that is, social data.

Be that as it may, with that paper of 1925 I carry some of the responsibility for Mannerism having become a term defining a certain style in art, a style with positive qualities like the Renaissance and the Baroque. In fact I am not the father of all this, as some people have recently said. The recognition of Mannerism as a style in its own right is due to Max Dvořák in Vienna about 1917, the publication of his views in 1921 and after, and to Wilhelm Pinder (who taught me the history of art) and his lectures of 1923 and 1924. But this is only for the record.

What is however needed before any attempt can be made to confront Elizabethan architecture and Mannerism is a definition of what I – and here I can now safely say, what we, that is, responsible scholars interested in the sixteenth century – understand by Mannerism. When the term was invented or rather transferred from a term of abuse to one of objective definition, it had become a necessity; for it had been recognised that the radical turn in Italian painting just before 1520 – the turn you see in the work of Michelangelo, Raphael, Correggio, and also the turn from, for instance, Andrea del Sarto to Pontormo and Rosso, was one as clearly away from the Renaissance as it was *not* towards the Baroque. Until the 1920s, Wölfflin's view had been held by all – that is, that the Renaissance was followed immediately by the Baroque, but that record was patently wrong. The characteristics of Michelangelo's *Libyan Sibyl* or *Jonah* in the ceiling of the Sistine Chapel, of Raphael's *Fire in the Borgo*, of Pontormo and Rosso and later of Parmigiano and so on to Tintoretto and Greco were obviously anti-Renaissance but they were not Baroque either. The early Cinquecento Renaissance – the High Renaissance, that is – is balanced, bodies are strong and broad faces, gestures, attitudes are noble, compositions are symmetrical, although not pedantically so; it is a world of ideal humanity, even where the divine is the goal. The Baroque, on the other hand – think of Caravaggio or Rubens or Bernini in the first place – is expansive and naturalistic. It exaggerates force, it is after violent sensations. Compositions are thrown out of symmetry, features are strained, details are copied from Nature to create a striking illusion of reality, light throws one thing into sudden relief and leaves others in semi-darkness. Very well – all this may be wildly generalised but it had to be because we are here not concerned with Renaissance or Baroque, only with the fact that Raphael's *Fire in the Borgo* or Tintoretto's *Miracles of St Mark* and his masterpieces in the Scuola di San Rocco or any painting by Greco have none or hardly any qualities of either style. Instead, what have they in common?

Single figures first: they are attenuated, sinuous, flower-stalk-like with small heads. The draperies are sinuous too or they are so ample that the body disappears in them. There is never a convincing display of physical strength, of physical stability almost, nor of staying power. The result can be of exceeding, dancer-like elegance or of immaterial spectral apparitions. The colours tend to be cold, either iridescent or jewel-like. Compositions are intertwined, difficult to see, difficult to understand. Often, for instance, the principal scene or figure is placed far back. Allegory and symbol attract the painters and the patron. You must be in the know to follow what is offered you. Nothing, to sum up, is simple, nothing is normal, nothing is real. Conceits are imposed just as patterns are imposed. This, so I would still argue, is the world of the Counter-Reformation. It is also the world of the growing absolute courts with their elaborate, highly artificial ceremonial. Just think, for example, of Elizabethan clothes and Elizabethan pageants to get the full flavour if it.

But wait: I said 'Elizabethan' and we have so far only been dealing with Italian painting. To clothes, these criteria apply internationally. They also apply unquestionably to Hilliard and Eworth and the others who painted stiff courtly portraits and court allegories in England. Yet Elizabethan England is utterly different from the Italy of the late sixteenth century.

This is really what brings me now to my immediate subject: architecture. After Mannerism as a positive style had been established in terms of Italian painting (and, incidentally, quite easily of sculpture as well, the sculpture of Cellini, Giovanni da Bologna and so on), the next step was to try it out on Italian architecture. And I did. I was again not the first. This was first done in 1932 by my late friend Ernst Michalski, also a pupil of Pinder. A few others followed. I did my bit as late as 1946 in a paper in that short-lived annual *The Mint*[1] and most of it has since gone into my old *Outline of European Architecture* which some of you will know. Mine was no more than the first attempt in English although it often differed in some ways from the others. What I found was this: Mannerism in painting and sculpture had come about in opposition to the Renaissance, an opposition which must have been conscious in many, especially those who were young about 1520. The opposition was directed against the this-worldliness of the Renaissance and against its ideal of a classic beauty at perfect rest and in harmony with itself. So artists broke the rules with which they had been brought up – complication instead of simplicity, difficult reading of the figure and the composition instead of perfect see-ability, if you'll excuse that term. Now did anything like this happen in architecture at the same moment?

It did and in a number of cases it was easy to show. Take Michelangelo's Medici Chapel designed in the 1520s and, even more, take his Laurentian Library, also designed in the 1520s which is really the *locus classicus*. The cold white and dark grey, which are the only colours, the extremely elongated proportions of the members, especially the brackets, as elegant and cold as any portrait by Bronzino, the pilasters which, instead of widening at the capitals, as you would expect, contract so that they are deprived of their visible strength to carry, and the paired columns incarcerated closely in recesses so that they have nothing to carry – here are deliberate illogicality and a use of Renaissance motifs in an anti-Renaissance way. The result is painful, it is an unresolved conflict – in short it is Mannerism.

For Mannerism never solves conflicts. The High Renaissance did not know them; the Baroque solves them triumphantly one way or another. This ambiguity of Mannerism is often expressed in a much less ingenious way in façades of palaces and churches by not allowing either height or breadth to dominate. Watch for instance for palaces which have no decided principal floor but instead, say, a ground floor, a mezzanine, another floor, another mezzanine – Vignola's great palace at Caprarola is an instance – and similarly Mannerist church faces have neither the balance of the few High Renaissance church faces nor the energetic pulling together of those of the Baroque. They spread unresolved, even if mostly without conflict.

But to go on with the extreme, most easily recognised, cases, there is Giulio Romano at Mantua, pupil of Raphael, painter and architect, with his Sala dei Giganti in the Palazzo del Te where the – painted – architecture falls round our ears, as we stand in amazement, and giants tumble down in the debris; or the real architecture of the court of the same palace, where the correct classical Doric frieze on its columns is every so often painfully interrupted by a triglyph being seemingly in the process of slipping down, or the courtyard in the castle of Mantua which has attached barley-sugar columns. Just try to think that out visually – attached barley-sugar columns – and you'll participate in the pain of the jarring details. What did Sebastiano Serlio, author of the first published illustrated treatise on architecture, write: 'To break and spoil *la bella forma*'? Even in terms of space I was able, I think, to show Mannerist qualities in Italian architecture, especially the liking for long, narrow vistas down to a distant closure – that is, not open to infinity as in the Baroque. The best-known example is the Uffizi courtyard in Florence by Vasari, so familiar to tens of thousands yet so rarely looked at as architecture. There you have the cold colours again, the indecision over the predominance of any one storey and in addition this impressive, tunnel-like vista along to the transparent galleries across the end. In Palladio's church interiors in Venice you find the same in the way the chancel ends in transparent arcading beyond which the building evidently goes on, although we don't know how.

Yet – and this is the next stage in my arguing – it would be forcing the evidence to say that Palladio's villas are Mannerist buildings. I admit that there are Mannerist features in them. Look at the back of the Villa Malcontenta, one of the two or three most familiar ones, or the front of the Villa Poiana or the courtyard of the Villa Sarego at Santa Sofia and you'll see motifs assembled into an ensemble that jars, a loggia front of completely unmoulded members, giant columns built up of rocky drums and so on – but they are exceptions of a passing phase. So you ought to return instead to the famous Villa Rotonda, absolutely symmetrical to all sides, with beautifully balanced fronts and with no tension, let alone any unresolved conflict. Mannerist? No – it must be admitted that taking him all in all, Palladio, exact contemporary of Tintoretto though he was, is not a Mannerist. But then, after all – is Veronese in painting? The difference, however, is that in painting the non-Mannerists in the age of Mannerism are an exception, in architecture less so. I'll just mention one more: Michele Sanmicheli of Verona. There has been an exhibition of his work in London recently and so some of you will remember that his palaces of the 1520s and his gates of Verona strike one as essentially Renaissance and not Mannerism, though Mannerist Giulio Romano motifs do occur. Finally, think of Vignola, this time at the end of Mannerism, the designer of the church of the Gesù in Rome, one of the most influential churches ever designed – but influential this time in terms of the Baroque and again not of Mannerism.

So here is a warning. Not everything, but nearly everything of importance in Italian painting and sculpture of about 1520 to 1600, is Mannerist. Not everything but a good deal of Italian architecture is. But among the exceptions there are several of the greatest. Some of you may even say that, after Michelangelo, Palladio on the one hand and Vignola on the other are the greatest. If this is the situation in Italy, what are we to expect of an outlying country like England? This is the question which I shall have to answer next time I talk to you.

1   Published by the poet Geoffrey Grigson.

Mannerism and Elizabethan architecture (PART 2)

Third Programme
THURSDAY 27 FEBRUARY 1964
Producer: Anna Kallin

It is an understandable desire of the historian to establish that one style rule at one time everywhere. A kind of mental tidiness demands it and also the historian's imperative faith in a *Zeitgeist* – that is, again, one character pertaining to one epoch. Moreover, this universal unity of style is what we have experienced in the case of the International Modern style of architecture, although with time lags. It is also true of the Romanesque and, with considerable national variations, of the

Gothic. Can it then also be established for Mannerism? This question is what made me (and, as I said in my previous talk, others before me) move from Italian painting and sculpture to Italian architecture and I confess that I felt some illicit satisfaction when I saw that at least in certain not unimportant features even Palladio could be included.

But Palladio for England means Inigo Jones, that is 1620, and Lord Burlington, that is 1720 – the two dates represent the beginning of the two phases of Palladianism – and it does not mean 1520 which is, as you remember, the approximate date when Mannerism started in Italy. What then is the situation in English architecture between 1520 and the early seventeenth century? May it be Mannerism? This pious hope led Dr Wüsten astray, the East German scholar whom I mentioned when I talked to you the other day and who sees in the architecture of Henry VIII, of Elizabeth I and largely of James I Mannerism and nothing but Mannerism.

It is my job today to check how right and how wrong such a view is and this can only be done by keeping firmly in mind the definitions of Mannerism as obtained from Italian painting and sculpture and confirmed by Italian architecture and then by comparing them and indeed the whole situation of architecture in the sixteenth century in Italy with that in England. This is the task with which we have to start. If one criterion of Mannerism is a deliberate incongruity in the juxtaposition of motifs and another criterion is a renewed sympathy with Gothic motifs, for instance in the paintings of Pontormo, does then a building like Layer Marney Towers in Essex of about 1520–25 not qualify? For here is a Gothic gatehouse with a large Perpendicular upper window and a kind of top battlement but the window has dainty Renaissance balusters on the mullions, some sort of cornucopia motif in the arches of the window lights instead of ogee arches, and upright shells instead of battlements. That sounds illogical and wilful enough for Mannerism, but do remember: in Italy, the case is one of deliberate incongruities and of a revived sympathy with a Gothic past. In England it is otherwise. The Gothic past is the Gothic present. Renaissance motifs are a recent import. They appear characteristically enough in the gatehouses of Hampton Court in 1521 as faience medallions of Roman emperors made by an Italian, Giovanni da

Majano, and inserted into the polygonal brick angle turrets as an alien body proudly introduced to show the King's appreciation of the superior world of Antiquity and Humanism.

Italy, when Gothic motifs reappear, had a hundred years of Renaissance on her shoulders. Italy, or at least Rome, but soon other parts as well, had left behind the graceful, exuberant decorative displays of the Quattrocento, happily carried on into the Cinquecento at Pavia, at Como, in the Veneto in the north of the country, and had turned to a severe classic and classical Romanita with Bramanto and Raphael and was now tired of it, bored with it, ready to explore the aesthetic possibilities of what jars, what shocks, what enrages. You see how completely different the psychological situation was. In England there was pleasure in a newly discovered happy beauty of decoration which made the Gothic standard motifs appear sour, thin, gauche. But this new pleasure in England was no more than a pleasure in fresh, natural and delicate ornament and the full understanding even of that was confined to a very few people with Humanist leanings. Layer Marney is the typical case of the courtier wanting to make use of the new fashion in ornament but blissfully ignorant of any unity of style behind it. Even at Hampton Court, the new – though a pure, truly Italian new – was set into the old. At Layer Marney the old is all. The Renaissance motifs are handled awkwardly. This is trying to speak Italian without command of grammar, syntax or vocabulary. So what at first may have seemed to me and others welcomely near to Mannerism is not Mannerism at all. It is the pidgin-Italian spoken by the sturdy Englishman of the Perpendicular – and Perpendicular, you must remember, was a version of the Late Gothic all English, without parallel anywhere abroad. Perpendicular was very strong and it had ruled England while Italy kept busy with its Quattrocento.

Layer Marney was my exhibit number one; number two is known to very few. It is the monument to Sir Robert Dormer at Wing in Buckinghamshire and it is dated 1552, thirty years after Layer Marney. Now this is a totally different story. Here is a sarcophagus with the classic Roman motif of ox's skulls and garlands, set in a generously dimensioned surround with pairs of noble fluted Corinthian columns carrying an ample, well-detailed entablature and cornice. This is a perfectly easy, competent handling of classical motifs and nothing but classical motifs – and moreover motifs emphatically no longer of the playful Quattrocento kind but of the grand Cinquecento kind, that is High Renaissance, and – let me add this at once – not a bit Mannerist. The nearest thing I know is the monument to Raphael's personal friend Cardinal Bembo in the main church of S. Antonio at Padua. Bembo died in 1547 and the monument was designed by Sanmicheli whom I mentioned the other day as one of the architects essentially Renaissance rather than Mannerist, and it is without question a Renaissance, not a Mannerist, monument.

But, you might say, it is ridiculous to assume that a man making a monument at Wing in Bucks should have been familiar with a monument at Padua. Well it isn't – and the two ways in which the connexion can be made are worth my telling you because they help you to see in the right perspective some of the England–Italy problems in architecture. One is that – as Dr Girouard told me – Sir Robert Dormer's son, who no doubt commissioned the monument, was the brother-in-law of the Duke of Northumberland and that the Duke was the first man we know of in England to send an artist specially to Italy to meet Italian architects and study Italian architecture. The man was one John Shute, the date was about 1550 – just the date we want – and in the end Shute published a kind of primitive treatise on the strength of his Italian experiences. Secondly – and this, I think, is just as interesting – two of the other English patrons of Renaissance architecture had actually studied at Padua about 1540, admittedly a bit early for our present purpose. One was Dr Caius, the founder of Caius College in Cambridge; the other Sir Thomas Smith, sometime provost of Eton.

Incidentally, Sir Thomas Smith was a *protégé* of Lord Protector Somerset who was an important patron of architecture himself and other *protégés* of his were two main actors in the story to follow: Sir John Tynne who built Longleat and William Cecil, Lord Burghley, who built Burghley House and was, as you know, the greatest statesman of the Elizabethan Age.

Both Longleat and Burghley were inspired by Protector Somerset's own London palace, Somerset House, begun in 1547. Now, Somerset

House is of importance to us here because it was the first English building designed with some understanding of what the Italian Renaissance was about. Until then 'Renaissance' had meant adding bits to Perpendicular houses. But now there was a symmetrical façade with a middle and two angle projections, with windows widely spaced and given pediments *all'antica* and a middle portal on the scheme of the Roman triumphal arch as revived by Bramante in the Belvedere Court of the Vatican. Somerset House also had orders of columns in two or three tiers and that also was an Italian motif but it had been taken over a generation before Somerset's in France in the chateaux on the Loire; and in France also the triumphal arch motif was, we know, being used at the same moment as that of Somerset House. Somerset indeed probably looked more to France than to Italy. France about 1545–55 was far ahead of England and had in Philibert Delorme a personality of so clear-cut a character as there were in no English architects before the seventeenth century. Delorme, there is no doubt in my mind, was indeed a Mannerist. France by then was ready for them. In fact at Fontainebleau, leading Italian Mannerists had been working in an extremely Mannerist style of painting and stucco decoration as early as the 1530s. There is nothing you could compare with that anywhere in England.

An unbiased look at the old illustrations, which is all that is left of Protector Somerset's Somerset House, will make it perfectly clear that Mannerist contrariness had no share in this design. The symmetry is arranged with ease, the triumphal arch motif and the window pediments are demonstrations of classicity and even the funny two oriels above the triumphal arch are only a sign that the Perpendicular past was still alive, not at all a sign of wilful English quotation in an Italian phrase. The English never get far away from the oriel.

There is really in the whole of Somerset House only one motif which I would be ready to accept as Mannerist. It is the tall paired chimney stacks. Their decoration is of the gay, busy, cut-brick Tudor kind familiar from Hampton Court and many other places but they carry an entablature and they seem to be meant to stand for Classical columns. If that is so, then it is a misuse of a Renaissance motif in the very spirit we find in Italian Mannerist designs. In the oldest surviving drawing of the building this is not quite clear, but the first of the great Elizabethan mansions, Sir John Tynne's Longleat, certainly interprets this motif in this way and has paired Tuscan columns as chimney stacks behind its top balustrade. And William Cecil's Burghley House also has them. But how far – this is now at last the crucial question – how far are Longleat and Burghley and the other Elizabethan palaces in the English countryside, how far are Kirby, Wollaton, Montacute, Hardwick and such Jacobean palaces as Hatfield and Audley End, Mannerist? I'll try next time to give my answer to this question.

Mannerism and Elizabethan architecture (PART 3)

Third Programme
FRIDAY 6 MARCH 1964
Producer: Anna Kallin

I ended last time by posing the crucial question of these talks of mine: how far can such houses as Longleat, Burghley, Wollaton, Hardwick, Hatfield, be called Mannerist? To answer this question we must first agree on what are their distinguishing characteristics. To me they are large windows with many mullions and one, two or even three transoms – that is, each a glazed grid; then bay windows and oriel windows, flat roofs perhaps punctuated by gables or turrets, a minimum of decoration except round the main entrance where you find columns, often in several tiers, and also that curious kind of ornament which is known as strapwork.

Now strapwork is a thoroughly Mannerist kind of ornament, *the* Mannerist ornament in fact. It is abstract, first of all, shapes of a sort reminiscent of thin wooden boards cut with a fret-saw or of leather cut with scissors and curling up at the ends or of cut parchment. Abstract ornament instead of the natural, beautifully but only slightly stylised foliage ornament of the Renaissance. Natural forms do occur with the strapwork as well but they are now grossly, unrestrictedly naturalistic, thick juicy fruits and vegetables and so on, obviously introduced for the contrast against the abstract strapwork and in such a way that the contrast remains in all its violence – a typically Mannerist attitude. This Mannerist ornament appeared for the first time at Fontainebleau and was then at once, in the 1540s, taken over by the Flemish. Elizabethan England, as you know, swarmed with Netherlandish artists. The leading painters, the leading sculptors and many decorators came from the Netherlands. From the Burghley papers we learn how an Antwerp master mason travelled forward and backward between his home town and England and how fully worked stones were shipped from Antwerp to England. In fact the decorative enrichments of Elizabethan and Jacobean interiors are often entirely Netherlandish in style, especially screens and chimneypieces and of course funerary monuments. Now these pieces with their strapwork and their bearded male caryatids or high-bosomed female caryatids growing out of sturdy tapering pillars are Mannerist in every sense – which shows that Mannerism as an overcrowded and confused accumulation of debased Renaissance motifs was welcome in England.

But did it represent a real conversion? I doubt it. Surely the large windows I have described in the first place are nothing if not English Perpendicular – only more so than the real Perpendicular of the fifteenth and early sixteenth centuries because then, at least at the top, each light had a little pointed arch where now there is nothing but horizontals and verticals, or, if you like, perpendiculars. And this bluntness and repetitiousness, these unrelieved horizontals and verticals, which had already distinguished the Early Tudor Perpendicular from any form of Late Gothic architecture on the Continent, has now spread to the plans and in some cases even the elevations as a whole. Take Hardwick as an extreme example – 'Hardwick Hall, more window than wall'. In plan it is an oblong with three square projections grouped round each of the short sides. The oblong is three-storeyed, the projections have four storeys and they end squarely and bluntly at the top, just with a minimum of pierced frilly strapwork. Surely there is here not a sign left of even a qualified sympathy with the Renaissance, be it with the Early Renaissance of Layer Marney or the High Renaissance of the monument at Wing. It is without any question anti-Renaissance – but is it Mannerist therefore? It is tempting to say 'Yes', pointing as an argument to the similar stiffness and angularity of contemporary dress. But I still think the temptation ought to be resisted and houses like Hardwick ought to be interpreted as triumphal proof of the power of survival and the sturdy health of the English Perpendicular.

Or take Hatfield, at least the side of the present-day entrance. Surely it is the same: rectangularity, directness and the absence of any of the artificialities and contradictions of Mannerism. Hardwick was begun in 1590, Hatfield in 1608 and completed in 1612. In the same year Bramshill in Hampshire was completed. It had been started in 1605 and is of the same unambiguous Perpendicular Englishness – except that here on the entrance side there is a frontispiece as Mannerist as anything anywhere: three tiers of paired stocky tapering pilasters, decorated with all kinds of motifs, and a top of wild big pierced strapwork. Inspiration for this frontispiece and the even more fantastical frontispiece of Charlton House, near Greenwich, was the craziest of all Mannerist pattern books, a German one of 1593.[1] But that Mannerist ornament could be accommodated and was enjoyed, we know already. What matters is that it did not affect the bones, the basic Perpendicular quality, of the buildings.

However, one thing has not yet been touched at all. It concerns something surely basic, the plans of the houses. Those of the Perpendicular manor houses had been informal and asymmetrical; now they are symmetrical. Not that symmetrically planned secular buildings had not existed at all before but they had been castles: Harlech and Bodiam for instance. But only with the early sixteenth century was symmetry of façade imposed on houses. The earliest example is Barrington Court in Somerset of about 1515 but most of you will remember more easily the entrance side of Hampton Court. Now Barrington and Hampton Court are pre-Renaissance in their forms. So this was an indigenous Late Perpendicular development, one of many signs to indicate that by 1515–30 the country was ready for the Renaissance – that is, began to appreciate an appearance of order and balance even at the expense of functional honesty. For the asymmetrical exterior of the earlier manor house had expressed unashamedly in size and place of openings what kind of room lay behind. Now the large bay window of the high-table end of a great hall might, for instance, be matched by another in its symmetrically appropriate place, even if no specially prominent room was behind. Such an illogicality has also by some been regarded as Mannerist.

But, again, surely, there is no justification for any of that. What is it that is Mannerist in planning in Italy? Two things, I think, one can single out: first, the tunnel-like spaces running into depth, of which I spoke the other day; and secondly the imposing on the plan of a pattern wholly independent of any regard for the uses of the rooms or the building – for example, the circular courtyard of the Emperor Charles V's new palace of the Alhambra at Granada or a hunting lodge outside Prague built by Italian workmen in the form of a six-pointed star.

Now, has England anything to compare with these Mannerist conceits of Italy? My answer is Yes. I think I can point to three features. First, surely, the Long Galleries of Elizabethan houses have the Mannerist quality of the tunnelled space, excessively long and always low, even if it must be admitted that they are not an innovation of the Age of Mannerism. They existed already about 1500, for instance in Henry VII's palace at Richmond in Surrey. Then, secondly, some of the curious entirely patternised plans of Mannerism also have their parallel in England, foremost Sir Thomas Tresham's highly curious Triangular Lodge at Rushden and John Thorpe's design, which needless to say remained on paper, of a house in the form of his monogram, J.T. The Triangular Lodge fits the Italian case particularly well for it was built for a fervent Catholic to be throughout (three gables to each side, trefoil windows and so on) a religious riddle, the solution of which is the Trinity. That is both the spirit of the Counter-Reformation and Mannerist conceitism. And, thirdly, if you want a total Mannerist conception of a house, take Wollaton – for two reasons: a plan almost as patternised as those I mentioned just now and some peculiar motifs of the exterior. The plan is not oblong as all the others without exception have been so far but instead a square with angular projections, and the Great Hall is in an unprecedented position right in the centre of the whole. This is revolutionary from the functional point of view but might perhaps be interpreted as a compliment to Renaissance all-round order rather than to Mannerist enforcement of a pattern. It is different with the motifs of the exterior of which I am thinking. Above the hall is a summer room and so the whole centre rises like a big central tower or really like a keep and the designer has indeed given that part corbelled-out angle turrets, as if it were a Scottish castle, and windows with a kind of half-understood Gothic tracery. Now this is very interesting. Here we have clearly not the *sur*vival of the Perpendicular but a self-conscious *re*vival, something like Spenser's archaic diction and the Arthurian allusions in some of the Queen's pageants, and a relished archaism is something entirely Mannerist. Nor is Wollaton a solitary case. There are others of this same Mannerist mediaevalism.

That is as far as I would go, and what it results in is this: England participated in the International Mannerism in dress and the ceremonial of the court, in painting and sculpture, in the funerary monuments especially, in much domestic decoration and here and there in certain architectural features and attitudes.

But basically the Elizabethan style was not a Mannerist style. Nor can it have been when you come to think of it. For Mannerism evolved in Italy as a revulsion against a hundred years of Renaissance and it belonged to the Counter-Reformation – that is, the Catholic revival – and to absolutist courts, both being forms of ruling people's lives in a spirit of distrust of human freedom and self-determination.

In England, architecturally speaking, the Italian Early Renaissance with its pretty and playful arabesque and candelabra shapes came in while the grave, noble, balanced High Renaissance held sway in Rome; the High Renaissance came into England when Mannerism was in full blast in Rome; but Mannerism also came in at the same moment, even if, as we have seen, only in this or that feature. That means that England accepted the Renaissance in the first place because it meant attractive, fresh and happily balanced ornament, in the second place because it meant grandeur and symmetry. The tiredness with a played-out Renaissance which was the strongest single cause of Mannerism in Italy obviously could not exist. If the English did not turn to the Italian Renaissance more universally and more convincedly, the reason was not, as was the case in Italy, that they were sick of what had been accepted by everybody for a hundred years but, on the contrary, that what they themselves had accepted for a hundred years – namely the English Perpendicular – was far too strong to be jettisoned.

What does it then all amount to? Italy in the sixteenth century was a tired country, capable still of great spiritual impetus but politically on the decline. England in the Elizabethan Age was full of zest, self-confident, boisterous. Not that there was no sophistication. There certainly is in men such as Sir Walter Raleigh. But, one thing one can say safely, I think. The prevailing mood was one of optimism all round with the political triumph over Spain and the triumph over Antwerp. Elizabethan architecture is scarcely ever as sophisticated as Elizabethan poetry can be; it is robust, lusty, even gross. That is not the spiritual and intellectual climate out of which Mannerism could evolve and so my verdict is that the term Mannerism which I helped to establish and popularise can be used for English architecture only to a severely limited extent.

1   By Wendel Dietterlin (1550/51–1599), a German artist and designer working mainly in Strasburg.

The Anti-Pioneers

Third Programme
SATURDAY 3 DECEMBER 1966
Producer: Leonie Cohn

I celebrate a memorable anniversary this year. I mean memorable for myself. It is just thirty years since I brought out my *Pioneers of Modern Design: from William Morris to Walter Gropius*. The book was originally called *Pioneers of the Modern Movement*; for what was in the book was supposed to be the complete prehistory of all that mattered in twentieth-century architectural design – the Modern Movement – and, as such, it has been compulsory reading for many a generation of architectural students in this country.

I needn't tell you how my argument went. First the theory of simplicity, honesty, service from Morris to the German Werkbund, then architecture and design on their way to these aims, including a chapter on Art Nouveau as the first effort to create non-period language and a chapter on the achievements of the engineers from the suspension bridges to the Eiffel Tower and beyond. My book goes only to 1914 because by then, in Frank Lloyd Wright's houses, in Tony Garnier's blueprint for an industrial town and more than in any other building in Gropius's Fagus Works, a style was ready and complete which was still the modern style of 1936.

But now, thirty years later, the young, it seems to me, have their doubts on the validity or at least the value of this interpretation of history. Reyner Banham – my pupil, I am glad to say and puzzled to say – was the first to cast doubts on it. I can sympathise with him and with the students of the 1960s, nearly two generations younger than I, nearly one generation younger than he. Someone ought to rewrite my book for them, keeping its main title and saying the very reverse. I can even give that someone the recipe. *Pioneers of Modern Design* for them ought to go like this: Chapter One would deal in retrospect with the fertility of Victorian architecture, its exuberance and its unbounded individualism, but it would end by saying the Victorian Age was still tied to historicism, the imitation of elements from style of the past. This would form the transition to Chapter Two: Art Nouveau. Art Nouveau broke these fetters. New ornament, new forms, great daring, the climax of course Gaudí. Then, however (Chapter Three) a bunch of spoil-sports came along and ironed it all out. They talked of social responsibility first (William Morris) and of industrial production and standards then (Muthesius and the German Werkbund) and they ended by preaching the false gospel of the cube. By 1914 they had driven out all the richness of personality. But then (Chapter Four) the convulsive experience of the First World War upset their rationalism and in came Expressionism with de Klerk and Piet Kramer in Holland, with Klint in Denmark, with Mendelsohn, with Poelzig, with Scharoun and Haering in Germany, years of fervour and boldness. Even Gropius caught fire but, alas, it soon spent itself and by 1924 Gropius re-emerged as the leader of the killjoys. At the same time, Le Corbusier committed himself to Cubist forms in villa architecture, even if he handled them less rigidly than Gropius, and Mies van der Rohe conceived the strictly rectangular glass skyscrapers which today are the standby of every architectural Tom, Dick and Harry. That this is so is due to the spreading of the Bauhaus style to all countries. By the 1930s, Russell Hitchcock could speak of the International Modern Style and I of the Modern Movement, meaning just that.

Because, you see, when I wrote my *Pioneers* in these thirties, what I thought I described was the coming of the Millennium. The Expressionists, in looking back at them from the safe port of 1936, were just ineffectual deviationists. Gropius had done the Fagus Works in 1910, the Bauhaus buildings in 1925. Why bother with some passing vacillation of his in between? So I could safely, I thought, end my book in 1914 and leave the Expressionists out entirely. To me what had been achieved in 1914 was the style of the century. It never occurred to me to look beyond. Here was the one and only style which fitted all those aspects which mattered, aspects of economics and sociology, of materials and function. It seemed folly to think that anybody would wish to abandon it.

But human feelings are inscrutable and what we are experiencing now is a new style completely, an anti-Pioneers style, if my pioneers are still valid, and a style alarmingly harking back in many different, even contradictory, ways to Art Nouveau and to Expressionism.

As I want you to realise that and to accept it, let me try to formulate what is Art Nouveau architecture and what is Expressionist architecture. It is necessary to do that, because to most people Art Nouveau is just decoration, wave, flame or tendril ornament and those odd typefaces which the West End is now so madly imitating, and Expressionism is just certain German painters Nolde, Kirchner, Beckmann, Franz Marc and so on and perhaps Rouault and the Picasso of *Guernica* as well. But Art Nouveau architecture exists and the pope of it was, as I said just now, of course Gaudí. Take the Church in the Colonia Güell near Barcelona – Santa Coloma di Cervelló, it is called. Take its pillars of all kinds of rough angular forms, of rubble or of brick, and set at all kinds of nightmarish angles or its roughly drop-shaped windows and its ambiguity of what is inside and what is outside the building proper – a building in *mood* Gothic but emphatically not in *vocabulary*. That was designed in 1898 and developed up to 1914 and yet tells you not only of the radicalism possible at that moment but also of the strongest anticipation of Expressionism twenty years in advance. For if you want a similar approach, you have to go to the Expressionism of Bartning's Stahlenkirche[1] of 1922 which also has piers which are not straight but leaning or rather swaying and windows of odd shapes. But for radicalism about 1900, you need not go so far afield. Few people know the church at Brockhampton-by-Ross in Herefordshire by Lethaby – 1901. Yet even if without any of the ferocious fantasy of Gaudí, here is another church Gothic only in mood and not in vocabulary. The closely set, sharply pointed stone arches across the nave rising nearly from ground level straight out of the walls are unforgettable.

But if Brockhampton and Santa Coloma have at least Gothic overtones (though really no more than Basil Spence's Coventry), Gaudí's two blocks of flats at Barcelona of 1905 have broken all ties with historicism. Rooms are curvaceous (to the detriment of wardrobes or cupboards you may wish to place against them), the façade bulges forward, the chimney stacks are like part of a specially cruel setting for Hansel and Gretel and are faced with broken tiles and the balcony railings are of such fanatically spiky wrought iron that tenants' trousers and skirts ought to be a special item in the householder's comprehensive policy. So here are ways in which the architecture about 1900 broke new ground and I have suggested that by doing so, inspiration was provided for the Expressionists of about 1920, including very emphatically *Dr Caligari*.

Now a few words on what the Expressionists actually did. I have already given you the names that mattered most and I'll now try to convey something of a few of their buildings. There is Mendelsohn's Einstein Tower near Berlin with its sensational streamlined shape – as if this astrophysical building would at any moment go into orbit itself. Then there are Mendelsohn's Hat Factory at Luckenwalde with its sharp and its obtuse angles in the roof and Hugo Haering's farm buildings at Garkau with their curves in plan and their one telling mono-pitch roof and de Klerk's Amsterdam housing with its random placing of windows and oriels of many shapes and sizes and Rietveld's furniture, primeval, chunky, with all joints exposed and Poelzig's monster theatre, a converted circus with its stalactite vaults. Even the International Moderns, before they finally turned to steel and glass and to the gospel of maximum performance with minimum mass, went in

for exaggeratedly massive concrete balcony railings and demonstrative
brick cubes sticking up or out.

That is the picture of the years immediately after the First World
War. And so now, as part of the *New Look Pioneers* which somebody
ought to write, I must do two things: show that the direct line of
descent from Art Nouveau and Expressionism to the 1950s–60s exists
and voice and define my acute discomfort about what has been going
on in architecture ever since the Unité and Ronchamp.

First Neo-Art-Nouveau. I have already mentioned the poster
designers and typography boys. Jewellery is just as obvious a case. But
in major architecture it also exists. I suppose John Johansen's American
Embassy at Dublin is the most immediately convincing case and he
does not deny himself that Gaudí was an inspiration for the rotundity
of the general shape, the curvaceous balconies and the twists of his
pre-cast concrete members. Neo-Expressionism is rarely that evident
but it is much more serious and – to me – alarming. I have more than
once placed before myself side by side pictures of, say, the
tremendously heavy and in this respect undeniably Expressionist
balcony and staircase parapets of Wells Coates's Lawn Road flats built
in 1934 but still in the style of the 1920s and equally heavy or even
heavier parapets say by Tange or Maekawa in the last ten years in
Japan. Or you might care to make a comparison of the unrelieved
vertical brick or concrete posts and the windows between them pulled
together into slit-like vertical shapes in the Chile House at Hamburg
of 1923 with, shall we say, James Gowan's new house in East Heath
Road, Hampstead. But that is not the whole story; if it were of cases
of imitation only, I would not worry.

What worries me much more is the development of radically
original architecture starting from Ronchamp, the Unité d'Habitation
in Marseilles, from the Maisons Jaoul in Paris and Chandigarh, i.e.,
from late Le Corbusier and leading right up to the present day. To put
it as simply as possible, I'll first speak of motifs only: Ronchamp means
random windows, random in shape and position, and walls and roof of
curvaceous sculptural shapes representing Le Corbusier the abstract
artist rather than Le Corbusier the architect. In the Unité, it is the
equally sculptural and personal roofscape and also the *béton brut*, the
passion for letting things appear raw and unbeautiful. The Maisons

Jaoul re-introduced arches, shallow arches scooped into big concrete blocks, heaviness in preference to lightness.

As for arches altogether, incidentally, that brilliant rogue Philip Johnson had by then already used them in the guest house to his purist, Cubist, all-glass house at New Canaan, Connecticut. That was in 1949 and his eccentric inspiration had been Soane. Philip Johnson is a virtuoso at playing with stylistic materials old and new, including the Victorian overtones of his recent New York State Theatre, so we'll leave him out, but Le Corbusier is of course a mightier matter, partly because of his genius and partly because of his universal influence. Chandigarh I have not seen but it can all the same serve to sum up what matters most today in architecture. It is, in my opinion, three things chiefly: one, self-expression of the artist-architect; two, a fervent avoidance of lightness, of anything that could be called elegant and also of anything that could be accounted for purely rationally; and three, forms of overpowering – what shall I say? – yes: brutality.

Brutalism has been used to mean much – too much, for the Hunstanton School with which Peter and Alison Smithson made their name and which served to launch the term is entirely unbrutal. It is symmetrical, clean, precise – in short, Mies van der Rohe and not Le Corbusier in origin, and the Smithsons' most recent and most conspicuous building, the *Economist*, in London, is again entirely unbrutal, a sensible and in its townscape aspects sensitive job, much less brutal for instance than, say, Richard Sheppard's Churchill College or Denys Lasdun's Royal College of Physicians. Churchill College, with the vaults of its high hall jutting forward on unmitigated concrete beams and tied together by two unmitigated concrete beams ruthlessly slammed on top and across the vaults; and the Royal College of Physicians, next to Nash's Regent's Park terraces, with two square concrete posts in front of one bigger square concrete post to mark the entrance – take it or leave it – and with the long-barrow of dark blackish-blue engineering bricks which marks the lecture hall – take it or leave, Mr Nash.

Now mind you, before going on, I should make it clear that I have the greatest respect and, as it happens, a quite exceptional personal liking for both Richard Sheppard and Denys Lasdun. But what they set out to do is Expressionism all the same, personality-cult all the same, and also in flat contradiction to the corpus of criteria to which I was committed when I wrote my *Pioneers* and to which I am still committed. But I am a historian and the fact that my enthusiasms can't be roused by Ronchamp or Chandigarh, by Churchill College and the Physicians, does not blind me to the existence today of a new style, successor to my International Modern of the 1930s, a post-modern style, I would be tempted to call it, but the legitimate style of the 1950s and 1960s. Very well; but the historian, if he does not shy away from the events of his own day, cannot help being a critic as well. In fact, the conscientious critic's methods are not all that different from the historian's. The procedure is in both cases to analyse many buildings of more or less one date or at any rate one phase, tabulate their qualities, find what they have in common (which is what we call 'style') and then measure them against their own intentions, the functional needs of the job and the social and economic conditions under which they have to exist.

So let me ask as a first question: am I entitled to speak of Neo-Expressionism today? And let me take as a test case one new English building. Wherever I have been abroad recently, the young know and praise the Engineering Building of Leicester University by James Stirling and James Gowan. I saw it for the first time last July and had a good look at it. It consists of a low oblong range with ridge-and-furrow daylighting throughout and, attached to it, two towers, one higher, one less high, set in a staggered way that they only touch at one angle. Both have, low down, but not at ground level, lecture theatres jutting out. They are of exposed concrete; the rest is faced with blue engineering bricks.

When I went over the building, it was fully in operation. Well – it functions, there is no doubt about that, although users of course nag for this reason or that and for good reasons or bad. For example, the ramp to what was meant to be the main entrance is perilously steep and people therefore don't much use it. But the architects needed the ramp for a ramp is a diagonal and diagonals are their line of attack. Take these curious prisms of glass which end each bay of the (incidentally, diagonally disposed) sky lighting of the low workshop range. I have tried in every way and yet I cannot see that they have any functional justification. They cannot let more light in or let light in in any other, more favourable, way. No – they are purely expressional and, as such, additional cost, but of course that in itself does not condemn them more than setting money aside for a piece of sculpture on a building. Only they must be admitted as expressional and James Stirling has himself admitted them as such. He is quoted to have said: 'to construct the shape of the roof and the complicated glazing that was fundamental to the design concept, a glazing bar had to be found which could adapt to the complicated geometry which resulted'. 'Design concept', you see – for that is what I imply if I say expressional. That the expression is aggressive, James Stirling may of course deny. Yet I see aggression in the diagonal undersides of the jutting-out lecture theatres and the chamfering of the higher tower and the angularly projecting aprons of the lower tower. Indeed, this aggressive angularity repeats all over the building. So you see, to me the Leicester Engineering Building is Expressionism, as much as Poelzig's Grosses Schauspielhaus and Taut's fantastic Stadtkrone. It is architecture heightened in its emotional effects by sharp stabbing angles, an expression not of the character of the building but of the architect – personality cult rather than self-effacement, such as comes naturally to the designer who thinks of the end user.

What I am objecting to in this case is the high pitch of emotion in a building which does not call for drama. Take Collins, Melvin, Ward and Partners' new university buildings at Sheffield in comparison. They are in the style of the 1930s – for that style, as we shall see, is by no means dead – and they are so much more neutral in expression without thereby in my opinion losing anything in aesthetic value. Their calm outline, their beautiful grouping and their precise detail reveal the excellence of their designer just as unmistakably as Stirling and Gowan's violent self-expression – and university buildings should perhaps rather convey calm and precision than ferocity.

One thing in any case is certain. University buildings should be designed with a view to the user rather than the architect. In this respect, I have nothing to say against Leicester but I have in another case, which seems to me instructive enough to dwell a little longer on. Paul Rudolph, a few years ago, designed the new building for the School of Art and Architecture at Yale, of which he was the director. I know the building well for I was actually invited to go over from

London and open it officially. I hesitated for I knew that I would have to be sceptical. But Paul Rudolph accepted that and said I should come along and do my damnedest. Of course I did not, but I did at one stage of my speech indicate that there were aspects under which I would regard that building as functionally at fault. However, I went on, as Paul Rudolph was the designer of the building and at the same time the director of the school, the building by Rudolph, the architect, for Rudolph, the client, must obviously be functionally right. So far so good. I admire the spatial intricacies inside, I could appreciate that the slabs of concrete, crossing or colliding, have a lot of force, but I had to insist to myself that the sculpture students had not enough overhead room and that, even for architectural students, to me a completely open plan with a spacious open well in the middle cannot be ideal because everything going on in one studio will be audible in the others, whether it be ragging or a serious and concentrated crit. However, if it satisfies Paul, there is no more to be said. But wait, for Paul Rudolph has now resigned and gone entirely into private practice. What a heritage he has left his successor! Every cubic foot of this building says 'Rudolph'. What can a successor, of different principles and maybe believing in a different routine, do with such a building? There you see, I hope, what I mean by the dangers of personality cult and the blessings of modesty, faith in service and a certain neutrality.

I think I ought to sum up this Rudolph argument and extend it a little. Just as in the 1930s, so today, nearly all that is being designed, whether it is a laboratory or a lecture block of a university or a university hall of residence or a block of flats or an office building or a factory or a hospital or a hotel or a department store, is designed not for an individual client, whose taste may respond immediately to that of the architect, but for groups of anonymous clients. What right has the architect then to make them monuments to himself instead of serviceable environments for the users? Any high pitch of emotion is as artificially thrown over such buildings as the giant columns of an Edwardian bank. Also, and here is the third argument, the structure of major buildings is usually of the simplest grid kind and what the architect of today does either hides or complicates that construction.

Mind you, I know I am generalising here. You could object that with concrete, the most gimmicky curves or angles can be done just as easily as the plainest. If you want an illustration of what I mean, take the new round skyscraper in Kingsway by Colonel Seifert. A round building I think is a mistake in a street anyway, because it breaks the unity of the building line – a mistake if you believe in a building in a town street being part of a greater whole – but that, though it is pertinent to my argument in general, is not what I am referring to at the moment. What I want to illustrate at this juncture is the fact that, once you build with cross-shaped pre-cast elements, it makes no difference to cost whether they are of a simple cross-shape or in addition formed so as to result, in the sum total, in a wildly jagged zig-zag. From the point of view of money spent and even from the point of view of the rational use of manufactured parts, there is nothing I could use as an argument against such aggressive details.

So in the end we are back at expression. But even in terms of expression, the critic can perhaps get a little beyond the purely subjective. Contrast for a moment not two buildings by different architects but four buildings by the same architect – the late Eero Saarinen's long, even office building for General Motors – first with his TWA Terminal at John Kennedy Airport. There is once again neutrality, the huge concrete loops left and right which make the TWA Building Expressionism. Now add to them the same Eero Saarinen's Styles and Morse Colleges at Yale, an intricate collegiate ensemble worthy of Oxford, and again the same Eero Saarinen's stiffly formal U.S. Embassy in London, with the superficial chequerboard rhythm of the window surrounds. How can one architect appear in so many guises? Was he a restless, never fully satisfied experimenter? In the case of Philip Johnson, who if anything is even more protean, his motive may be less experimenting than the itch to astonish his sophisticated public with every new building. But in comparison with the attitude of architects about 1930, is this refusal to believe in one style not a lack of firmness of conviction? Are we not, though on the whole in terms unmistakably of the twentieth century, back at the attitude of the nineteenth-century architect who designed a villa in Jacobean, a club in Cinquecento, a church in Gothic and a town hall in a kind of French? I'll come back to the Victorian parallel later.

As for Saarinen and Philip Johnson, they might say (and you might agree) that different buildings demand indeed different expressions. What is suited to General Motors is not suited to TWA. But surely that argument, even if accepted in principle, does not apply to this particular case. Why should an airline departure and arrival building rise to such heights of expression? Surely the spiritual function, if you call it that, of an airline terminal is neither elating nor edifying. Does anybody want to receive information on Flight 230 from a trim girl busy inside a coral reef?

So this is a case of function contradicting form. But there are other buildings where the spiritual function would justify the antics of TWA. Take the Sydney Opera House designed by Jörn Utzon and whose gigantic concrete loops – structurally entirely unnecessary – are causing so much worry. They swallow more and more money and Nervi, the greatest designer in concrete now alive, objects to them and says that *he* always tried in his sweeping concrete shapes to arrive not only at the structurally but also at the economically most advantageous solution. Utzon certainly did not do that. Even so, it could be said that, however expensive, the Sydney loops are fully justifiable because they express the fact that here is a building which deserves a more than utilitarian appearance and the architect in a curious and to me somewhat alarming way has satisfied both practical and emotional needs by keeping the useful and the useless, the auditoria and the loops, completely separate. The halls are down below, the loops are over and above. This distinguishes Sydney from, for instance, Hans Scharoun's Berlin Philharmonie where the foyers, the staircases, the auditorium itself are all forced into highly Expressionist shapes. Not for nothing did Scharoun when he was young himself belong to the Expressionists of the 1920s. In the Berlin Philharmonie, the forms interfere with the functions. It is for instance not at all easy to keep one's bearings, to find one's staircase and so on. Here, surely, to let forms detract from function is a sin, today as thirty years ago, however thrilling the forms – a sin against the users, committed for the sake of self-display of the architect.

At Sydney, that criticism does not apply, just as in my opinion it does not apply at Ronchamp, the most famous building of the last twenty years – though for different reasons. Scharoun allows display to interfere with function; Utzon keeps function and display separate; at

Ronchamp the function is so simple and straightforward that, whatever brilliant play of forms Le Corbusier has created, it does not do damage to the function of the pilgrimage chapel.

Yet there is one doubt I want to introduce even here, although this one is a purely personal one and I shan't be able to convince anyone of it who does not react as I do. As far as I am concerned, I want my emotions to be created in a church by the communication with eternity and in the opera house by the power of music – not by the architect's mood. I don't want to be bowled over before I have even handed in my coat at the cloakroom, quite apart from the question of how, say, Gluck will tune in with the vast sails of Sydney. But, once again, we can let that stand. It is a matter of subjective involvement, not of objective criticism.

So I am ready to grant Sydney certain privileges and Ronchamp all the privileges, although isn't there something uncomfortable in the admission that 1960 uses one style for church and concert hall, another for the hotel or hospital, the offices and the flats – one style for Sundays, another for weekdays? I know there is logic in that division. I also agree that it has to be taken more seriously than the Proteans' thesis of a style a building. But I still feel that it betrays little of that firmness of grip which the less self-indulgent architects of the 1930s had wielded. And, to move yet one further step in my argument: are we in the end entitled altogether to accept the existence of a historical contrast between 1930 and 1960 such as I have so far all the time presupposed? Can we say, as the young tend to say, 1930 was 1930 and belongs to the past? Surely we can't. 1930 is very much alive and kicking. The Sheffield University Library and Arts Tower is only a couple of years old, Sir Robert Matthew and Johnston Marshall's New Zealand House is recent, so is Arne Jacobsen's St Catherine's College in Oxford. Couldn't one, instead of one style for Sundays, one style for weekdays, say: one style in the succession of what had been evolved and established between 1900 and 1930, one style in opposition to it?

Now if we try that distinction, who will win, as it were? That is: who will convince 1990 when 1990 looks back over the whole century? Of course, perhaps something yet quite different will be done then which we can't guess at all. But one thing seems certain to me: the style of 1930 is not played out yet. I had already emphasised that arguments of function, of anonymity of use, of industrial production and so on are the same now as they were then. So in my opinion, what we are experiencing now may well be another interlude such as Art Nouveau and Expressionism. The historian has a right to call them interludes. Art Nouveau appeared very rarely before 1890; it flourished in the 1890s and up to about 1905 at the latest. Then the fireworks had burnt themselves out. And Expressionism really belongs to ten years at most: 1917–27. How long is the excessive pitch of emotion likely to be kept up this time?

I don't want to prophesy, especially because – as you have no doubt noticed a long time ago – I am party. I don't evaluate and criticise only. I am irritated – irritated by the loops of TWA and Sydney as much as by the arbitrary rhythms of normal windows and slit windows where there are just large rooms of even plan behind, irritated by the sudden jutting-forward balconies in an odd position here, an odd position there, on high blocks, where no functional accents correspond to the balconies, irritated by the gargantuan chunks of concrete where less material would do structurally perfectly well, irritated by all the jerks and stabs of many English jobs.

This is a subjective matter and I should perhaps have kept quiet about it to put up a better case. But as I have started this talk with subjective matters, I may be allowed to finish with subjective matters and the last of them takes me back to what I began with, the *Anti-Pioneers* which someone could write today. For there is one embarrassing thing in this not-yet-existing book – embarrassing for me, I mean. The author of the *Anti-Pioneers* would more likely than not quote in a footnote that I was one of the first in England to draw attention to Gaudí – it was in 1952 – and that I have written several papers, long and short, on Victorian architecture. How unbecoming, he would say, and you could say, for the Chairman of the Victorian Society to attack a change of style in architecture which is a patent parallel to the current reassessment of the Victorian style including the current craze for Gaudí. I know, I would have to answer – but then, what else could I say? Well, I would say that Gaudí is a case of an explosion of genius which cannot fail to impress the historian, whenever and however it happens. It has absolutely nothing to do with the question of whether I would personally like to live in the Casa Battlo. Le Corbusier was another such case and it does not matter whether I like Chandigarh. Objective evaluation wins without effort over subjective. Rubens was a painter of supreme genius even if Rembrandt has more to give *me*. Cézanne was a painter of genius even if van Gogh has more to give *me*. And, if a historian notices that an artist of genius has remained unknown to lots of people, he gets going, which is what I did some fifteen years ago.

The Victorian problem is different. Here it was not the unexpected genius, though unrecognised genius came into it as well. It was by and large the challenge of the unrecognised *period*, the period people laughed at and refused to know. So the need for the historian was to discover and to convert, to convert people to what deserves to be appreciated – and there is plenty of it: the churches of Bodley and Pearson, for instance, every bit as good as, and often better than, the parish churches of the thirteenth century everybody runs to admire. And discoveries were lying ready to be made everywhere because the kind of research which has gone on for ages for the earlier periods just didn't exist yet for the Victorian decades. That naturally tempts a historian and the converting should also tempt a good historian. I at least have always regarded it as just as much the architectural historian's job to guide to appreciation as to find out and present information. Besides, surely, the historian should not be denied a privilege which you all enjoy, I mean the privilege to be fascinated by certain things of the past which you would not therefore necessarily want to be revived? These are my personal arguments. But I wouldn't for a moment deny that the spectacular growth of the Victorian Society over the last two or three years is due to other causes as well, such as the scarcity and high price of antiques which have raised the Victorian wash-stand to the status of an antique, the delight of putting just one fanciful object into a white and rational interior and – especially among our young members – the feeling of affinity between the Victorian Age and that arbitrary, highly personal and highly self-confident style of today which, as you have seen, irks me so much.

And now it is high time for me to sum up. For, as I have tried to show you, what irks me lies also open to attack on objective grounds. And you should be familiar with them, even if it is irrelevant to you how one individual – myself – reacts. My theses then are these. What is happening in architecture today is in the line of descent of the High Victorian style, of Art Nouveau and of Expressionism, not of the International Modern of Gropius and Mies. It is ill suited for most architecture now because the majority of buildings are built of industrially produced – that is, impersonal – materials, because the majority of buildings are built for large numbers of anonymous clients and because the first concern of the architect must therefore be with their practical and emotional needs and not with the expression of his own personality. And finally, the style of today is unlikely to last, just as Art Nouveau and Expressionism didn't last, because phases of so excessively high a pitch of stimulation can't last. We can't, in the long run, live our day-to-day lives in the midst of explosions.

1   The Stahlenkirche (literally 'Steel Church') in Cologne was one of several evangelical churches designed in the round by the Dutch architect Otto Bartning (1883–1959) in the 1920s. Its principal materials were glass, steel and concrete. Bartning became director of the Weimar State School for Architecture in 1925 after the Bauhaus moved to Dessau.

Reynolds's *Discourses*

Third Programme
TUESDAY 21 JANUARY 1969
Producer: Leonie Cohn

Go to the Wallace Collection and have a long look at Reynolds's *Nelly O'Brien*, sitting and facing you, perfectly relaxed, her pet dog in her lap just as perfectly at ease. She appears attractive but not unduly and no one could doubt that in life she looked exactly like this. It is a masterpiece of the rendering of individuality and a masterpiece also of brushwork: bold, lively, sketchy, seemingly spontaneous yet the result of a painter's great experience. The colouring is as subtle: a subtle pale pink rug over her knees, her shirt and cuffs striped white and light blue, her bodice black, her straw hat with a light blue ribbon and the nose of her white dog, black.

Now, when you have seen *Nelly*, look up Reynolds's pronouncements and this is what you'll find: portraits belong to the departments
of painting which do not make high pretensions. They can only be
raised in value by being raised to a general idea. If you want to have
it in his own words: 'If the painter is not satisfied with the exact
similitude of every feature and the minute peculiarities of the dress'
and if he succeeds in 'approaching [his work] to a general idea' and if
he changes the dress 'from a temporary fashion to one more
permanent', if he paints 'not linen, nor silk, satin, or velvet, but just
drapery – nothing more', then he may yet 'ennoble the character of
the countenance' and approach his work to that of the great masters
who painted the great subjects in the great style.

And 'the great style' really means, though Reynolds does not say it
in so many words, 'the great style' means that a painter must not paint
as a painter.[1] The great masters are masters of sculpture (the Ancients
with a capital A and Michelangelo) or else they are masters of the
outline (Raphael in his frescoes, the Carracci and the other painters of
Bologna). They ought to be recognised as perfect and infallible guides.
They ought to be followed carefully. At the age of about fifty
Reynolds painted himself with a bust of Michelangelo in the
background. It is a noble portrait and it shows that Reynolds had
studied a great master – but that master is Rembrandt and of
Rembrandt, Reynolds said the only time he mentions him that he
took individual nature just as he found it – and that, as we have seen,
is a grave fault.

Is it all hypocrisy? No: the Reynolds problem is not as simple as
that. First of all you must remember that *Nelly O'Brien* is of about
1760 and the *Self-Portrait* very probably of 1773 and that in between,
in 1768, the Royal Academy had been founded, that Reynolds had
been instrumental in establishing the Academy and that he was elected
its first President. And with an eye to the Academy exhibitions,
Reynolds painted such portraits as Lady Blake as Juno, Mrs Crewe as
St Genevieve, Mrs Quarrington as St Agnes, the three Montgomery
girls as the Graces adoring Hymen. They are all painted more
smoothly, with conventional browns as the dominant colours and
with conventional attitudes too, extremely competently but, I would

say, less animated, less subtle even. But this change is one in accordance with the very rules Reynolds was laying down.

If there is a scale of subjects, starting at the top with 'the highest style of history', the 'art of animating and dignifying figures with intellectual grandeur', and if a portrait qualifies to an acceptable position only on these terms, then – surprising as it may seem to us – Lady Blake as Juno is more worthwhile as a painting *qua* Juno than *qua* Lady Blake. And moreover, as we have also seen, 'the Roman, the Florentine and the Bolognese' are the best schools and the Venetians rank lower because 'it cannot be disputed [that one should] give the preference to him who represents the heroic arts ... of man [over] him who by the help of meretricious ornaments ... captivates the sensuality'. Reynolds's examples where he says this explicitly include Venice. And so the least he could do on that score was to paint in a more dignified, that is, a more general way. Admittedly, the likeness may suffer just a little but as Reynolds says: 'it is very difficult to ennoble the character of a countenance but at the expense of the likeness'.

All this is academic theory and it is time now to remind you what the Royal Academy was founded for. Broadly speaking it was for three goals. It was to provide ample exhibition space for the artists to show their wares; it was to raise the status of certain artists to a higher level by Royal patronage – but, as against the French academies, not by Royal interference – and also to raise the artist's status by the intellectual cachet which the term 'academy' bestows; and finally it was to teach. Part of that teaching was to be by drawing classes as they had already been held, privately and by artists' societies, before; the other part was modelled on the powerful Paris Academy.

Professors were appointed for Anatomy, Perspective, Architecture and also Painting and they were to give lectures. Reynolds's, being the President's, were of a special kind. They were discourses held at the prize-giving ceremonies. The first was held on January 2nd, 1769, the fifteenth and last on December 10th, 1790. These discourses, it must be remembered, were not like the President of the Royal Academy's speeches now, briefly reported in the papers the next day, read with approval or exasperation and forgotten. To Reynolds's *Discourses* the civilised world listened. The first was at once translated into French

and German. Numbers One to Seven were published in England in
1778 and also translated, first into German, then into French.

So although they were directed to students, they were read by all
and sundry including the Empress Catherine of Russia. But directed
to students they were. What Reynolds intended to do was to pass on
to the students the accepted, current theory of art as it had been
developed in Italy in the sixteenth and seventeenth centuries and
brought to a climax in the Paris of Louis XIV, Colbert and Lebrun.
All this business of the scale of value of subjects from mythology and
history down to portrait, landscape and still-life comes from Paris
where Roger de Piles had even drawn up a *Balance des Peintres*: full
marks 80, Raphael and Rubens 65, Carracci 56, Domenichino 56,
Lebrun 53, Poussin 51 and so on, to Michelangelo who gets only 36.
Reynolds's grading would have been a bit different but then de Piles
preceded him by sixty and more years and, besides, Reynolds would
no doubt have been afraid of appearing ridiculous with such a mark-
sheet – and personal dignity meant much to him. But essentially he
agreed, except that Poussin, though giving his paintings more 'of the
air of Antique Painting' than anyone else, has a 'dryness of manner';
that Rubens can only be fully appreciated if one takes him all in all,
forgetting his 'want of that nicety of distinction ... which is required
in the higher walks of painting'.

So the distance between Paris and London is short and if Reynolds
cautions his students 'against being too much captivated' by 'the
seducing qualities' of Veronese and Tintoretto, he is actually more
classically Parisian than de Piles who wrote about 1700. Reynolds goes
back to the theory of Lebrun in the great age of Colbert who had
created the French academies. About 1700, the veneration of Raphael
– or in French terms of Poussin – was no longer unchallenged. The
Rubenistes (the Rubens-men) were making themselves heard against
the Poussinistes (the Poussin-men) and achieved a compromise.
Reynolds's intention – that will not be obvious to you – was to
provide his Academy with a code of behaviour like that of the Paris
Academy at its most dogmatic and to overcome the time lag in
respectable art theory which, in the absence of an academy, had
existed between France and England.

But Reynolds was not only the P.R.A.; he was Reynolds as well and what makes the *Discourses* so much more rewarding than the *Conférences* of the Paris Academy is what he added to the common corpus of his own personal observations, his own personal uncertainties about the validity of the academic principles and occasionally even his own personal self-searching.

The uncertainties may not have been noticed much by the students for they occur usually as contradictions between one discourse and another. For instance, in *Discourse Six*, the students are told: 'All the inventions of the Ancients, whether conveyed to us in statues, bas-reliefs, intaglios, cameos, or coins, are to be sought after and carefully studied', but in *Discourse Twelve*, Reynolds warns that 'as such studies are by their very nature long, tedious and complex, the student ought to employ himself during a study journey upon whatever he has been incited to by an immediate impulse'.

This contradiction is only one illustration of a much worse confusion and one from which not only Reynolds suffered, the confusion over the basic terms with which Reynolds operates: over truth, rules of art, nature, taste and genius. Here is an anthology of passages to document this confusion: 'The natural appetite or taste of the human mind is for Truth' and truth has 'unalterable and fixed foundations in nature and [can therefore be] investigated by reason, and known by study'. But there is side by side with real truth also 'apparent truth, or opinion, or prejudice' and Reynolds by no means despises them; for, as 'the art whose office is to please the mind as well as instruct it, must direct itself according to opinion', opinion cannot be discounted: and the rule that Reynolds is ready to make is that 'the longer opinions have been held, the nearer do they approach to certainty'. So in the end he is ready to say: 'They deserve, on account of their duration and extent, to be considered as really true.' This is slippery ground.

Nor is one better off concerning not truth but rules. Rules, says Reynolds 'for ever will elude our search' – that is, rules to satisfy reason. But here again, the secondary truth comes in conveniently and Reynolds says: 'What has pleased, and continues to please, is likely to please again; hence are derived the rules of art, and on this immovable foundation they must ever stand.' What has pleased and pleases now – an immovable foundation! Surely this is admitting total defeat – and indeed the one rule which Reynolds never abandons is the very elementary: 'All arts have the same general end, which is to please.' But there is pleasing and pleasing. 'A picture should please at first sight' – yes, but it should please the mind, not merely the senses. 'It is the lowest style only of art ... that may be said ... to be naturally pleasing. The higher efforts ... do not affect minds wholly uncultivated. This refined taste is the consequence of education and habit.'

So there we have reached taste and taste is acquired. What else does Reynolds say of taste? Taste is 'the power of distinguishing right from wrong in works of art' and 'the first idea of what is fixed ... in taste, is ... the general idea of nature' – the general idea as against the mere imitation of common nature. 'A mere copier of nature can never produce anything great.' The artist must endeavour 'to improve his imitations by the grandeur of his ideas'. That is what Reynolds means by general nature and what he means when he says: 'The works ... of painters which are built on general nature live for ever.'

And now after taste genius: 'It is not the eye, it is the mind which the painter of genius desires to address.' But: 'All arts have the same general end, which is to please and addressing themselves to the same faculties, through the medium of the senses.' 'Whatever pleases has in it what is analogous to the mind, and is therefore, in the highest and best sense of the word, natural.' It seems a hopeless tangle, especially as genius is again not clearly separated from taste, as *we* would feel to be imperative: 'Genius and taste ... appear to be very nearly related,' says Reynolds: 'The difference lies only in this, that genius has super-added to it a habit or power of execution; or we may say, that taste, when this power is added, changes its name and is called genius.' All right, but if that is so, does it make sense to say that Raphael had more Taste, Michelangelo more Genius? It really is just going in circles. Only once, as far as I can see, does Reynolds get nearer the true character of genius. It is where he says: 'Genius consists in the power of expressing, whatever it may be, as a whole.' That allows him to admit that 'a work may justly claim the character of Genius, though full of errors'.

His great test case is Gainsborough. The fourteenth *Discourse*, which is almost entirely an obituary of Gainsborough, shows Reynolds masterly as an observer and expositor, condescending and unbeknown to himself, highly arrogant as the P.R.A. – and again, with all his laying down the law, painfully uncertain of himself. 'In discoursing on the talents of the late Mr Gainsborough, my object is . . . to draw from his excellencies and defects matters of instruction to the Students.' The excellencies are brilliantly analysed: 'the unfinished manner'; 'This hatching manner', which gives his portraits such a 'striking resemblance' – 'the imagination supplies the rest'; 'Those odd scratches and marks' which seem 'chaos' from nearby but 'at a certain distance assume form'. This technique, Reynolds says, is intuitive, 'the work of an artist who had never learned from others'. And that is what was wrong with Gainsborough. He developed 'without the assistance of an academic education'. Reynolds himself did of course too, as there was no academy then. But Gainsborough in contrast to Reynolds also never visited Italy. However, in spite of that, he succeeded in conveying 'the powerful impression of nature'. But to give an impression of nature belongs, as we have seen, to 'a lower rank of art'. So Reynolds can speak of 'the humble attempts of Gainsborough', adding however immediately that he prefers them to 'the works of [many of] the regular graduates in the great historical style'. And Gainsborough knew that the learned subjects of the grand manner were not for him. His range goes from portrait and landscape to those 'little beggar-children' whose 'interesting simplicity and elegance' Reynolds praises so nicely and not beyond.

Reynolds did occasionally go beyond, in *Ugolino* after Dante, in *Cymon and Iphigenia* and a few other canvases but they are rare and the result does not look one little bit like Raphael and Michelangelo. So if he ended this obituary *Discourse* as he did, he cast doubts on his own at the same time as on Gainsborough's achievements:

> However we may apologise for the deficiencies of Gainsborough (I mean particularly his want of precision and finishing), who so ingeniously contrived to cover his defects by his beauties; and who cultivated that department of art, where such defects are more easily excused; you are to remember, that no apology can be made for this deficiency, in that style which this Academy teaches, and which ought to be the object of your pursuit. It will be necessary for you, in the first place, never to lose sight of the great rule and principles of the art, as they are collected from the

full body of the best general practice, and the most constant and uniform experience; this must be the groundwork of all your studies: afterwards you may profit, as in this case I wish you to profit, by the peculiar experience and personal talents of artists, living and dead; you may derive lights, and catch hints, from their practice; but the moment you turn them into models, you fall infinitely below them; you may be corrupted by excellencies, not so much belonging to the art, as personal and appropriated to the artist; and become bad copiers of good painters, instead of excellent imitators of the great universal truth of things.

It is pathetic. With this final warning Reynolds conveys the students back into the universal truth which he could not define, which meant nothing to them and which he himself was unable to live up to. However, what makes one forgive him, what makes one even respect him all the more, is that he knew it and in those very *Discourses* confessed it. Michelangelo and Raphael he always presented as the supreme examples. Raphael he called the 'foremost of the first painters' and Michelangelo 'the exalted Founder of Modern Art ... which he carried at once to its highest point of possible perfection'. Yet he warned students that 'at their first setting out' to see and study Michelangelo they 'should be prepared for disappointment ... and they must be cautioned that probably they will not, at first sight, approve'. And *à propos* his own first meeting with Raphael's frescoes, he wrote in a letter: 'I am of opinion that a relish for the higher excellencies of art is an acquired taste which no man ever possessed without ... great labour ... On such occasions [as seeing Raphael's *School of Athens*] we are often ashamed of our apparent dullness as if it were expected that our minds like tinder should instantly catch fire from the divine spark of Raphael's genius.' And so he recommends to 'feign a relish, till we find a relish come'.

What he naturally does not tell his students is that he himself, when in Rome at the age of twenty-eight, painted a parody of Raphael's *School of Athens* populated by the caricatures of two dozen English visitors. The Reynolds who did that was smothered by the Academician but also by the successful portrait painter. And it is the conflict between these two which I have to illustrate to you in my last set of quotations. Already in 1770, in the third *Discourse*, the one in which he contrasts the Grand Style against the mere copying of nature, ideal beauty against nature with 'blemishes and defects', and addressing the mind against addressing the eye, Reynolds says at the very end: 'A man is not weak, though he may not be able to wield the club of Hercules; nor does a man always practise that which he esteems the best, but does that which he can do best.' And at the very end of his *Discourse*, taking leave of the Academy at the age of sixty-seven, in that encomium of Michelangelo from which I have already quoted, he said:

> I have taken another course, one more suited to my abilities and to the taste of the times in which I live. Yet, however unequal I feel myself to that attempt, were I now to begin the world again, I would tread in the steps of that great master; to kiss the hem of his garment, to catch the slightest of his perfections, would be glory ... enough for an ambitious man.

This remained in his eyes his justification for having taught British artists: 'Keep your attention fixed upon the higher excellencies. If you compass them, and compass nothing more, you are still in the first class ... You may be very imperfect, but still you are an imperfect artist of the highest order.'

It is true that it was Reynolds's advice which sent Fuseli to Rome to become a painter in the grand style; it is true that James Barry had begun his wall paintings in the Royal Society of Arts in 1777, eight years after the first *Discourse*, and it is true that Boydell's Gallery (begun in 1786) and Macklin's Gallery (begun in 1788) might never have been assembled but for Reynolds's plea. But take the three greatest English artists born in the years between Reynolds's thirtieth and sixtieth year and who are they? Two, Constable and Turner, were landscape painters and the third, William Blake wrote: 'I consider Reynolds's *Discourses* as the Simulations of a Hypocrite who smiles particularly when he means to betray.'

1 This talk, one of his last for the BBC, was written to mark the two hundredth anniversary of the founding of the Royal Academy but was held back for broadcast until the following year. In it, Pevsner returned to one of his first themes – not architecture or art but art theory and its relationship to personality. Sir Joshua Reynolds was the most important force in eighteenth-century painting and a powerful influence on the Europeanisation of British tastes. For at least fifteen years, Reynolds personified the seal of approval of British academic art and the transformation in the

status of artists. What fascinates Pevsner, however, is the image of Reynolds as Polonius, a powerful but insecure man forced – not necessarily unwillingly – into hypocrisy and pretension.

Reynolds (1723–92) was the foremost portrait painter of his day, first President of the Royal Academy, primary expositor of the eighteenth-century grand manner in England and one of the strongest influences on the course of British painting. He was born in Plympton, Devonshire, learned portraiture in London and then set up as a portraitist in Devon. In 1749, he sailed to Europe and travelled round Italy, studying the great masters and the Antique and learning the lessons of contemporary art theory which elevated history painting and encouraged painters to improve on nature. Setting up in London in 1753, he soon attracted notice for his society portraits and became the first English painter to achieve social recognition for his work. He himself favoured the company of writers to that of painters and by his hard work and success as a businessman he was able in 1764 to found London's Literary Club. Four years later he became first President of the Royal Academy of Arts and was knighted in 1769. In 1769 also he delivered the first of his annual *Discourses* (published 1778) to the students of the Academy which became the definitive word on art in Britain and made him art's ultimate academic authority.

Of his own work, his reputation rests on his portraits and even though his professionalism allowed the use of assistants to paint his drapery and skies, he repeatedly achieved a versatile and direct response to each of his sitters, a richness of colour and a mood of calm dignity. His later history paintings are less successful. Blindness stopped him painting in 1790 and he died two years later.

Of all the historical figures who shaped Britain's culture, it may have been Reynolds with whom Pevsner identified most, for many of the dilemmas that Reynolds faced as writer, teacher and theorist are issues that relate to Pevsner. At issue in this talk, in addition, is the quality of Reynolds's thought and the endurance of his legacy. Pevsner's judgement on both of these may have reinforced that sense of identification.

The golden days of the Vienna Secession

Radio Three
TUESDAY 2 JANUARY 1971
Producer: Leonie Cohn

When I think of poetry of the Geoffrey Grigson generation, I think of objects in Nature just named and, by their naming, conjured up with an intensity which more than just naming would weaken. So let me try and do the same with Vienna of the brief golden days of the Secession.[1] In the Secession's own terms, they are the architect Otto Wagner, born 1841, the senior of them all; of Olbrich, the architect of the Secession building, born in 1867; of Josef Hoffmann, the most successful Secession architect; and of Adolf Loos, passionately anti-Secession, both born in 1870; and of Gustav Klimt, the most startling and bewildering of all Secession painters. He was born in 1862. Kolo Moser, the wizard of the Wiener Werkstätte, in 1868. But that isn't all. And here is what I want simply to name in order to conjure it up. Freud, born 1856, his classic on *The Interpretation of Dreams*, 1900. Mahler, born 1860, director of the Vienna Opera from 1897. Schoenberg, born 1871. Peter Altenberg, the essayist and his *As I See It*, 1896 – so charming, so Viennese. Schnitzler, born 1862. Hofmannsthal, born 1874. Karl Kraus, the fierce journalist, born 1874. And Hermann Bahr, born 1863.

Now Bahr in 1900 published a book called *Secession* composed of articles of his from 1896–1900 and dealing with the arts in Vienna before and after the creation of the Secession. The name 'Secession', incidentally, means the breaking away of the young from the establishment and it had been anticipated in Munich in 1892 when another breaking away had taken place. Franz von Stuck had been one of the founders in Munich, a sensation-mongering painter in the Classicist vein. But only the Vienna Secession succeeded in getting at once a building of their own.

What happened, so I'm told, is that the young people had founded the Secession on 3 April 1897, and were able to hold their first exhibition early in 1898. They took 100,000 crowns. The building cost 80,000; it was put up in six months. So there they were. At the suggestion of Otto Wagner, Olbrich, aged thirty-one, was chosen to be the architect although Klimt – one of the twenty founders – must have had something to do with it as well for there is in the show a drawing of his which is in certain features much like the building, although in other more startling ones it isn't. As for the building, I'll tell you more about that presently.

Bahr dedicated his book to 'Master Olbrich' – I'm quoting – 'Master Olbrich, with his featherweight cane, his raillery, his good humour, ready to cope with anything, a veritable sorcerer'. The book blames the older artists of Austria for their exhibitions being a mere matter of trade and their painting just so many goods. Concurrently, Bahr blames the architects for their houses being designed for show. 'A house is to live in,' he says; 'our houses are a fraud.'

For those of you who before they saw the exhibition were not even familiar with Klimt, let me indicate what Hermann Bahr praised of art other than Austrian. Klinger in Germany, Besnard and Rodin in France, van Rysselberghe and the Belgian pointillistes, and Whistler and Brangwyn from England. And the leaders of decorative art – Gallé, Tiffany, van de Velde. Their names convey some idea of Bahr's programme and the Secession's programme. That programme, incidentally, did not exclude Impressionism, as the presence of Whistler of course shows. Engelhardt was the leading local Impressionist, relatively weak and not well represented in the exhibition. So the programme was: 'Workers towards new goals unite' – unite against academicism. By the way, this absence of animosity of Post-Impressionists against Impressionists and vice versa is just as noticeable in the associations of artists in other countries and especially, as I have shown in my *Pioneers of Modern Design*, in the new art journals. The Secession started a journal as well, at once, in 1898. It was called *Ver Sacrum* – 'Sacred Spring' – and it is one of their finest achievements, in contents as well as design. But before I try to tell you something of Secession design, I must have a few minutes for Vienna and Secession architecture.

The protagonist of innovation in Vienna in the 1890s was an architect, Otto Wagner, over fifty-five when the Secession started. In 1895 and even earlier, he had pleaded against the Renaissance in favour of a *naissance* – against all historicism, 'against' – I'm quoting – 'artists dissecting the dead instead of feeding the living'. 'Nothing that is not practical', he wrote on another page, 'can be beautiful.' It's very curious for in that same year, 1895, Wagner himself still designed in a kind of free Austrian Baroque, that kind of Baroque which in an English version we also get over here in the Victorian decades, I mean in Belcher's Institute of Chartered Accountants or Mountford's Old Bailey. But in 1894–95, Wagner was commissioned to design buildings for the Danube canal and the Vienna Métro, novel jobs calling for novel architectural forms. That liberated him. And it may well be true that he was helped in this breaking away from the Baroque by a pupil who worked in his office in those years. Now that pupil was Olbrich and Master Olbrich in 1898 built the Secession building, one of the most daring buildings of those years in the world – severely cubic, severely symmetrical, with smooth window-less surfaces and culminating in a pure hemispherical dome. True, this radical geometry is given the required connotation of art and artists by the dome being open-work – gilt, iron laurel leaves – and the plain surfaces round the central entrance have that kind of flat tree-and-leaf decoration which at that time Townsend had done at the Bishopsgate Institute four or five years earlier. Olbrich's building is represented in the exhibition by a delightfully dainty model. Hermann Bahr enthused about the building. 'It is', he writes, 'as functional as a good bicycle: everything in it is as necessary and seems a matter of course. Such a building as this', he goes on, 'is not a question of pleasing or not pleasing but of true or false. The interior', he says, 'cleanses us of everyday cares and turns us to the eternal. The exterior succeeds in being both true and decorative.'

'Both true and decorative.' How does the unquestionable star of the Secession painters, how does Klimt fit into these categories and indeed into this building? Into the building I would say admirably. The Secession exhibition of 1903, with eighty works by Klimt, must have been a feast. But into the programme of truth and decoration, Klimt fits only with many reservations.

Here lies the problem of Klimt's art and of his stature and the exhibition illuminates this admirably. Klimt, like Otto Wagner, started from the Baroque, the neo-Baroque, gorgeously brandished about in Vienna by Markart, the painter of huge flamboyant machines, of such historical subjects as *Cleopatra on the Nile* or *The Entry of Charles V into Antwerp*.

Now Klimt, the successful painter of ceiling and wall decoration, discovered for himself in the mid-1890s the sensational modern German Classicists – Stuck of Munich and Klinger of Leipzig. Klimt's *Pallas Athene* of 1898, a sombrely coloured, heavily stylised archaic idol, is all Stuck. Klimt's poster of the first exhibition with *Theseus and the Minotaur*, all in linework with no tonality at all, is all Klinger. Only after that, about 1900, did Klimt find himself. The climax of his work, in my opinion, is the mosaic decoration of the dining room of Josef Hoffmann's fabulous Palais Stoclet in Brussels – like Olbrich's Secession, one of the most daring buildings of its date, 1905–11, with its external panels of white marble edged with gilt metal strips and its internal surfaces of white marble, black marble, green marble, severely smooth but superbly precious. Now Klimt's decoration of which a full-scale cartoon is the *point de vue* of the central axis of the exhibition, also combines superb preciousness with severe reduction to two dimensions. But where Josef Hoffmann succeeded, did Klimt succeed? Hoffmann stands as a pioneer of the international twentieth-century style; Klimt does not. His mosaic is the finest flower of Austrian Art Nouveau – it is an end rather than a beginning. The true pioneer work of the Stoclet years – that is, the years 1905–11 – is Picasso's *Demoiselles d'Avignon*; the continuation is Cubism.

Now, in a curious way, Klimt seems en route towards Cubism but Picasso's and Braque's ruthlessness and Rouault's ruthlessness and the ruthlessness of the Brücke in Dresden is absent in the Stoclet mosaic, which pays tribute incidentally to Symbolism by its title *Expectation and Fulfilment*. Instead, what have we got? Faces and hands are entirely naturalistic – pretty faces, slender hands, almost the clichés of the fashion magazines. The draperies and the like are interpreted as flat surfaces and covered with little triangles, little squares, little circles, scrolls, dots – Cubist if you like, but all in gay often rather sweet colours, I might almost say boiled-sweet colours. So the mood of the figures and the mood of the patterned surfaces may be the same but aesthetically speaking the two never merge. Perhaps one shouldn't ask for them to merge, perhaps that is a pedantic demand, perhaps one should just enjoy so *raffinée* a display, such exquisite piquancy.

One thing is certain. Klimt is eminently Austrian, being radical yet never heavily serious. His drawings, of which there are many in the Royal Academy, show his sensitivity and also they show a range greater than the paintings would make one expect. That is what distinguishes him from his most brilliant follower Egon Schiele who died, aged twenty-eight, in the same year as Klimt. Schiele's line is more incisive, his stylisation, especially in his landscapes and his tree studies, is more forceful, his concern with sex is almost obsessive. Yet he also never strays far from elegance. That changed only with Kokoschka. Of course Kokoschka's *Dreaming Boys* – that enchanting little picture book of his of 1908 – is Klimt both in origin and in mood. But the great portraits which follow immediately have a psychological insight never accessible to Klimt or Schiele and a vehemence and resourcefulness of technique leaving all Secession conventions behind. But alas, Kokoschka is inadequately represented in the exhibition – rightly so, because he, being all his life ferociously critical of Austria, never showed in the Secession until as late as 1955.

The discovery for most visitors will be Kolo Moser. He and Josef Hoffmann were the creative force in the Vienna Workshops – the Wiener Werkstätte – which had been founded in 1903, thanks to financial support from Dr Wärndorfer.

Now that brings another strand into the work of the Secession. Late in 1900, Mackintosh and his wife had shown in one of the exhibitions. Their unique synthesis of sinuous line with rigidly rectangular framing and their subtle delicate colours were a sensational success and Mackintosh pieces included in the Royal Academy show stand out from the much heavier Viennese furniture. It is true that Hoffmann himself was already on the way from Art Nouveau to rectangularity before the Mackintoshes became known to him but it is also true that Mackintosh inspired him decisively. One can see that in Hoffmann's austere black grandfather clock. To me, incidentally, the finest Hoffmann piece in the show is the ebony and mother-of-pearl commode with its curious stepping-back sides.

Where Vienna in my opinion is at its best is in the two-dimensional work, the dainty stationery of the Werkstätte and the set of posters of the Secession exhibitions, all very long and narrow and of a most enjoyable variety of approaches and styles. Of course it's true that the conversion of the poster into a vehicle of high decorative art had been done several years before the Secession by Cheret and Toulouse-Lautrec in France and by Pryde and Nicholson in England, the best of them all if you ask me. But Vienna holds its own beside them. Nowhere do the Viennese graphic qualities come out more convincingly than in the numbers of their journal *Ver Sacrum*, which appeared from 1898–1904. I have a number of it at home inherited from my mother. It is Volume Two, Number Eight, and its chief article deals with the Hofpavillion Station of Otto Wagner's Métro, the nearest Wagner came to Olbrich's Secession even if so much more exuberant. The illustration shows certain details of the building which are of a high originality – a carpet, a light fitting, a fireplace, a wild lamp standard. Otherwise there is still some Klinger – mostly nudes – and also there is some Mucha. In another number is a piece written by Rilke.

Among the four editors of *Ver Sacrum* were Olbrich and Kolo Moser. So we are back to Moser. What the exhibition shows is, apart from his furniture which strikes me as rather heavy-handed Art Nouveau, some delightfully pretty silverwork and jewellery, some textiles with long sinuous lines and some marbled book papers. These book papers are to me one of the summits of the show. They are put together – eight or ten each – in two large framed panels and if I could walk away with just one item of this whole exhibition, it would be one of these two panels.

There are also two large paintings of Kolo Moser and they betray another Secession source – the Swiss painter Ferdinand Hodler who did such groups of excessively stylised figures in meaningful actions ever since 1890. Hodler, Klimt, Stuck – what else to reconstruct the pedigree? Munch, the Norwegian, as is painfully patent from Richard Gerstl's full-length portrait. And of course, time and again, England. The catalogue of the exhibition has a whole section of about twenty items by corresponding members from Great Britain. Who are they? C.R. Ashbee must be mentioned first only because his delicate silverwork is most patently reflected in that of the Viennese but also because his Guild of Handicraft first operating from the East End of London, then from Chipping Campden, was the inspiration of the Wiener Werkstätte which was intended to be – I quote – 'a community of artist-craftsmen for the production of articles of craft'. The objects produced were signed by initials of the designers and also of the craftsmen. By 1905 there were thirty-seven such executant craftsmen.

Second strongest among British influences, apart from Mackintosh, was Beardsley. Other British corresponding members were Brangwyn and Clausen, Walter Crane, John Lavery, Nicholson, Sargent, Walton, Whistler. There is in fact in the exhibition a letter in English from Klimt to Whistler asking him to accept honorary membership. But the reflections of Britain are really everywhere although of course most concentratedly in the showcase of Austrian Arts and Crafts. There's a lot to enjoy if you take your time.

Josef Hoffmann was the most fertile designer but curiously enough,

Adolf Loos is represented too in spite of his violent sustained campaign against the Secession and against Hoffmann in particular. A correspondent wrote to Loos in 1903: 'if I understand you rightly, you want to wring the neck of the Secession'. He did. And why? Because he regarded them as superficial in every sense of the word, as self-satisfied in mere decoration, as incapable of getting down to matters of principle of the ethics of architecture. Yet there is that one piece on show by Loos and it makes indeed much of the rest of that showpiece appear as *Kunstgewerbe* – as Applied Art. It's a very large brass clock – an exposed piece of clockwork in a glass case, the bevelled glass panels framed in glass. There is no ornament whatsoever 'for ornament', Loos had written in the famous article of 1908, 'for ornament equals crime'. The clock is a demonstration of extreme functionalism in the original sense that you see it function.

Loos and Kokoschka were close friends. A few years ago, Kokoschka devoted the money he had received for the Erasmus Prize to the financing of the first monograph on Loos, the one of which Thames and Hudson did an English edition. In fact, Loos and Kokoschka marked the way out of the Secession into the full twentieth century. But the Royal Academy exhibition does not stop at 1914 as I think it should. Instead, it goes on to the present day with in fact nearly twenty-five per cent of the total of about 600 items being of after 1945. The Secession exhibition in London simply becomes a survey of Austrian art. However, objects called 'Space Filler', 'Sculpto-Furniture' and 'We and Our Skin' have nothing to do with Olbrich's building, nothing to do with Klimt and Kolo Moser and Schiele. They just show that in painting and sculpture, as in architecture, the twentieth century defeats the national nuance. The Secession of the golden days was as much a demonstration of Austrianness as William Morris and the Arts and Crafts were of Englishness.

---

1   The occasion of this talk was an exhibition at the Royal Academy in London of work by artists, architects and designers associated with the Vienna Secession.

South Kensington: a memorial to Albert

Radio Three
SUNDAY 30 MAY 1976
Producer: Not known

Faulkner's *History of Kensington* came out in 1820.[1] At that time, Kensington was almost entirely rural. There were country houses large and small, mostly small. There were farmhouses, village nuclei such as Brompton, and tree nurseries and a lot of market gardening. As for anything urban, Kensington Square, so close to Kensington Palace, had existed ever since the eighteenth century, incongruously townish in these rural surroundings.

Now in the ten years after Queen Victoria's coronation, development seemed to be in terms of relatively small houses and terraces, two-storeyed and stuccoed, in off-white or beige, pretty and really quite cosy. But in 1850, a change of scale – not of style but of scale – took place. Stucco terraces of four of five storeys were put up by developers on the pattern of Brighton, in Paddington as well as Kensington.

Now in Kensington, the best position would obviously be on Kensington Gore, or close to Kensington Gore, and Kensington Road – that is, close to the main road from Knightsbridge to Earls Court, Hammersmith and so to the west. There, in 1850, Hyde Park Gate and Kensington Gate were built, west of the future Albert Hall; and Hyde Park Terrace, even closer to the future Albert Hall; and Prince's Gate, east of the Albert Hall. The type of house is familiar – cream-coloured, of great height and with porches of two detached columns. Clearly, that was going to be the future of Kensington.

But then, a totally unforeseeable event deflected that development. The Exhibition of 1851 placed its premises – the Crystal Palace – in the Park, opposite and quite close to Prince's Gate.

Now the Crystal Palace meant two things: a building of glass and iron and not brick and stucco; and objects exhibited which were made industrially or by craftsmen, clever in skill but very often ghastly in taste. A few English critics were aware of this collapse in taste. Their leaders were Henry Cole, a young civil servant, and Richard

Redgrave, a painter. Without Cole, it is safe to say, there would have been no 1851 Exhibition. Their views had already begun to appear in a journal which they founded and which started in 1849. There, and later in criticisms of the Crystal Palace exhibits, you find terms such as 'absurd', 'abomination', 'floral tinsel' and so on. Another critic of the exhibits, Ralph Nicholson Wornum, blamed for their inferiority the uneducated taste of the producers.

Well, if their taste was uneducated, what could be done about it? The answer was: educate taste. And how can you educate taste? Prince Albert knew: 'by applying most efficiently the fine arts to our manufactures, in order to wed high art to mechanical skill'. Here then was a challenge – and Cole was just the man to accept it.

This is what happened. The exhibition ended with a surplus of £186,000. That money ought to be spent on fostering the cultural aims of the Exhibition. Prince Albert in 1851 presented a programme. Land should be bought and on it, schools of instruction and exemplary collections should be housed. The aim ought to be, as Prince Albert put it, 'to extend the influence of science and art upon productive industry' – in short, to create an industrial university. 'By such means, in the end, Britain', he said, 'would become the headquarters of the skilled industry of the world.' So land was bought, rural land, roughly between the Park and what is now South Kensington station. And in addition, a department was created which in 1852 was called the Department of Practical Art and then soon, the Department of Science and Art. Henry Cole was made Superintendent of the Department of Practical Art and then, from 1853–73, Secretary of the Department of Science and Art and General Superintendent of the South Kensington Museum. And so the building up of the estate began.

The first thing, however, was not brick and mortar but grand planning on a large scale. Professor Donaldson, the great Professor Cockerell and James Pennethorne, who was architect to the Office of Works, took part in a kind of competition. All three applied to their designs the grandiose language of Durand and other French architects of the late eighteenth and early nineteenth centuries – a language inspired by the Baths of the Roman emperors, usually with a rotunda somewhere and halls with an apse or two, and perhaps an oval or two.

Only Henry Cole did something more realistic. He had a scheme which included, for example, a testing ground for experiments and also students' hostels. Cole was a man of tremendous energy and of a ruthlessness which made him highly unpopular. Lord Derby called him 'the best-abused man in England'. Cole was convinced that to improve standards of design, a museum was needed to offer inspiration to manufacturers and a school to train suitable designers and craftsmen. Back in 1849, he had said, perhaps despairingly: 'I don't think schools of art in England were created for aesthetic purposes or for general educational purposes. I apprehend that the age is so essentially commercial that it hardly looks to promoting anything except for commercial purposes.'

So the museum started first and it is typical of Cole that instead of that grand architecture that had been proposed, he had his museum built of corrugated sheet iron, painted for decoration with green and white stripes. 'The Brompton Boilers' is what Londoners called it. But whatever its appearance, the museum grew rapidly – and in a direction that must have baffled Cole. The Sheepshanks Collection of nineteenth-century paintings was donated and soon after that, space had to be found for the Vernon Collection and the Turner Bequest. They were all gifts of paintings, you see, although the museum was supposed to inspire manufacturers. So to the north of the Boilers, to hold these collections, two brick ranges were erected, very plain but with blank round arches – what the Germans call the *Rundbogenstil* – the round-arch style. Between 1859–62, the brick ranges grew – first the South Court, then the North Court, and what is now the principal inner court, the Quadrangle, was also started. It is there that the style first appeared and is usually called 'South-Kensington'. It is the style of a new man in the Department, Francis Fowke. He was Cole's favourite, perhaps because he was not an architect. He was in fact a young captain in the Royal Engineers. Fowke had a passion for multi-colour terracotta and faience. Your best examples are the north side of the Quadrangle of the Museum, the splendid ceramic staircase inside the Museum and the façade of the Huxley Building, round the corner from the main front, which was the first science building on the site.

Fowke died young and the Huxley Building was actually designed by his successor, another Royal Engineer, Colonel Scott, later General Scott. The Fowke style was derived from the style of the early Cinquecento in northern Italy, say, from the Certosa of Pavia, and among the elements are vivaciously decorated pilasters and equally decorated balusters taking the place of columns. The Museum went on growing but it remains a maze of exhibition halls without a clearly marked axis and – until about 1900 – without any façade.

The early designs for the whole estate had suggested a large concert hall. For Cole, this was the next thing to be provided and when he couldn't convince the authorities, undaunted character that he was, he decided to build it at his own risk. He worked out a scheme by which private people would contribute the necessary funds and receive in return seats in perpetuity. And this is how we got the Albert Hall, huge, oval, red-brick, with a typical frieze of dark-brown terracotta – a frieze alas too high up to recognise the figures and their actions.

That is one of the great differences between the Albert Hall and the Albert Memorial, which went up at the same time, facing the Hall. Also, there is of course the difference of style: the Gothic of the Memorial versus the Italianate – for the Albert Hall is still in the Fowke and Scott style. By the way, don't get mixed up between the famous George Gilbert Scott who designed the Albert Memorial and our General Scott. In the Albert Memorial, the figure of the Prince is placed under a Gothic canopy as if the statue were part of an altar. The Memorial celebrates Prince Albert as the great promoter of art, science and social virtues. And so, apart from conventional groups of ladies representing, say, the Four Continents or Commerce, Industry, Agriculture and Engineering, there is a frieze all along the podium which portrays heroes of the arts including architects, painters, writers, musicians. I'll name only those whom I found surprising but you should really go and look for yourselves; the frieze is large enough and near enough to read it easily.

Now among architects, the French cathedral master masons Jean Deschamps and Robert de Courcy appeared, and Abbot Suger of St Denis; and in England William of Sens and William of Wykeham. And then for the Elizabethan style, John Thorpe and so on to Pugin, to Barry, to Cockerell and in fact to Scott himself. But you would look in vain for Soane and in vain for Schinkel.

Among painters, Turner is in and Constable is out. Two of the three Carracci are in, Guido Reni and Domenichino are out. It's altogether an eminently telling chapter of the history of taste.

But in spite of the Albert Memorial, the Gothic never struck roots in South Kensington. There are only two churches – Butterfield's St Augustine, fully flavoured and highly idiosyncratic, and Holy Trinity by Bodley.

Now, the whole of this epic of Kensington is told – and beautifully told – in the latest volume of the *Survey of London*. It is a masterly account of the building of the whole estate. But what comes through to me most strikingly is that, during the decades of the greatest prosperity of Britain, the South Kensington scheme was carried on in such a bitty way. Think of the British Museum and the National Gallery, built only a generation earlier. Where had that pride and that generosity gone? In fact it did return but surprisingly late – really after the prosperity of the country had been challenged by America and Germany. The operative date is 1871, when the British Museum began a new building for its natural history collections and placed it in Kensington, miles away from its Bloomsbury home. The Natural History Museum is in my opinion the best building on the whole estate. It's the work of Alfred Waterhouse and it was completed in 1881. The façade is long, uniform and symmetrical and where the Fowke style had been pretty, Waterhouse's style is hard and determined. Yet Waterhouse did not mean to fight Fowke. He took notice of the Fowke characteristics and very intelligently made use of them. His façade is faced with terracotta and his style is a *Rundbogen* style. But where Fowke had gone to the Italian Quattrocento, Waterhouse went to the twelfth and early thirteenth century, north of the Alps. For an architect who, until then, had had all the successes in the neo-Gothic, that was quite a daring thing to do. But Waterhouse was not sold on any one style of the past, as George Gilbert Scott was sold on Gothic. In fact, if one studies Waterhouse's work, as I have done a bit, one is surprised to see with what freedom he handled period precedent, putting use before style. The Great Hall inside the Natural History Museum has the same largeness, the same hardness, as the façade. The grand stair at the far end of the Hall comes as a complete surprise. It flies up, seemingly unsupported. If you ask me, it's one of the finest Victorian staircases.

Now, other buildings on a comparable scale followed. Most monumental and resourceful was the Imperial Institute by Collcutt, of which now only the tower survives. The function of the Imperial Institute has never been clearly defined. What was it for? Exhibitions of colonial products? Commercial contacts? I can't say. But I do remember the long and broad empty corridors echoing under my feet.

Quite a number of other institutes established themselves on the Commissioners' land, none of them architecturally especially valuable: the City & Guilds College, the Royal College of Music, the School of Mining, the Imperial College. The last two are by Aston Webb but Aston Webb's most conspicuous contribution to South Kensington is the façade range of the Victoria and Albert Museum. Conspicuous, yes – but not in my opinion a major piece of architecture.

I need hardly add that there is no bridge from here to the style of our century. The first South Kensington building which discarded historicism – that is, the imitation of the motifs of past styles – was the Science Museum. Don't be deceived by the columns on its façade. Go inside and there is a reinforced concrete skeleton, fully exposed.

Now the date of the Science Museum is 1914–28. After that, what I have still to add is mostly destruction. Just as London University in Bloomsbury, so the Imperial College in South Kensington needed more and more space and so buildings went down. It's a great pity that the replacements of 1956 and the following year are so confused in grouping and so neutral in design. It's a melancholy end to this story of colleges and museums – but it isn't quite the end, for in my references to the sequence of Victorian styles, I have neglected so far the domestic parts of the Commissioners' estate – terraces of houses along the fringes, such terraces as I have mentioned before. You remember Prince's Gate, facing the Park, and built in 1850.

The new terraces were built with stuccoed brick again but they were four or five storeys high and the motifs a transition between the early nineteenth-century Classical and a subdued Victorian Italianate. This kind of house, once introduced, remained static right to the year 1874. The prosperous people – lawyers, merchants, industrialists –

who moved to South Kensington must have liked these particular architectural conventions.

1874 was a crucial year. In that year, an architect called Dawkes did Numbers 197–200 Queen's Gate in the conventional Italianate and, in that same year, Mr. J.P. Heseltine commissioned Norman Shaw to build for him Number 196 and that was intended as a challenge to its neighbours. It is of red brick, unstuccoed and with a big gable. The style is Netherlandish of about 1630 or English derived from the Netherlandish. Shaw had made his appearance on the Commissioners' estate a year earlier with Lowther Lodge, which is now the Royal Geographical Society. The stylistic origin here was the same but the house is detached and really rather a country house than a town house. In Queen's Gate, other gabled houses followed. Shaw's Number 180 was particularly interesting, in a free Tudor with some unexpected curlijigs by the gable. Number 185 is the last one of Shaw's houses and that he built in 1891.

In 1891, the *British Architect and Architectural Journal* praised that house as a 'knock-down blow to the heavy philistinism opposite'. In fact, the professional press and the professional critics had been anti-stucco and anti-terraces much earlier. The *Building News*, for instance, in 1876 spoke of 'the dismal and insufferable barrack-like monotony that invades these terraces' and yet much earlier, Henry Cole's *Journal of Design* had hit out at 'the stucco abomination'.

I'm stressing this passing of the style of the stucco terraces and this recognition that with 197–200 Queen's Gate we meet their end because whether that is so or not has had some interesting repercussions in recent years. The story I am referring to seems to me quite instructive.

The accommodation provided for the Royal College of Art on the Commissioners' estate had throughout been extremely miserly. They got proper and functionally satisfactory well-designed premises only in 1960–64. The architects were H.T. Cadbury-Brown, Sir Hugh Casson and R.Y. Goodden. The building – black metal, brick and glass – is sombre and strictly rectangular in its motifs reflecting the serious rather than the clever work of the College. But even this new made-to-measure building was from the beginning too small. Britain's only state school of design urgently needed extension and so they cast their eyes on an area to the immediate west of their new building – Number 25 Kensington Gore and, round the corner, our Numbers 197–200 Queen's Gate. Now remember what I told you about these houses. It will make you understand that the Royal College of Art was convinced that they would get permission to demolish Numbers 197–200 and to build their extension.

The proposed new building went to several versions of design and after some time reached a final form. Meanwhile, however, the opposition against demolition had hardened. A public inquiry was demanded and granted – that is, the Secretary of State for the Environment called in (that's the technical term), called in the design and an inspector was allocated to the inquiry. He reported to the Secretary of State that the Royal College should get its licence but the Secretary of State did not accept the view of his inspector, which is a relatively rare thing to happen, and the Royal College of Art was turned down.

Experts felt passionately about it all. The Victorian Society was delighted but a group of distinguished architects was sufficiently shocked to write to *The Times* that permission ought to have been granted. The letter seemed to me unwise because it must have been hard for the architects not to be biased. I didn't say anything at the time but now I want to.

Let me put my arguments to you. First, the corner in question is not Kensington stucco at its best; it is, as you have seen, the fag end. Moreover, it is a stump. The stucco terraces, in Kensington or Paddington, need a certain length to make their point – and plenty of long terraces of course survive. But there is just as much to be said against the new building. The architects – the same who built the earlier Royal College building – intended to make it modern and yet to achieve some harmony with the Norman Shaw gables. In my opinion, the steep gables of the new design – if you call them gables – fail to read in any Norman Shaw way. The sharp skyline appears to me arbitrary and even eccentric. Yet as far as I am concerned, I would not hesitate to allow the design with the glass pyramids to be built. Why? Well there is my principal argument – an argument which to the best of my knowledge has not been put forward in that long-drawn-out battle.

If we speak of South Kensington, we don't think in the first instance of stucco terraces. We think of a large number of public buildings, close together and in a variety of styles, some of them of great architectural value. But whatever their value, it is the variety that matters. The new volume of the *Survey of London* makes that – in my opinion – abundantly clear.

So you see in what scrape an honest historian and an honest critic may land himself if he is equally concerned with the architecture of the past and the situation of architecture today. What it amounts to in my particular case is that as the Chairman of the Victorian Society, I found myself in opposition to my committee and as a critic I found myself pleading for a building which I don't really like.

1   Pevsner's talk was prompted by the publication of the Kensington volume of the *Survey of London* and by a public controversy about an application to extend the Royal College of Art which involved the demolition of Italianate houses of the mid-1870s.

Truly a municipal palace

Radio Three
TUESDAY 13 SEPTEMBER 1977
Producer: Not known

The Manchester Town Hall is indeed one of the proudest town halls of England and its architect, Alfred Waterhouse, is one of the most important and enlightened architects of the mid-Victorian age and moreover he is far too little known, even though his principal buildings may be known individually.[1]

As I regard him that highly, and some respected colleagues of mine don't, I want to present my case to you, telling you about Waterhouse's style, his attitude to historicism, his rationalism and his large practice which yet never made him jettison his principles.

Among Waterhouse's main buildings, there is the Prudential in Holborn – red-brick and it seems to me the best-known of his buildings. Others are the University College Hospital with its diagonally set cross-shaped plan; and the National Liberal Club, originally with a gorgeous spiral stair by Waterhouse; the Natural History Museum; Eaton Hall in Cheshire, the largest of all English country houses; and of course our Manchester Town Hall.

Now let me say straight away that much of what I'm going to tell you comes from an admirable Ph.D. thesis presented in 1970 by a pupil of mine, Dr Stuart Smith, who is now Professor at the University of New Brunswick – and may that thesis soon be published.

But we must start at the start. Waterhouse was a north-country man, born in Liverpool in 1830. The family were Quakers and well-connected in commercial circles – the Barclays, the Gurneys, the Buxtons, the Peases were near-relatives or distant relatives – and so Waterhouse was never short of jobs. But what brought him to the notice of wider and more influential patrons was his design for the Assize Courts in Manchester which he won in a competition with over a hundred participants in 1859. The building, which was destroyed during the war, was in the Gothic style of the thirteenth century. The style is more or less the same in the Town Hall. That public buildings could be Gothic or, rather, could be anything other than Grecian was due to the terms of the competition for the Houses of Parliament in 1835: designs would only be admitted, so the terms of the competition stipulated, if they were in the Gothic or Elizabethan style. The winner was Charles Barry, working with Pugin, and they chose the Perpendicular Gothic and not the thirteenth-century Gothic. For the Manchester Town Hall also, a competition was held. Waterhouse was thirty-eight when he won it.

Victorian competitions were questionable affairs. No dignity could be expected. There was not yet any code of professional behaviour. Architects fiercely attacked each other in the architectural journals. Now, the judges of Manchester were Street and Professor Donaldson, the first a convinced Gothicist, the second of Italianate leanings. The result, as far as Waterhouse was concerned, according to the judges: for merit from an architectural point of view, Waterhouse came fourth but for plan, for lighting and ventilation and for the estimates he came first and that meant that on a total adding up, he turned out to be the winner. The *Manchester Guardian* protested that the winning design should be what they called an imperfect piece of architecture.

Others were of a different view, for example, Manchester's Member of Parliament John Bright who said: 'it is truly a municipal palace ... whether you look at its great proportions outside or its internal decorations, there is nothing like it that I know of in the United Kingdom and I doubt whether there is in any of the great famous old cities of the Continent of Europe.'

I agree. In my opinion, Waterhouse amply deserved the prize. The site of the Town Hall was spacious but decidedly awkward – a steep triangle with the base – that is, the façade – to Albert Square, 306 feet long; the sides of the triangle 336 and 373; the apex – that is, the east side – was truncated and so it was very short. The style is that of the Assize Courts – that is, the style of the thirteenth century, with windows, either lancet or of two lights with geometrical tracery. The style was at the time called Second Pointed or Middle Pointed. It was the favourite style of Street, of Gilbert Scott and of many others.

The total impact of the exterior of the Town Hall is dour and that is characteristic of Waterhouse – there is nowhere any amplitude of ornament. The façade is nearly symmetrical but not quite. You see that for example in the end pavilions of the Albert Square front. The tower – 260 feet high – is nearly in the middle but not quite. The principal rooms are on the first floor but the most ornate façade feature is on the ground floor – the portal of five orders – with foliage in the arch. The short east side is symmetrical and has a tower in the middle, less conspicuous than that to Albert Square. The two long sides north and south are less monumental, in fact rather crowded. The south side cannot be seen well now because of the annexe of the 1930s. On the north side alone, close to its west end, is a major asymmetry. There are two gabled portals side by side and the windows above them, and left and right, differ. Also on that side of the building are two oriel windows. They rest on big brackets and the brackets are connected by segmental arches. Now, segmental arches do exist in genuine thirteenth-century work but very rarely. Do remember this, as I'll have to come back to that.

But first, the interior. The interior is logically planned – you feel that at once. You enter from Albert Square and find yourself in a large, rather low, rib-vaulted entrance hall. The vaults are of stone, not of wood or stucco imitating stone. To the left and right of the entrance hall are the two main staircases, both with an apsidal intermediate landing. Subsidiary staircases are of the newel or spiral type and this duality results in thrilling vistas in several directions. On the main floor, the centre is the great hall, wide and high and with the famous wall paintings by Ford Madox Brown as its main decoration. The other main rooms are along the front – Council Chamber, Committee Room, Ante-Room, Reception Room and Dining Room. The Lord Mayor's dwelling is round the corner on the second floor. The most powerful of the principal suite is the Ante-Room – square with four sturdy free-standing granite columns and a rib vault. The long sides of the Great Hall give on to two inner courtyards. All the main corridors of the building run along these courtyards, which makes it easy to find one's way.

Waterhouse designed much of the interior furnishings and details himself. I wish I knew whether these splendid boldly stylised sunflowers of the Dining Room curtains were his. Stylised leaves occur in several contexts, especially in the wooden ceiling of the Great Hall, but much of the decoration is abstract. That evidently suited Waterhouse.

Now, if I add that Waterhouse made use of iron and that he liked terracotta facing of the walls, I think I have pointed out some of the most characteristic features but I must for a moment go back to the segmental arches of the north side – a motif, as I told you, not anti-thirteenth century but rare in the thirteenth century and that did not worry Waterhouse. He must have been convinced that these depressed arches would tell us of the weight of the oriels above and that expressional effort mattered to him more than any historicist arguments, for Waterhouse was not a strict historicist. It is true that once in 1890 he said this: 'The introduction in the same building of parts, avowedly made to look as though designed by different people in different ages, ought to be deprecated.' Yet Waterhouse also said à propos the Assize Courts – and this is a very important statement: 'The mouldings and details are thirteenth-century in their general charac-teristics but whenever I thought that the particular object in view could not be best obtained by a strict obedience to precedent, I took the liberty of departing from it.' The 'object in view' surely means the function of the building. And indeed Waterhouse addressing students in 1878 said this: 'First find out exactly what is wanted. Never think about elevations until you have ascertained this, and embodied it in your plans as fully and perfectly as you can.'

Now that sounds a positive attack on historicism and historicism was of course the most Victorian of all Victorian bugbears. I need not explain to you what historicism means: choose for your building a suitable style of the past and follow it. It was only at the end of the nineteenth century and the beginning of the twentieth century that all historical adherence was abandoned. Yet the Victorians did realise that every age ought to have its own style. Proof of Waterhouse's realising it is this passage of 1888: 'It is certain that the past did not respect its own past as we do ours, and our practice, commendable as I think it is, has no doubt its dangers. If we are forever dwelling on the past, we shall never be self-reliant, and if we are not self-reliant, we shall never be bold, originating architects.'

Now on another occasion, he said the same thing even more radically – and I'm quoting it again:

> The Greeks spent their powers as artists perfecting their own work, not resuscitating a dead style. Our mediaeval brethren spent theirs in the marvellous development of their own phase of architecture. The artists of the Renaissance, in spite of that name, were likewise originators. It has been left to us to pillage ancient monuments by reproducing old forms with more or less ability but also with more or less inappropriateness.

Now, for every Victorian Gothicist, the application of such principles had its consequence in the field of restoration. There again, it is worth listening for a moment to Waterhouse. In 1878 he said: 'What is needed is a firm determination to keep our ancient buildings as they are – that is, to retain not only Elizabethan stallwork and Jacobean panelling but even the pews and galleries which marked the era of our Hanoverian sovereigns.' But what did that come to in reality? At Balliol College in Oxford, Waterhouse built two blocks after having pulled down their predecessors because, he said, they were of little or no interest architecturally; and he intended to go even further than that. At Pembroke College in Cambridge he wanted to remove

Christopher Wren's Chapel and in London, in his competition designs for the new Law Courts, he expressed the hope that the Church of St Clement Danes would be removed. Happily, both these buildings are still with us.

The competition for the London Law Courts took place in 1866. Street won the competition. I am inclined to say 'Just as well' as far as Waterhouse is concerned for he had begun work on the designs for the Natural History Museum in 1866 and, after all, the competition for the Manchester Town Hall started in 1867. I need not remind you that the Law Courts, just as the Manchester Town Hall, are Second Pointed in style and so had been the Assize Courts and so also had been Eaton Hall, the country palace of the Dukes of Westminster which has been demolished. But just because you know all that, you should remember that Waterhouse was by no means a one-style man. Take the Natural History Museum in South Kensington and you find a different style and, by the way, a different material. As for style, the façade of the Museum is consistently round-arched – that is, in its inspiration it is German of the latest Romanesque. Now why did Waterhouse choose that style? His argument is curious. His predecessor, the architect of the big public buildings in South Kensington, Captain Fowke, was a partisan of the Italian Early Renaissance and that style of course was committed to the round arch. It was also committed to terracotta or maiolica or faience as a facing material – so Waterhouse, convinced of the superiority of the Middle Ages over the Renaissance, found his compromise – terracotta and Romanesque. Romanesque, incidentally also, but Italian Romanesque, is Waterhouse's best church – Reddish in Lancashire, started in 1882, one year after the completion of the Museum. It is high and broad with exposed brick inside as well as outside and short, stubby piers between nave and aisles.

By the way, in making use of the Romanesque, Waterhouse could rely on his travel notes and sketches, for he travelled a lot, often in France and often in Germany. He also knew Italy, he knew Sicily, Catalonia, Spain and Prague and Scandinavia and even Istanbul.

But there are other things about the Natural History Museum which you have to observe fully, to appreciate Waterhouse. One is the main staircase in the central hall. It rises in one flight and at the intermediate landing it breaks by ninety degrees to left as well as right – and all this is seemingly unsupported. To me it is one of the finest staircases of Britain. Surely, this piece alone makes Waterhouse a great architect.

Two more points I want to make. They concern materials and they establish Waterhouse as a believer in technological innovations. They are the use of an iron skeleton and, as I have already mentioned, the use of terracotta as a facing material. Both take us back once more to the Manchester Town Hall. Iron Waterhouse found useful for structural reasons; terracotta he favoured in particular in the form of slabs with raised relief motifs. Now, both these materials are industrially produced and not dependent on craftsmen. The rationale of this attitude fits Waterhouse's rationale in choosing styles. For this, let me give you one last example. It refers to his work in 1867–68 at Caius College, Cambridge. If you are sufficiently familiar with Cambridge, you will remember walking along King's Parade towards Caius College. In walking, you have the big Gothic church of St Mary on your right, the Georgian Senate House on your left. But between them rises the strongest accent of the whole group – Waterhouse's tower block of Caius. Neither St Mary nor the Senate House can compete with that four-storeyed tower. In style it is François I – that is, the style of Blois and of Chambord. And if you now ask in despair why in the very years of the Gothic Law Courts and the Gothic Eaton Hall and the Romanesque Museum, why he should have turned to the Loire, the answer which Waterhouse gave is this: 'The style of Chambord is an exclusively domestic style and a style which can be looked at as a link between Gothic and Georgian.' This is of course rather a specious argument but it sounds like rational justification and this is what Waterhouse needed. It is more rational, anyway, than Gilbert Scott using the Second Pointed for St Pancras Station and Hotel. Scott's choice at St Pancras has only aesthetic argument to rely on; Waterhouse's has just that little more.

And now to conclude, I have told you a lot about the Town Hall and about other buildings by Waterhouse but I have not told you much about Waterhouse the man. When the *Building News* in 1867 asked its readers whom they would consider the leading British architect, ninety per cent named Waterhouse and as for professional recognition, he was made an honorary member or honorary fellow of the academies of Antwerp, Berlin, Brussels, Milan, Paris and Vienna. But towards the end of his life, journalists as well as students did not appreciate him any longer. His style was called extremely florid, lacking in repose and lacking in simplicity. Yet no one had any doubt about Waterhouse's character. His professional integrity was proverbial. Stuart Smith in his thesis tells us that when, in a case in 1888, the estimate was exceeded, Waterhouse paid the difference himself. That was one side. Another side was praised time and again by the obituarists: his unaffected kindliness, we read; his sincerity of manner; his inexpressible charm.

Yet one enigma remains. Looking at the tower of Caius College, has it inexplicable charm? Surely not. What it has is a stunning self-confidence. That Waterhouse must have felt. St Mary's? The Senate House? I can do as well as they did. And with this assertiveness I will end. For self-assertiveness is also a dominant – a domineering – feature of the Manchester Town Hall, only there one is ready to applaud it because it stands for the pride of a flourishing city.

1 'Truly a municipal palace' was delivered on the centenary of the completion of Manchester Town Hall in 1877.

Appendix

Pevsner's BBC Radio Talks

Pevsner's BBC Radio Talks

The list below attempts to give a comprehensive record of all Pevsner's written talks for the BBC. As well as his more substantial broadcasts, it includes a number of pieces effectively written as 'fillers' – short talks of only a few minutes – designed for regional and foreign services. Nonetheless, it gives a sense of the breadth and scale of his activity down the years, and of his relationships with the various producers with whom he worked.

The list does not include interviews and other programmes in which Pevsner may have taken part as a guest or speaker. Most talks were repeated; repeat dates are not included. Repeats of the Reith Lectures went out on the Third Programme.

Title *(First broadcast, Service, Producer)*

Le Corbusier and Frank Lloyd Wright *(9 February 1945, Home, Unknown)*
The rise of academies *(25 May 1945, Home, Unknown)*
The function of craft *(27 January 1946, Pacific, Noni Bright)*
Modern homes *(26 March 1946, Home, Unknown)*
Building now *(11 April 1946, Home, Unknown)*
Reflections on ruins *(3 May 1946, Home, Unknown)*
Art and the state *(16 June 1946, Pacific, Noni Bright)*
Ruins *(1 July 1946, Pacific, Noni Bright)*
Britain can make it *(10 October 1946, Third, Basil Taylor)*
Soft furnishings in the 1940s *(26 November 1946, Services Education: Light, Robert Waller)*
Richard Payne Knight *(16 January 1947, Third, Basil Taylor)*
The architecture of Washington *(10 July 1947, Third, Basil Taylor)*
The renaissance of the English public house *(2 November 1947, Home, T.B. Radley)*
The Adoration of the Kings *(26 January 1948, Third, Basil Taylor)*
The Imaginary Museum *(23 February 1948, Third, Basil Taylor)*
The Dukeries *(7 November 1948, Third, Basil Taylor)*
Danish art *(13 November 1948, Third, Basil Taylor)*
Public buildings *(23 December 1948, Services Education: Light, Robert Waller)*

From William Morris to Walter Gropius *(16 June 1949, Third, Basil Taylor)*

German painting of the Age of Reformation *(16 July 1949, Third, Anna Kallin)*

Goethe and architecture *(19 November 1949, Third, Anna Kallin)*

Sir Matthew Digby Wyatt *(8 December 1949, Third, Anna Kallin)*

Villard de Honnecourt *(18 February 1950, Third, Anna Kallin)*

The golden age of English architecture *(21 May 1950, German, Unknown)*

Revivalisms in architecture *(12 June 1950, Third, Basil Taylor)*

Baroque painting in Italy *(21 January 1951, Third, Leonie Cohn for Roger Cary)*

How to judge Victorian architecture *(4 July 1951, Third, Anna Kallin)*

Pugin, Ruskin, Scott *(11 July 1951, Third, Anna Kallin)*

Churches and public buildings and the neglect of the common man *(19 July 1951, Third, Anna Kallin)*

The Late Victorians and William Morris *(25 July 1951, Third, Anna Kallin)*

Splendeurs et misères *(30 November 1951, Third, Anna Kallin)*

Modern architecture and the Church *(6 January 1952, Third, Anna Kallin)*

Anglo-German friendship *(23 May 1952, German, Unknown)*

Lumley Castle, County Durham *(15 June 1952, Home, R.E. Keen)*

Bolsover Castle, Derbyshire *(22 June 1952, Home, R.E. Keen)*

Strawberry Hill *(29 June 1952, Home, R.E. Keen)*

Antoni Gaudí *(31 July 1952, Third, Anna Kallin)*

Reflections on not teaching art history *(19 October 1952, Third, Leonie Cohn)*

Strawberry Hill *(19 February 1953, General Overseas Service, Roger Cary)*

At Aspen in Colorado *(31 August 1953, Home, Anna Kallin)*

Reconstruction in France *(15 November 1953, Third, Anna Kallin)*

A pilgrim's church in France *(24 December 1953, Third, Prudence Smith for Anna Kallin)*

The picturesque and the twentieth century: modern town planning *(31 January 1954, Third, Prudence Smith)*

County guides *(25 January 1954, German, Unknown)*

Arts and commerce promoted *(21 March 1954, Home, Lorna Moore)*

Bavarian Rococo – or the eloquent in art *(17 November 1954, Third, Leonie Cohn)*

Dam building in the Dolomites *(3 December 1954, Third, Leonie Cohn)*

The geography of art *(16 October 1955, Home, Donald Boyd)*

Hogarth and observed life *(23 October 1955, Home, Donald Boyd)*

Reynolds and detachment *(30 October 1955, Home, Donald Boyd)*

Perpendicular England *(6 November 1955, Home, Donald Boyd)*

Blake and the flaming line *(13 November 1955, Home, Donald Boyd)*

Constable and the pursuit of nature *(20 November 1955, Home, Donald Boyd)*

The genius of the place *(27 November 1955, Home, Donald Boyd)*

A setting for St Paul's *(6 May 1956, Home, Leonie Cohn)*

Some thoughts on German painting *(13 May 1956, Third, Leonie Cohn)*

New trends in architecture *(9 May 1957, German, Unknown)*

Untitled (in the series 'Hier Spricht England') *(25 July 1957, German, Unknown)*

City of tomorrow *(30 July 1957, Third, Anna Kallin)*

King Ramiro's churches *(13 March 1958, Third, Leonie Cohn)*

The ingratiating chaos *(11 November 1958, Third, Anna Kallin)*

New Zealand *(11 January 1959, German, Unknown)*

The Penguin story *(14 January 1959, German, Unknown)*

Bauen und Planen *(1 February 1959, German, Unknown)*

Sir Basil Spence *(12 April 1959, German, Unknown)*

Contemporary British architecture *(30 October 1959★, French, Unknown)*

Claydon House *(5 November 1959★, Home (Southeast Region), Colin Nears)*

Eltham Hall and Eltham Lodge *(5 November 1959★, Home (Southeast Region), Colin Nears)*

Layer Marney *(5 November 1959★, Home (Southeast Region), Colin Nears)*

Deutscher Geist in England *(8 November 1959, German, Unknown)*

Bedford Park *(12 January 1960★, Home (Southeast Region), Colin Nears)*

Ladbroke Estate *(12 January 1960★, Home (Southeast Region), Colin Nears)*

St John's College Library *(12 January 1960★, Home (Southeast Region), Colin Nears)*

Bloomsbury *(17 March 1960★, Home (Southeast Region), Julia Bearder)*

Long Melford *(17 March 1960★, Home (Southeast Region), Julia Bearder)*

The Norfolkness of Norfolk building *(23 May 1960, Home (Midlands), Paul Humphreys)*

Sources of the twentieth century *(24 November 1960, Third, Leonie Cohn)*

Argentinian Edwardian *(24 December 1960, Third, Leonie Cohn)*

Dark gold *(16 January 1961, Third, Leonie Cohn)*

Geistige Auslese *(9 February 1961, German, Unknown)*

The return of historicism *(11 February 1961, Third, Prudence Smith)*

Ernst Barlach *(11 May 1961, Third, George MacBeth)*

Any old Bauhaus *(31 December 1962, Third, Anna Kallin)*

Skidmoring around New York *(4 August 1963, Third, Anna Kallin)*

Mannerism and Elizabethan architecture (1) *(21 February 1964, Third, Anna Kallin)*

Mannerism and Elizabethan architecture (2) *(27 February 1964, Third, Anna Kallin)*

Mannerism and Elizabethan architecture (3) *(6 March 1964, Third, Anna Kallin)*

Hogarth (*22 October 1964, German, Unknown*)

Westminster Abbey (*11 November 1965, German, Unknown*)

News from Split (*3 March 1966, Third, Leonie Cohn*)

The Anti-Pioneers (*3 December 1966, Third, Leonie Cohn*)

Kara Dag and Alahan (*17 February 1967, Third, Leonie Cohn*)

Germany and I (*24 March 1968, German, Unknown*)

Gothic – Early to High (*26 May 1968, Radio Three, Leonie Cohn*)

Charles Rennie Mackintosh (*7 June 1968, Scottish Home Service, George Bruce*)

An appeal for the Historic Churches Preservation Trust (*17 November 1968, Radio Four, B. Maxwell*)

Reynolds's *Discourses* (*21 January 1969, Radio Three, Leonie Cohn*)

The golden days of the Vienna Secession (*26 January 1971, Radio Three, Leonie Cohn*)

A personal talk (*13 June 1972, German, Unknown*)

The enigma of Sir William Chambers (*18 September 1972, Radio Three, Leonie Cohn*)

Is there an English Baroque? (*9 February 1973, Radio Three, Unknown*)

South Kensington – a memorial to Albert (*30 May 1976, Radio Three, Unknown*)

Truly a municipal palace (*13 September 1977, Radio Three, Unknown*)

★ Recording date: broadcast date not known.

INDEX